REFORM AND CHANGE I

HIGHER EDUCATION DYNAMICS

VOLUME 8

Series Editor
Peter Maassen, *University of Oslo, Norway, and University of Twente, Enschede, The Netherlands*

Editorial Board
Alberto Amaral, *Universidade do Porto, Portugal*
Akira Arimoto, *Hiroshima University, Japan*
Nico Cloete, *CHET, Pretoria, South Africa*
David Dill, *University of North Carolina at Chapel Hill, USA*
Jürgen Enders, *University of Twente, Enschede, The Netherlands*
Patricia Gumport, *Stanford University, USA*
Mary Henkel, *Brunel University, Uxbridge, United Kingdom*
Glenn Jones, *University of Toronto, Canada*

SCOPE OF THE SERIES

Higher Education Dynamics is a bookseries intending to study adaptation processes and their outcomes in higher education at all relevant levels. In addition it wants to examine the way interactions between these levels affect adaptation processes. It aims at applying general social science concepts and theories as well as testing theories in the field of higher education research. It wants to do so in a manner that is of relevance to all those professionally involved in higher education, be it as ministers, policy-makers, politicians, institutional leaders or administrators, higher education researchers, members of the academic staff of universities and colleges, or students. It will include both mature and developing systems of higher education, covering public as well as private institutions.

The titles published in this series are listed at the end of this volume.

REFORM AND CHANGE IN HIGHER EDUCATION

Analysing Policy Implementation

Edited by

ÅSE GORNITZKA

Norwegian Institute for Studies in Research and Higher Education,
Oslo, Norway

MAURICE KOGAN

Brunel University, Centre for the Evaluation of Public Policy and Practice,
Uxbridge, UK

and

ALBERTO AMARAL

University of Porto and CIPES,
Portugal

 Springer

A C.I.P. Catalogue record for this book is available from the Library of Congress.

ISBN-10 1-4020-5536-6 (PB)
ISBN-13 978-1-4020-5536-2 (PB)
ISBN-10 1-4020-3402-4 (HB)
ISBN-13 978-1-4020-3402-2 (HB)
ISBN-10 1-4020-3411-3 (e-book)
ISBN-13 978-1-4020-3411-4 (e-book)

Published by Springer,
P.O. Box 17, 3300 AA Dordrecht, The Netherlands.

Printed on acid-free paper

TABLE OF CONTENTS

v

LIST OF CONTRIBUTORS

ALBERTO AMARAL is professor at the University of Porto and director of CIPES. He is chair of the Board of CHER, vice-chair of EUA's steering committee on institutional evaluation, life member of IAUP, and a member of EAIR and IMHE. He was the rector of the University of Porto for the period 1986–1998. Recent publications include articles in *Quality Assurance in Education, Higher Education Quarterly, Higher Education Policy, Higher Education in Europe* and *European Journal of Education*. He is editor and co-editor of several books.

NICO CLOETE is currently a full-time director of CHET. He was previously research director of the National Commission on Higher Education and coordinator of the Post Secondary Education Report of the National Education Policy Investigation (NEPI) and the Policy Forum of UDUSA. He has worked at numerous South African universities including the Universities of the North, Transkei and Witwatersrand where his teaching and research were mainly concerned with psychology and student services. He was actively involved in academic staff organisation as general secretary of UDUSA (1993–94) and president of the Wits Staff Association (1991–92). He has served on the Minister's Advisory Council for Universities and Technikons. Dr Cloete has published widely in psychology, sociology and education.

HARRY DE BOER, a public policy analyst at the Center for Higher Education Policy Studies, University of Twente, has carried out research and consultancy projects for national advisory and international organisations such as the Dutch Advisory Council for Science and Technology Policy, the International Fellowship Program of the Ford Foundation and the Deutsche Forschungsgemeinschaft. He has been a consultant on several national evaluation projects for the Dutch educational ministry and has frequently published on these subjects.

ELAINE EL-KHAWAS is professor of education policy at George Washington University. She has previously served as professor of higher education at the University of California, Los Angeles and as vice-president for policy analysis and research at the American Council on Education. A sociologist who earned her masters and doctoral degrees at the University of Chicago, she is a former president of the Association for the Study of Higher Education, a member of the board of trustees of Emmanuel College, and currently serves on the editorial boards of the *Review of Higher Education, Higher Education Management* and other academic journals.

JÜRGEN ENDERS is professor of higher education policy studies and director of the Center for Higher Education Policy Studies at the University of Twente, the Netherlands. He is a member of the board and secretary of the Consortium of Higher Education Researchers (CHER) as well as a member of the editorial board of the book series 'Higher Education Dynamics' and the journal *Higher Education*. His research interests are in the areas of the sociology of education and the professions, organisational studies, governance and management of higher education and research, higher education and the world of work, and the academic profession.

ÅSE GORNITZKA is a political scientist and senior researcher at ARENA, Centre for European Studies at the University of Oslo and at NIFU STEP. She received her doctoral degree from the University of Twente in the Netherlands. Her main research interests include the Europeanisation of higher education and research policy, and studies of change processes in higher education and research institutions.

GRANT HARMAN is emeritus professor of education management at the University of New England, Armidale, NSW, Australia. He holds a PhD in political science from the Australian National University and has held academic positions at the University of New England, the Australian National University and the University of Melbourne. His research interests are mainly in higher education management and policy and he is currently editor-in-chief of the journal *Higher Education,* published by Springer in the Netherlands.

ALICIA D. HURLEY is the director of NYU's Office of Federal Policy, overseeing the university's interaction with policy makers in Washington, DC. Dr Hurley earned her doctorate from NYU in the field of higher education administration with an emphasis on policy. She was a researcher for the Alliance for International Higher Education Policy Studies. Her dissertation is titled, "The Federal Role Recast: Politics, Policy and American Higher Education in the 1990s".

RICHARD JAMES is a higher education policy researcher and associate professor at the University of Melbourne, Australia. He is involved in a wide-ranging research programme into the student experience of higher education that is examining the decision making of prospective university students, the transition to university and the first year experience, and the nature of graduate outcomes.

ROLLIN KENT is professor of public policy and educational management at the University of Puebla, Mexico. He studies comparative policy and organisational change in higher education. Currently he is participating in the Alliance for International Higher Education Policy Studies, a multi-year project funded by the Ford Foundation focusing on the determinants of policy effectiveness in higher education in the NAFTA countries throughout the 1990s (see http://www.nyu.edu/iesp/aiheps).

MAURICE KOGAN is professor emeritus of government and director of the Centre for the Evaluation of Public Policy and Practice at Brunel University where he has been dean of the Faculty of Social Sciences and acting vice-chancellor. He graduated with first class honours in history at Cambridge University and was placed first in the Civil Service Administrative Class Examination. He joined Brunel after some years service in the Department of Education and Science. He is the author of several books and articles on higher education and science, health and local government policy. His most recent major works are in a five volume publication (2000), with Swedish and Norwegian colleagues, on changing policies and practices in higher education in the three countries; and the joint editorship, with Mary Hawkesworth, of the second edition of the Routledge *Encyclopedia of Politics and Government* (2003). He holds honorary doctorates from Brunel University and the University of Hull.

SVEIN KYVIK is a senior researcher at the Norwegian Institute for Studies in Research and Education – Centre for Innovation Research. He holds a PhD in sociology, and his current research focuses on the development of a non-university higher education sector in Norway and on the academic researcher role.

LIV LANGFELDT is a senior researcher at NIFU STEP in Oslo. She holds a doctoral degree in political science from the University of Oslo. She has been affiliated to NIFU since 1991 and has carried out studies on research policy related topics, including peer review decision-making processes and bias, research evaluation and quality, research council organisation, research policy instruments, policy making at higher education institutions, and the internationalisation of research. She has also been a research assistant at the Department of Political Science, University of Oslo and a visiting scholar at the Department of Science & Technology Studies, Cornell University.

INGVILD MARHEIM LARSEN is a senior researcher at NIFU STEP – Studies in Innovation, Research and Education. Her main research interests are on reforms and change processes in higher education, more specifically the steering and organisation of the higher education system, leadership and management of higher education institutions, institutional response and adaptation to change, the role of the governing body in higher education institutions, and the relationship between academic and administrative staff.

GIUNIO LUZZATO is the director of CARED, an interdisciplinary Center for Educational Research at the University of Genoa, and leads CONCURED, a committee coordinating all analogous centres in Italian universities. As a consultant to the ministry of education, he has contributed in defining the structure of the two-tier system (Bologna process) and a new system of teacher education, both adopted by Italian universities.

PETER MAASSEN is a senior fellow at the Center for Higher Education Policy Studies (CHEPS), University of Twente, the Netherlands. He was the director of CHEPS from January 1997 to March 2000. He specialises at CHEPS in the public governance (including policy reform and institutional change) of higher education.

He has published numerous books, book chapters and articles (in 6 languages) in journals of higher education, political science, management studies and policy analysis. In 1998 he was awarded a fellowship by the Society for Research on Higher Education (SRHE).

ANTÓNIO MAGALHÃES is associate professor at the University of Porto, and a senior researcher at CIPES. His main interests are the regulation mechanisms of education and the relationships between state and higher education. He has published articles in *Higher Education Policy, European Journal of Education*, and *Globalisation, Societies & Education, Educação Sociedade & Culturas* among other journals. He has also published some books and chapters with *Peter Lang, Fundação Calouste Gulbenkian* and *Edições Afrontamento*, among other publishing houses.

SUSAN MARTON is a researcher at the Center for Public Sector Research (CEFOS) at Göteborg University and an assistant professor at the Department of Political Science, Karlstad University. In 2000, she received her PhD from the Department of Political Science at Göteborg University with a dissertation entitled, "The Mind of the State: The Politics of University Autonomy in Sweden, 1968–1998". Her recent work focuses on research policy and education reform policies in general.

CRAIG MCINNIS is a higher education policy researcher and associate professor at the University of Melbourne, Australia. He is involved in a wide-ranging research programme into the student experience of higher education that is examining the decision making of prospective university students, the transition to university and the first year experience, and the nature of graduate outcomes.

JOSÉ-GINÉS MORA is director of the Centre for the Study of Higher Education Management (CEGES) at the Technical University of Valencia (UPV). He is president of EAIR and a member of the governing board of the IMHE Programme of the OECD. His research is focused on economics of education, the labour market, higher education and quality assurance. Currently, he is responsible for Assessment of Technology, Universities and Science in the Regional Government of Valencia.

ROBERTO MOSCATI is a full professor of sociology of education at the University of Milano-Bicocca, Department of Sociolog, with previous teaching activities at the Universities of Catania, Trieste and Milano (State University). He has professional experience as coordinator of ministerial programmes for the cultural development of southern regions in Italy at FORMEZ (a centre for studies and training activities in the Mezzogiorno), Roma. He is a member of the editorial boards of the *European Journal of Education* and *Tertiary Education and Management* and a member of evaluation groups at the University of Pavia and IULM (Free University of Languages, Milan).

JOHAN MULLER is professor of education in the School of Education at the University of Cape Town. He is also director of the Graduate School of Humanities and deputy dean for Research and Postgraduate Affairs. He teaches sociology of knowledge and curriculum, as well as higher education policy. His book *Reclaiming Knowledge: Social Theory, Curriculum, and Education Policy* was published by RoutledgeFalmer in 2000.

HANS PECHAR is an associate professor at the Faculty for Interdisciplinary Studies (IFF), University of Klagenfurt, and head of the Department for Higher Education Research. He is a research associate at the Center for Studies in Higher Education, UC Berkeley and at the Centre for Policy Studies in Higher Education and Training, University of British Columbia. His research topics are comparative higher education and economics of higher education.

RICHARD C. RICHARDSON Jr is professor of higher education at NYU and chair of the Department of Administration, Leadership and Technology. He directs a Ford funded project, the Alliance for International Higher Education Policy Studies, that examines linkages between public policy and higher education outcomes in the US, Mexico and Canada. The project also focuses on training younger policy scholars.

PAUL SABATIER is a political scientist who received his PhD from the University of Chicago in 1974. Since that time, he has been a member of the Faculty of the Department of Environmental Science & Policy at the University of California, Davis (USA). He is best known for his work on policy implementation and on policy change and learning over periods of a decade or more. The chapter in this book describes this change in research focus which occurred during the 1980s. Most of Professor Sabatier's empirical research has dealt with environmental policy, including coastal land use planning in Britain, France and California, automotive pollution control in the US, and watershed planning in California and Washington.

BJØRN STENSAKER is a programme director at NIFU STEP in Oslo. He holds a doctoral degree from the School of Business Administration, Technology and Public Administration at the University of Twente, the Netherlands, and has a special interest in studies of quality, leadership and organisational change in higher education. Stensaker is the editor-in-chief of *Tertiary Education and Management (TEAM)*, one of the editors of *Quality in Higher Education*, and has written extensively on issues related to quality assurance and organisational change.

JOHN TAYLOR is professor of higher education management and policy at the University of Southampton and director of the Centre for Higher Education Management and Policy at Southampton (CHEMPaS). After a successful career in higher education management at the Universities of Leeds, Sheffield and Southampton, he moved to the University of Bath before returning to his present position in Southampton. His main research interests lie in higher education policy; higher education management, especially strategic planning, resource allocation and research management; and the comparative, international study of higher education.

JUSSI VÄLIMAA is professor of higher education. He works at the Institute for Educational Research, University of Jyväskylä, Finland. He is the head of the higher education research team and one of the coordinators of a national doctoral training programme.

JAVIER VIDAL (PhD) is professor of research methods in education at the University of Leon, Spain. Since 2004 he has been vice-rector for Planning and Institutional Assessment at the University of Leon. He has been a member of the Coordination Committee of the Plan for the Quality of the Universities, at the Spanish Council of Universities. His fields of research are the assessment and quality improvement of higher education and the relations between education and employment.

DON F. WESTERHEIJDEN coordinates research on quality management at CHEPS, University of Twente, the Netherlands. He is an executive editor of the journal *Quality in Higher Education*. He has published articles and books on quality issues in higher education. His research interests include impacts of evaluation of quality in Europe amongst others focusing on the Bologna process, transformation of higher education in Central and Eastern Europe, and methodological issues.

PREFACE

The Consortium of Higher Education Researchers (CHER) is a community of researchers that meets each year to share new research insights and explore new research frontiers. The 2003 meeting in Porto intended to strengthen this emphasis of the annual CHER Conference.

This book contains some of the contributions made to the 2003 Conference of the Consortium of Higher Education Researchers. It had as its main theme *change in higher education* and took as its starting point a critical appraisal of the seminal work by Ladislav Cerych and Paul Sabatier *Great Expectations and Mixed Performance: The Implementation of Higher Education Reforms in Europe* (1986).

The Conference attracted about 100 scholars from 21 countries. They gave a total of 49 papers on a wide range of subjects.

Three opening presentations, which we publish here, by Paul Sabatier, Åse Gornitzka and Maurice Kogan, discussed what had been learned since the publication of the Cerych and Sabatier book. There was also provision for the pursuit of other parallel themes, mainly expressed through accounts of current policy developments and their impacts in the different countries. The national case studies were based on the implementation of national higher education policies over the last twenty years and authors had been invited to address the three basic questions of the Cerych and Sabatier book:

1. How did the reform originate and what were its official goals?
2. To what extent have those objectives been attained over time? What other politically significant impacts has it had? Have additional objectives emerged? If so, with what effects?
3. What principal factors affected those objectives?

Between them, the national case studies provided a rich source for secondary comparative analysis of contemporary trends. Many also provided the potential for empirical questioning and illumination of the main themes of the Conference, although not all attempted an analysis of factors affecting the implementation process and the attainment of formal goals.

The tracks focusing on different aspects of change in higher education were:

- *Governance* covering the relationship between government and higher education, funding, steering mechanisms, quality and accreditation.
- *Institutional dynamics* covering institutional management and governance structures, middle management organisation, the role of deans and heads of

departments, and stakeholder participation. Under this theme there were also contributions on managerialism.

- *Students and staff* covering issues related to degree programmes (e.g. introduction of new structures and programmes at different levels), and the learning and teaching dimension.

In this book we have been able to reproduce only a minority of these papers; fortunately many others will find their way into journals and other forms of publication. We are confident that the present volume will be just the initial one in a series that will give public notice of relevant research in the increasingly consolidated area of higher education policy studies.

Alberto Amaral
Chair of the Board
CHER

and

Jürgen Enders
Secretary
CHER

Porto
November 2004

ÅSE GORNITZKA, MAURICE KOGAN AND ALBERTO AMARAL

INTRODUCTION

1. THE PURPOSE OF THIS BOOK

The traditional forms of higher education put a high premium on continuity, on the careful accretion and testing of knowledge, in which teaching and learning are conducted within a well-understood and respected framework of institutional and teacher-student relationships. Within such stable and assured frames, major advances in knowledge and the techniques for acquiring it could be confidently secured. In more recent decades, however, the social contexts within which universities work have changed. Most systems have experienced and have had to come to terms with the turbulence associated with enormous increases in their scale and a great widening of client groups, together with major changes in modes of central and institutional government and the higher education objectives of government.

These changes, which can be matched by examples across the whole policy spectrum, have given rise to consideration, by both policy makers and academic policy scientists, of the ways in which policies might be generated and implemented. For higher education, the work of Cerych and Sabatier (*Great Expectations and Mixed Performance: The Implementation of Higher Education Reforms in Europe*, 1986) proved to be a landmark attempt in this area.

As the chapters in this volume by Sabatier (Ch. 1), Gornitzka, Kyvik and Stensaker (Ch. 2) and Kogan (Ch. 3) show, there has been substantial development of implementation theory since then. CHER decided that the time was ripe to revisit Cerych and Sabatier's book, and thus reopen the debate on classical implementation frameworks. Many policy makers and academic analysts still encounter the key problems raised in 1986 which include two main areas of analysis:

- Reform and change – how far does reform translate into change, and what are the appropriate conditions favouring an effective relationship between the two?
- Expectations and results – do results, in general, correspond to expectations, and what conditions favour or hinder a good match? Or do expectations evolve and become adapted along the implementation process?

The choice of areas included in this book follows the range of offerings made at the Conference; selection was also based on the extent to which contributions were

1

Å. Gornitzka et al. (eds.), Reform and Change in Higher Education, 1-14.
© 2007 Springer.

focused on the main theme of the Conference. The structure of the debate followed in this volume is that three general chapters (Sabatier; Gornitzka, Kyvik and Stensaker; and Kogan) present views on the initial work of Cerych and Sabatier from a critical standpoint, followed by a number of national case studies describing chosen examples of implementation of higher education policies.

2. THE DEVELOPING ARGUMENT

Gornitzka, Kyvik and Stensaker's and Kogan's papers note the large repertoire of alternatives to the original top-down implementation theory. Sabatier himself has moved on from the original implementation theory towards the creation of a theory of the role and working of advocacy coalitions. This looks for alternatives to the staged heuristic, and a synthesis of top-down and bottom-up models. The process involves actors at several levels who might operate through advocacy coalitions which share beliefs and activities. In this there are differentiations between levels. Many types of groups are involved in advocacy coalitions which are driven by two causal drives: core values and external perturbations.

Some of the national case studies in this volume directly address the issue of implementation theories and provide an assessment of the usefulness of the Sabatier and Cerych framework for the cases they address (Kyvik, Ch. 4; El-Khawas, Ch. 16; Harman, Ch. 10; James and McInnis, Ch. 13; and Kent, Ch. 11).

Whilst some of Cerych and Sabatier's conclusions and empirical cases remain secure after an interval of nearly 20 years, and their frame of analysis still offers useful perspectives, their top-down treatment of policy development and implementation has been overtaken by alternative accounts. Taylor (Ch. 5), for example, notes how his account of the implications of funding reductions on institutional management in the UK fits the framework for change of depth, functional breadth and level of change. A similar attempt with two cases in the Netherlands, however, concludes that "great expectations and mixed performance" might be due to an analysis that takes the "missionary statements of policy reform too literally" (De Boer, Enders and Westerheijden, Ch. 6). Later accounts depict the multiple ways, levels of systems and the interest groups through which policies are created. They have been well epitomised as multi-level governance, a multi-actor playing field and interactive and dynamic policy processes and the blurring boundaries between different public and private sectors (Enders et al. 2003).

Other heuristics include Trowler's (2002: 3) policy implementation staircase which also illustrates how different groups, advancing different perspectives, emerge at different stages. He notes the differences between change, innovation, initiatives and intervention which come not in tightly defined packages but in confused 'bundles'. Definitions of many similar categories appear in Välimaa (Ch. 14). In the general literature, there are several versions of the new institutionalism (see e.g. Hall and Taylor 1996 for a comprehensive critical review) offering insights into the issue of policy development and implementation. Borrowing from neo-institutional theory, Marton (Ch. 18) uses a framework alternative to the analysis of implementation proposed by Cerych and Sabatier in her account of the implementation of the triple helix relations in Swedish universities. She sees implementation as a process of organisational change and considers how change can be seen as primarily coercive, normative or mimetic. The South African case study looks at implementation from the perspective of shifts in governance. Cloete, Maassen and Muller (Ch. 12) introduce four different governance approaches to discuss implementation processes in South Africa since 1994. Policy processes are analysed as part of shifts in governance, where governance arrangements are seen as the set of institutions and steering capacity used to influence the behaviour of individuals and organisations in society.

The original authors of *Great Expectations*, and the distinguished author of the Foreword to their book, Clark Kerr, had hoped that such studies could be useful in creating successful policies. It is relevant to question, however, how far attempts to *predict* outcomes or to create a theory attempting to do so have proved successful. This would run counter to the sophisticated scepticism put up by earlier generations of policy scientists such as Braybrooke and Lindblom (1963). Lindblom (1990) has more recently posited instead the seeking of information and the resolution of future policies through negotiation.

The usefulness of creating *heuristic* models of the ways in which policy is formulated and the processes by which it then produces outcomes and impacts is not contested. In contention, however, is the extent to which predictive models can be created. So, too, is the aspiration to create a causal theory. In Kyvik's comparison (Ch. 4) of the failure of the late 1960s with the success of the 1990s merger reforms in Norway he attributes the later success to changes in the political and socio-economic climate, but notes, laconically, that the case offers 'probably nothing' to those seeking to add to their knowledge of policy implementation. He is sceptical about our ability to develop a general theory "or a list of factors conducive to the achievement of reform objectives. Every implementation process is unique ..." Kogan expresses similar doubts and Gornitzka, Kyvik and Stensaker recount some of the critique to be found in the literature. The current volume can, however, be read as a step towards gathering and juxtaposing several national experiences and analyses with a long perspective on the relationship between reform and change and the capacity of governments to adopt and implement policies.

3. THE NATIONAL CASE STUDIES – GEOGRAPHICAL AND THEMATIC RANGE

The empirical case studies offered here provide rich sources for potential overarching analyses, through up-to-date accounts of what is happening in many countries in Western Europe (Austria, Finland, Italy, Netherlands, Norway, Portugal, Spain, Sweden and UK), Australasia (Australia), South Africa and America (the US and Mexico). The chapters offer insight into a broad range of policy issues and developments that clearly demonstrate the growing expectation directed at higher education systems in many countries. Several chapters offer analyses of policies over a time span of 20 to 30 years, and refer to the implementation of major or broad policies and major reform packages in higher education (see Harman's chapter for the Australian case (Ch. 10) and Pechar's (Ch. 15) for the Austrian case). Also the Spanish case offers the long-term perspective on changes in higher education. Starting from the impact of external events, notably the transition to democracy and a new definition of 'the state', Mora and Vidal (Ch. 8) analyse the implementation and impact of the higher education reform of 1983, and the reactions to and embryonic impact of a new legal framework for higher education institutions introduced in 2001.

Others give accounts of more specific policies. Kyvik (Ch. 4) for instance examines a major structural reform of the non-university sector in two phases – more specifically the attempt to bring about major amalgamation of Norwegian colleges. This example of two attempts at reform at a thirty-year interval points to a general criticism of implementation studies, that is, that such processes are analysed over too short a period which affects the validity of conclusions concerning success or failure.

Many of the chapters focus on the policies of national governments, but the importance of multiple layers in both policy making and implementation is noted in most of them which between them take in the institutional, intermediary, regional and state as well as the federal levels, where that applies. Also the international layer is seen as relevant in the policy process in some of the chapters. Clearly the contributions in this book provide ample examples of the importance of incorporating into the analysis the multiple layers and actors involved in implementation processes.

The chapters exemplify the rich range of experiences through which countries are moving. Although the rhetoric of reform is often universal, the starting points and active preoccupations of main actors differ greatly between systems. Some case studies concern issues of *access and equity*, for example, federal access policies in the US are treated by Richardson and Hurley's chapter (Ch. 17) focusing on the policy of expanding educational opportunity in the US. Government attention to access and equity in higher education is also a main feature in one of the Australian chapters (James and McInnis, Ch. 13), the Portuguese case (Amaral and Magalhães, Ch. 7) and Mexican cases (Kent, Ch. 11). Others address patterns of *state-university relationships* (e.g. Spain, UK, Austria). The push for *accountability* of higher education is treated by several of the authors as a key aspect of the government-higher education relationship. Chapter 16 (El-Khawas) offers an analysis of accountability policy processes and implementation at state level in the US, describing how the mid-1980s and onwards became a 'time for results' for American public universities and colleges. Changes in *funding arrangements* are also a recurring theme in many of the case studies, some more dramatic than others. Taylor (Ch. 5), for instance, discusses the impact of the drastic cutbacks in funding for UK higher education institutions, 1981 being the crucial moment. This case study analyses the long-term consequences through an empirical study of universities' response to the cutbacks in government funding. Marton (Ch. 18) looks at more subtle shifts in the funding of university research in Sweden as a source of change in universities.

4. GENERALISING FROM THE EMPIRICAL CASES

Higher education as a field of study is not alone in renewing its interest in the issue of implementation. In the field of public policy research and public administration in general there are several signs of a revitalised interest in implementation of public policies (see e.g. Hill and Hupe 2002; Barrett 2004; Schofield and Sausman 2004). Also in the area of European integration studies there is a burgeoning contemporary literature that does not hesitate to study implementation of European policies (see e.g. Knill and Lenschow 1998; Lampinen and Uusikylä 1998; Smit 2002; Sverdrup 2004). This book indicates that studies of implementation are not a dead-end enterprise but that implementation as object of investigation does not necessarily have to be undertaken within a limited set of analytical frameworks. Implementation studies include a variety of frameworks that refer to conceptual developments more generally. The contributions of this volume direct our attention to various aspects of implementation in higher education some of which have been given considerable attention in the classical implementation approaches, while others have not. It is not possible to offer a cross-country analysis or summary of what these cases contain within the compass of this Introduction. Can we learn something new from the national case studies? It is not our purpose to update or re-write Cerych and Sabatier's conclusions but to point out to the reader some of the general themes that emerge from the national case studies. Below we highlight some core general points that can be based on the national case studies presented in the chapters.

4.1. Changing Context of Implementation

Issues of policy implementation and formation in higher education cannot be severed from an understanding of the overall political conditions for reform and change. There were considerable changes in the 'implementation context' – from the 1960s and 1970s to the 1980s and 1990s, specifically in the changes in political dynamics and the new political landscape (Kogan, Ch. 3). This is well exemplified in the accounts of long-term and comprehensive reform, for example, Australia (Harman, Ch. 10), the USA (El-Khawas, Ch. 16), Norway (Kyvik, Ch. 4) and South Africa (Ch. 12). Several chapters report on the importance of looking at policies and the implementation of them in the context of regime changes. The Spanish (Ch. 8) and Portuguese (Ch. 7) cases analyse policy processes against the backdrop of transition to democracy. In Cloete, Maassen and Muller's chapter (Ch. 12), the transition from the apartheid regime to the new South African democracy is at the heart of their analysis. Several other chapters refer to significant changes in the overall *political climate* as a key factor in understanding the various elements of the policy process in higher education. Kyvik (Ch. 4) notes this in his analysis of how the policy to merge colleges was successfully implemented the second time around. Also several note the impact of shifts in interest and political ideology of ministers (e.g. the Portuguese case, Ch. 7) as hampering the implementation of policies, as the political backup and attention of ministers are lost in the process of putting policies into practice. Both the Finnish (Ch. 14) and Mexican (Ch. 11) cases exemplify the importance of changes in the general *economic climate*, in describing how a general economic crisis can be a lever for policy implementation and source of change.

Furthermore, national higher education policies cannot be seen in isolation from other national policies. The national case studies point to the interconnectedness of policies, either implicit or explicit. A number of the empirical chapters reveal how what we term as higher education policies or reforms are part of economic policy and public sector reform programmes. Many of the empirical cases refer to equity and access policies as being guided primarily by efficiency objectives. Richardson and Hurley (Ch. 17) describe how access policies were affected by changing policy frames of higher education at the federal level in the US, as higher education policy went from being linked to defence policy in the 1950s, to the federal 'war on poverty' in the 1960s, to an equity focus from the perspective on institutional *performance* in the mid-1980s. The latter is also described by El-Khawas in Ch. 16.

4.2. The Many Layers and Actors of Policy Processes

Much recent literature in general policy sciences and higher education studies has pointed to the need to see policy and change processes from a multi-level perspective involving a range of actors. Policy making is becoming increasingly complex where actors move between different levels of action and where authority is dispersed across multiple tiers (Hooghe and Marks 2001). The chapters in this volume provide ample exemplifications of the multi-actor/multi-layered aspect of the policy processes in higher education. For instance when looking at accountability policies in the US, El-Khawas (Ch. 16) makes it clear that the considerable changes triggered by the introduction of such policies were created by the actions of multiple policy actors and should be seen as the 'cumulative effort' as actors sustained the accountability effort over time. In this case the multiple actors supporting the state authorities in this effort were other states, federal government, accreditors and independent policy organisations. The actors and layers involved in policy making and implementation need not be fixed. There seems to have been a significant increase in the complexity of the policy process over time. The Mexican experience (Ch. 11) is a case at hand. Here the policy processes are marked by the entry of new actors in the system, and demonstrate how the emergence of such actors was a deliberate effort to restructure the central government with respect to higher education. Especially important was the establishment of a rectors' association that acted as a mediator between government and institutional leaders. New actors also include the presence of international bodies as relevant for Mexican higher education policy. The Spanish case also offers a tangible expression of the multi-layered aspects of policy implementation and decision making relevant to various aspects of university life. Mora and Vidal (Ch. 8) analyse several specific issues of which most are salient policy in general, including, funding policy, policy for academic staff issues, as well as curriculum and university governance reform.

A more specific issue offered by the Spanish case is the increasing complexities of the policy landscape in higher education due to the impact of the European level and in particular the *regionalisation* of higher education. The Spanish case brings to the forefront the impact of regionalisation on higher education, and also how central government is trying to retrieve some of its lost powers through legal reforms (Mora and Vidal, Ch. 8). Implementing policies was marked by tensions between the various levels and the actors representing them. For instance decisions with respect to academic personnel made in the Spanish systems involve a web of four levels – central and regional government, university level, and the level of collegial bodies – and this is stated as a permanent source of discord and conflict. However, these tensions have not prevented reforms concerning academic staff issues having an impact in universities; rather the legal changes made in the 1980s are described as an 'earthquake' in the traditional structure of Spanish universities. Finnish higher education reforms from the 1970s to the end of the 1990s also brought on stage changes in terms of number and types of actors, such as academic trade unions (the case of degrees reform) and various regional actors (the case of the establishment of the polytechnics). Also European influence is noted in Finnish higher education.

For the most part it is noticeable that the professoriate is hardly involved in all of these power shifts and actions.

The multiple layers are not merely activated in the implementation of nationally instigated policies. Larsen and Langfeldt (Ch. 19) provide an account of 'in-house' implementation in their study of strategic planning at four Norwegian universities. Even though the focus here is on the plans that are formulated and implemented within the universities, Larsen and Langfeldt show how such plans are clearly related to the priorities that are set in the national research policy for the universities. A university's own strategic plans merge with the implementation of national reforms.

4.3. Expectations

That policies as implemented often seem different from policies as initially adopted is a major conclusion that has been drawn from implementation studies in general. Contributions in this volume also corroborate this conclusion with respect to higher education, and give indications as to why there are such discrepancies. A policy is not a given entity; studying implementation of a policy without looking at how those policies come about, divorcing our understanding of implementation from our understanding of the processes that generate policies may be a fruitless exercise. Policy implementation involves giving meaning to words, political compromises, intentions and expectations that are not always consistent and clear. And besides, policies are not simply instruments and guidelines for action, often they are expressions of what policy makers believe in and what they find virtuous. They may also be read and analysed as symbols and affirmations of values (cf. Baier, March and Sætren 1988).

What do the chapters in this book say about the *expectations* of governments as expressed in government policies? Governments express in general high expectations of their capacity to shape the direction of higher education – all the chapters included in this volume describe in various ways policies as the embodiment of the official objectives of policy makers. They have expectations that policies will make a difference. It is still often assumed that once a policy is adopted it will be carried out in one way or another, so that part of the policy process is, in effect, wishful thinking. The case of the Portuguese private sector higher education gives fuel to the idea that policy implementation is seriously marked by the wishful thinking of policy makers. Establishing a private sector in Portugal was assumed to be a way to create higher education institutions that were more responsive to regional needs. This turned out to be a false assumption as the private institutions pursued completely different interests, mainly providing low risk and low cost higher education that did not involve any greater societal responsiveness.

The long-term perspective taken by most of the national cases clearly demonstrates the multiple and changing character of such expectations. Objectives are adjusted according to changes in attention, changes in preferences and learning. This is especially clear in the South African and Portuguese cases. Some cases also demonstrate how governments sometimes learn through the process of implementation, not only about success or failure of policies, but about their objectives. We find accounts of policy learning and a feedback driven strategy (where policy makers have little control over the factors that affect the policy outcomes) and policy experimentation (see especially the Finnish case study, Ch. 14). Others, again, give accounts of high ideals – opening of access (South Africa, Ch. 12), devolved and more open government (Spain, Ch. 8), curriculum reform (Italy, Ch. 9) – and how poor analysis of what must be done to secure them has led to a poor return for the effort. It is difficult, indeed, to produce conceptualisations to account for weak development and implementation which arise from governmental ineptitude.

The considerable time span that the national case studies give to their analyses thus underlines the appropriateness of giving attention to policy modification. Policies are not stable over time – the expectations of governments and other actors relevant for policy making and implementation in higher education change, while the overall theme might remain the same. El-Khawas notes a considerable modification of accountability policies in the course of implementation; policies were modified by shifts in political circumstances and in the political interests of new state governors, shifts in economic circumstances and also through universities and colleges actively pushing for changes in the practices and procedures of accountability. Shifts in goals are also clearly underlined in the area of access and equity policies (see Richardson and Hurley, Ch. 17; Cloete, Maassen and Muller, Ch. 12; and James and McInnis, Ch. 13). The national case studies indicate that this is an area of higher education policy where expectations are revised and objectives are abandoned as 'sour grapes', that is, what one cannot get one ceases to want (Richardson and Hurley, Ch. 17; and Cloete, Maassen and Muller, Ch. 12). Some objectives may be sacrificed to obtain a dominant one (see e.g. the Portuguese case study).

Also there are accounts in this book of changing conflicts, interests and actor constellations. The study of US access policies indicates how initial consensus in a policy area disintegrates over time and leads to a shift in goals and instruments of policy. In this instance the goals of the federal government shifted from aiding access to higher education for students from low income families: "Over time the

1972 access and opportunity reforms have been transformed into initiatives that offer more for the middle class than for the original targets" (Ch. 17). Richardson and Hurley attribute this change, or possible displacement, of policy goals to the shifting interests of federal politicians and their wish to cater for the interest of the American 'median voter', though the original interest in the low income social classes still remains an interest of federal policy makers with respect to equity policy in the US.

If governments change their expectations of what policies are supposed to accomplish according to what they learn they can achieve, or shifts in political interests, then the Austrian case can partly be seen as a case where policies are temporarily modified. The Austrian case (Ch. 15) looks at two broad reforms (referred to as the 1st and 2nd reform cycle) in higher education – and this is a case of implementation 'by force', as legal instruments were used to push through a reform despite heavy opposition among academics. Austria's first reform cycle changed the relationship between the state and the universities permanently, and eroded the implicit agreement between the two (Pechar, Ch. 15). Introducing what Pechar refers to as structures inspired by new public management into the higher education relations was easy when establishing new institutions (*Fachhochschulen*). However, doing the same with respect to the traditional universities was quite another matter. With respect to the universities the initial policies for reorganisation were modified and 'softened' in 1993, but it turned out that this was temporary and the full modernisation of the management structure of Austrian universities was passed by parliament decision in 2002. According to Pechar, this was made possible because new groups of academics (rectors and deans) that gained power through the previous reform in 1993, had interests and values that differed from the position taken by academics traditionally. Thus the implementation of one reform had as a major consequence a shift in the power balance relevant to higher education policy making. Starting in 2004, Austrian universities will no longer be state agencies, but will acquire corporate autonomy and have the status of 'legal subjects under public law'.

4.4. Reform and Change

The chapters in this volume raise the issue of the relationship between government reform and change – how government attempts to impact on higher education by design and how that is related to processes of change and (stability) in higher education, its institutions and its basic processes. Government reforms can be seen as integrated parts of ongoing processes of change, where policies of governments can be as much a response to change as a source of change.

The case studies raise questions about the sources of change. If we adopt Burton R. Clark's formulation (1983) – see also Becher and Kogan 1983 – change in higher education emanates from activities at the base of the system. While this certainly remains true of changes in perceptions of the nature of knowledge, of curricula, and of modes of learning and teaching (although governments have been taking an increasing interest in the latter two), the main structural reforms concerning institutional diversity, access, modes of government and financing, together with a host of other reforming intentions, must be attributed to government and particularly to the emergence of non-consensus seeking and heroic ministers (see below).

To put it more negatively, if it had been left to academics, few of the major structural changes would have occurred. Whilst a top-down conceptualisation of policy process was less appropriate when the Cerych-Sabatier text first emerged, the cases presented here give plenty of evidence that it is alive and well in current practice, although it works in parallel with other more interactive processes. This raises interesting questions on how far changes at the base – of the nature of knowledge, of curricula, and of modes of learning and teaching – percolate into policy formation. What would be the kind of issue important at the operational base that might lend itself to aggregation and attempted resolution at the system level? And what might be the mechanisms through which this would happen? The analyses in this book indicate that there is an interplay between conscious political action and more general processes of change in current higher education systems. Consequently, it is hard to isolate the effects of specific government policies. That does not necessarily imply that governments have lost their ability to act autonomously. For instance, the UK case study (Ch. 5) discusses the side effects of policies rather than the officially declared expectations of the effects of changes in a funding regime. The reduction in funding prompted many important changes, especially in the management practices of the institutions. In this sense, the power of policy was considerable as the effects on institutions' responses can still be felt 20 years later. However, as noted by several chapters in this book, and in many of the reviews of the implementation approach, the impact of a policy especially over time mingles with the impact of other forces of change and other policy initiatives which are added.

4.5. Central Intentions, Heroic Acts and Local Resilience

In this shift of the location of the power and intention to initiate change, the earlier aspirations towards rationality in policy formulation have to some extent given way to more impulsive and spontaneous intentions of politicians. Thus, the Cerych and Sabatier insistence on the necessity for deliberative setting of objectives for reform is not observable in many of the reforms. As Marton (Ch. 18) puts it, in using the triple helix to discuss Swedish reforms, which she attributes to coercive forces in the system, "there is no evidence that a system of norms based on market-determined success has taken over".

But in the almost headlong rush away from top-down explanations it has been too easy to overlook the persistence of the institutions and organisations which remain as the custodians of continuing values and social processes. This aspect of the policy process has been captured in many different ways in neo-institutionalist thinking which has as yet hardly penetrated the political science of higher education. The Australian case study of equity policy (James and McInnis, Ch. 13) refers to 'policy ossification'. The authors attribute failures to incompatible objectives, of market, student choices and diversity. In the US, too, state accountability policies began with diffuse goals and lacked implementation tools for their achievement (El-Khawas, Ch. 16). A similar account of the South African 'implementation vacuum' points to lack of adequate preparation (Cloete, Maassen and Muller, Ch. 12).

The obstinacies of both higher education and political institutions are well captured in the case studies of Spain (Mora and Vidal, Ch. 8), Italy (Luzzatto and Moscati, Ch. 9) and Austria (Pechar, Ch. 15). These cases run counter to the judgment that "Colleges and universities are purposive organisations designed by their creators to maximise opportunities in the policy environments where they operate" (Richardson and Hurley, Ch. 17). The national case study of Portugal (Ch. 7) notes one of the specific conditions of implementation of policy in the higher education sector in its analysis of forces of academic drift in the polytechnic sector. This case indicates some of the difficulties in a system in keeping the formal expectations of government and other stakeholders aligned with the natural inclination of higher education institutions to shift their activities towards the perceived traditional university model. System diversity as a political concern seems variably to come up against this driver for change. The Portuguese case portrays how the clear original expectations directed at the polytechnics became blurred by academic drift within the institutions.

Somewhat different, but an aspect of residual 'top-downness', is the strengthened and more heroic role of politicians – well exemplified in the case of Australia and John Dawkins (Harman, Ch. 10) – who have in recent decades seemed able to secure major structural reforms often with a minimum of consultation (Kogan, Ch. 3). Such minister-enforced changes raise interesting questions about the ends of the policy process. Given the well-attested obduracy of academics in the face of proposed change, and the dependence of their socio-technology on working through at the basic level, will full implementation be secured? And, for that matter, at what point can one be sure that the process is completed and closure secured?

Harman's chapter looks at the extensive reform package introduced in the Australian higher education system in 1987 that eventually involved significant structural change from a binary to a unified national system, change in the internal management system at the universities, reform of academic employment and work as well as the reintroduction of student fees. This is the story of a reform that carried with it major changes and triggered major controversies that still linger over a decade later, yet can be seen as reform that was successfully implemented. Some of the factors pointed to in Harman's analysis are echoed in other chapters, especially the importance of the commitment and sustained attention from the central political leadership at the national level. In the Australian case a major factor in successful implementation is attributed to the personal effort of the minister of education, Dawkins, in combination with a reorganisation of the government office to make it reform friendly; it was a high speed and complex yet compact reform package that made it hard for opponents to attack successfully. Furthermore the institutional opposition and possible inertia were successfully handled by letting the reform contain sufficient attraction for institutional leaders by eliciting an anticipation that more funding would be available in the future through the reform. The implementation process was thus marked by the mustering of several political resources that made implementation possible.

The analysis of Australian equity policy, however, does not share the same story of successful implementation. James and McInnis (Ch. 13) give a telling account of policy modification and permutation. They point to Australian equity policy as a 'moving target' that has been stretched to accommodate shifts in attention and interest while consensus over the overarching value of social equity has remained.

The main conclusion of the Norwegian national case study on mergers in the college sector highlights two elements as important for understanding the differences between the two reform attempts. Firstly, commitment at a high level in the ministry to the second reform – a centrally positioned actor who acted as a true fixer in the implementation process. Secondly, shifts in political ideology with a much stronger emphasis on efficiency and streamlining organisation and strengthening the institutional management capacity in the higher education sector as well as in the public sector in general. Thus the general change in the political-ideological climate set the stage for the 'heroic' ministers to act and carry policies into practice.

5. NOTES FOR FUTURE RESEARCH

These essays open up several themes for further work. As indicated in the national case studies where national policies do play a role, the changes described in higher education are caused by dynamic, interactive processes. The focus in earlier versions of implementation studies placed too much energy on identifying gaps between original formulation and outcome, and put too much emphasis on one actor. Future research should do justice to the complexities of the changed relationship between policy makers and policy objects. These complexities are amply identified in this volume.

Why should there be an analytical interest in government policies? Can we on the basis of the chapters argue for a continued research interest in not only policies as such but in the way that policies interact with the practices of higher education? Broadly speaking, governments have tried to alter structure rather than content although recently some have put their shoulders behind learning and teaching change. A relevant research topic would assess the impact of structural changes on content and vice versa.

An issue which applies to all study areas that rest on policy problems and where domains rather than disciplines are the appropriate approach is the extent to which empirical case studies feed into or rest on theoretical approaches. The richness of materials presented here invites the thought that whilst many studies in our field make use of theories and concepts from the social sciences, not enough is done to make sure that they themselves feed into the developing and testing of theory. Rich sources of empirical data which could refresh and test theory thus go unused. That is an issue which future conferences would do well to pick up.

Central on the agenda will then be to renew our interest in the public policies of higher education. We need to find ways of looking at the relationship between policies and practice in higher education so as to include studies of implementation and of the significance of public policies for understanding change processes in higher education.

There remain the conflicting perspectives of top-downers and bottom-uppers (see Gornitzka, Kyvik and Stensaker, Ch. 2; and Kogan, Ch. 3). There is a case, to judge by our empirical examples, for taking an eclectic and case by case approach on this question. It would thus be difficult to construct a combined model, unless one could specify those areas of policy that are likely to be top-down (e.g. those deriving from broader social and economic policies) and those deriving from the substantives of higher education activity (e.g. learning and teaching) which would be bottom-up. It would then be necessary to analyse ways in which they are connected or converted into policies and practices.

REFERENCES

Baier, V.E., J.G. March and H. Sætren. "Implementation and Ambiguity." In March, J.G. (ed.). *Decisions and Organizations*. Oxford: Basil Blackwell, 1988, 150–166.

Barrett, S.M. "Implementation Studies: Time for a Revival? Personal Reflections on 20 Years of Implementation Studies." *Public Administration* 82 (2004): 249–262.

Becher, T. and M. Kogan. *Process and Structure in Higher Education*. London: Heinemann, 1983.

Braybrooke, D. and C.E. Lindblom. *A Strategy for Decision*. Glencoe: The Free Press, 1963.

Cerych, L. and P. Sabatier. *Great Expectations and Mixed Performance. The Implementation of Higher Education Reforms in Europe*. Stoke-on-Trent: Trentham Books, 1986.

Clark, B.R. *The Higher Education System: Academic Organization in Cross-National Perspective*. Berkeley, CA: University of California Press, 1983.

Enders, J., M. Jeliazkova, A. McGuinness and P. Maassen. "Higher Education Policy Formulation and Implementation: A Framework for Case Analysis." Paper presented at the 16th CHER Annual Conference, Porto, 4–6 September, 2003.

Hall, P.A. and R.C.R. Taylor. "Political Science and the Three New Institutionalisms." *Political Studies* XLIV (1996): 936–957.

Hill, M. and P. Hupe. *Implementing Public Policy: Governance in Theory and Practice*. London: Sage, 2002.

Hooghe, L. and G. Marks. *Multi-level Governance and European Integration*. Lanham: Rowman and Littlefield, 2001.

Knill, C. and A. Lenschow. "Coping with Europe: The Impact of British and German Administrations on the Implementation of EU Environmental Policy." *Journal of European Public Policy* 5 (1998): 595–614.

Lampinen R. and P. Uusikylä. "Implementation Deficit – Why Member States do not Comply with EU Directives?" *Scandinavian Political Studies* 21 (1998): 231–251.

Lindblom, C.E. *Inquiry and Change. The Troubled Attempt to Understand and Shape Society*. New Haven, London and New York: Yale University Press and Russell Sage Foundation, 1990.

Schofield, J. and C. Sausman. "Symposium on Implementing Public Policy: Learning from Theory and Practice – Introduction." *Public Administration* 82 (2004): 235–248.

Smit, A. "Managing EU Structural Funds. Effective Capacity for Implementation as a Prerequisite." *International Review of Administrative Sciences* 68 (2002): 472–475.

Sverdrup, U. "Compliance and Conflict Management in the European Union: Nordic Exceptionalism." *Scandinavian Political Studies* 27 (2004): 23–43.

Trowler, P.R. (ed.). *Higher Education Policy and Institutional Change: Intentions and Outcomes in Turbulent Environments*. Buckingham: SRHE and Open University Press, 2002.

OVERVIEW

PAUL SABATIER

FROM POLICY IMPLEMENTATION TO POLICY CHANGE: A PERSONAL ODYSSEY

1. INTRODUCTION

Building upon the pioneering work of Pressman and Wildavsky (1973), the decade from the mid-1970s to the mid-1980s represented the 'golden era' of implementation research in OECD countries. This was the period of the development of 'top-down' implementation frameworks by Van Meter and Van Horn (1975) and Sabatier and Mazmanian (1979, 1983). That work stimulated a wave of 'bottom-up' critiques by Hjern and Hull (1982), Barrett and Fudge (1981), Berman (1978) and Hanf and Scharpf (1978). *Great Expectations and Mixed Performance: The Implementation of Higher Education Reforms in Europe*, by Ladislav Cerych and myself, was published in 1986, at the end of this period.

The purpose of this conference, as I understand it, is to assess the field of implementation studies of higher education reforms since the *Great Expectations* book: What has happened to implementation theory? Are scholars still engaged in the top-down/bottom-up debate, or has some new conceptual framework come to the fore? What have we learned about the factors affecting the implementation of higher education reforms?

In this chapter, I shall first review the implementation literature and the broader 'policy cycle' or 'stages heuristic' out of which it emerged. I shall then discuss the development and basic principles of the Advocacy Coalition Framework (ACF), which represents my attempt to synthesise the advantages of the 'top-down' and 'bottom-up' approaches to implementation research in order to understand policy change over periods of a decade or more. Finally, I shall discuss the implications of the ACF for the study of higher education policy.

2. IMPLEMENTATION STUDIES: CONTRIBUTIONS AND LIMITATIONS

Implementation scholars during the 1970s and 1980s made some important contributions to our understanding of policy implementation and the broader policy process. Much of this was a product of the debate between 'top-down' and 'bottom-up' approaches to implementation studies. While applied research has continued, in my view the field essentially ground to a halt in the late 1980s, at least at a theoretical level. There have been several attempts to revive it (Matland 1995; Lester and Goggin 1998; De Leon and De Leon 2002), but none appears to have

Å. Gornitzka et al. (eds.), Reform and Change in Higher Education, 17-34.

been successful. In this section, I first review the broader stages heuristic out of which implementation research emerged, and then focus on the top-down/bottom-up debate.

2.1. The Policy Cycle/Stages Heuristic

Throughout the 1970s and 1980s, the most influential framework for understanding the policy process – particularly among American scholars – was what Nakamura (1987) termed 'the textbook approach', what May and Wildavsky (1978) termed 'the policy cycle', and what I have termed 'the stages heuristic' (Sabatier 1991). As developed by Lasswell (1971), Jones (1970), Anderson (1975) and Brewer and De Leon (1983), it divided the policy process into a series of stages – usually agenda setting, policy formulation and legitimation, implementation and evaluation – and discussed some of the factors affecting the process within each stage. The stages heuristic served a useful purpose in the 1970s and early 1980s by dividing the very complex policy process into discrete stages and by stimulating some excellent research within specific stages – particularly agenda setting (Cobb, Ross and Ross 1976; Kingdon 1984; Nelson 1984) and policy implementation (Pressman and Wildavsky 1973; Hjern and Hull 1982; Mazmanian and Sabatier 1983).

The stages heuristic has, however, been subjected to some rather devastating criticisms (Nakamura 1987; Sabatier 1991; Sabatier and Jenkins-Smith 1993, 1999):

- It is not really a causal theory since it never identifies a set of causal drivers that govern the process within and across stages. Instead, work within each stage has tended to develop on its own, almost totally oblivious to research in other stages.
- The proposed sequence of stages is often descriptively inaccurate. For example, evaluations of existing programmes affect agenda setting, and policy formulation/legitimation occurs as bureaucrats attempt to implement vague legislation (Nakamura 1987).
- The stages heuristic has a very legalistic, top-down bias in which the focus is typically on the passage and implementation of a major piece of legislation. This neglects the interaction of the implementation and evaluation of numerous pieces of legislation – none of them pre-eminent – within a given policy domain (Hjern and Hull 1982; Sabatier 1986). The assumption of a single policy cycle focused around a major piece of legislation oversimplifies the usual process of *multiple, interacting cycles* involving numerous policy proposals and statutes at multiple levels of government. In such a situation – which is common – focusing on '*a* policy cycle' makes very little sense.

The last point in particular led me to conclude that the stages heuristic was fundamentally flawed, even though much of the work on policy implementation was quite useful. The stages heuristic needed to be replaced with a framework that sought to explain an overall policy process within a given policy domain that would usually be composed of a variety of initiatives at different stages of the policy cycle.

2.2. Top-Down and Bottom-Up Approaches to Implementation Analysis

2.2.1. The Top-Down Perspective
The essential features of a top-down approach were developed by Pressman and Wildavsky (1973), starting with a definition of 'implementation' as 'the carrying out of a policy decision'. This approach starts with a policy decision by governmental (often central government) officials and then asks (Mazmanian and Sabatier 1983):

- To what extent were the actions of implementing official and target groups consistent with (the objectives and procedures outlined in) that policy decision?
- To what extent were the objectives attained over time, that is, to what extent were the impacts consistent with the objectives?
- What were the principal factors affecting policy outputs and impacts, both those relevant to the official policy as well as other politically significant ones?
- How was the policy reformulated over time on the basis of experience?

The Sabatier and Mazmanian framework (1979) was probably the most detailed of the top-down approaches. It first identified a variety of legal, political and 'tractability' variables affecting the different stages of the implementation process. It then sought to synthesise this large number of variables into a shorter list of six sufficient and generally necessary conditions for the effective implementation of legal objectives:

1. *Clear and consistent objectives.* Taken from Van Meter and Van Horn (1975), clear legal objectives were viewed as providing both a clear standard of evaluation and an important legal resource to implementing officials.
2. *Adequate causal theory.* Borrowing the fundamental insight of Pressman and Wildavsky (1973) that policy interventions incorporate an implicit theory about how to effectuate social change, Sabatier and Mazmanian provided some useful guidelines about how to ascertain the adequacy of the causal theory behind a policy reform.
3. *Implementation process legally structured to enhance compliance by implementing officials and target groups.* Borrowing again from Pressman and Wildavsky (1973), the authors pointed to a variety of legal mechanisms including the number of veto points involved in programme delivery, the sanctions and incentives available to overcome resistance, and the assignment of programmes to implementing agencies which would be supportive and give them high priority.
4. *Committed and skilful implementing officials.* Recognising the unavoidable discretion given implementing officials, their commitment to policy objectives and skill in utilising available resources were viewed as critical (Lipsky 1971; Lazin 1973). While this could partially be determined by the initial statute, much of it was a product of post-statutory political forces.

5. *Support of interest groups and sovereigns over time.* This simply recognised the need to maintain political support from interest groups and from legislative and executive sovereigns throughout the long implementation process (Downs 1967; Murphy 1973; Bardach 1974; Sabatier 1975).

6. *Changes in socio-economic conditions which do not substantially undermine political support or causal theory.* This variable simply recognised that changes in socio-economic conditions, for example, the Arab oil boycott or the Vietnam War, could have dramatic repercussions on the political support or causal theory of a programme (Hofferbert 1974; Aaron 1978).

In short, the first three conditions can be dealt with by the initial policy decision (e.g. a statute), whereas the latter three are largely the product of political and economic pressures during the subsequent implementation process.

In the five years following the 1979 publication of the framework, Sabatier and Mazmanian sought to have it tested – by themselves and others – in a variety of policy areas and political systems. The framework was critically applied to at least twenty cases (Sabatier 1986), including several involving environmental policy in the US and the seven higher education reforms in Europe that were published in the *Great Expectations* book. What did they find?

First, the emphasis of the framework on legal structuring of the implementation process – one of its major innovations – has been confirmed in numerous studies. This is particularly gratifying since one of the most frequent criticisms of the framework was that the emphasis on legal structuring is unrealistic, that is, that the cognitive limitations of policy makers and the need for compromise at the formulation stage preclude careful structuring (Majone and Wildavsky 1978; Barrett and Fudge 1981). The evidence suggests that, while fairly coherent structuring is difficult, it occurs more frequently than critics realise and, when present, proves to be very important.

Likewise, two of the major contributions borrowed from Pressman and Wildavsky (1973) – veto points and causal theory – were confirmed in many studies. For example, the much greater success of the British Open University than the French IUTs (*Instituts Universitaires de Technologie*) in reaching projected enrolments can be partially attributed to the better theory utilised by policy formulators in the former case (Cerych and Sabatier 1986).

Perhaps the best evidence of the potential importance of legal structuring is that the two most successful cases studied to date – the California coastal commissions (at least during the first decade) and the British Open University – were also the best designed institutions. That is, they structured the process to provide reasonably consistent objectives, a good causal theory, relatively few veto points, sympathetic implementing officials, access of supporters to most decisions and adequate financial resources.

Second, the relatively manageable list of variables and the focus in the framework on the formulation-implementation-reformulation cycle encouraged many of our case authors to look at a longer time-frame than was true of earlier implementation studies (i.e. ten years instead of four). This, in turn, led to a discovery of the importance of learning by programme proponents over time as they became aware of deficiencies in the original programme and sought improved legal and political strategies for dealing with them. For example, the supporters of the French IUTs greatly improved their understanding of the factors affecting student choice over time (Cerych and Sabatier 1986).

Third, our focus on legally mandated objectives – particularly when combined with the ten-year time span for assessing programme effectiveness – helped produce a less pessimistic evaluation of governmental performance than was true of the first generation of implementation studies. On the one hand, the focus on legally mandated objectives encouraged scholars to carefully distinguish the objectives contained in legal documents from the political rhetoric surrounding policy formulation – the criticism of the 'failure' of the Open University to meet the needs of working class students being a case in point. In addition, the longer time-frame used in many of these studies meant that several which were initially regarded as failures – US compensatory education and the French IUTs – were regarded in a more favourable light after proponents had had the benefit of a decade of learning and experimentation (Kirst and Jung 1982; Mazmanian and Sabatier 1983; Cerych and Sabatier 1986).

2.2.2. Criticisms of the Top-Down Perspective

Despite these strengths, several years' experience with testing the Sabatier/Mazmanian framework has also revealed some significant flaws.

First, the focus placed on 'clear and consistent policy objectives' needs to be reconceptualised. Experience has confirmed the critics' charge that very few programmes meet this very demanding criterion, either initially or after a decade (Majone and Wildavsky 1978; MacIntyre 1985). Instead, the vast majority incorporate a multitude of partially conflicting objectives. This does not, however, preclude the possibility for assessing programme effectiveness. Instead, it simply means that effectiveness needs to be reconceptualised into the 'acceptability space' demarcated by the intersection of the ranges of acceptable values on each of the multiple evaluative dimensions involved. This can be illustrated by the case of the Norwegian regional colleges: they were supposed to serve students from the local region and to foster regionally relevant research at the same time that they were also mandated to be part of a national educational system in which the transfer of student credits among institutions and the evaluation of faculty research by peers in other institutions had to be protected. While the institutions after a decade were receiving 'excellent' ratings on very few of these dimensions, the evidence suggests they were satisfactory on all of them (Cerych and Sabatier 1986).

On a related point, most implementation scholars have followed Van Meter and Van Horn (1975) in assuming that, *ceteris paribus*, the probability of effective implementation of a reform is inversely related to the extent of envisaged departure from the status quo ante. One of the most significant conclusions of the *Great Expectations* book was that the relationship is not linear but rather curvilinear. They suggest that very incremental reforms – for example, the Swedish 25/5 Scheme for adult admission to universities – simply do not arouse enough commitment to get much done, while those such as the German Gesamthochschulen which envisage a comprehensive reform of the entire system arouse too much resistance to get off the ground. Instead, those reforms – for example, the British Open University – which are ambitious enough to arouse intense commitment from proponents but are rather limited in their effects on the entire higher education system stand the best chance of success.

Second, while Sabatier and Mazmanian encouraged a longer time-frame and provided several examples of policy-oriented learning by proponents over time, their framework did not provide a good conceptual vehicle for looking at policy change over periods of a decade or more (Goodwin and Moen 1981; Browning, Marshall and Tabb 1984; Goggin 1984; Lowry 1985). This is primarily because, as we shall see below, it focused too much on the perspective of programme proponents, thereby neglecting the strategies (and learning) by other actors. This was a major flaw in the Sabatier/Mazmanian model which hopefully was improved by the ACF.

The assessment thus far has been from the point of view of Sabatier/Mazmanian or other sympathisers of a top-down perspective. It is now time to examine the more fundamental methodological criticisms raised by 'bottom-uppers'.

2.2.3. The Bottom-Up Perspective

The fundamental flaw in top-down models, according to Hjern and Hull (1982), Hanf (1982), Barrett and Fudge (1981), Elmore (1979) and other bottom-uppers, is that they start from the perspective of (central) decision makers and thus tend to neglect other actors. Their methodology leads top-downers to assume that the framers of the policy decision (e.g. statute) are the key actors and that others are basically impediments. This, in turn, leads them to neglect strategic initiatives coming from the private sector, from local implementing officials and from other policy subsystems. While Sabatier and Mazmanian are not entirely guilty of this – in particular, their focus on causal theory and hierarchical integration encourages the analyst to examine the perspectives of other actors – this is certainly a potential Achilles heel of their model.

A second, and related, criticism of top-down models is that they are difficult to use in situations where there is no dominant policy (statute) or agency, but rather a multitude of governmental directives and actors, none of them pre-eminent. As this is often the case, particularly in social service delivery, this is a very telling criticism. While Sabatier and Mazmanian can recognise such situations – through the concepts of (inadequate) causal theory and (poor) hierarchical integration – they have very little ability to predict the outcome of such complex situations except to say that the policy they are interested in will probably not be effectively implemented.

A third criticism of top-down models is that they are likely to ignore, or at least underestimate, the strategies used by street-level bureaucrats and target groups to get around central policy and/or to divert it to their own purposes (Weatherly and Lipsky 1977; Elmore 1978; Berman 1978). A related point is that such models are likely to neglect many of the counterproductive effects of the policies chosen for analysis. While a really skilful top-downer can attempt to deal with such deficiencies, there is little doubt that these, too, are important criticisms.

The bottom-uppers were able to advance some telling arguments against the top-down approach. Have they also been able to accomplish the more difficult task of developing a more viable alternative?

The bottom-up approach of Hanf, Hjern and Porter (1978) starts by identifying the network of actors involved in service delivery in one or more local areas and asks them about their goals, strategies, activities and contacts. It then uses the contacts as a vehicle for developing a networking technique to identify the local, regional and national actors involved in the planning, financing and execution of the relevant governmental and non-governmental programmes. This provides a mechanism for moving from street-level bureaucrats (the 'bottom') up to the 'top' policy makers in both the public and private sectors (Hanf, Hjern and Porter 1978; Hjern and Porter 1981; Hjern and Hull 1982).

The approach developed by Hanf, Hjern and Porter (1978) has several notable strengths.

First, they have developed an explicit and replicable methodology for identifying a policy network ('implementation structure'). In the small firms study, for example, they started with a random sample of firms in an area, and then interviewed key officials in each firm to ascertain their critical problems, the strategies developed to deal with each, and the persons contacted to execute each of those strategies. They then used those contacts via a networking technique to identify the 'implementation structure' (Hull and Hjern 1987). It is this intersubjectively reliable methodology which separates Hanf, Hjern and Porter from the vast majority of bottom-up (and even top-down) researchers.

Second, because Hanf, Hjern and Porter do not begin with a governmental programme but rather with actors' perceived problems and the strategies developed for dealing with them, they are able to assess the relative importance of a variety of governmental programmes vis-à-vis private organisations and market forces in solving those problems. In contrast, a top-down approach is likely to overestimate the importance of the governmental programme which is its focus. For example, Hanf's (1982) bottom-up analysis of pollution control in the Netherlands concluded that energy policies and the market price of alternative fuels had more effect on firms' air pollution control programmes than did governmental pollution control programmes – a conclusion which would have been difficult for a top-downer to reach.

Third, this approach is able to deal with a policy/problem area involving a multitude of public (and private) programmes, none of them pre-eminent. In contrast, such cases present substantial difficulties for top-down approaches.

For all these strengths, however, the Hanf, Hjern and Porter approach also has its limitations.

First, just as top-downers are in danger of overemphasising the importance of the centre vis-à-vis the periphery, bottom-uppers are likely to overemphasise the ability of the periphery to frustrate the centre. More specifically, the focus on actors' goals and strategies – the vast majority of whom are at the periphery – may underestimate the centre's indirect influence over those goals and strategies through its ability to affect the institutional structure in which individuals operate (Kiser and Ostrom 1982). In short, one of the most basic shortcomings of the Hanf, Hjern and Porter approach is that it takes the present distribution of preferences and resources as given, without ever inquiring into the efforts of other actors to structure the rules of the game.

Second, Hanf, Hjern and Porter fail to start from an explicit theory of the factors affecting its subject of interest. Because their approach relies very heavily on the perceptions and activities of participants, it is their prisoner. Their networking methodology is a useful starting point for identifying many of the actors involved in a policy area, but it needs to be related via an explicit theory to social, economic and legal factors which structure the perceptions, resources and participation of those actors.

2.3. Attempts at a Synthesis: An American Perspective

Since 1986, there have been at least four attempts in the US to synthesise some of the best features of the top-down and bottom-up approaches into a new conceptual framework of the implementation process. There may have been additional efforts in other OECD countries, but I am simply not aware of them.

The first such effort was by Richard Elmore (1985), right at the end of the 'golden era'. He combined his previous work on 'backward mapping' – one of the bottom-up classics – with what he termed 'forward mapping', essentially a top-down perspective. He argues that policy makers need to consider both the policy instruments and other resources at their disposal (forward mapping) and the incentive structure of ultimate target groups (backward mapping) because programme success is contingent on meshing the two. Elmore's paper is primarily concerned with aiding policy practitioners by indicating the need to use multiple perspectives in designing and implementing policies. At that very practical level, it is excellent. It does not purport, however, to provide a model of the policy process which can be used by social scientists to explain outcomes in a wide variety of settings.

The second attempt at synthesis was made by Malcolm Goggin et al. (1990). They developed a communications model of intergovernmental implementation in the US. In their views, states are the critical actors. They receive messages from both 'the top' (the federal government) and 'the bottom' (local actors). Goggin et al. applied their framework to a number of cases, but, to my knowledge, no one else has seriously applied it. In the late 1990s, Lester and Goggin (1998) stimulated a brief flurry of essays on implementation research, but no new theoretical syntheses and no programme of empirical research.

Midway through the 1990s, Richard Matland (1995) sought to combine top-down and bottom-up approaches by arguing that they were applicable to four different situations:

- In situations of low goal conflict and low technical ambiguity, 'administrative implementation' is the appropriate strategy. This was essentially a top-down approach. As long as resources are provided, implementation should be relatively straightforward.

- In situations of high goal conflict and low technical ambiguity, actors know how to accomplish policy objectives but they cannot agree on the appropriate objectives. He terms this, 'political implementation'. Again, a top-down model is appropriate once policy makers can decide on the appropriate goals.
- In situations of high technical ambiguity and low goal conflict, the emphasis should be on facilitating learning – what Matland terms 'experimental implementation'.
- In situations of high goal conflict and high technical ambiguity, coming to agreement on anything is extremely difficult. Letting local actors find local solutions (essentially the bottom-up perspective) is appropriate. He terms this 'symbolic implementation'.

Unfortunately, to my knowledge, no one – including Matland – has seriously applied Matland's framework.

More recently, De Leon and De Leon (2002) have called for a revival of implementation research using essentially a bottom-up approach but linking it more closely to prospects for public participation.

To the best of my knowledge, none of these post-1985 attempts at synthesising top-down and bottom-up approaches has stimulated the development of a coherent theory linked to programmes of empirical research by a body of scholars. In Lakatos' (1978) terminology, then, none of them represents a 'progressive research programme'.

All is not bleak, however. For a fifth approach, the ACF was developed in the late 1980s as an explicit effort to combine the best features of top-down and bottom-up approaches to implementation research with contributions from a number of other literatures, mainly social psychology and policy subsystems. It is a relatively coherent theory which is constantly expanding and which has stimulated approximately 35 applications by a wide variety of scholars (Sabatier and Jenkins-Smith 1999). It is to the ACF that we now turn.

3. AN ADVOCACY COALITION FRAMEWORK OF POLICY CHANGE

One of the major contributions of Mazmanian and Sabatier (1983) was their contention that the relatively short time span (4–5 years) used in most implementation studies was inadequate. Not only did it lead to premature judgments concerning programme failure, but it also missed some very important features of the policy process, namely, the extent of policy-oriented learning. While this top-down approach did a good job of illustrating learning by reform proponents, its top-down assumptions made it difficult to focus equally on learning by opponents. This deficiency can be remedied, however, by investigating bottom-uppers' strategies for improving goal attainment. This points to a synthesis which combines top-down and bottom-up approaches in the analysis of policy change over periods of a decade or more.

3.1. Elements of the Synthesis

The elements of such a conceptual framework are at hand. Consistent with the bottom-uppers, one needs to start from a policy problem or subsystem – rather than a law or other policy decision – and then examine the strategies employed by relevant actors in both the public and private sectors at various levels of government as they attempt to deal with the issue consistent with their objectives. The networking technique developed by Hanf, Hjern and Porter can be one of the methods for determining the actors in a subsystem, although it needs to be combined with other approaches to include the actors who are *indirectly* involved.

Likewise, the concerns of top-down theorists with the manner in which legal and socio-economic factors structure behavioural options need to be incorporated into the synthesis, as do their concerns with the validity of the causal assumptions behind specific programmes and strategies. This leads to a focus on (1) the effects of socio-economic (and other) changes external to the policy network/subsystem on actors' resources and strategies; (2) the attempts by various actors to manipulate the legal attributes of governmental programmes in order to achieve their objectives over time; and (3) actors' efforts to improve their understanding of the magnitude and factors affecting the problem – as well as the impacts of various policy instruments – as they learn from experience.

Attention thus shifts from policy implementation to policy change involving numerous policy initiatives over a period of 10–20 years. The longer time span creates, however, a need to aggregate actors into a manageable number of groups if the researcher is to avoid severe information overload. After examining several options, the most useful principle of aggregation seems to be by belief system. This produces a focus on 'advocacy coalitions', that is, actors from various public and private organisations who share a set of beliefs and who engage in a non-trivial degree of coordinated behaviour in order to realise their common goals over time.

In short, the synthesis adopts the bottom-uppers' unit of analysis – a whole variety of public and private actors involved with a policy problem – as well as their concerns with understanding the perspectives and strategies of all major categories of actors, not simply programme proponents. It then combines this starting point with top-downers' concerns with the manner in which socio-economic conditions and legal instruments constrain behaviour. It applies this synthesised perspective to the analysis of policy change over periods of a decade or more. This time-frame is required to deal with the role of policy-oriented learning – a topic identified as critical in several top-down studies. Finally, the synthesis adopts the intellectual style (or methodological perspective) of many top-downers in its willingness to utilise fairly abstract theoretical constructs and to operate from an admittedly simplified portrait of reality.

3.2. Overview of the Framework

The ACF starts from the premise that the most useful aggregate unit of analysis for understanding policy change in modern industrial societies is not any specific governmental organisation but rather a policy subsystem, that is, those actors from a variety of public and private organisations who are actively concerned with a policy problem or issue, such as higher education (Heclo 1974; Jordan and Richardson 1983; Milward and Wamsley 1984; Rose 1984; Sharpe 1985).

Figure 1. 1998 diagram of the Advocacy Coalition Framework

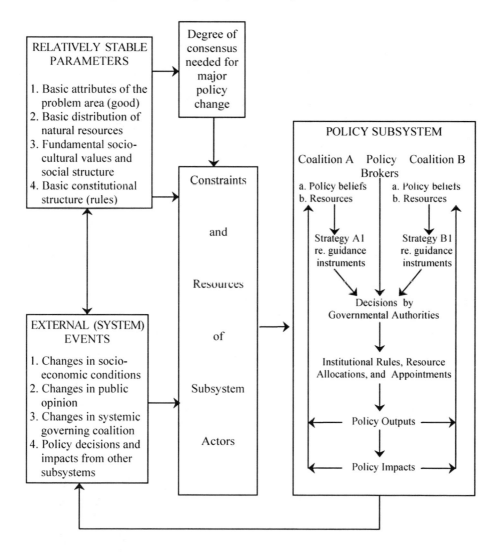

Figure 1 presents a general overview of the framework. On the left side are two sets of exogenous variables – the one fairly stable, the other dynamic – which affect the constraints and resources of subsystem actors. Higher education policy, for example, is strongly affected by very stable factors, such as the overall income and educational levels in a society, plus cultural norms about elitist vs. egalitarian strategies governing access to higher education. But there are also more dynamic factors, including changes in socio-economic conditions and in system-wide governing coalitions, which provide some of the principal sources of policy change. These are all features drawn from top-down models which 'structure' policy making.

Within the subsystem, the framework draws heavily upon the bottom-up approach. It assumes, however, that actors can be aggregated into a number of advocacy coalitions – each composed of politicians, agency officials, interest group leaders and intellectuals who share a set of normative and causal beliefs on core policy issues. At any particular point in time, each coalition adopts a strategy(s) envisaging one or more changes in governmental institutions perceived to further its policy objectives. Conflicting strategies from different coalitions are mediated by a third group of actors, here termed 'policy brokers', whose principal concern is to find some reasonable compromise which will reduce intense conflict. The end result is legislation or governmental decrees establishing or modifying one or more governmental action programmes at the collective choice level (Kiser and Ostrom 1982; Page 1985). These in turn produce policy outputs at the operational level (e.g. graduation rates in different disciplines). These outputs at the operational level, mediated by a number of other factors (most notably, the validity of the causal theory underlying the programme), result in a variety of impacts on targeted problem parameters (e.g. employment patterns of higher education graduates), as well as side effects.

At this point, the framework requires additional elements not central to the implementation literature. By far the most important of these is the ACF's model of the individual, that is, its assumptions about actors' goals, information processing capabilities and decision rules. First, in contrast to frameworks drawn from micro-economics, the ACF does not assume that all actors seek to maximise their self-interest all the time. Instead, it argues this is an empirical question, but clearly allows for the possibility of some concern for collective welfare. Second, consistent with Simon's (1979) work on bounded rationality, the ACF assumes that actors have only a limited capacity to process information and thus seek to use all sorts of simplifying 'heuristics'. Third, consistent with the literature on cognitive dissonance and biased assimilation (Festinger 1957; Lord, Ross and Lepper 1979), the ACF assumes that actors perceive the world through a set of beliefs that filter in information consistent with pre-existing beliefs and filter out dissonant information. This makes belief change difficult. In addition, it means that actors with different perceptual filters will perceive the same piece of information in different ways. This, in turn, leads to suspicion about opponents' intellectual integrity, reasonableness and capacity to engage in reasoned argument. Finally, the ACF adopts the central proposition of prospect theory (Quattrone and Tversky 1988), namely that actors value loses more than gains. This means that actors will remember defeats more than victories and, in turn, exaggerate the power of opponents. Combining the last two points results in 'the devil shift', the proposition that actors in a political conflict view opponents as more nefarious, less reasonable and more powerful than they probably are (Sabatier, Hunter and McLaughlin 1987). That, in turn, exacerbates the potential for belief change and compromise across coalitions (who, by definition, are composed of actors with different beliefs).

Some aspects of public policy clearly change far more frequently than others. In order to get a conceptual handle on this, the framework distinguishes the core from the secondary aspects of a belief system or a governmental action programme. Recall that coalitions are seeking to get their beliefs translated into governmental programmes, so the two concepts can be analysed in similar categories. The extent to which a specific programme incorporates the beliefs of any single coalition is, however, an empirical question and will reflect the relative power of that coalition within the subsystem.

The ACF conceptualises the belief systems of policy elites as a tripartite structure. At the deepest and broadest level are *deep core beliefs.* These involve very general normative and ontological assumptions about human nature, the relative priority of fundamental values such as liberty and equality, the relative priority of the welfare of different groups, the proper role of government vs. markets in general (i.e. across all policy subsystems), and beliefs about who should participate in governmental decision making. The traditional Left/Right scales operate at the deep core level. Largely the product of childhood socialisation, deep core beliefs are very difficult to change. At the next level are *policy core beliefs.* These are applications of deep core beliefs to an entire policy subsystem, such as French higher education policy, and include such topics as the priority of different values, whose welfare counts, the relative authority of governments and markets, the proper roles of the general public, elected officials, civil servants, experts, etc., and the relative seriousness and causes of policy problems in the subsystem as a whole. The general assumption is that policy elites are very knowledgeable about relationships within their policy subsystem and thus may be willing to adjust the application of certain deep core beliefs to that subsystem. For example, while American conservatives generally have a strong preference for market solutions, many of them recognise the desirability of state-funded mass higher education institutions. Because policy core beliefs are subsystem-wide in scope and deal with fundamental policy choices, they are also very difficult to change. The final level consists of *secondary beliefs.* Secondary beliefs are relatively narrow in scope (less than subsystem-wide) and address, for example, detailed rules and budgetary applications within a specific programme, the seriousness and causes of problems in a specific locale, public participation guidelines within a specific statute, etc. Because secondary beliefs are narrower in scope than policy core beliefs, changing them requires less evidence and fewer agreements among subsystem actors and thus should be less difficult.

The ACF argues that legislators, agency officials, interest group leaders, researchers, and intellectuals with similar policy core beliefs will form an advocacy coalition in an effort to coordinate their behaviour and bring about changes in public policy. In any given policy subsystem, there may be 2–5 advocacy coalitions. Among members of a given coalition, trust is common and belief change is relatively easy on secondary beliefs. Given the 'devil shift', however, belief change *across* coalitions is hypothesised to be extremely difficult. Thus there is a strong tendency for coalitions to be rather stable over periods of a decade or more. In fact, until recently, the ACF argued that major (policy core) policy change within a subsystem would occur *only* when significant perturbations from other policy areas or socio-economic conditions changed the resources or the core beliefs of major actors, and essentially led to the replacement of the previously dominant coalition by a previously minority coalition (Sabatier and Jenkins-Smith 1993: 34).

While changes in the policy core are usually the result of external perturbations, changes in the secondary aspects of a governmental action programme are often the result of policy-oriented learning by various coalitions or policy brokers. Following Heclo (1974: 306), policy-oriented learning refers to relatively enduring alterations of thought or behavioural intentions which result from experience and which are concerned with the attainment or revision of policy objectives. Policy-oriented learning involves the internal feedback loops depicted in figure 1, as well as increased knowledge of the state of problem parameters and the factors affecting them. Since the vast majority of policy debates involve secondary aspects of a governmental action programme – in part because actors realise the futility of challenging core assumptions – such learning can play an important role in policy change. In fact, a principal concern of the framework is to analyse the institutional conditions conducive to such learning and the cases in which cumulative learning may lead to changes in the policy core.

A more extensive exposition of the ACF can be found in Sabatier (1998) and Sabatier and Jenkins-Smith (1999). This overview should, however, indicate how it synthesises important elements from both top-down and bottom-up perspectives within the implementation literature, and combines them with a model of the individual drawn heavily from social psychology.

4. IS THE ACF USEFUL IN UNDERSTANDING HIGHER EDUCATION REFORMS IN EUROPE AND ELSEWHERE?

The ACF was designed to deal with what Hoppe and Peterse (1993) have termed 'wicked' policy issues, that is, those characterised by high goal conflict, high technical uncertainty about the nature and causes of the problem, and a large number of actors from multiple levels of government. As of 1999, the ACF had been applied to at least 34 published cases, most of them energy, environmental or social policy disputes involving goal conflict, technical uncertainty and intergovernmental actors (Sabatier and Jenkins-Smith 1999: 126; Sabatier 1998: 100). None of them involved higher education reforms. Why? While I obviously cannot provide any definitive answers, let me offer a few speculations:

- My perception is that most higher education reforms do not involve high goal conflict and competing belief systems. Instead, almost everyone views expanding higher education as desirable, but they disagree on the distribution of resources to different institutions or programmes. The exception are disputes with high potential for class conflict, for example, the German gesamthochschulen or affirmative action programmes designed to increase access to underprivileged groups.
- The ACF assumes that researchers and agency officials involved in a policy subsystem are not neutral but instead are members of advocacy coalitions.

This conflicts with the image of the Weberian civil servant. I have previously expressed my scepticism of this argument. But it is possible that the neutral role is more applicable to the higher education sector.

- It is possible that many higher education researchers do not stay abreast of theoretical developments in the general public policy literature. To the extent that is true, hopefully this volume will provide a stimulus to be more open to the potential utility of theory.
- It is possible that the ACF is not very useful for understanding anything, and higher education researchers have been quicker to grasp this point than colleagues in other policy sectors.

I would like to close with the fascinating story of Jasmin Beverwijk, a PhD student at the University of Twente. Her dissertation involves an application of the ACF to, of all things, higher education reform in Mozambique.

Ms Beverwijk's research is fascinating to me because it represents an enormous expansion of the external validity of the ACF. Almost all ACF research to date involves OECD countries where there really is a set of stable system parameters, where democratic institutions and the ability to form opposing coalitions are accepted, where most policy subsystems are relatively mature, and where coalitions have been fighting for decades. None of this is true with respect to higher education in Mozambique. Yet, Jasmin is convinced that the ACF is more useful than alternative explanatory frameworks because (1) it avoids the pitfalls of the stages heuristic; and (2) its focus on beliefs, resources and interdependencies provide the building blocks to understand the dynamics of coalition development and policy change (Fenger and Klok 2001).

The greatest satisfaction of a theoretician is to see one's ideas fruitfully applied by someone over whom one has absolutely no control to a situation completely beyond the ideas' original scope of application. If the ACF can be used to understand higher education reform in Mozambique, there is some hope for its application to higher education reforms in OECD countries.

NOTES

[1] For a recent effort to link the ACF to the literature on alternative dispute resolution in order to explain policy de-escalation and consensus, see Sabatier et al. (in press).

[2] This scepticism has been reinforced by a private communication from Daniel Kuebler (University of Zurich) indicating that Swiss bureaucrats involved in drug policy have had no difficulty seeing themselves as members of coalitions.

[3] The exceptions are (a) Magnus Anderson's dissertation on environmental policy in Poland in the 1980s and 1990s; and (b) Chris Elliot's (2001) paper on forest certification in Indonesia. But both of these countries are much more advanced on a 'developing nation' scale than Mozambique.

REFERENCES

Aaron, Henry. *Politics and the Professors*. Washington, DC: Brookings Institution, 1978.
Anderson, James. *Public Policy-Making*. New York: Holt, Rinehart and Winston, 1975.
Bardach, Eugene. *The Implementation Game*. Cambridge: MIT Press, 1974.
Barrett, Susan and Colin Fudge (eds). *Policy and Action*. London: Methuen, 1981.

Berman, Paul. "The Study of Macro- and Micro-Implementation." *Public Policy* 26 (1978): 157–184.
Beverwijk, Jasmin. "Policy Change in the Mozambican Higher Education Sector." Unpublished paper, CHEPS, University of Twente, the Netherlands, 2003.
Brewer, Gary and Peter de Leon. *Foundations of Policy Analysis*. Homewood, ILL: Dorsey Press, 1983.
Browning, Rufus, Dale Marshall and David Tabb. *Protest Is Not Enough*. Berkeley: University of California Press, 1984.
Cerych, Ladislav and Paul Sabatier. *Great Expectations and Mixed Performance: The Implementation of Higher Education Reforms in Europe*. Stoke-on-Trent: Trentham Books, 1986.
Cobb, Roger, Jennie-Keith Ross and Marc Ross. "Agenda Building as a Comparative Process." *American Political Science Review* 70 (March) (1976): 126–138.
De Leon, Peter and Linda de Leon. "What Ever Happened to Policy Implementation: An Alternative Approach." *Journal of Public Administration Research and Theory* 12.2 (2002): 467–492.
Downs, Anthony. *Inside Bureaucracy*. Boston: Little, Brown and Company, 1967.
Elmore, Richard. "Organizational Models of Social Program Implementation." *Public Policy* 26 (Spring) (1978): 185–228.
Elmore, Richard. "Backward Mapping." *Political Science Quarterly* 94 (Winter) (1979): 601–616.
Elmore, Richard. "Forward and Backward Mapping." In Hanf, K. and T. Toonen (eds). *Policy Implementation in Federal and Unitary Systems*. Dordrecht: Martinus Nijhoff, 1985, 33–70.
Fenger, H.J.M. and P-J. Klok. "Interdependency, Beliefs, and Coalition Behavior." *Policy Sciences* 34.2 (2001): 157–170.
Festinger, Leon. *A Theory of Cognitive Dissonance*. Evanston: Row, Peterson, 1957.
Goggin, Malcolm L. "Book Review of *Implementation and Public Policy*, Daniel A. Mazmanian and Paul A. Sabatier (eds)." *Publius* 144 (1984): 159–160.
Goggin, Malcolm L., Ann O'M. Bowman, James Lester and Laurence O'Toole. *Implementation Theory and Practice: Toward a Third Generation*. Glenview, ILL: Scott Foresman and Co., 1990.
Goodwin, Leonard and Phyllis Moen. "The Evolution and Implementation of Federal Welfare Policy." In Mazmanian, D. and P. Sabatier (eds). *Effective Policy Implementation*. Lexington, MA: D.C. Heath, 1981, 147–168.
Hanf, Kenneth. "The Implementation of Regulatory Policy: Enforcement as Bargaining." *European Journal of Political Research* 10 (June) (1982): 159–172.
Hanf, Kenneth, Benny Hjern and David Porter. "Local Networks of Manpower Training in the Federal Republic of Germany and Sweden." In Hanf, K. and F.W. Scharpf (eds). *Interorganizational Policy Making: Limits to Coordination and Central Control*. London: Sage, 1978, 303–344.
Hanf, Kenneth and Fritz Scharpf (eds). *Interorganizational Policy Making: Limits to Coordination and Central Control*. London: Sage, 1978.
Heclo, Hugh. *Modern Social Policies in Britain and Sweden*. New Haven: Yale University Press, 1974.
Hjern, Benny and Chris Hull. "Implementation Research as Empirical Constitutionalism." *European Journal of Political Research* 10 (1982): 105–116.
Hjern, Benny and David Porter. "Implementation Structures: A New Unit of Administrative Analysis." *Organization Studies* 2 (1981): 211–227.
Hofferbert, Richard. *The Study of Public Policy*. Indianapolis: Bobbs-Merrill, 1974.
Hoppe, Robert and Aat Peterse. *Handling Frozen Fire*. Boulder: Westview Press, 1993.
Hull, Chris and Benny Hjern. *Helping Small Firms Grow*. London: Croom Helm, 1987.
Jones, Charles. *An Introduction to the Study of Public Policy*. Belmont, CA: Wadsworth, 1970.
Jordan, A.G. and J.J. Richardson. "Policy Communities: The British and European Political Style." *Policy Studies Journal* 11 (June) (1983): 603–615.
Kingdon, John. *Agendas, Alternatives, and Public Policies*. Boston: Little, Brown and Company, 1984.
Kirst, Michael and Richard Jung. "The Utility of a Longitudinal Approach in Assessing Implementation: Title I, ESEA." In Williams, Walter (ed.). *Studying Implementation*. Chatham, NJ: Chatham House, 1982, 119–148.
Kiser, Larry and Elinor Ostrom. "The Three Worlds of Action." In Ostrom, E. (ed.). *Strategies of Political Inquiry*. Beverly Hills: Sage, 1982, 179–222.
Lakatos, Imre. *The Methodology of Scientific Research Programmes*. Edited by John Worrall and Gregory Currie. Cambridge, UK: Cambridge University Press, 1978.
Lasswell, Harold. *A Pre-View of Policy Sciences*. New York: American Elsevier, 1971.
Lazin, Frederick. "The Failure of Federal Enforcement of Civil Rights Regulations in Public Housing, 1963–71." *Policy Sciences* 4 (1973): 263–274.

Lester, James and Malcolm Goggin. "Back to the Future: The Rediscovery of Implementation Studies." *Policy Currents* 8 (Sept.) (1998): 1–10. (See also the January 1999 and April 1999 issues of *Policy Currents*.)

Lipsky, Michael. "Street Level Bureaucracy and the Analysis of Urban Reform." *Urban Affairs Quarterly* 6 (1971): 391–409.

Lord, Charles, Lee Ross and Mark Lepper. "Biased Assimilation and Attitude Polarization." *Journal of Personality and Social Psychology* 37 (1979): 2098–2109.

Lowry, Kem. "Assessing the Implementation of Federal Coastal Policy." *Journal of the American Planning Association* 51 (Summer) (1985): 288–298.

MacIntyre, Angus. "The Multiple Sources of Statutory Ambiguity." In Hibbeln, H. Kenneth and Douglas H. Shumavon (eds). *Administrative Discretion and the Implementation of Public Policy.* New York: Praeger, 1985, 66–88.

Majone, Giandomenico and Aaron Wildavsky. "Implementation as Evolution." In Freeman, Howard (ed.). *Policy Studies Review Annual 2.* Beverly Hills: Sage, 1978, 103–117.

Matland, Richard. "Synthesizing the Implementation Literature: The Ambiguity-Conflict Model of Policy Implementation." *Journal of Public Administration Research and Theory* 5.2 (1995): 145–174.

May, Judith and Aaron Wildavsky (eds). *The Policy Cycle.* Beverly Hills, CA: Sage, 1978.

Mazmanian, Daniel and Paul Sabatier. *Implementation and Public Policy.* Chicago: Scott Foresman and Co., 1983.

Milward, H. Brinton and Gary Wamsley. "Policy Subsystems, Networks, and the Tools of Public Management." In Eyestone, Robert (ed.). *Public Policy Formation and Implementation.* Boston: JAI Press, 1984, 3–25.

Murphy, Jerome. "The Education Bureaucracies Implement Novel Policy: The Politics of Title I of ESEA." In Sindler, Allan (ed.). *Policy and Politics in America.* Boston: Little, Brown, 1973, 160–199.

Nakamura, Robert. "The Textbook Process and Implementation Research." *Policy Studies Review* 1 (1987): 142–154.

Nelson, Barbara. *Making an Issue of Child Abuse.* Chicago: University of Chicago Press, 1984.

Page, Ed. "Law as an Instrument in Center-Local Relations." *Journal of Public Policy* 5.2 (1985): 241–265.

Pressman, Jeffrey and Aaron Wildavsky. *Implementation.* Berkeley: University of California Press, 1973.

Quattrone, George and Amos Tversky. "Contrasting Rational and Psychological Analyses of Political Choice." *American Political Science Review* 82 (Sept.) (1988): 719–736.

Rose, Richard. "From Government at the Center to Nationwide Government." *Studies in Public Policy* No. 132, University of Strathclyde, Glasgow, 1984.

Sabatier, Paul. "Social Movements and Regulatory Agencies." *Policy Sciences* 8 (1975): 301–342.

Sabatier, Paul. "Top-Down and Bottom-Up Models of Implementation Research." *Journal of Public Policy* 6 (Jan.) (1986): 21–48.

Sabatier, Paul. "Toward Better Theories of the Policy Process." *PS: Political Science and Politics* 24 (June) (1991): 147–156.

Sabatier, Paul. "The Advocacy Coalition Framework: Revisions and Relevance to Europe." *Journal of European Public Policy* 5.1 (1998): 98–130.

Sabatier, Paul, Susan Hunter and Susan McLaughlin. "The Devil Shift: Perceptions and Misperceptions of Opponents." *Western Political Quarterly* 40 (Sept.) (1987): 449–476.

Sabatier, Paul and Hank Jenkins-Smith. *Policy Change and Learning: An Advocacy Coalition Approach.* Boulder: Westview Press, 1993.

Sabatier, Paul and Hank Jenkins-Smith. "The Advocacy Coalition Framework: An Assessment." In Sabatier, Paul (ed.). *Theories of the Policy Process.* Boulder: Westview Press, 1999, 117–168.

Sabatier, Paul, William Leach, Mark Lubell and Neil Pelkey. "Theoretical Frameworks Explaining Partnership Success." In Sabatier, Paul, Will Focht, Mark Lubell, Zev Trachterberg, Arnold Vedlitz and Marty Matlock (eds). *Swimming Upstream.* Cambridge, Mass: MIT Press, ch. 6, in press.

Sabatier, Paul and Daniel Mazmanian. "The Conditions of Effective Implementation." *Policy Analysis* 5 (Fall) (1979): 481–504.

Sharpe, L.J. "Central Coordination and the Policy Network." *Political Studies* 33 (1985): 361–381.

Simon, Herbert. *Models of Thought.* New Haven, CT: Yale University Press, 1979.

Van Meter, Donald and Carl van Horn. "The Policy Implementation Process: A Conceptual Framework." *Administration and Society* 6 (Feb.) (1975): 445–488.

Weatherly, Richard and Michael Lipsky. "Street Level Bureaucrats and Institutional Innovation: Implementing Special-Education Reform." *Harvard Educational Review* 47.2 (1977): 171–197.

ÅSE GORNITZKA, SVEIN KYVIK AND BJØRN STENSAKER

IMPLEMENTATION ANALYSIS IN HIGHER EDUCATION[1]

1. INTRODUCTION

1.1. Revisiting the Missing Link – Implementation Analysis in Higher Education

In many countries higher education is undergoing fundamental changes concerning its governance, structure, funding and organisation. Often-mentioned forces triggering these changes are effects of the post-industrial society on higher education and the current invasion of 'the market' in higher education (Williams 1995; Slaughter and Leslie 1997). These change processes seem to point in the direction of a future for higher education institutions that is likely to consist of more self-regulated, dynamic and innovative organisations. Consequently, in the attempts to analyse and document the current changes in higher education, there is a tendency not to focus on the analysis of governmental policies. This is understandable, due to the current attention given to other forces affecting change in higher education, for example, the possibilities of new technologies in teaching and learning, corporate-based lifelong learning schemes blurring the boundaries between education and employment, and the effects of globalisation on higher education.

However, governments are far from silent and paralysed by the developments described above. Even though over the last few years the way in which politicians and public authorities have participated in shaping the future of higher education has changed, the involvement as such has not become less (Neave and Van Vught 1991; Neave 1998). Under labels such as 'managerialism' (Henkel 1991), 'new public management' (Pollitt 1993) and 'the evaluative state' (Neave 1988), one can find new policies, ideas and concepts on how politicians and public authorities would like to see higher education develop. Even though many observers seem to agree that the role of the state in higher education is changing (Neave and Van Vught 1991; Dill and Sporn 1995; Neave 1998; Henkel and Little 1999), this fact does not imply that the role and impact of the state on higher education are less relevant than before. A look at the pace and scope of the many public reforms and policy initiatives in higher education throughout the OECD area gives strong indications of a rather proactive state, where new actions are taken continuously as a response to the changing environment for higher education. The increasing role higher education institutions seem to play in the socio-economic and technological development of

Å. Gornitzka et al. (eds.), Reform and Change in Higher Education, 35-56.

our societies is an indication that the public interest in influencing higher education will continue in the years to come. Not surprisingly, this public interest in higher education is often combined with concerns about the efficiency, quality and effectiveness of this sector. In the end, it is exactly these objectives that guide public policy making in higher education. In a situation where tight public budgets, accountability claims due to new social demands, and output of higher education are on the agenda, policy analysis and, in particular, implementation analysis should be squarely at the centre of the research interest of students of the sector.

However, it could be questioned whether this is the case. Even if policy analysis still interests many researchers in higher education, and policy documents, white papers and other policy initiatives often are analysed and commented upon, there are few thorough studies that analyse and 'follow' a given policy through the implementation process. When Pressman and Wildavsky coined the term 'implementation studies' in political science with their seminal book *Implementation,* in 1973, it was argued that well-founded and theoretically based implementation analysis, that is, what happens after decisions have been made and policies are put into action, was a 'missing link' in policy studies conducted at that time (cf. Hargrove 1975). Over 25 years later this still seems to be a valid argument with respect to research in higher education. Implementation studies could, however, be particularly interesting in the present situation for higher education, since it seems evident that public policy, to a great extent, still is shaped during the implementation process.

First, with the amount of resources spent on higher education and with the social expectations now being put on higher education, there is a need for analysis that informs the public on the effectiveness of policy processes that distribute these resources in the sector. To know what those resources are being used on, and their effects, is of great interest to the society in general and stakeholders in higher education in particular. Second, even if the state and public officials are active in policy making and in reform-initiating activities, it is likely that current globalisation, 'technification' and 'marketisation' processes in the sector influence the policy implementation process in new and less known ways. And when the environment for public policy making is changing, it should be more important than ever to analyse how policy is affected by these forces, and to try to identify factors that stimulate or hinder the policy initiatives taken. Third, with new stakeholders entering and influencing higher education, that is, new categories of students, new forms of knowledge producing actors and new types of 'consumers' of higher education, a new territory for policy making is being shaped where little knowledge about cause and effect relationships exists – something that a thorough analysis of the implementation process could help to uncover. The aims of higher education researchers attracted to this field should, thus, perhaps still echo those that initiated this kind of research (O'Toole 1986): to contribute to the development of theories of effective implementation of policy goals, and to aid those involved in policy formulation and implementation processes by developing empirically based recommendations on how the aims of programmes and reforms could be accomplished. Therefore, this chapter will explore the practice and potential of applying implementation analysis for studying change processes in higher education.

The purpose of this chapter is to review the theoretical, empirical and practical advances of the implementation approach in higher education policy studies. In part two, it discusses the development of implementation studies in higher education with references to the general literature in the field. Part three starts by asking why there seems to be so little interest in implementation analysis in current higher education research. We continue the discussion by reviewing some major current policy studies in higher education and their way of handling and exploring changes in higher education policy. However, questions and some comments are made regarding the potential relevance of using some of the basic insights of an implementation perspective in current research efforts. Part four closes the chapter with a discussion of the extent to which a renewed interest in implementation analysis could be of practical relevance to policy makers in higher education. Some suggestions are given on what kind of research is still needed in this area to fill our existing gaps in knowledge.

2. HISTORY, PERSPECTIVES AND CRITIQUE RELATED TO IMPLEMENTATION ANALYSIS IN HIGHER EDUCATION

2.1. Introduction

Although there is a long tradition in higher education research, as in other social sciences, for studying the relationship between goals and outcome and explaining what went wrong, it is fair to say that the explicit focus on the implementation process as a distinct field of study in social science first took off in the mid-1970s. The book by Pressman and Wildavsky, *Implementation*, first published in 1973, represents a benchmark in this respect. Based on a study of the Economic Development Administration's employment effort in Oakland, California, two general policy recommendations were put forward in order to facilitate implementation of public programme goals. First of all they showed that an implementation process can include a large number of decision points, and that each required clearance point adds to the probability of stoppage or delay. The number of such points should therefore be minimised wherever possible. Second, the authors recommended that as much attention should be paid to the creation of organisational machinery for executing a programme as for launching one. Another important contribution of this book was its emphasis on an adequate underlying causal theory of the relationship between means and ends in a reform process. This and other case studies, which drew rather pessimistic conclusions about the ability of governments to effectively implement their programmes, were followed by a large number of papers that aimed to investigate the conditions necessary for trying to achieve the objectives of a particular policy. Various attempts were undertaken to build general theories on effective implementation, or how public agencies should proceed to ensure that their policy objectives could be accomplished. Still, empirical evidence on the effectiveness of these models was in general missing. One could, therefore, say that the tendency of trying to identify implementation failure and the related lack of thorough empirical investigations into how implementation processes actually could succeed was one of the major reasons why a large multi-national research project on policy implementation in higher education in Europe was launched in the late 1970s and early 1980s (Cerych and Sabatier 1986). It is still the most comprehensive and explicit analysis using an implementation approach; it is also a central study in the implementation literature in general. A major question guiding this research project, led by Ladislav Cerych and Paul Sabatier, was: Are contemporary societies really as incapable of planned change in higher education as the pessimists suggest? In their own comment to this question, they concluded that centrally initiated reform initiatives indeed were possible, and that such initiatives also could be characterised as a success under certain conditions (Cerych and Sabatier 1986: 242–254).

However, research efforts, such as the Cerych and Sabatier study, mainly built on a top-down perspective, clearly illustrate the complexity of analysing policy implementation. The latter study could still be criticised for underestimating these problems. Those who argued for developing theoretical models that tried to incorporate the complexity related to implementation processes focused instead on how those who actually worked with putting the policy into action experienced the process. Not surprisingly, this way of analysing implementation soon became known as the bottom-up perspective. A debate by those favouring a top-down or a bottom-up perspective when analysing implementation processes then followed for years. Some attempts at combining these two perspectives were later undertaken, before the theoretical development seemed to come to a halt.

Premfors (1984) has shown that the top-down/bottom-up distinction has been used in three rather different contexts. First, the scholarly debate has concerned the most appropriate way of *describing* implementation processes. Is the top-down perspective more relevant than the bottom-up approach? A second and related question concerns the *methodology* used in implementation research. How should research be undertaken? Finally, much implementation research has a *normative* purpose. How can research help governments to attain the goals of programmes or reforms? The differences in approaches in what became the field of implementation studies, are centred upon the following aspects:

1. What is implementation? Is there a start and a finish to it? And if so, where do you draw the line?
2. What constitutes a 'policy', or what is the object of implementation?
3. What is failed and what is successful implementation?
4. What are the best instruments for implementation?

With these questions in mind, in this section we will give a brief overview of the perspectives, models and critiques of implementation research (for a more extensive overview, see e.g. Sabatier 1986; Lane 1993; Parsons 1995).

2.2. Cerych and Sabatier – The Classic Implementation Study in Higher Education

The major contribution to the field of implementation research in higher education is undoubtedly the book *Great Expectations and Mixed Performance. The*

Implementation of Higher Education Reforms in Europe by Ladislav Cerych and Paul Sabatier. This book was published in 1986 and was the final outcome of a large research project encompassing nine specific reforms initiated during the 1960s.[1] All these reforms sought explicitly to make important changes in the higher education systems of their countries. Three types of objectives predominated in these reforms: a) to widen access to higher education; b) to increase the relevance of higher education to regional development; and c) to develop more vocationally oriented and short-term higher education. The main purpose of the project was to analyse reasons for the success or failure of these reforms by applying policy implementation analysis (see also Cerych and Sabatier 1992). In the conceptual framework that guided the research project, Cerych and Sabatier distinguished between policy formulation, policy implementation and policy reformulation as the three stages major changes in public policy pass through (Cerych and Sabatier 1986: 10):

1. A period of policy formulation involving an awareness of inadequacies in the existing system, followed by the examination of one or more means of redressing the situation, and culminating in a formal (legal) decision by the cabinet or parliament to establish a new program or institution.

2. The program is then assigned to one or more organisations for implementation. In higher education reforms, these will almost always include the Ministry of Education and the affected establishments of higher education. Other institutions such as local governments or private employers may also be included, if the program involves the creation of new universities or efforts to employ graduates. Within the implementation stage one can normally distinguish an initial phase involving the elaboration of regulations and the creation of new structures necessary to translate the cabinet-parliamentary decision into actual practice from a subsequent phase involving day-to-day applications and adjustments of the initial decisions.

3. Based upon various actors' evaluations of the implementation experience and reactions to changing conditions, there will follow what may be termed the reformulation stage, in which efforts are made to revise program goals, to change the implementing institutions or, in extreme cases, to abandon the program altogether. Such reformulation may be based on elaborate studies of the outcomes of the program or simply on perceptions of such effects or on changes in the general political climate. Whereas major revisions will often involve formal decisions by the cabinet or the parliament, they may sometimes proceed solely from the discretionary authority vested in the education ministry or the affected institutions of higher education. Program reformulation may also be the product of a more subtle process involving cumulatively important changes largely imperceptible to people outside the implementing institutions.

Special emphasis was laid on the analysis of goals, their comparisons with outcomes, and the factors affecting policy implementation, particularly the attainment of formal goals. These factors were listed as follows (Cerych and Sabatier 1986: 16):

1. Legal (official) objectives. a) Clarity and consistency b) Degree of system change envisaged;
2. Adequacy of the causal theory underlying the reform;
3. Adequacy of financial resources provided to implementing institutions;
4. The degree of commitment to various program objectives among those charged with its implementation within the education ministry and the affected institutions of higher education;

5. Degree of commitment to various program objectives among legislative and executive officials and affected groups outside the implementing agencies;
6. Changes in social and economic conditions affecting goal priorities or the program's causal assumptions.

This list is fairly similar to those presented in the general implementation literature by Sabatier (1986) and others.

With respect to the goals of the reforms, the authors took as a starting point that their success or failure was dependent upon two aspects of the goals themselves: the amount of system change envisaged and their internal clarity and consistency. The larger the change decided upon, the lower the degree of accomplishment of the reform; and the more clarified and consistent the aims of the change are, the more easily the objectives could be fulfilled. However, Cerych and Sabatier also suggested that vague and somewhat conflicting goals are often the price to be paid for obtaining agreement in the policy formation process, and that ambiguity facilitates adjustments to changing circumstances during the implementation stage.

On the basis of the analyses of the various higher education reforms, the authors came to the conclusion that ambiguity and conflict in goals are in many cases unavoidable, and in addition that a precise goal does not guarantee superior implementation. They therefore suggested that instead of focusing on clear and consistent objectives, implementation analyses ought to identify an "acceptable mix of outcomes" (p. 243).

With respect to the effect of degree of change on the outcome, Cerych and Sabatier stated that a more complex conceptualisation of the scope of change was necessary to capture the processes. They suggested a three-dimensional framework that they called depth of change, functional breadth of change and level of change. *Depth of change* indicates the degree to which a new policy implies a departure from existing values and practices. *Functional breadth of change* refers to the number of functional areas in which a given policy is expected to introduce modifications, while *level of change* indicates the target of the reform: the system as a whole, a particular sector of the system, or a single institution. Lessons learned from the comparative study indicated some interesting conclusions:

- Policies implying far-reaching changes can be successful if they aim at one or only a few functional areas of the system or an institution.
- It is easier to change a single (or to create a new) institution than a whole system.
- Reforms projecting a very low degree of change both in terms of depth and functional breadth are often unsuccessful, essentially because they do not galvanise sufficient energy to overcome inertia in the system.

In the theoretical outline of their project, Cerych and Sabatier also stressed the importance of an adequate causal theory or a set of assumptions about means and ends.

> If goals are to be realized, it is important that causal links be understood and that officials responsible for implementing the program have jurisdiction over sufficient critical linkages to make possible the attainment of objectives. Only when these two

conditions have been met, the basic decision establishing the reform can be said to 'incorporate' a valid causal theory (p. 15).

They concluded that it was startling to observe how many of the reforms examined were based on wrong assumptions. However, they also admit that not everything can be foreseen and advocate that systematic evaluation ought to be an integral part of implementation as a means of correcting errors, reformulating implementation strategies or even goals.

2.3. The Central Debate: Top-Down or Bottom-Up?

The complexity issue raised, *inter alia*, by the Cerych and Sabatier study, serves as a good introduction to the central debate in implementation research: what are the essential factors furthering or hindering the fulfilment of the objectives of a given reform initiative? The effort made by Cerych and Sabatier to create a set of 'critical' variables in understanding implementation success was a procedure followed by many researchers involved in implementation analysis, both inside and outside higher education. The central characteristic for these kinds of studies was the belief that implementation processes could be centrally controlled and steered if just the number of relevant variables and their interconnectedness were disclosed. A study by Van Meter and Van Horn (1975) is an illustrative example of this type of thinking. In their model of how to analyse the implementation process, 'critical' variables were a) *policy standards and objectives*; and b) *policy resources*. In addition, four other factors were included: inter-organisational communication and enforcement activities; the characteristics of the implementing agencies; the economic, social and political environment affecting the jurisdiction or organisation within which implementation takes place; and the disposition of implementers:

- Policy standards and objectives: The objectives of the reform are obviously the starting point for the analysis of implementation processes. As Pressman and Wildavsky (1973: xiv) noted, "implementation cannot succeed or fail without a goal against which to judge it". In general, clear and unambiguous goals are easier to implement than a set of vague, complex and contradictory goals. In addition, if general guidelines are the foundation for a reform, the probability is relatively high that different interpretations will make implementation difficult. In addition, Van Meter and Van Horn assumed that implementation will be most successful where only marginal change is required and where goal consensus is high. Furthermore, of these two variables, goal consensus will have a greater effect on effective implementation than will the level of change. The likelihood of effective implementation will accordingly depend in part on the nature of the policy to be carried out, and the specific factors contributing to the realisation or non-realisation of policy objectives will vary from one policy type to another. Thus, characteristics of the objectives of an initiative may be assumed to be important for the possibilities for implementing an initiative in line with its objectives.

- Policy resources: Policies also make available resources for the implementation of a reform, through funds or other incentives, which facilitate the administration of a programme. It is general wisdom that funds are usually not adequate, making the accomplishment of policy objectives difficult to achieve.
- Inter-organisational communication and enforcement activities: In the context of inter-organisational relations, two types of follow-up activities are most important. First, technical advice and assistance should be provided. Second, superiors should rely on a wide variety of sanctions – both positive and negative.
- Characteristics of the implementing agencies: This factor consists of both the formal structural features of organisations and the informal attributes of their personnel. Van Meter and Van Horn mention the competence and size of an agency's staff, the degree of hierarchical control of processes within the implementing agencies, etc.
- Economic, social and political conditions: General economic, social and political conditions have been shown to be important for the relationship between objectives and results. Political measures are often undertaken without sufficient analysis of financial consequences. Furthermore, economic conditions change continuously, and it is not unusual that it will be difficult to put through a measure in line with its original intentions. Political support for a reform can also change over time, due to new power constellations or to changes in priorities.
- Disposition of implementers: This could concern the motivation and attitudes of those responsible for implementing the reform. Experience has shown that key persons in an organisation, or 'fixers' in Bardach's (1977) terminology, can be very influential for the success or failure of a reform.

A number of papers followed in the wake of the Van Meter and Van Horn contribution, and they were basically aimed at improving the list of factors important for the effective implementation of programme goals. Several of these first attempts at developing theoretical contributions in the field of implementation analysis were to a large extent confined to discussions of which factors were important to study in implementation processes. O'Toole (1986) lists more than 100 studies from the late 1970s and early 1980s that were merely dedicated to identify important variables. In some cases, the authors also linked the variables in more complex theoretical models (e.g. Sabatier and Mazmanian 1980).

The first wave of implementation researchers' attempts at developing conceptual and methodological frameworks for theoretical and practical implementation purposes was soon heavily criticised. One line of criticism was that these approaches mainly identified important variables or a checklist of factors without specifying a model of implementation (see O'Toole 1986). Others argued that the number of variables were too long and that there was a need for research which could identify which variables were most important and under which circumstances (see Lester et al. 1987). The emphasis on clear and consistent policy objectives as a precondition for effective implementation was soon criticised. Several scholars argued that the lack of clear and consistent programme goals is more the rule than the exception. Instead, "objectives are characteristically multiple (because we want many things, not just one), conflicting (because we want different things), and vague (because that is how we can agree to proceed without having to agree also on exactly what will be done)" (Majone and Wildavsky 1978: 108).

The insistence on 'adequate causal theory' as a policy recommendation to practitioners can also be criticised for lack of realism. In many policy areas the cognitive demands put on policy making are very high. Arriving at the 'adequate causal theory' is not only difficult in view of political controversy, but also when cause and effect relations are disputed in professional or scientific communities. The list of difficulties for those who want to build policy upon an adequate policy theory is rather long. Still, the early implementation researchers were right in trying to unravel the underlying logic of policy decisions, and the attention given to this aspect of policy (but not the conclusions drawn) fits the later 'cognitive turn' in the social sciences (cf. DiMaggio and Powell 1991; Scott 1995). The attention given to underlying 'policy theory' is certainly worth keeping in mind. In essence this point brings up the issue of what constitutes the knowledge basis for policy making. In the present context it gives grounds for higher education researchers to reflect on their own role as information and knowledge providers for decision makers.

The main criticism directed at the first wave of implementation studies was that they represented a 'top-down' approach to implementation analysis, which was not very adequate in explaining real-life implementation processes (Hanf, Hjern and Porter 1978; Barrett and Fudge 1981; Hjern and Hull 1982). Thus, the top-down approach represented an instrumental and rational understanding of organisations. Certain goals are to be realised through particular measures. It is presumed that changes in organisational structure, authority relations, decision-making principles and communication patterns will lead to desired results. The studies applying a bottom-up approach would refer to and distance themselves from the top-downers before presenting an alternative way of addressing the issue of implementation. They represented a break with the earlier implementation approach, theoretically, methodologically and normatively, to the extent that they took great pains to avoid a 'hierarchical' terminology and focus. Clearly, such a critique should be at the heart of the interests of higher education policy researchers who devote their scholarly attention to a sector that traditionally has been viewed as particularly 'bottom-heavy' and where core functions of the institutions are seen as naturally defying hierarchical structures.

One line of criticism aimed at the top-down perspective was attacking the belief in the implementation process as a technical procedure. Sabatier (1986) summarised this as a three-part problem. The first problem is the emphasis on central objectives and decision makers and the tendency to neglect initiatives coming from local implementing officials, from other policy subsystems and from the private sector. Second, top-down models are difficult to use in situations where there is no dominant policy or agency, but rather a multitude of governmental directives and actors. Third, top-down models are likely to underestimate the strategies used by street-level bureaucrats and target groups to divert central policy to their own purposes. In this respect, Dunleavy (1981) stressed the important role of professionals in the implementation chain. Teachers, doctors, planners, engineers, social workers, etc. all have discretion in how they carry out their work. The relevance of such an observation to the policy and practice in higher education should be obvious to anyone familiar with how colleges and universities work.

In contrast to the top-down approach, the bottom-up researchers start by mapping the network of actors at the bottom of the implementation chain, asking them about their goals, strategies, activities and contacts. The contacts are then used as a means to identifying the network of actors involved in the execution of a public policy at the local level. A key proponent of this approach is Elmore (1980, 1985). He challenges the mythology of the top-down perspective on grounds that it is an inappropriate way of describing real-life policy implementation, and because central control over processes at the local level is not necessarily desirable. In implementation processes bargaining is claimed to be crucial not only to adjust but also to create the goals of social programmes. The disparity between formal policy decision and practice that in the first wave of implementation studies was seen as erring behaviour and 'goal displacement' is now considered as a natural part of implementing policy. It is also put forward as a prescriptive strategy for researchers and decision makers. In a bottom-up perspective the 'intentions in Oakland' are not hierarchically subordinate to the 'goals in Washington'. One further illustration of such an approach is found in the work of Hjern and his colleagues (see Hanf, Hjern and Porter 1978; Hjern and Hull 1982).

The bottom-uppers' research question is rather different from the top-downers'. They ask how actors go about solving societal problems in different areas and see what role government measures play in that. The criterion of successful implementation is then not focused on a degree of match or mismatch between formal intentions and actions of the implementers, or on the possible 'deviant behaviour' of the agencies that are trusted to put policy into practice. Their democratic ideal also comes across as different, in the sense that they see the 'local' flair in handling societal problems as an expression of a well-functioning democracy, and not as undemocratic actions of agencies that run wild or undermine the decisions made by democratically elected bodies. Here we can draw a useful parallel to the discussion on legitimacy in higher education relationship with the state and other stakeholders. The attention given to the traditional concept of institutional and individual academic freedom sets this sector apart from other sectors of society where governments have exerted a stronger steering.

2.4. Adjusting to Complexity – The Development of Combined Models

Partly as a result of the discussion between top-downers and bottom-uppers, and partly as a result of obvious weaknesses in the early top-down approaches, various attempts at building more comprehensive hybrid models took place (see e.g. Lane 1993 or Parsons 1995 for an overview). In a later edition of Pressman and Wildavsky's *Implementation* (1984), Wildavsky and colleagues incorporate some of the criticisms of the top-down approach to present a revised view on implementation. They reject the idea that goals and programmes are reifications:

goals should not be viewed as static. Goals often change over time, partly because of weaknesses in the ideas themselves, partly because of the fact that ideas change, and also because of new circumstances. On the other hand they are not willing to reduce the status of policies to only a collection of words, and they reject the interactionist idea that the function of the implementation process is to satisfy the needs of the participants regardless of the actual policy results. Majone and Wildavsky point to an essential problem when they state that (1978: 114):

> Implementation is evolution. Since it takes place in a world we never made, we are usually in the middle of the process, with events having occurred before and (we hope) continuing afterward. At each point we must cope with new circumstances that allow us to actualise different potentials in whatever policy ideas we are implementing. When we act to implement a policy, we change it.

Implementation thus often implies the carrying out of goals as well as the reformulation and re-design of original intentions and plans. Implementation in this sense has also been conceptualised as *mutual adaptation* (Browne and Wildavsky 1984a) and a *learning process* (Browne and Wildavsky 1984b), and implementation as negotiation and interaction (Barrett and Fudge 1981). The later work of Sabatier (1986) has suggested that implementation studies could be undertaken within 'an advocacy coalition framework'. This approach is based on the premise that the most useful aggregate unit of analysis for understanding policy change is a policy subsystem or policy segment, that is, those actors from a variety of public and private organisations who are actively concerned with a policy problem or issue, such as higher education. Sabatier (1986) proposes to adopt the bottom-uppers' unit of analysis assuming that "actors can be aggregated into a number of advocacy coalitions which share a set of normative and causal beliefs and which dispose of certain resources". Together with a keen focus on the legal instruments and socio-economic conditions that constrain behaviour as the legacy from the top-down perspective, he suggests a synthesised model for the study of implementation processes.

2.5. Some Concluding Comments

The body of scholarly literature on implementation has provided rather disparate answers to the questions we outlined earlier. First, there is a distinction between those who see implementation as a rather narrow process with a start and a finish, versus those who view implementation as a process without a decision to launch it or a goal line that marks the ending of putting policy into practice. And second, there is a distinction to be made between viewing processes in terms of phases or stages gone through, versus seeing policy implementation and formation as intertwined where the defining and negotiating over intentions and objectives are continuous and infinite. For the latter scholars what is to be accomplished is something to be bargained over and not a given attribute of policies/programmes under implementation. That is to say, policy intentions are not fully developed until they are negotiated. Consequently, the criteria for determining policy success or failure differ significantly according to the approach used. Likewise for the issue of what is 'democratic' or not. The difference between the two approaches becomes most apparent with respect to the policy recommendations that they carry. Where top-downers prescribe an adequate policy theory, more control, goal clearance and fixers to push the policy through, the bottom-uppers would recommend local knowledge and user control and policy outcomes measured against local objectives. Given this state of affairs, implementation research has been criticised for its theoretical pluralism, for its restricted nature and for being non-cumulative (Lester et al. 1987; Lane 1993).

The top-down emphasis on central control as a means to secure successful implementation could be seen as a scholarly anachronism in the sense that such government strategies are both ideologically and in practice increasingly replaced by, or modified by, indirect means of control. Nevertheless, one of the major contributions of the first wave of implementation studies was the emphasis on the importance of inter-organisational arrangements and the characteristics of the formal ties between programme/policy issuers and the implementing institutions. Studying the impact of formal hierarchical arrangements between institutions is important both from a scholarly (echoing the neo-institutional theory development) and a practical perspective. For students of higher education policy it is crucial. Clearly, implementation in times of new relations between agencies/public institutions and central authorities will continue to arouse interest. What are the consequences for implementation when the formal levers of control between government and underlying institutions have been changed? This is a highly pertinent issue that should lead to careful examination of the actual changes in formal arrangements and the consequences of such changes. A focus on decisions and legal resolutions does not represent an obsolete area of interest. Rather, it directs attention to central determinants of political administrative action, also with respect to higher education. Furthermore, national governments continue to formulate policies for higher education with the expectation that such initiatives are translated into practice in the field. Also supranational organisations, such as the EU and NAFTA in North America, have ambitions of effectiveness with the programmes and policies they formulate with respect to higher education. The relationship between policy issuers and the units that policies are directed at in the higher education sector is in many cases undergoing formal alterations. And as such the attention to such arrangements is important to incorporate into a study of implementation of specific policies.

A lasting and important contribution of the bottom-uppers is the highlight they put on the organic aspects of implementation, the informal processes and spontaneous constellations that spring out of processes, the strong element of negotiation and the political aspects of processes also outside the central political apparatus. However, not unlike other behavioural approaches in the study of politics, it tends to overlook the weight carried by institutions as a powerful frame of human action. The bottom-uppers' change of focus from the policy decision fixation to organic processes clearly served to sensitise the student of implementation processes to the danger of reifying policy and adding mythical properties to the power of a policy decision and programme. However, the complete relaxation of a special focus on authoritative policy decisions at a central level is also ill advised. A policy decision then has the same status as other 'environmental factors' that play a role, with no higher rank order. It is not the trigger of the processes one is studying, as it would for the top-downers. This might be a good approach in areas where government initiatives are many and scattered, but 'ignoring' the importance of formal government decisions and the momentum that such decisions carry both symbolically and as a driving force in implementation processes seems empirically errant.

3. BUILDING ON THE PAST? CURRENT EMPIRICAL POLICY RESEARCH IN HIGHER EDUCATION

3.1. Introduction

Why has implementation research in higher education not boomed after the seminal work offered by Cerych and Sabatier? Several reasons could be identified, including the complexity of the research task and the lack of a unified perspective in the field due to the debate between bottom-uppers and top-downers. Furthermore, studies of the implementation of higher education reforms have also to a large extent been undertaken in a European context. The relatively few studies of American reforms applying an explicit implementation approach have been explained by system differences. Clark (1986) states that reforms in American higher education, in contrast to Europe, typically are not planned and enacted through the national centre. Because the American system is so large and decentralised, reforms are usually generated at lower levels. In Clark's words: "If authority is extensively decentralized, then opportunities to innovate are decentralized; higher levels find levers of change usually beyond their reach" (1986: 260). Instead, reforms occur incrementally, have small expectations, depend considerably on local initiative and are often market-driven.

In addition, implementation of higher education reforms may be more difficult to accomplish than reforms within other sectors of society. Cerych and Sabatier (1986: 256) have discussed this question. They argue that the special problems posed by higher education reform implementation are set primarily by the many autonomous actors present, and by the diffusion of authority throughout the structure. Even in a centralised state, higher education is more 'bottom-heavy' than other social subsystems and certainly more than lower educational sectors. Policy implementation then becomes very interactive, and implementation analysis becomes a study of the respective interactions. Higher education policy implementation is increasingly complicated by its ambiguous and multiple goals. Although the system is concerned primarily with knowledge, it has been called upon to assume many new functions only indirectly related to its traditional responsibility for producing, extending and transmitting knowledge. It is now supposed to actively promote social equalisation, to provide more vocational training, to assist in regional development, to cater increasingly for the adult student, and so on. Cerych and Sabatier conclude that there is no general consensus regarding these new functions and, if and when they become specific policy objectives, they are immediately questioned and openly contested.

Implementation studies of higher education, as in other sectors, might have been undertaken in other contexts and under other labels, for example, evaluation studies. This is an argument also raised in general by Ham and Hill (1986: 111). They indicate that there are many studies with a policy focus but without the implementation label, that could be of great relevance to the implementation field. The latter explanation brings us to the possibility that policy studies, in which implementation analysis is a central part, also depend very much on the content and type of policy and how it is enacted. The lack of perceived interest in implementation analysis in higher education may be a result of changes in public policy in higher education from the mid-1980s. One major change is, for example, the shift towards new public management doctrines emphasising privatisation, deregulation and evaluation (see e.g. Henkel 1991; Neave 1988). As a consequence, it is possible to identify a change in the way public policy is framed, that is, that only broad frameworks and objectives are specified, leaving much discretion to local organisation and implementing agencies (see Van Vught 1989). Even if it may be difficult to differentiate sharply between internal and external forces in the developments within policy studies, one could argue that changes in public policy have influenced policy and implementation studies. This development has resulted in a change in the way policy and implementation studies are conducted, and not in a declining interest in the implementation 'theme' as such, even if the label has changed.

The development in political ideology and practice sets the focus on rather different aspects of policy making and implementation compared to the analytical focus of the first wave of implementation studies. Rather, one could see the interest in new research questions as related to changes in public policy making. How, for instance, is policy shaped in this new multi-organisational framework in which different stakeholders try to affect policy and policy realisation (Neave 1995)? What are the efficient policy instruments in a situation where the degree of governmental control is loosened (Van Vught 1997)? Undoubtedly this represented a significant shift of the ideology of public policy, and such policy developments impinge on the definition of relevant research issues. However, if we look beyond the rhetoric of 'self-regulation' the transition from one state to the other is not unequivocal. At the level of actual policy in many Western countries the formal structures of the former state control models linger on alongside the ideological and practical decentralised and autonomised structures (Gornitzka and Maassen 2000). Most of these systems are still in a 'hybrid' state where remnants of old systems are blended with the new. The complexity of public policy and political (sub)systems poses serious challenges to the student of implementation, when ideas of self-regulation mix with continued aspirations and practices of central control, and when structures of responsibility and governance are unclear. Consequently, the new policy developments have undoubtedly had an impact on policy studies, yet the 'old' issues are not obsolete and irrelevant within new landscapes of public policy and models of state governance.

Given the changes in higher education policy, the question then becomes: How do current policy studies handle this changing policy landscape? A search through the current higher education literature paying special attention to studies that try to analyse the relationship between a formally defined or specified policy or reform on the one hand, and institutional responses, adaptation or practice on the other, shows that these questions are at the very core of many studies. On the European scene, it is possible to identify several research projects that are of great interest to the implementation field. However, many studies seem to have a normative purpose when analysing public policy initiatives, without much empirical evidence. Other studies often lack a theoretical framework to structure the analysis, and thus represent empirical descriptions with little contribution in terms of generalisable knowledge. Still, as a result of changes in higher education policy, current empirically oriented 'implementation studies' seem to change according to the development outlined earlier. Some typical examples of recent studies are given below.

3.2. The Organisational Theory Approach

The use of organisation theory for studying change in higher education is hardly a new development. However, one could actually reverse the statement, claiming that several important studies in organisation theory have grown out of studies of higher education (Rhoades 1992: 1884). In recent studies of 'putting policy into practice' that are framed by organisation theory, the investigation has focused not merely on the implementation of higher education policy or reform; rather, implementation is seen as a case of organisational change in higher education institutions.

The most novel element when it comes to applying organisation theory to the study of change is an expansion of the analytical scope of the studies carried out. While organisation theorists traditionally analysed changes *within* organisations, such theoretical frameworks are today often used to study inter-organisational relationships, that is, between organisations and different stakeholders in the organisational environment. The recognition that organisations are dependent on their environment is the main factor behind this development. For organisation theory to be applicable to the study of policy implementation, the latter recognition is essential. An interesting example is that of Goedegebuure (1992), where a resource dependency perspective is applied to understand merging activities in the college sector in Australia and the Netherlands. In both countries, the initiative to amalgamate small institutions into larger ones came as a direct result of governmental policies, with the governments spelling out certain incentives to guide the merging process, that is, increasing institutional size would trigger increased funding (Goedegebuure 1992: 3–6). On the basis of the political objectives, and by outlining theoretical propositions on the basis of the resource dependency framework, these are then tested empirically using a range of data. The results of the analysis show, *inter alia*, that governmental policies relating funding mechanisms to the mergers in the two countries were highly successful (Goedegebuure 1992: 225). However, the study also argues that the merging activity depended on other environmental factors in addition, and that the extent to which a given institution engaged in a merger depended on "the overall environmental situation as perceived by the institutions" (Goedegebuure 1992: 226). This result could be interpreted positively both by top-downers and bottom-uppers in an implementation perspective. For top-downers, the existence of well-defined policy means, that is, economic incentives that guided the successful implementation of the mergers, must certainly be encouraging. For bottom-uppers, the notion that successful implementation depended on how institutions perceived their general situation could be an argument for analysing potential merger activity by some form of backward mapping. In general, the resource dependency framework proved to be a fruitful perspective for analysing and understanding the institutional behaviour that took place after the policy initiatives in the two countries, accounting for the role of the environment in producing organisational change as well as focusing on the organisational capacity to influence environmental conditions under which they had to operate (Goedegebuure 1992: 223–224).

A project with relevance for students interested in implementation is a large comparative study of governmental policies and programmes for strengthening the relationship between higher education institutions and the national economy (TSER-HEINE project) (see also Gornitzka 1999; Gornitzka and Maassen 2003). The main research question is how higher education organisations change in response to or in interaction with government policies and programmes. The research involves an examination of how government policies and programmes act as impetuses for change in higher education organisations. The approach used is not identical to the set-up of a top-down implementation study. It does not follow a given policy from formation to implementation, to the effects of the policy in question, assuming a linear causal chain of events. The focus of this study is on public policy initiatives as possible inputs to organisational change processes at an institutional level. The conceptual framework applied in this study is built around two theoretical perspectives on organisational change: resource dependence theory and neo-institutional theory. The framework rests on two main assumptions. First, organisational response to environmental expectations is shaped by inter-organisational factors, such as power distributions and institutional values, identities and traditions. Second, organisational actors seek actively to interact with environmental constituents in order to shape and control dependency relations.

The TSER-HEINE project framework echoes the classic implementation studies in the sense that it pays special attention to characteristics of government policies that are directed at institutions in higher education. It assumes that such aspects are of importance in the study of how state action serves as an impetus for organisational change. Policies are more than just 'a collection of words'. Furthermore, their approach does not see the state as 'just another actor'. The research takes as its point of departure that governments are essential in furnishing and maintaining an overall governance system within which the day-to-day relationship between higher education and government takes place. Such system-level characteristics are studied as part of the significant institutional and historical context within which policies and programmes are developed and organisational change processes are positioned. Methodologically, the TSER-HEINE project takes a two-step comparative approach to the study of institutional change. National policies within the selected subject area are studied and compared in an independent analysis (cf. Gornitzka and Maassen 2000). Second, the main empirical basis is found in a set of case studies at an institutional level in the seven European countries that are part of the project, which in turn are analysed cross-nationally. In these case studies, government policies are analysed as part of the many factors that may affect change processes at an institutional level. This study exemplifies a multi-level comparative approach, with an explicit focus on government decisions and actions as part of a frame of order within which organisational adaptation takes place. The approach used is also compatible with an interest in issues of implementation in the sense that types of policy and systems of state control and steering are seen as important to understanding the responsiveness of universities and colleges. One of the outcomes of the study demonstrates that most of the governmental policies that were studied were not directly linked in a linear causal way to outcomes at the institutional level. Nonetheless, the value of national policies for institutional level change processes is more than 'just' symbolic. The normative and cognitive content of policies certainly affect the sets of values and norms of the institutional actors involved in institutional adaptation and change. Furthermore, a central conclusion refers to the importance of viewing the success or failure of implementing specific policies in relation to the governmental steering approach within which these policies are embedded (Van Heffen, Verhoeven and De Wit 1999: 291).

3.3. The Network Approach

Central to these types of studies are the attempts to couple actor and structure relationships, establishing the 'missing link' between the micro and macro level of analysis. In the words of Lane (1990: 39), these models are high on realism, but have weaknesses when it comes to analytical stringency. One of the projects using a network/field approach to study policy change is a comparative research study, where national policy developments in Swedish, Norwegian and UK higher education are analysed and compared over the last decades, with a special focus on the extent to which public reforms have affected the values and behaviour of academics within higher education institutions (see Kogan and Hanney 2000; Henkel 2000; Bleiklie, Høstaker and Vabø 2000; Bauer et al. 1999; Kogan et al. 2000). The theoretical foundations for these studies can be pinpointed quoting Kogan and Hanney (2000: 20–21), when they state that

> it has proved virtually impossible to make an adequate match between micro analysis, in which the verities of close-grained empirical studies can be demonstrated, and macro analysis, in which more generally applicable propositions can be announced and interrogated. The world of knowledge has increasingly accepted that more than one incommensurate or apparently inconsistent proposition can be advanced simultaneously. In the social domain, in particular, reality does not pile up in well-connected hierarchies of paradigms and theorems.

Thus, it is argued that the problem of traditional implementation studies of both a top-down and a bottom-up character is the question of how the levels are related to one another. Consequently, both the top-down and the bottom-up perspectives are rooted in a hierarchical model limiting the dynamics of policy making and policy shaping (Bleiklie, Høstaker and Vabø 2000: 15). To fully understand the changes higher education has gone through in the three countries, the authors instead develop theoretical frameworks using metaphors like arenas, frames and space of action (Bauer et al. 1999: 31), or 'fields of social action' (Bleiklie, Høstaker and Vabø 2000: 15). Even if it may be difficult to disagree with the arguments put forward, one could claim that this type of policy analysis is (again) engaging some of the classical problems in the history of implementation analysis, where the number of independent variables is difficult to limit, especially since the dependent variable that the comparative project aims at explaining – change in higher education – is difficult to operationalise. As such, these studies are not restricted to the process where policies are put into practice, but also have an interest in studying how policies come about. The political context is quite different in the three countries studied. The UK policy direction is perhaps the most exceptional, where higher education institutions shifted from state-subsidised independence to increased dependence on, and deference to, state policies (Kogan and Hanney 2000: 234). Nonetheless, political similarities can also be detected. Thus, rather identical conclusions can be identified between the countries when it comes to how policies and reform attempts seem to have been created, being a product of a complex interplay of context, ideologies, ministers and bureaucracies. The findings in the UK illustrate that it is difficult to identify a traditional policy community in this country (Kogan and Hanney 2000: 237). A point Kogan and Hanney make is that in the UK the processes of national policy do not interact directly with the academic system so much as they act as separate systems producing fields of force between them (p. 238). The factor explaining much of the developments seems to be that of historical continuity – in all three countries. Because of the longitudinal character of the studies, the processes of historic continuation may be followed more easily, showing extensive explanatory power (Kogan and Hanney 2000: 238; see also Bleiklie, Høstaker and Vabø 2000: 307; Bauer et al. 1999: 266).

When it comes to identifying the forces of change, quite similar conclusions are also reached. To quote the conclusion from the Norwegian study:

> Changes that have taken place were not the outcome of political reforms alone. They should be considered part of more comprehensive demographic, socio-structural and political-institutional processes of change. Within this context the reforms have been both the driving forces behind and the responses to change (Bleiklie, Høstaker and Vabø 2000: 307).

4. CONCLUSIONS AND CHALLENGES FOR FUTURE RESEARCH

Policy realisation and political reform are predominantly studied as a part of a comprehensive change process, and not as the sole cause of change. Apparently, policy studies in Europe to an increasing degree take the same path as current studies of organisational change in the US. In the eye of an American scholar, this is a theoretical position where "people (and organisations) are understood to be constructed and to act in the light of socially constructed and defined identities, which are understood to be made up of cultural ideas … Their sovereignty, boundaries, and control systems are similarly embedded in cultural material" (Meyer 1996: 243). These observations are valid also for many of the studies of policy and change in the area of higher education. The empirical studies referred to above point to the following directions of current and future studies. First, the development is clearly going from a single theoretical framework towards applying a multi-theoretical framework. The direction of change is seen as non-linear rather than linear. Institutional and systemic change are analysed as a result of dynamic interactive processes rather than as the product of a centrally determined design. The theoretical perspectives applied have gone from viewing implementation as a separate process towards seeing policy making and implementation as integrated processes. Similarly, we note a renewed interest in the formal structures that frame action.

While since the mid-1980s a large number of studies on higher education policy issues have been conducted, explicit implementation studies have become rare phenomena in the field. How can this be explained? We have pointed to changes in the relationship between governments and higher education as a key factor that can be regarded as part of the explanation. However, the knowledge that governments keep up their efforts to reform higher education should still trigger interest by researchers in studying the processes that bring about the effects of governmental policies. While the nature of the relationship between government and higher education has changed over the last decade or so, this change was not an expression of the withdrawal of the government from higher education, or the end of public reforms in higher education. Instead, it can be argued that the overall relationship between governments and higher education institutions has changed, leading to different conditions for putting governmental policies into effect. This obviously poses challenges to research on implementation processes. While these challenges are by no means novel in the field of implementation studies in general, specific developments in higher education make it even more urgent to deal with them seriously. Related to the rise of the 'stakeholder society' (Maassen 2000), policy making and reform implementation tend to take place more and more in a network structure that replaces traditional bilateral relationships between the government and higher education institutions. Instead of looking at implementation process in the traditional (causal) way, implementation processes should be perceived as *interactive* processes. Furthermore, 30 years of implementation research has amply demonstrated the lack of realism in assuming that policies and reform initiatives move from government to objects of implementation unaffected by the road they travel. Assumptions of governmental omniscience and omnipotence are not helpful as a point of departure for implementing policies in practice, nor for studying such processes. Also, in many cases, a policy or a given reform is not necessarily the start of change, but a reflection of it; in other words, the government may 'legitimise' changes by developing policies or new laws responding to developments in the higher education system. Understanding implementation in higher education is taking notice of how policies and reforms often are formal political confirmation of developments in the field, and not some kind of alien phenomenon that is thrust upon 'unsuspecting' institutions. Based on these considerations, future research should pay attention to the following topics. Policy and reform studies in higher education should in principle use a multi-level approach. This implies that implementation studies have to be transformed, for example, into studies that examine the relationship between the authority responsible for policy making and the policy object, that is, from policy implementation to policy interaction. Implementation studies should include a much more careful analysis of the processes of formulating governmental policies, and ask, for example, how the nature of the policy relationship affects the way the policy object is involved in the policy making, feels responsible, and feels committed to the agreed upon policy. Also, one should give special attention to the different interests of institutions in higher education and who the winners and losers are in the process of shaping government policies and reforms. Certainly, the structures of policy making may be seen as a network, but that does not make issues of power, interests and conflicts over policy irrelevant in explaining institutional responses to initiatives from government or supranational bodies.

NOTES

[1]   We are grateful to David Dill for constructive comments. This chapter is based on: Gornitzka, Åse, Svein Kyvik and Bjørn Stensaker. "Implementation Analysis in Higher Education." In Smart, John C. (ed.). *Higher Education: Handbook of Theory and Research, vol. XVII.* Dordrecht: Kluwer Academic Publishers, 2002, 381–423, and reprinted with the kind permission of Kluwer Academic Publishers.

[2]   Separate case studies were undertaken as part of this project: the British Open University (Woodley 1981), the Swedish 25/5 Admission Scheme (Kim 1982), the University of Umeå in Sweden (Lane 1983), the Polish Preferential Point System, the University of Tromsø in Norway (Bie 1981), the Norwegian Regional Colleges (Kyvik 1981), the French *Instituts Universitaires de Technologie* (Lamoure 1981), the University of Calabria in Italy (Coppola-Pignatelli et al. 1981) and the German *Gesamthochschule* (Cerych et al. 1981).

REFERENCES

Bardach, E. *The Implementation Game.* Cambridge: MIT Press, 1977.
Barrett, S. and C. Fudge (eds). *Policy and Action: Essays on the Implementation of Public Policy.* London: Methuen, 1981.
Bauer, M., B. Askling, S.G. Marton and F. Marton. *Transforming Universities. Changing Patterns of Governance, Structure and Learning in Swedish Higher Education.* London: Jessica Kingsley Publishers, 1999.
Bie, K.N. *Creating a New University: The Establishment and Development of the University of Tromsø.* Oslo: Institute for Studies in Research and Higher Education, 1981.
Bleiklie, I., R. Høstaker and A. Vabø. *Policy and Practice in Higher Education. Reforming Norwegian Universities.* London: Jessica Kingsley Publishers, 2000.
Browne, A. and A. Wildavsky. "Implementation as Mutual Adaptation." In Pressman, J. and A. Wildavsky (eds). *Implementation.* Berkeley: University of California Press, 1984a, 206–231.
Browne, A. and A. Wildavsky. "Implementation as Exploration." In Pressman, J. and A. Wildavsky (eds). *Implementation.* Berkeley: University of California Press, 1984b, 232–256.
Cerych, L., A. Neusel, U. Teichler and H. Winkler. *Gesamthochschule – Erfahrungen, Hemmnisse, Zielwandel.* New York: Campus Verlag, 1981.
Cerych, L. and P. Sabatier. *Great Expectations and Mixed Performance. The Implementation of Higher Education Reforms in Europe.* Stoke-on-Trent: Trentham Books, 1986.
Cerych, L. and P. Sabatier. "Reforms and Higher Education: Implementation." In Clark, B.R. and G. Neave (eds). *The Encyclopedia of Higher Education, vol. 2, Analytical Perspectives.* Oxford: Pergamon Press, 1992, 1003–1013.
Clark, B.R. "Implementation in the United States: A Comparison with European Higher Education Reforms." In Cerych, L. and P. Sabatier (eds). *Great Expectations and Mixed Performance. The Implementation of Higher Education Reforms in Europe.* Stoke-on-Trent: Trentham Books, 1986, 259–267.

Coppola-Pignatelli, P. et al. *Rapporto sull'universita della Calabria.* Roma: Gruppo di Ricerche sull'edilizia per l'Istruzione Superiore (GREIS), 1981.
Dill, D.D. and B. Sporn (eds). *Emerging Patterns of Social Demand and University Reform: Through a Glass Darkly.* Oxford: Pergamon Press, 1995.
DiMaggio, P. and W.W. Powell. *The New Institutionalism in Organizational Analysis.* Chicago: University of Chicago Press, 1991.
Dunleavy, P. "Professions and Policy Change: Notes Toward a Model of Ideological Corporatism." *Public Administration Bulletin* 36 (1981): 3–16.
Elmore, R.F. "Backward Mapping: Implementation Research and Policy Decisions." *Political Science Quarterly* 94.4 (1980): 601–616.
Elmore, R.F. "Forward and Backward Mapping: Reversible Logic in the Analysis of Public Policy." In Hanf, K. and T.A.J. Toonen (eds). *Policy Implementation in Federal and Unitary Systems.* Dordrecht: Martinus Nijhoff Publishers, 1985, 33–70.
Goedegebuure, L.C.J. *Mergers in Higher Education.* Utrecht: Uitgiverij LEMMA BV, 1992.
Gornitzka, Å. "Governmental Policies and Organisational Change in Higher Education." *Higher Education* 38 (1999): 5–31.
Gornitzka, Å. and P. Maassen. "National Policies Concerning the Economic Role of Higher Education." *Higher Education Policy* 13 (2000): 225–230.
Gornitzka, Å. and P. Maassen. "Europeiske universiteter mellom marked og myndighet." In Larsen, I.M. and B. Stensaker (eds). *Tradisjon og tilpasning. Organisering og styring av universitetene.* Oslo: Akademisk forlag, 2003, 35–58.
Ham, C. and M. Hill. *The Policy Process in the Modern Capitalist State.* London: Sage Publications, 1986.
Hanf, K., B. Hjern and D. Porter. "Local Networks of Manpower Training in the Federal Republic of Germany and Sweden." In Hanf, K. and F.W. Scharpf (eds). *Interorganizational Policy Making. Limits to Coordination and Central Control.* London: Sage Publications, 1978, 303–341.
Hargrove, E.C. *The Missing Link. The Study of the Implementation of Social Policy.* Washington: The Urban Institute, 1975.
Henkel, M. *Government, Evaluation and Change.* London: Jessica Kingsley Publishers, 1991.
Henkel, M. *Academic Identities and Policy Change in Higher Education.* London: Jessica Kingsley Publishers, 2000.
Henkel, M. and B. Little (eds). *Changing Relationships between Higher Education and the State.* London: Jessica Kingsley Publishers, 1999.
Hjern, B. and C. Hull. "Implementation Research as Empirical Constitutionalism." *European Journal of Political Research* 10 (1982): 105–115.
Kim, L. *Widened Admission to Higher Education in Sweden – the 25/5 Scheme. A Study of the Implementation Process.* Stockholm: National Board of Universities and Colleges, 1982.
Kogan, M., M. Bauer, I. Bleiklie and M. Henkel. *Transforming Higher Education – A Comparative Study.* London: Jessica Kingsley Publishers, 2000.
Kogan, M. and S. Hanney. *Reforming Higher Education.* London: Jessica Kingsley Publishers, 2000.
Kyvik, S. *The Norwegian Regional Colleges: A Study of the Establishment and Implementation of a Reform in Higher Education.* Oslo: Institute for Studies in Research and Higher Education, 1981.
Lamoure, J. *Les Instituts Universitaires de Technologie en France.* Paris: Institute of Education, 1981.
Lane, J.E. *Creating the University of Norrland. Goals, Structures and Outcomes.* Umeå: CWK Gleerup, 1983.
Lane, J.E. *Institutional Reform. A Public Policy Perspective.* Aldershot: Dartmouth, 1990.
Lane, J.E. *The Public Sector: Concepts, Models and Approaches.* London: Sage, 1993.
Lester, J.P., A.O'M. Bowman, M.L. Goggin and L.J. O'Toole. "Public Policy Implementation: Evolution of the Field and Agenda for Future Research." *Policy Studies Review* 7 (1987): 200–216.
Maassen, P. "The Changing Roles of Stakeholders in Dutch University Governance." *European Journal of Education* 35 (2000): 449–464.
Majone, G. and A. Wildavsky. "Implementation as Evolution." In Freeman, H. (ed.). *Policy Studies Review Annual 2.* Beverley Hills: Sage, 1978, 103–117.
Meyer, J.W. "Otherhood: The Promulgation and Transmission of Ideas in the Modern Organizational Environment." In Czarniawska, B. and G. Sevón (eds). *Translating Organizational Change.* New York: Walter de Gruyter, 1996, 241–252.

Neave, G. "On the Cultivation of Quality, Efficiency and Enterprise: An Overview of Recent Trends in Higher Education in Western Europe, 1986–88." *European Journal of Education* 23.1/2 (1988): 7–23.

Neave, G. "The Stirring of the Prince and the Silence of the Lambs: The Changing Assumptions Beneath Higher Education Policy, Reform and Society." In Dill, D.D. and B. Sporn (eds). *Emerging Patterns of Social Demand and University Reform: Through a Glass Darkly.* Oxford: Pergamon Press, 1995, 54–71.

Neave, G. "The Evaluative State Reconsidered." *European Journal of Education* 33.3 (1998): 265–284.

Neave, G. and F.A. van Vught (eds). *Prometheus Bound. The Changing Relationship Between Government and Higher Education in Western Europe.* Oxford: Pergamon Press, 1991.

O'Toole, L.J. "Policy Recommendations for Multi-actor Implementation: An Assessment of the Field." *Journal of Public Policy* 6 (1986): 181–210.

Parsons, W. *Public Policy. An Introduction to the Theory and Practice of Policy Analysis.* Aldershot: Edward Elgar, 1995.

Pollitt, C. *Managerialism and the Public Services: Cuts or Cultural Change in the 1990s?* Oxford: Blackwell, 1993.

Premfors, R. (ed.). *Higher Education Organization. Conditions for Policy Implementation.* Stockholm: Almqvist & Wiksell International, 1984.

Pressman, J.L. and A. Wildavsky. *Implementation.* Berkeley: University of California Press, 1973.

Pressman, J.L. and A. Wildavsky. *Implementation.* 3rd edn. Berkeley: University of California Press, 1984.

Rhoades, G. "Governance: Models." In Clark, B.R. and G. Neave (eds). *The Encyclopedia of Higher Education, vol. 2, Analytical Perspectives.* Oxford: Pergamon Press, 1992, 1376–1383.

Sabatier, P.A. "Top-down and Bottom-up Approaches to Implementation Research: A Critical Analysis and Suggested Synthesis." *Journal of Public Policy* 6 (1986): 21–48.

Sabatier, P.A. and D.A. Mazmanian. "The Implementation of Public Policy: A Framework of Analysis." *Policy Studies Journal* 8.(special issue) (1980): 538–560.

Scott, W.R. *Institutions and Organizations.* Thousand Oaks, CA: Sage, 1995.

Slaughter, S. and L.L. Leslie. *Academic Capitalism: Politics, Policies, and the Entrepreneurial University.* Baltimore: Johns Hopkins University Press, 1997.

Van Heffen, O., J. Verhoeven and K. de Wit. "Higher education policies and institutional response in Flanders: Instrumental analysis and cultural theory." In Jongbloed, B., P. Maassen and G. Neave (eds). *From the Eye of the Storm – Higher Education's Changing Institution.* Dordrecht: Kluwer Academic Publishers, 1999, 263–295.

Van Meter, D.S. and C.E. van Horn. "The Policy Implementation Process. A Conceptual Framework." *Administration and Society* 6 (1975): 445–488.

Van Vught, F.A. (ed.). *Governmental Strategies and Innovation in Higher Education.* London: Jessica Kingsley Publishers, 1989.

Van Vught, F.A. "The Effects of Alternative Governance Structures." In Steunenberg, B. and F.A. van Vught (eds). *Political Institutions and Public Policy. Perspectives on European Decision Making.* London: Kluwer Academic Publishers, 1997, 115–137.

Williams, G.L. "The 'Marketization' of Higher Education: Reforms and Potential Reforms in Higher Education Finance." In Dill, D.D. and B. Sporn (eds). *Emerging Patterns of Social Demand and University Reform: Through a Glass Darkly.* Oxford: Pergamon Press, 1995, 170–193.

Woodley, A. *The Open University of the United Kingdom.* Paris: European Cultural Foundation, 1981.

MAURICE KOGAN

THE IMPLEMENTATION GAME

1. INTRODUCTION

Ladislav Cerych and Paul Sabatier must be feeling ambivalent about this event. It is good that we should refresh ourselves about the classics in our field, and honour those who produce them. At the same time, they will know better than most that a great deal of water has flowed under the bridges since they produced their book (Cerych and Sabatier 1986); indeed, Paul Sabatier in particular takes a leading role in implementation studies in political science more generally, and his development of the advocacy coalition framework (1998) is one of the more important contributions to political science of the last decade. It is also several generations on from the formulations offered in the original work of 1986.

2. AN APPRECIATION OF CERYCH AND SABATIER, AND SOME RESERVATIONS

Let me first acknowledge the importance of the original work. It opened up an important agenda, even if, in doing so, its perspectives now seem rather limited in that it did construe reform as largely a top-down process. It provided us with a generous range of case studies of examples of higher education developments that fed our knowledge of the present and future range of structures and provision.

My reservations about the tradition which they exemplified can be summed up as follows:

a) The preliminary chapters assumed that the most important changes were created and seen through by the most important people. Let me quote (p. 10):

> Parliaments have the legal authority to strongly affect the implementation process by stipulating clear and consistent policy goals, assigning implementation to sympathetic institutions, giving sympathetic officials sufficient sanctions and inducements to convince recalcitrants to alter their behaviour, providing sufficient financial resources and so on.

Not only Cerych and Sabatier but Martin Rein's excellent essay (1983), too, took it for granted that policy begins or is greatly modified in parliaments or through legislation. This has not been the case in the UK or, I suspect, in Australasia or probably other countries, too. They all provide

Å. Gornitzka et al. (eds.), Reform and Change in Higher Education, 57-66.

strong examples of top-down changes, but emanating from the executive rather than parliament.

In this kind of account, too, the whole sequence of policy generation is depicted as much more visible and in the public domain than I think it has been. They assume a clarity and determination to create policies that are not always there. There is often quite a casual drift into policies.

b) They assume that it is possible to enumerate factors or variables associated with success in implementation. But for the most part these do not seem to work. For example, the clear statement of goals is one of the declared factors. But these occlude complexity not only of values but also of the role of interests.

c) A self-imposed limitation occurs in Cerych and Sabatier, which was intended "to apply policy implementation analysis to higher education by looking closely at deliberate and planned change in higher education" (p. 4). But they explicitly did not include reforms dealing with the curriculum and with management and decision-making structures. Nor did they look at the role of non-deliberated and unplanned change, mainly created from the academic base of the system, which historically we have regarded as the main source of change in higher education.

d) They used as examples cases that were concerned mainly with changes in structure and provision. In this they shared the limitations of most of the higher education research of their time which took a long time to understand that the true indicators of change must include the substantive content of higher education, that is, the work and values of academics. This linkage has been made since, and, I would modestly claim, informed quite a deal of the work that our small group of colleagues attempted in the 1980s and perhaps more directly in our multi-national study of England, Norway and Sweden (Boys et al. 1988; Kogan et al. 2000).

e) They remark that the success or failure of goals depends on the amount of system change envisaged and their internal clarity and consistency. They accept that ambiguity and conflict are unavoidable and that a precise goal does not always secure success. Therefore look for an 'acceptable mix of outcomes', 'an acceptability space'. So far so good. But are they right to assume that big changes are more difficult, or that ambiguity does not pay off? In the 1990s we had a new political climate which gave confidence to politicians about their ability to change the world. Certainly, British ministers, and some Norwegian and Swedish ones, were able to create seismic changes without consultation and very quickly. These were daring actors forging forward even when the context offered no particular excuse or rationale for what they were doing.

Our authors were daring in producing middle range propositions. (This is a procedure about which I have doubts to which I will return.) They were:

1. Far-reaching changes work only if they aim at one or a few functional areas of the system. Our recent histories demonstrate this to be untrue. We have experienced enormous and wide-scale changes which seem to stick.
2. It is easier to change or create a new institution rather than a whole system. Again, this is empirically not a robust conclusion. In Austria, Greece, Norway and the Netherlands, for example, binary systems have been created and new statuses created wholesale.
3. Reforms projecting a low degree of change are often unsuccessful because they do not galvanise sufficient energy to overcome inertia. Well, OK.

A further part of the study attempts to clarify an adequate causal theory or set of assumptions about means and ends. This chimes in with the current concerns of some of our colleagues that implementation theory should prove useful to policy makers, an ambition that I do not share, on roughly the grounds of John Maynard Keynes' observation that "Practical men who believe themselves to be quite exempt from any intellectual influence are usually the slaves of some defunct economist". They (Cerych and Sabatier 1986: 15) wrote:

> If goals are to be realised, it is important that causal links be understood and officials responsible for implementing the programme have jurisdiction over sufficient critical linkages to make possible the attainment of objectives. Only when these two conditions have been met can the basic decision establishing the reform be said to 'incorporate' a valid causal theory.

Although they concede that not everything can be foreseen so it is important that policy makers correct as they go along, it means that they have to have secure knowledge that certain measures will secure change. I think this is a hopeless task. We know that coercion often works, and that pouring large sums of money into projects will cause changes at a certain, surface, level of reality. Whether they are then instantiated is another question. So much depends on the changes that are sought. Take two examples. A £100m attempt to embed enterprise into higher education curriculum in the UK had no effects. The insistence on quality assurance in teaching and learning had major effects but some of them, for example, in the restructuring of power within institutions were unexpected (Henkel 2000). It succeeded because it became a public process with penalties.

In both cases, these initiatives attempted to enter the entrails, the private life, of higher education. In each case, success has to be defined, and the impact analysis has to be multi-value and multi-perspective. Some of us would hate systems in which benchmarking and outcome measures, and the enterprise culture, were successful. But even by governmental instrumental criteria it will take decades to know whether value systems and practices have changed permanently and in the full range of subjects and institutions.

More fundamentally, this predictive ambition faces the objections put up by Braybrooke and Lindblom (1963) in attempts to play god, to create general welfare functions. Muddling through and disjointed incrementalism may not be good enough but something like them may be the best we can hope for.

3. WHERE THE ARGUMENT NOW STANDS

I have perhaps spent too long in criticising this pioneering work, but only do so because so much of it could plausibly return as relevant and, indeed, in one respect, its emphasis on the power of central institutions has proved to be more right than the revisionists'. To bring us up to where we now are, we have to take note of a strong political science literature on the subject and of scholarship which goes well beyond the field of higher education. It would be tiresome, and perhaps unnecessary in view of the excellent NIFU (Norwegian Institute for Studies in Research and Higher Education) survey (Gornitzka, Kyvik and Stensaker 2002) to do more than refer to only a small sample of the literature. The analysis of relevant literature provided by our three Norwegian colleagues is itself a substantive contribution to the debate.

Martin Rein's early but formative essay on implementation (1983), Sabatier's recent work on advocacy coalitions (1998), the many versions of new institutionalism (Hall and Taylor 1996), Paul Trowler's recent essay (2002) on the policy staircase and David Dill's recent critique (2003) of it give us plenty to work on. We also have more empirical treatments of national policy developments by the three teams in the Anglo–Norwegian–Swedish national and comparative studies that provide something of a contrast to the abstractions of the theorists.

In its simplest terms, these works all emphasise the non-linear nature of both policy making and implementation and the extent to which they might move through phases where different interest groups exercise key roles. Martin Rein (1983: 114–115), for example:

> posit(s) a ... view about implementation ... that emphasizes the interrelationship between the process and the product rather than the roles of the different actors who dominate in a competitive field. Policy and administration ... are continuously co-mingled. Purposes are redefined at each stage of the implementation process ... This continuity enables the contending views held by different interest groups to be worked out at each stage on the policy-practice continuum. Interest groups responsible for the development of policy may differ quite substantially from those that enter the process at the stage of implementation ... Implementation is interpreted as an expression of an accommodation to institutional realities. The imperatives in the law are redefined to take account of the problems faced in practice.

Other accounts, too, for the most part emphasise complexity, evolution, mutual adaptation and a learning interactive and negotiative process. Sabatier's latest work (e.g. updated version 1998) advances the role of advocacy coalition frameworks. This looks for alternatives to the staged heuristic and a synthesis of top-down and bottom-up models. The process involves actors at several levels who might operate through advocacy coalitions which share beliefs and activities. In this there are differentiations between levels. There are the deep core of belief systems, policy core beliefs and policy-oriented learning. Coalitions' principal glue are the core beliefs. There is resistance to changing them and they need strong evidence before admitting change. Many types of groups are involved in advocacy coalitions. The advocacy coalition field has two causal drives: core values and external perturbations.

This is a creative and sustained contribution to the argument. Not all of it is brand new. My criticism of it is applied to all of the principal theories within this arena: it seeks generalisations that simply do not apply through all the cases one could contemplate.

Trowler (2002) also deals with the procession of the implementation process. In countering the rational-purposive account of policy making and implementation he notes that there is only a limited distinction between them and that policy is made as it is put into practice. He offers us the implementation staircase where the roles different groups play at different times in influencing higher education policies can be located.[1] The substance of public policies is frequently transformed as policies descend from 'the staircase from adoption to implementation' and this helps to explain, as Pressman and Wildavsky (1973) first suggested, why the outcomes of public policy frequently fail to achieve their goals. Trowler (2002) argues for a fuller understanding of university environments, disciplinary cultures and the nature of academic organisation as input to policy design in higher education. These processes are not much studied and so, he thinks, not helpful to policy makers. They are indeed plainly part of the deep context which may trigger change. But I repeat that usefulness to policy makers, other than adding to their deeper wisdom and sensitivity to contextual issues, is not likely to directly emerge.

New institutionalism presents some of the more sophisticated versions of policy formation and is already a whopping industry, brilliantly summarised for us by Hall and Taylor (1996). In Lane's (1987) new institutionalist approach, the factors are physical and demographic structure, historical development, development of personal networks and temporal structure. A perspective is that change is possible as long as the institutional core is not threatened.

Theories of institutionalism are contended between academic traditions; between historical institutionalism, rational choice institutionalism and sociological institutionalism. The first group saw the institutional organisation of the polity or the political economy as the principal factor structuring collective behaviour. Institutions provide moral or cognitive templates for interpretation or action. The historical institutionalists acknowledge the asymmetries of power that institutions help to structure as well as the importance of social and economic contexts to the role that institutions play.

The rational choice institutionalists see politics as:

> A series of collective action dilemmas ... An actor's behaviour is likely to be driven, not by impersonal historical forces, but by a strategic calculus [which] will be deeply affected by the actor's expectations about how others are likely to behave as well. Institutions structure such interactions (Hall and Taylor 1996: 945).

The sociological institutionalists argue that:

> Many institutional forms and procedures should be seen as culturally specific practices ... so as to include not just formal rules, procedures or norms, but the symbol systems, cognitive scripts and moral templates that provide 'the frames of meaning' guiding human actions (Hall and Taylor 1996: 947).

This range of studies could be criticised in terms of NIFU's point that although it provides several potential frames for denoting the origins and roles of institutions it does not add to our knowledge of internal governmental processes, and this at a time when central authorities are more proactive. The institutionalists do not meet that challenge at the empirical level but, between them, present a range of conceptual choices within which closer grained empirical work might be framed. I think, however, that the Norwegians underestimate some work that is relevant to our quest, such as the US work on the nature of policy makers in general (e.g. Linder 1981; Caplan 1977) and some of our own recent work in our three country study. We tried (Kogan and Henkel 1983; Kogan et al. 2000) to depict the ways in which the nature of governments affects their commissioning and use of the results of research, and in doing so did reflect on the internal nature of government and how they dealt with the knowledge they created. We (Bleiklie, Høstaker and Vabø 2000; Kogan and Hanney 2000) have also tried to describe the ways in which different groups affect the genesis and outcomes of higher education policies, in three different countries. Bleiklie (2000) suggests that the design of the reforms actually adopted was influenced by the different nature of the policy networks in the three countries. In the UK we tested the extent to which three groups of influencers – the academic elites, the coopted elites and the institutional leaders – affected policy and showed that they were less important than heroic ministers. This could be compared with a similar scrutiny of elites in Norway and an assessment of the ways that successive waves of reform were handled (Bleiklie, Høstaker and Vabø 2000).

But NIFU is right to suggest that there are few thorough studies that analyse and follow through a given policy through the implementation process and identify factors that stimulate or hinder the policy initiatives taken. Whether such studies will produce knowledge about cause and effects I have already doubted. I am also doubtful about Pressman and Wildavsky's (1973) advocacy of an adequate causal theory of relationships between ends and means in a reform process for the possibility of goal attainment.

4. ELABORATING FURTHER

What can we piece together from all this? I have implied considerable reservations about much of the general scholarly work that has gone in parallel with mainly empirical attempts in the field of higher education. Before expressing them, let me acknowledge that Cerych and Sabatier were unusual in attempting to theorise on the basis of empirical studies. However, let me make my reservations explicit about theories of implementation in general.

We look at these theories with respect but then have to ask the naïve question: Do they apply to the cases we know? We must try to generalise but attempts to create generalised implementation theories in such a culturally saturated area as higher education are likely to fail because national policy-making and implementation systems are different from each other. This lesson is being learned the hard way by the Bolognaists who are seeking to impose uniformities on many countries. Moreover, higher education policy making is not only country specific but also sub-sector specific. Reform of the curriculum is likely to enter wholly different power and value terrains from those of, say, student financing.

In reaching generalisations, we have to take account of the points from which policies started. The origins of a policy give many clues not only on substantive content but what interests might be lined up for or against it, Martin Rein's point. It is like a yacht race. The starting point largely determines the finish. One could generalise for example that where the state historically had been least obtrusive – again as in the UK and Australasia – the 'reforms' have been most drastic; they had further to go. Historical contexts are all important. Political dynamics have changed. Our authors were reflecting on a period when politicians felt they had to be negotiative and gradualist if they were not to fall outside the democratic and Fabian conventions of the time. We work now within a different political landscape. The three country study exemplifies enormous shifts in ministerial styles and ambitions from the 1970s.

The recent literature on implementation adds up to a case for eclectic approaches. It is now obvious, and has been for a long time, that policy making does indeed go through several stages and emerges from several sources. I would widen them to include more explicitly the stage of *issue emergence* (Lowi 1972; Premfors 1980). This is a stage when often inchoate and emerging needs and wants, and discontent with the present order of things, are beginning to emerge as an issue that will eventually be identified, contested and settled in the political arena. It is the stage most often missed by higher education analysts who may be too anxious to get to the point quickly. I am not at all sure that one could then go on to produce a list of generalisable factors affecting implementation.

To analyse issue emergence, one has to go back into the deeper history. Thus, in the case of the expansion of higher education in the UK, analysis would show that the schools were getting restless with a system that could not accommodate increased numbers of qualified school leavers. This would lead us back to the increased bourgeoisification of British society and enhanced democratisation of expectations during the Second World War.

Or if we take the democratisation of European universities involving the end of the chair systems and the enfranchisement of junior staff and students in decision making, we would have to trace the impacts of radical sociology of knowledge on academic authority, as well as deeper changes in the national political psyches.

Then we must ask whether reforms emerging from the political and social ether are beginning to gell and are likely to generate wider social and political support to the point where some temporary minister takes them up as a good opportunistic policy. We would then have to ask whether their internal content is likely to survive the many other contingent factors that will affect outcomes and implementation, such as the constituency to which it might appeal. So, for example, we would judge that expansion will appeal not only to a huge constituency but that it wins on its multiple value content; it supports equality, the economy and individual development. Other examples would have to appeal to a far narrower constituency and value system. Thus we get back to the framework-actor duality.

That leads us to distinguish between the underlying factors and the factors that trigger change. The triggering factors are of two kinds. First, they are rarely parliamentary action but political opportunism. More than most systems, higher education if left to itself seeks and probably needs stability and continuity rather than change and reform. Its primary aim will be to sustain academic values through the pursuit of knowledge and this requires exception from the pursuit of reformist ambitions. Pursuing and disseminating knowledge are not easily performed under the glare of public policy activities. What are called reforms in higher education have derived more from public and social policy than from academic development.

The second kind of reform is that developing from changes in the knowledge landscape and affecting curricula and research agendas. Their impact will differ between that on existing elite institutions and new and more demotic institutions. Some changes are both social and academic; quality assurance is the obvious example, with its connotations of accountability but with its deep implications for academic work. I suggest that in such mixed cases it will be the politicians who insist on change, though institutional leaders soon recruited themselves to the QA banner but for managerial rather than academic reasons.

The more traditional top-down descriptions of policy making are not always wrong. For example, the insistence on formalised quality assurance came from politicians and not from the academy. Many of the so-called reforms of the last two decades were imposed without consultation or interaction with interest groups and straight from the heads of radical politicians. To canvass the field fully we need work on new styles of politicians and academic leadership and the power networks they create.

Attempts to show the impact of higher education policies have mainly concerned the impact on governmental and organisational structures, and on provision. Some of us did attempt to show how government-inspired policies affected the curriculum (Boys et al. 1988) and more recently we have the studies of the impacts on academic identities (Henkel 2000). Impact analysis is not easy. It requires a long time span and empirical access enabling many dimensions to be assessed. Moreover, impacts will be, to borrow Marton, Howell and Entwistle's terminology (1984), deep or shallow. Big bang changes, imposed by ministers, may do little to shift the basic essentialism of higher education's content and power structures. Small changes might have insidious effects.

So Cerych and Sabatier deserve high praise for opening up the field, for producing revealing and important case studies which, as the historians say, 'feed the mind' but do not add significantly to grand theory, although Clark Kerr, in his Foreword (p. xvi), thought that there would be a burst of new advance in the 1980s and that "when that time of renewed progress comes, this study ... may seem not just an interesting record of times past but a useful guide to times future". Well I am not too sure that it contributed to either regional development or vocational and short-cycle education. And it is unlikely that it contributed to what now seems inevitable in the widening of access. But that would be true of most of what most of us do.

This may all cast doubt on the utility of theory. It may yield little predictive power. But if taken carefully, like curry sauces, it can illuminate the experiences uncovered by empirical work. Probably it is time for a wholesale review of where higher education studies stand and should stand as against the more highly esteemed theory drawn from the disciplines.

NOTES

ᴵ I thought (Kogan 1975) the metaphor of the staircase too rigid a descriptor of the relationship between one stage of policy making and another.

REFERENCES

Bleiklie, I. "Policy Regimes and Policy Making." In Kogan, M., M. Bauer, I. Bleiklie and M. Henkel (eds). *Transforming Higher Education – A Comparative Study*. London: Jessica Kingsley Publishers, 2000, 53–87.

Bleiklie, I., R. Høstaker and A. Vabø. *Policy and Practice in Higher Education. Reforming Norwegian Universities*. London: Jessica Kingsley Publishers, 2000.

Boys, C., J. Brennan, M. Henkel, J. Kirkland, M. Kogan and P. Youll. *Higher Education and the Preparation for Work*. London: Jessica Kingsley Publishers, 1988.

Braybrooke, D. and C.E. Lindblom. *A Strategy for Decision*. Glencoe: The Free Press, 1963.

Caplan, N. "The Use of Social Research Knowledge at the National Level." In Weiss, C.H. (ed.). *Using Social Research in Public Policymaking*. Lexington, MA: D.C. Heath, 1977, 183–197.

Cerych, L. and P. Sabatier. *Great Expectations and Mixed Performance. The Implementation of Higher Education Reforms in Europe*. Stoke-on-Trent: Trentham Books Ltd, 1986.

Dill, David, D. "Book Review of *Higher Education Policy and Institutional Change. Intentions and Outcomes in Turbulent Environments*, P.R. Trowler (ed.)." *Higher Education Quarterly* 57.4 (2003): 396–400.

Gornitzka, Åse, Svein Kyvik and Bjørn Stensaker. "Implementation Analysis in Higher Education." In Smart, John C. (ed.). *Higher Education: Handbook of Theory and Research, vol. XVII*. Dordrecht: Kluwer Academic Publishers, 2002, 381–423.

Hall, P.A. and R.C.R. Taylor. "Political Science and the Three New Institutionalisms." *Political Studies* XLIV (1996): 936–957.

Henkel, M. *Academic Identities and Policy Change in Higher Education*. London: Jessica Kingsley Publishers, 2000.

Kogan, M. *Educational Policy Making*. London: Allen and Unwin, 1975.

Kogan, M., M. Bauer, I. Bleiklie and M. Henkel (eds). *Transforming Higher Education – A Comparative Study*. London: Jessica Kingsley Publishers, 2000.

Kogan, M. and S. Hanney. *Reforming Higher Education*. London: Jessica Kingsley Publishers, 2000.

Kogan, M. and M. Henkel. *Government and Research*. London: Heinemann Educational Books, 1983.

Lane, J-E. *Bureaucracy and Public Choice*. London: Sage, 1987.

Linder, S.H. "Perceptions of the Policy-Making Environment." Unpublished, 1981.

Lowi, T. "Four Systems of Policy, Politics and Choice." *Public Administration* 32.4 (1972): 298–310.

Marton F., D. Howell and N. Entwistle (eds). *The Experience of Learning*. Edinburgh: Scottish Academic Press, 1984.

Premfors, R. *The Politics of Higher Education in a Comparative Perspective: France, Sweden, United Kingdom*. Studies in Politics 15. Stockholm: University of Stockholm, 1980.

Pressman, J.L. and A. Wildavsky. *Implementation*. Berkeley: University of California Press, 1973.

Rein, M. "Implementation: A Theoretical Perspective." *From Policy to Practice*. Armonk, NY: M.E. Sharpe, 1983, 113–137.

Sabatier, P. "The Advocacy Coalition Framework: Revision and Relevance for Europe." *Journal of European Public Policy* 5.1 (1998): 98–130.

Trowler, P.R. *Higher Education Policy and Institutional Change. Intentions and Outcomes in Turbulent Environments*. Buckingham: SRHE and Open University Press, 2002.

NATIONAL CASE STUDIES

SVEIN KYVIK

THE IMPLEMENTATION OF THE NORWEGIAN COLLEGE REFORM

1. INTRODUCTION

One of the case studies in *Great Expectations and Mixed Performance. The Implementation of Higher Education Reforms in Europe* (Cerych and Sabatier 1986) is based on the establishment of the Norwegian district colleges in the late 1960s. As a collaborator in the comparative project and the author of the report that Chapter 7 in that book is primarily based on (Kyvik 1981), I have later had the opportunity to reflect on some of the conclusions drawn in the book and its contributions to implementation theory.

The report and the chapter cover the first 10 years of the development of this reform, which started with the establishment in 1965 of a governmental committee on postsecondary education to assess the future needs for higher education in Norway. One of the proposals of the committee was that all non-university institutions in each of twelve regions should be administratively and organisationally integrated in study centres called *district colleges*.[1] Concurrently, these new colleges should develop short-term vocationally oriented education as an alternative to the universities and the traditional institutions for teacher training, health education, technology, social work, etc. The issue of integration was, however, postponed and later abandoned by the government, and the district colleges were established as autonomous institutions on the basis of new types of short-term vocationally oriented programmes and some first-year university programmes. The evaluation of this reform, conducted by myself and Cerych and Sabatier, concluded that the establishment of district colleges as autonomous institutions had, on the whole, been successful during the first decade.

The non-implementation of the proposal to merge postsecondary schools in each region was explained by the resistance from some of the institutions involved, and that it was easier to establish new study programmes in a new institution not hampered by cultural and social traditions. Both I and Cerych and Sabatier concluded that the merger failed because the degree of system change envisaged was too large.

Today, the district colleges no longer exist as autonomous entities, and the original reform proposal to integrate non-university tertiary education in multidisciplinary institutions has been implemented. In 1987, the integration issue was revitalised by the next governmental commission on higher education (the

69

Å. Gornitzka et al. (eds.), Reform and Change in Higher Education, 69-82.
© 2007 *Springer.*

Hernes-Committee), and in 1994, 98 non-university colleges in Norway – including
the district colleges and the colleges for teacher training, health education, social
work, technology, etc. – were merged into 26 state colleges.

The two questions I will address in this chapter are why the merger of
institutions was carried through in the early 1990s and not in the late 1960s, and
whether the analytical framework developed by Cerych and Sabatier is still useful to
explain change processes in higher education.

2. THE PROPOSAL TO ESTABLISH DISTRICT COLLEGES

In 1965 a governmental committee on postsecondary education (the Ottosen-
Committee) was established to assess future needs for higher education in Norway.
The government foresaw the necessity of introducing major structural reforms in
order to cope with the changing and increasing demands for education at this level.
The committee was appointed for various reasons. First, the relative number of
young people seeking tertiary education had increased considerably, and an
increasing number were refused admittance to universities and colleges. Second,
there seemed to be a lack of balance between university education and vocationally
oriented short-term tertiary education. There were strong indications that the
universities represented a second choice for many secondary school graduates.
Third, the development of the postwar society had created new kinds of work and
jobs that required new kinds of skills. The traditional theoretical university
programmes did not satisfy the need in industry, commerce and the public services
for practical and vocational knowledge. Fourth, tertiary education was mainly
located in the three largest cities, Oslo, Bergen and Trondheim. However, the
political climate changed remarkably in this period in favour of geographic
decentralisation of tertiary education. While only 9 per cent of the Norwegian
population considered regional policy to be one of the three most important political
issues in 1957, this percentage increased to 27 per cent in 1965 and 59 per cent in
1969 (Valen and Martinussen 1972). The importance of viable local communities
was stressed as a reaction to the tendency of centralisation in the past years. Though
the short-term tertiary educational institutions were dispersed throughout the
country, this situation made people concerned with educational policy want to create
new institutions at college and university level outside the three urban centres. These
two trends, the regional and the vocational, thus should form the basis for major
innovations in Norwegian higher education (Kyvik 1983).

The Ottosen-Committee presented five reports from 1966 to 1970. The first
report outlined some of the main problems of the future educational policy and some
estimates of the total need for places in tertiary education. In its second report in
1967 the Ottosen-Committee proposed some changes in the organisation of
postsecondary education outside the university sector. The proposal was based on
two ideas: (a) development of short-term vocationally oriented education as an
alternative to the universities and the traditional institutions for teacher training,
health education, technology, social work, etc.; and (b) organisational and
administrative coordination of all short-term tertiary education in each of twelve

regions. Existing institutions and new study programmes were to be integrated in a new type of multidisciplinary institutions called *district colleges*. Norway has 19 counties; only six of these were to form a region of their own. The core of each district college was to be located in a study centre, recruiting 1500 to 4000 students. The main arguments for this integration were that a study centre would offer students a broader choice of courses; a broader and better milieu for the teaching staff; and a better utilisation of buildings, libraries and welfare installations.

In the various regions the proposal immediately aroused great interest and enthusiasm. Some planning committees were set up on local initiative, and from spring 1966 several local plans regarding location and establishment of district colleges were submitted to the Ministry of Education. Also at the national level, the proposal met with strong political support. In its third report, the committee had planned to discuss the future role and organisation of continuing and adult education. However, the Ministry of Education, and later on Parliament, requested that the committee expedite the work with a report on district colleges. This resulted in a postponement of the report on continuing education. Instead a special report on the district colleges was prepared, containing practical proposals on organisation and administration. A key person in this process was the Minister of Education, Kjell Bondevik. He represented the Christian People's Party, a political party that gained its strongest support in the rural regions, and which was part of a liberal/ conservative government coalition. Bondevik was working actively to stop the centralisation tendencies in the elementary school system and to establish study places in tertiary education outside the university cities.

The Ottosen-Committee presented its third report in March 1968. The committee defined a district college as an organisational superstructure of short-term tertiary education in a region. This meant that a district college did not necessarily have to be situated in one place, but could be located in different parts of the region. However, the committee recommended that a college should be concentrated in one place in order to obtain an integration of the various short-term institutions.

The first part of the proposal, development of new types of short-term job-oriented education in the various regions, was strongly supported both locally and by the Ministry of Education and Parliament. This was probably due to the fact that such a reform was seen more as a potential instrument in regional development than as an innovation in higher education. Representatives from all parts of Norway took part in the debate and emphasised the need for a district college in their respective counties. The other part of the proposal – integration of existing institutions and new study programmes in each region – met with immediate resistance from some of the colleges concerned and their affiliated professional organisations. The resistance was particularly strong at the colleges of teacher training and the colleges of social work. They wanted no integration in a common organisation that could limit their autonomous position. In addition, they claimed that administrative and organisational integration of the various institutions in a region would lead to practical difficulties. Different professional and administrative traditions and different teaching methods would impede an integration process.

Partly as a result of this resistance, the political decision to merge these institutions was postponed and later abandoned (Sørheim 1973). Instead, the

Ministry of Education proposed to establish district colleges as autonomous institutions without any formal ties to other institutions. In 1969, Parliament decided to establish district colleges for a trial period until 1974. From 1975 on, the district colleges became permanent institutions.

The Ottosen-Committee had stressed the importance of treating their different reports and proposals for a reorganisation of tertiary education in Norway as a whole. However, the proposal for the development of short-term vocationally oriented programmes was taken out of the total reform proposal, and the process led to the establishment of district colleges as autonomous institutions. The original proposal to develop an integrated educational system at the regional level was to be reconsidered at the end of the test period. After the withdrawal of this proposal, the reform did not directly concern the existing institutions. Their autonomous position remained unchanged. The postponement of the difficult integration question and the enthusiasm at all political levels thus made the planning and the establishment of district colleges a speedy process.

Within the Ministry of Education, a district college section was established to attend to matters of planning and administration. In addition, a central advisory board on district college matters was established in 1969. The advisory board was to be concerned with development within the colleges, partly by appointing committees and working groups to prepare curricula in new subjects. At the local level, each college would have a board of which the majority would be external representatives.

The central advisory board on district college matters supported the idea of an integrated college system. In a report to the Ministry of Education in 1972, the board stated that short-term higher education in each region ought to be located in a study centre. Only under special circumstances should this pattern be deviated from. On the other hand, the board emphasised that the future pattern of location ought not to be tied to the 12 regions proposed by the committee.

3. THE ESTABLISHMENT OF A REGIONAL COLLEGE SYSTEM

In 1972, the Labour Party government was replaced by a new liberal/conservative government coalition. This government submitted a white paper to Parliament on the future structure of higher education. However, contrary to the Labour Party government, the new coalition did not agree to the proposal of the Ottosen-Committee for an integrated college system. On the contrary, it proposed that the various institutions, for example teacher training colleges, technical colleges and social work colleges, should keep their autonomous position and be located in different parts of each region. This attitude must not only be regarded as recognition of the individual institutions and their distinctive character; the emphasis on a decentralised location pattern was as much an expression of the general regional policy carried out by this government as of its educational policy. While it was the policy of the Labour Party government to build up centres of a certain population size in each region, the coalition was more inclined to support a dispersed location pattern. In line with this policy, the liberal coalition also changed the number of regions from 12 to 17. It stated that each of the 19 counties should constitute a region for tertiary education with two exceptions.

The general election in 1973 brought the Labour Party government back into power. The report to Parliament prepared by the previous coalition was withdrawn and replaced by a revised version. However, the government retained the division into 17 regions. This was seen as natural, as the division in counties was used for most administrative purposes. Besides, this policy was in line with the persistent reform work within local administration in Norway. The counties were strengthened both politically and administratively in this period. However, contrary to the previous liberal/conservative coalition, the government stated that the various institutions should as far as possible be concentrated in one geographical area. The idea of the Ottosen-Committee for an integrated regional college system was accordingly maintained. The proposal implied a decentralisation of power from the Ministry of Education to a common organisation for non-university tertiary education in each region.

The report was discussed in Parliament in 1975. The result of the negotiations was a compromise between the Labour Party and the Conservative Party. A decision was made to establish common boards for district colleges, teacher training colleges, technical colleges, and social work colleges in each of 17 regions. In addition, plans were made to include the rest of the short-term postsecondary institutions under the jurisdiction of these boards. However, the Conservative Party stressed that the internal autonomy and the professional, distinctive quality of the individual colleges should be maintained.

The regional boards for non-university higher education were established in 1976. The main task of these boards was to ensure that planning, establishment and development of all short-term tertiary education in a region should be considered as a whole. However, the various institutions were still independent of each other, administratively, educationally and financially. Most of the institutions also had a rather negative attitude towards the regional boards. The boards were often regarded as bureaucratic and superfluous organisations standing between the individual institutions and the Ministry of Education. Thus, the boards had limited power, and the tertiary education system at the regional level was nearly as fragmented as before.

Why then did the integration in each region not succeed? As mentioned, the original proposal of the Ottosen-Committee met with immediate opposition from some of the colleges concerned and their affiliated professional organisations. They wanted no integration which could limit their autonomous position. The resistance was particularly strong in the teacher training colleges and in the social work colleges. In addition, several specialised colleges in Oslo and the neighbouring county wanted to be exempted from this administrative arrangement. Some of them argued that they covered a national need for qualified manpower. For that reason they found it unnatural to be subject to a board with the purpose to assess and plan for the cover of regional needs.

The Ministry of Education continued to work with the question of integration after the establishment of the first colleges. But the initiatives taken still met with opposition (Kyvik 1981). In addition to resistance on a professional basis, it was argued that organisational integration of the various short-term institutions would lead to practical difficulties. The colleges operated under different conditions, different administrative traditions and different teaching methods. The speed of the introduction of the reform therefore made it easier to establish the district colleges as separate institutions. But the fact that the question of integration was also postponed complicated the further integration process. During the test period the district colleges appeared as autonomous institutions with distinctive professional and administrative characteristics different from those of the colleges of teacher training, technology and social work. Integration of all short-term tertiary education in each region and establishment of study centres therefore seemed more problematic than ever before.

In addition, the district colleges soon sought to be compared with the universities and not with the other non-university institutions. Several of the subjects taught at the colleges offered special qualifications not covered by other educational institutions. These courses were national in character and both students and teachers maintained that 2–3 years of study was too short a time to provide a satisfactory education. Some of the colleges were therefore working consciously to expand their courses to make them comparable in standard to, although different in content from, higher degree courses at the universities.

The speed of the introduction of the reform in 1968–69 led to the postponement of a thorough discussion of the role of the district colleges in the future structure of higher education in Norway. This was partly because Parliament regarded the establishment of the new colleges not only as a matter of innovation in tertiary education, but also as a part of the regional policy issue. Besides, the change of governments in this period led to repeated revisions of the preparatory work in the Ministry of Education. In 1968, Parliament decided that a report on the development of the district colleges should be submitted for discussion as soon as possible. This report was however long in coming. Not before 1975 was this report discussed in Parliament. The district colleges had then existed for seven years.

4. THE MERGER OF REGIONAL COLLEGES INTO STATE COLLEGES

The reorganisation issue was revitalised by a governmental commission set up in 1987 to evaluate the goals, organisation and priorities of higher education and research (the Hernes-Committee). The commission pointed out several reasons as to why the earlier attempts at regional reorganisation had failed. First, the functional division into educational categories based on links to the professions intensified the local geographical disintegration of institutions. Further, the various vocational courses were administered by different offices in the Ministry of Education, and partly even by different ministries. Arguments for coordination were opposed by the colleges, and arguments for mergers were defeated by local political interests. Second, the various colleges had different study traditions, curricula, course structures, and staff members with heterogeneous obligations and rights. Third, earlier merger attempts had resulted in disputes concerning qualifications, and in some cases in personal conflict. The commission stated that the significance of such problems had been overemphasised, and that the time now was ripe for reducing the number of independent colleges through mergers within each region.

The white paper that followed supported the commission's recommendations. Right from the time when the proposal to integrate all college education into study centres was launched, the Ministry desired to have fewer institutions to manage. The large number of colleges under its auspices created considerable administrative capacity problems. Seen from the viewpoint of the Ministry, the regional boards were a poor compromise. It was for this reason that an amalgamation of institutions was included as one of the premises in the commission's mandate. In 1993, the government decided that the existing colleges in each of the regions should be merged into new units, named *state colleges*. The historic most comprehensive reform of Norwegian higher education became a fact. In the meantime it had taken almost 30 years from when the proposal for mergers had first been aired until 26 state colleges were inaugurated. The conditions for bringing about this reform were also considerably different in the early 1990s than at the end of the 1960s. The weaknesses of the college system were manifest, and the political opposition to such a change in the educational system had become considerably less. In this respect Norway placed itself within an international trend aiming at reducing the number of many small, specialised, single-purpose colleges, and creating a smaller number of larger, multipurpose, multidisciplinary institutions (Goedegebuure and Meek 1997).

In 1994, 98 regional colleges were amalgamated into 26 new state colleges encompassing the previous colleges of teacher training (25), engineering (15), health education (27) and social work (3), as well as the district colleges (14), and various other institutions offering a specialist range of teaching programmes (14). The purpose of the reorganisation was to enhance the quality of administrative functions and academic work through the creation of larger administrative and academic units, to break down barriers between the former colleges, and to develop new and broader study programmes. In addition, economies of scale would lead to more efficient use of physical resources.

Another aim of the reform, though not officially stated, was to prevent the two largest district colleges from achieving university status. These two colleges had for many years attempted to become universities, but the Minister of Education, Gudmund Hernes, was very intent to curb the tendencies to institutional drift and to limit the number of universities to the four established institutions. By establishing a binary system with two distinct higher education sectors, and by amalgamating these colleges with the professionally oriented non-academic colleges in each of their regions, he hoped to put an end to their university ambitions.

We can broadly distinguish between two stages in the implementation of this reform: the merger process conducted by the Ministry of Education, and processes taking place in the colleges after the mergers in order to accomplish (or counteract) the objectives of the reform. The first stage – the restructuring of the non-university college sector – can be regarded as a set of organisational changes undertaken to achieve the various academic, administrative and economic goals. First, the number of colleges was reduced to one fourth. Next, the internal organisation of each of the new state colleges was decided upon through the division into faculties and departments as well as by the establishment of new administrative structures.

Finally, a university-like management system was introduced. In the second stage – after the state colleges were established – it was generally the responsibility of the individual colleges to implement the measures necessary to fulfil the academic, administrative and economic objectives of the reform.

A condition for most of the objectives of the reform to become realised was that the state colleges were co-localised. However, the geographical location of each of the 98 original colleges made it politically unacceptable to move all course programmes within each of the regions to a single centre. In most cases teaching still takes place at the sites where the original colleges were located, even though those institutions have been merged into one common institution. Many of the colleges are in fact superstructures of faculties located far from each other.

The reorganisation was a result of a long and extensive political decision-making process that was undertaken according to a parliamentary resolution. The reform process was instigated by the Ministry of Education in order to implement this political resolution. In the Ministry, a small group of dedicated people was established to carry the mergers through. The regional boards for higher education were asked to organise the amalgamation process in their region according to directives and lines of guidance developed by the Ministry. In the first phase, the main issue was to come to an agreement on which institutions were to be merged within the various regions. The regional boards were the driving force in this process. They had worked for many years for closer regional integration of the different higher education institutions in their regions. The various colleges were less enthusiastic, but accepted somewhat reluctantly the inevitable outcome of this process. Still, some colleges worked actively to avoid the amalgamation, but for a variety of reasons. Some argued that the distance to the administrative centre of the new state college would be too far, while other colleges feared that their ambitions to be granted university status would be effectively stopped by the incorporation into a state college. The Ministry directed the merger processes, but negotiations between the regional boards and their affiliated colleges gave room for local adjustments.[2]

5. WHY WAS THE MERGER IMPLEMENTED IN 1994 AND NOT IN 1969?

This chapter has two purposes. First, to explain why the merger of the non-university tertiary education institutions was not implemented in the initial stage of the college reform, but 25 years later. Second, to discuss whether the analytical scheme by Cerych and Sabatier is a useful tool in this analysis.

As a starting point in their comparative project, the two authors developed a conceptual and analytical framework as a guide for the national case studies of implementation processes. On the basis of the analyses of the various reforms, Cerych and Sabatier concluded that it is a mistake to focus on *clear and consistent objectives*. They reduced the importance of an *adequate causal theory* for a successful outcome, and the comparative project indicated that *adequate financial resources* were of less importance than expected to ensure successful implementation. Still, they seemed to mean that two factors might be more important than others for a successful implementation of goals: a *moderate extent of change*, and the long-term presence of a *'fixer'* committed to the fulfilment of the reform.

Cerych and Sabatier initially pointed to the seemingly obvious fact that major changes are more difficult to implement than minor ones. They suggested that the degree of system change hoped for by a reform be conceptualised in terms of the number of institutions affected, the proportion of individuals within each institution whose behaviour would have to change, and the amount of behavioural change required of the staff. In their conclusion they stated however that a more complex conceptualisation of the scope of change was necessary to capture the process: *depth of change* indicates the degree to which a new policy implies a departure from existing values and practices of higher education. *Functional breadth of change* refers to the number of functional areas in which a given policy is expected to introduce more or less profound modifications, while *level of change* indicates the target of the reform: the system as a whole, a particular sector or segment of the system, a single institution or an institutional sub-unit.

The two authors concluded that the relationship between the scope of change and implementation success seems to be curvilinear. Policies with a very wide functional breadth and extensive depth of change encounter strong opposition, whereas those with a narrow functional breadth and small depth of change do not galvanise sufficient energy to overcome inertia in the system: "Thus reforms visualising a moderate scope of change are likely to be more successfully implemented than those with a very high or a very low scope" (p. 248).

In its report in 1968, the Ottosen-Committee proposed that all postsecondary education institutions in each of 12 defined regions should be merged. However, during the political process the number of regions were increased to 17. In its report in 1988, the Hernes-Committee suggested that the number of colleges should be reduced through amalgamations, and presented some examples on mergers. These examples indicated that the number of colleges might be reduced to about 55. The Ministry of Education (where Gudmund Hernes now was Minister of Education) thought this to be a too large number of entities, and suggested in a white paper to Parliament that 20 to 30 colleges would be a more appropriate number.

The Hernes-Committee and the Ministry of Education were less specific than the Ottosen-Committee in terms of which colleges should be merged, and the suggested number of new institutions was much lower than proposed by the Ottosen-Committee. One might therefore possibly conclude that the implementation of the 1994 merger was facilitated by *a less clear vision* of the final outcome and *a lower degree of system change*. There is after all a big difference between ending up with 26 and not 12 colleges (or 17 which was the outcome of the political process). On the other hand, the number of institutions, staff and students affected by a merger were far fewer in the late 1960s than in the early 1990s. In 1965, less than 10,000 students were enrolled in non-university tertiary education compared to 70,000 in 1994. Not only had 14 district colleges been established, but the number of colleges for various professional studies had also expanded considerably. The degree of system change in the 1994 merger therefore was probably greater than that of a similar reform in the late 1960s would have been. To use the terminology of

Cerych and Sabatier: depth of change, functional breadth of change, and level of change were all substantial. In theory, the likelihood of such a revolutionary structural reform to achieve the necessary political support and be implemented should thus be very low.

A too large extent of system change was a very convincing explanation for the merger failure in the late 1960s; an explanation that of course has to be modified in the light of later events. So, what was different in the early 1990s? *Adequacy of causal theory* is included in the analytical scheme by Cerych and Sabatier. But to the extent that it is in this respect possible to apply this term, there is no great difference in the logic behind the reform proposal on the two occasions. *Adequacy of financial resources* to secure a successful implementation of a reform is another factor, but it cannot explain the differences in implementation success. As opposed to the first merger proposal, one of the aims of the 1994 reform was to reduce public expenditures in the college sector through economies of scale in the larger merged institutions. In line with this assumption, the government anticipated a more cost-efficient state college system and reduced appropriations to the new colleges (Kyvik 2002a). The unimportance of adequate funding for the implementation of this reform corroborates in this respect the conclusion drawn by Cerych and Sabatier.

The big difference between the situation in the late 1960s and the early 1990s is *the degree of commitment to the objectives* of the reform proposals as suggested by the two committees. While the colleges and their staff opposed the merger proposal on both occasions, the Hernes-Committee attained general political support for the merger issue. Moreover, the chairman of this committee, Gudmund Hernes, was given the opportunity to restructure Norwegian higher education according to his own visions by being appointed Minister of Education. Reforms are not self-executing: someone has to be in charge of their implementation. It is generally regarded as important for goal attainment that those agents who are responsible for the implementation of the reform are highly committed to their task. Cerych and Sabatier particularly emphasise the importance of having a strong leader – a so-called 'fixer' (Bardach 1977) – committed to the reform. Such 'fixers' were also present in most of the higher education reforms they studied. However, their role was usually limited to policy formulation and adoption and restricted to the early phase of the implementation process. Cerych and Sabatier therefore suggested that many difficulties that arose later could have been overcome if the 'fixers' had been in charge for a longer period. Gudmund Hernes was accordingly a true 'fixer' in the implementation of the reform.

But why did the merger proposal by the Hernes-Committee attain general political support? What was different on the later occasion from the situation in the late 1960s? The answer can be found primarily in *changes in the political and socio-economic environmental climate*, which is one of the important factors influencing policy implementation in the analytical scheme of Cerych and Sabatier. The authors noted that social and economic conditions which originally motivate the adoption and launching of a reform may change, and that this new climate may either undermine its implementation or give it a new and unforeseen orientation. In the reforms studied, a changing climate often contributed to a shift in emphasis among multiple goals of a reform. Cerych and Sabatier concluded that the effects of changed socio-economic environments on policy implementation are highly complex:

> No clear direction can be identified in which worsened social, economic and financial conditions influence higher education reform implementation. Sometimes the impact was negative; often it was not. Occasionally, it facilitated implementation because the generally worsened conditions were in fact favourable in an unforeseen way to the realisation of a policy. When the impact was negative, however, it was never the only factor in failure (p. 254).

These changes can in a Norwegian context be interpreted as a mixture of increased emphasis on *efficiency*, *standardisation* and *regionalisation* in public administration. The reorganisation of the non-university higher education sector in 1994 accordingly has to be viewed in a broader national context in order to understand the objectives of the reform and the processes that took place.

At the end of the 1980s, to a larger extent than hitherto, higher education institutions came to be regarded as regular state agencies subject to a common steering system. This change in thinking was widespread in other European countries and came to influence Norwegian public policy in important ways. This applied in particular to the 'new public management' ideas developed by the OECD, and, in line with recommendations by this organisation, the government introduced a general programme for renewal of the civil service. The main steering principle is that more decision-making authority and administrative tasks should be transferred from the government to the individual institutions. Further, increased importance should be attached to a market orientation, either through increased demands for self-financing, or through the introduction of market and quasi-market mechanisms. The condition for the implementation of these governmental objectives in the non-university higher education sector was that the governance and the management system in the colleges be strengthened. This could best be achieved by creating larger institutions, which would also generate economies of scale and be more cost-efficient than the smaller institutions.

Another important factor is the general trend in society towards coordination of human activities through *standardisation* (Brunsson and Jacobsson 2000). In most countries the development of a tertiary education system has been a balancing act between diversity and convergence (Meek et al. 1996). From a political point of view the shaping of a diversified tertiary education system with a combination of academic and vocational studies as well as long and short programmes usually is regarded as important to meet the varied demands of society for skilled labour and the needs of a heterogeneous mass of young people for education. On the other hand there is an administrative need for standardised regulations of the educational system. Moreover, the tendency towards institutional and academic drift among vocationally oriented education institutions and their staff in the long run favours convergence, not diversity.

The district colleges were established as higher education institutions, while the existing postsecondary institutions did not have that status. During the period 1973–81 the various vocational schools were upgraded to higher education institutions. This process started with the colleges of teacher training. In 1977, the colleges of engineering and health education were upgraded, and various other small institutions in 1981. Simultaneously, the teaching programmes were extended from two to three years.

In this perspective the development of the non-university tertiary education sector in Norway can be described as a large number of *standardisation processes*. There has been a standardisation of steering and organisation principles in this sector, a standardisation of structure and content in teaching programmes, a standardisation of admission criteria, and also of working conditions and career structure among academic staff (Kyvik 2002b). Gradually, the various programmes became more similar with respect to practice demands, teaching and examination, and more emphasis on theory. These standardisation processes have taken place over a very long period irrespective of policy aims of creating and maintaining a diversified higher education system, and probably without any clear vision by policy makers at different points in time. In this respect, standardisation processes in the tertiary education sector can be viewed as a reflection of similar processes in public administration in general. Convergence in the regional college sector facilitated the merger process, and the reform in itself was part of a radical standardisation process in Norwegian higher education.

A third factor is the tendency towards *regionalisation* of public services. The regional level gradually increased its importance to the detriment of the local level and the state level in most public sectors. The same trend can be found within the tertiary non-university sector. While the national policy for higher education until the early 1980s supported the establishment of new colleges in local communities without such institutions, this policy changed in the 1980s in favour of regional concentration of study places. Several reasons can be put forward to explain this process. First, the governmental educational administration was functionally overloaded, and decentralisation of tasks and authority to the local and regional level had been an objective for many years. Second, the government assumed that economies of scale could be obtained by the concentration of study programmes in regional centres due to better utilisation of buildings and administrative capacity. Third, the government assumed that large educational units would be conducive to high quality teaching and research as well as quality in administrative services, and fourth, that the co-localisation of study programmes would have positive effects on collaboration patterns between staff across different disciplines. This policy coincided with, and was partly inspired by, the introduction of new steering principles in the public sector. The private concern with its divisional structure became a model for the organisation of public administration. In this respect, the establishment of a relatively small number of colleges – one in each region through mergers – was in line with new trends in public policy. In addition, there was a growing consciousness in the regions themselves that higher education institutions should contribute to a larger extent in developing the local economy, and that one large and visible institution would be better equipped to undertake such a role, than many small entities.

6. CONCLUSION

The political decision to undertake large-scale mergers in the regional college sector, and the successful implementation of this decision in the early 1990s, were facilitated by changes in the environmental climate. The proposal to establish fewer and larger state colleges through mergers was consistent with prevailing trends in political and administrative thinking about how the public sector should be organised. The existence of a 'fixer', who in this case proposed the reform as well as implemented it, was an additional factor which guaranteed a successful outcome of the political decision. However, the reform with great probability would have been implemented even without Gudmund Hernes in charge of the Ministry of Education. The ministerial bureaucracy was intent on carrying this reform through and was backed by a unanimous political decision.

What can we learn from this case to extend our knowledge about implementation of higher education reforms? I am inclined to conclude that the results are probably of limited value. We might of course have concluded that a large-scale structural reform can be successfully implemented even if the affected institutions and their staff oppose it, as long as the reform is consistent with the prevailing political and bureaucratic ideology of how higher education should be organised. But I am not sure whether such a conclusion would have any theoretical bearing, nor be of any practical relevance. I am sceptical as to whether it is possible to develop 'a general theory of effective implementation of policy decisions', or even a list of factors conducive to the achievement of reform objectives. Every implementation process is unique, taking place under different conditions and with different actors involved.

On the other hand, a specific implementation process is also a unique learning process. It is important to have in mind that objectives often are formed without detailed knowledge of their consequences. Decisions leading to public goals and plans are not necessarily rational. The classical theory of the rational actor presupposes that the decision maker has complete knowledge of alternatives and their consequences, that the actor is capable of ordering his/her preferences, and that the actor can choose the appropriate means to reach the desired results. This theory has been attributed to individual human beings, but as we all know, there are strong cognitive limitations to individual rationality. Public policy, however, is unlikely to result from the choice process of one individual. Policy formulation is usually the result of interaction among actors with different interests, goals and strategies. Yet, the theory of the rational actor is often attributed to groups of individuals within a common decision system. But if there are indeed limits to individual rationality, then these will apply as well to organisations. Imperfect ideas may therefore produce unsatisfactory results if the goals are not changed or reformulated through experience.

The use of systematic analysis and evaluation of problems and challenges in the course of the implementation phase of a reform therefore increases possibilities for a successful outcome. In that respect, I agree with Cerych and Sabatier when they suggest in their conclusion that "evaluation ought to be an integral part of implementation. With few exceptions, evaluation in practice is rarely used as a means of correcting errors, identifying unforeseen constraints, and reformulating implementation strategies or, if necessary, even goals" (p. 249). However, in accordance with the general shift from implementation analysis to evaluation (cf. Gornitzka, Kyvik and Stensaker 2002), I should like to turn this statement around and contend that implementation analysis should be an integral part of evaluation of public reforms. I think it is in this context the relevance of the implementation approach will turn out to be greatest in the future.

NOTES

[1] The Norwegian name of these colleges is 'distriktshøgskoler'. Kyvik (1981) and Cerych and Sabatier (1986) used the standard translation of this name – regional colleges. I now prefer to use the term district colleges, because all tertiary non-university colleges were later given the umbrella name 'regionale høgskoler' (regional colleges).

[2] The outcome of the reform in relation to its objectives has been analysed elsewhere (Kyvik 2002a), and this stage of the implementation process is not part of the present analysis.

REFERENCES

Bardach, E. The Implementation Game. Cambridge: MIT Press, 1977.

Brunsson, N. and B. Jacobsson. A World of Standards. Oxford: Oxford University Press, 2000.

Cerych, L. and P. Sabatier. Great Expectations and Mixed Performance. The Implementation of Higher Education Reforms in Europe. Stoke-on-Trent: Trentham Books, 1986.

Goedegebuure, L. and V.L. Meek. "On Change and Diversity: The Role of Governmental Policy and Environmental Influences." Higher Education in Europe 12 (1997): 309–319.

Gornitzka, Å., S. Kyvik and B. Stensaker. "Implementation Analysis in Higher Education." In Smart, J.C. (ed.). Higher Education: Handbook of Theory and Research, vol. XVII. Dordrecht: Kluwer Academic Publishers, 2002, 381–423.

Kyvik, S. The Norwegian Regional Colleges. A Study of the Establishment and Implementation of a Reform in Higher Education. Report. Olso: Norwegian Institute for Studies in Research and Higher Education, 1981.

Kyvik, S. "Decentralisation of Higher Education and Research in Norway." Comparative Education 19 (1983): 21–29.

Kyvik, S. "The Merger of Non-University Colleges in Norway." Higher Education 44 (2002a): 53–72.

Kyvik, S. (ed.). Fra yrkesskole til universitet? Endringsprosesser i høgskolesektoren. Bergen: Fagbokforlaget, 2002b.

Meek, V.L., L. Goedegebuure, O. Kivinen and R. Rinne (eds). The Mockers and Mocked: Comparative Perspectives on Diversity, Differentiation and Convergence in Higher Education. Oxford: Pergamon, 1996.

Sørheim, I.Ø. "The Norwegian Regional Colleges." In Furth, D. (ed.). Short-Cycle Higher Education. A Search for Identity. Paris: OECD, 1973, 45–82.

Valen, H. and W. Martinussen. Velgere og politiske frontlinjer.

JOHN TAYLOR

THE LEGACY OF 1981: AN ASSESSMENT OF THE LONG-TERM IMPLICATIONS OF THE REDUCTIONS IN FUNDING IMPOSED IN 1981 ON INSTITUTIONAL MANAGEMENT IN UK HIGHER EDUCATION

1. INTRODUCTION

In the last 25 years, UK higher education has undergone fundamental change. Key developments have included:

- The movement from a highly selective, elitist system to one based on mass participation, prompting a significant reduction in the unit of resource per student and changes in the methods of student finance. In particular, the UK has moved towards the introduction of fees for undergraduate education.
- Increasing accountability in the use of funds, including a strong focus on 'value for money' and new transparency in resource allocation with consequences for institutional management. New financial arrangements have challenged the traditional autonomy of UK institutions.
- The emergence of increasing selectivity and quality-related funding, especially in research, with major consequences for institutional diversity and the interrelationship of teaching and research.
- Increasing commercialisation of university activities, including a new awareness of market forces and of the need for generating alternative sources of finance.

Against this background, the year 1981 is widely recognised as a turning point. A period of growth and expansion had come to an end and had been replaced by cuts in expenditure. 1981 is also seen as the start of other, deep changes in the direction, organisation and management of higher education, both in government and within institutions. Maurice Kogan and Stephen Hanney describe 1981 as a 'year of drastic policy change'; an interviewee in their study of reform in higher education states that "July 1981 was the crucial date. Before then, there was very little government policy for higher education. After 1981, the Government took a policy decision to take policy decisions, and other points such as access and efficiency moves then followed" (Kogan and Hanney 2000: 87). For those working in the system at the time, the shock was enormous. There were fears that not only would jobs be lost but that whole institutions would close; a period of crisis management commenced. Of

Å. Gornitzka et al. (eds.), Reform and Change in Higher Education, 83-96.

longer term significance, many of the key changes in UK higher education towards the end of the twentieth century are often traced back to the cuts in 1981 and to their impact on universities.

Over 20 years later, with all the benefits of hindsight, how significant was 1981 in shaping UK higher education as it exists today? Research has been undertaken to examine the priorities and internal management of individual institutions. The result is a study of policy implementation in higher education, the extent to which that policy has short-term and longer term implications, and the extent to which it has both planned and unplanned consequences. In particular, the research aims to assess how significant were the financial cuts in 1981 on the development of UK higher education and to what extent are the changes which were prompted at that time still an influential factor in university management.

To this end, it is helpful to examine first of all the views expressed by the universities themselves soon after the cuts were announced. In 1983–84, the UK government through its Department of Education and Science (DES) funded a research project looking into the response of universities to the financial reductions announced on 1 July 1981. This project took the form of a number of case studies, covering nine different universities. Institutions were asked to consider the impact of the reductions in 1981 compared with other changes which had occurred in the preceding period. In particular, they were asked to identify the consequent changes in academic planning and resource allocation procedures and to describe other policy implications, especially examples of 'good' and 'unsatisfactory' management practice; reference was to be made to academic departments, academic related services, administration and central services, buildings and estates, student amenities and welfare and non-government income. Using the reports compiled at this time, it is possible to consider in each of the nine universities concerned to what extent the changes which were introduced in 1981 continue to influence their operation in 2003.

2. BACKGROUND

In attempting to answer this question, it is necessary to look back at the period immediately before 1981. The 1960s and early 1970s was a period of unprecedented growth in UK higher education. In 1961–62, the number of full-time and sandwich students in universities stood at 113,000 and the total number of higher education students was about 192,000. The government's acceptance of the Robbins Report in 1963 resulted in a 'policy led' expenditure programme for higher education which funded a decade of expansion during which the number of full-time and higher education students more than doubled to 453,000 in 1971–72. University numbers increased by 63% to 184,000 during the 1962–67 quinquennium. As Clive Booth (1982: 33) has emphasised "... the Robbins Report secured a niche for higher education in the [government's expenditure] plans from which it was able to withstand onslaughts on public expenditure during the late 1960s and the early 1970s" with the result that, not only did resources accompany the increases in student numbers, but the 1967–72 quinquennial settlement provided for a 10% increase in student unit costs.

This optimism continued with the 1972 White Paper *Education: A Framework for Expansion* which included further projections of growth. However, in reality, the 'golden age' was already coming to an end. The government assumed that, because student numbers would be expanding through the 1970s, it would be possible to increase efficiency in terms of tightening staff:student ratios and reducing unit costs whilst maintaining academic students. Thus, the White Paper envisaged some 30% growth in full-time student numbers in universities over the 1972–77 quinquennium, with recurrent grants falling by 2% in real terms per student. There were other warning signs of things to come, with the government beginning to offer advice, at this stage in very broad terms, about subject mix and discouraging the development of whole new departments.

There followed a period of very significant change, even before 1981. In 1973–74, the economic crisis prompted by international cuts in oil production resulted in significant cuts in government expenditure. This included half the increase in recurrent expenditure for the universities for 1974–75 and for the subsequent years of the 1972–77 quinquennium. Under these pressures, the quinquennial planning system effectively came to an end. 1975–76 was another very difficult year in financial terms. At this time, therefore, universities became accustomed to dealing with financial stringency. However, most universities saw such requirements as a temporary measure; Shattock and Rigby (1983: 10) commented as follows:

> With the benefit of hindsight the UGC and the universities should have paid more attention to the events and public statements of the 1974–75 crisis. Many universities set up wide-ranging economy committees to find ways of reducing expenditure ... But only one university of the number we have studied fundamentally amended its planning and resource allocation structure as a result of the crisis. In retrospect the pressures of 1974–75 look rather like a profound warning to the universities which the universities did not heed.

Further important shifts in government policy were presaged from 1977–78 when the government decided that a higher proportion of university general recurrent income should be obtained from fees and a smaller proportion from the Exchequer grants. At this time most full-time students were in receipt of mandatory awards from local authorities which covered fees and maintenance. The shift towards fees was in effect a transfer in the burden of funding from central to local government. Nevertheless, part of the rationale was that funding should follow the student, an early acknowledgement of the power of student demand in shaping higher education finance in the UK.

In 1979, following the election of the Conservative government led by Margaret Thatcher, government support for overseas students was withdrawn, replaced by guidance to universities to charge fees to cover full tuition costs to such students. For many universities, the implications were very serious, requiring further savings and staff economies. However, there were further important consequences. In particular, many universities rapidly adopted new ways of working in order to attract international students, including specialist marketing and a new awareness of competition on the basis of fees as price rather than cost.

Thus, before 1981, universities had become familiar with the pressure on funding, even if their managerial arrangements may not have been prepared for the shock of 1981. This is significant, however, because, in responding to the DES research project, many universities pointed to the 1970s, rather than 1981, as a crucial time in which they began to develop their academic planning procedures. Many of the universities studied had academic plans in place and contingency financial plans; the emphasis, however, was on academic planning rather than overall strategic or corporate planning, and on the short-term rather than any longer term vision.

3. THE CUTS OF 1981

The late 1970s were a time of nervous foreboding; Edward Parkes, who became Chairman of the University Grants Committee, immediately identified 'symptoms of malaise in the university system'. There were many signs of an imminent change in fortune for higher education and for particular universities, but little action was taken and many clung to a mistaken view that things would get better. After 1979, such complacency was shaken forever. Soon after the change in fees policy for international students, the government announced a cut of 8.5% in the recurrent grant spread over 1981–82 to 1983–84, bringing the total cut since 1979 to about 15%. In December 1980, the government announced a reduction of £30 million (3.5%) in the recurrent grant for 1981–82, rapidly followed in May 1981 by a further 5% for 1982–83 and 1983–84.

The University Grants Committee (UGC) took the lead in implementing these reductions, ignoring those who argued that the Committee should have resigned rather than follow the government line. It emphasised that no universities should be closed but that courses and whole departments should be reviewed; student numbers would be reduced accompanied by a shift in the balance of student numbers towards the sciences. Letters were sent to individual universities providing detailed advice on the closure of particular activities or the expansion of others, and asking for a full response on the action to be taken, including the staffing implications.

The cuts announced in 1981 varied widely between institutions. In the DES study under consideration, the reductions in grants varied (see table 1).

Table 1. Reductions in institutional grants 1981

Institution	%
Bath	3
Heriot-Watt	13
Sheffield	14
Hull	20
Sussex	21
Aberdeen	23
Stirling	27
Aston	31
Salford	44

Taken together with the withdrawal of funding for international students, universities overall lost 13–15% of their total income over the period 1981–84.

4. THE IMPACT ON UNIVERSITY MANAGEMENT

In responding to the DES research project, universities outlined how they had gone about planning for the new financial scenario with which they were faced. The reductions in funding prompted many important changes in management practice. To what extent are these changes still a factor in university management? Do the cuts of 1981 continue to exert an influence in UK higher education?

Several key points emerged, upon which the universities concerned have now commented afresh:

- The importance of high quality management was emphasised in 1984 in order to overcome institutional inertia. This included both day-to-day control and resource management, but also a new emphasis on leadership, especially for the motivation of staff, the maintenance of morale and the capacity to provide long-term vision. It was increasingly recognised that, in selecting a new vice-chancellor, universities needed to look for a leader and a manager; an outstanding academic record continued to be important in order to ensure credibility within the academic community but it was no longer the prime or sole determinant in securing an appointment. At the same time, the universities indicated the need to balance such central leadership and direction with the development of decentralised structures which provided incentives and encouraged initiative and entrepreneurship. The role of the vice-chancellor was increasingly to provide the overall vision and direction, but also to create an environment within which this could also flourish. It was the explicit recognition of these roles and, in particular, the need to be proactive in their pursuit, which made such an impact on institutional management immediately after 1981.

  Today, the universities concerned continue to recognise the importance of such leadership. Most still see this as one of the most crucial changes consequent upon the cuts of 1981, especially within those universities most adversely affected. The cuts required universities in filling senior appointments to look for skills of management and leadership as well as academic distinction. This necessity continues today. To this end, universities now devote very significant effort, not least through the use of 'head hunters' to secure the 'right' appointment. Many new pressures and demands have emerged, but there is no doubt that events in 1981 and immediately thereafter placed new expectations and responsibilities on the role of the vice-chancellor or principal in UK universities which have continued to the present time. No longer simply *primus inter pares*, the vice-chancellor began to emerge as a 'Chief Executive' and as an 'Accounting Officer', directly responsible for the management and direction of their institutions.

It is unlikely that this was the deliberate outcome of the 1981 cuts in expenditure, but it was a vital and enduring part of the response of universities. A new emphasis was placed on leadership, management and responsibility. The extent to which individuals were equipped to undertake this role varied, of course, and concerns about the quality of institutional leadership remain today. Such concerns, in part, have prompted the recent establishment by Universities UK of the Leadership Foundation, a body charged with improving management in higher education.

- The need for a critical evaluation of an institution's portfolio of subjects and courses resulting in a plan which emphasises selectivity in the use of resources was also clearly identified in 1984. Many universities for the first time began to use performance indicators in order to compare academic performance between different departments and, where possible, with external comparators. As a management tool, benchmarking began to emerge in many universities. Information was often imperfect and techniques for analysis were still emerging, but universities were forced by financial stringency to face a key fact which had always been known but whose consequences had always been suppressed, namely, that standards and quality varied both between and within institutions. It is interesting that, in response to the 1981 cuts, universities in 1984 were commonly using terms like 'evaluation' and 'selectivity', ahead of the first Research Selectivity Exercise or the formal assessment of teaching.

Today, the universities studied continue to pursue such policies, but they attribute these requirements to the impact of teaching and research assessment, the effect of market forces and the need to build on strengths. For those involved in responding to the 1981 cuts and still in senior management, there is a strong view that the forces for selectivity in the 1990s and more recently are much more powerful than existed after 1981, mainly because of the public nature of assessments and performance indicators. The Research Assessment Exercise, Teaching Quality Assessments, 'league tables' in the national press and the vagaries of student demand are all seen as key factors in driving selectivity; few people draw a conscious, direct link with 1981.

The 1981 cuts in expenditure compelled universities to examine critically their portfolio of activities with a view to reaching management decisions on whether to maintain, develop or run down particular areas. This differed from what went before when there had been a common assumption that universities could ride the storm and everything would be better in the end. However, the response to 1981 in most universities remained an essentially internal exercise; institutions retained the view that 'they knew best' how to respond. Today, whilst such views remain strong and institutional autonomy continues to be a cornerstone of the higher education system, many decisions are effectively driven by external judgments and assessments. It takes a strong management supported by a large, diverse and discretionary funding base to pursue alternative policies.

- The development of strong, cohesive management teams, with clearly defined responsibilities and capable of high levels of effort and imagination is a characteristic of the universities surveyed in 1984. Universities had traditionally been run by individuals, often working in isolation and without any clear management framework; the autocratic baronial, professional head of department, who went his (and it was almost exclusively his) own way, is, perhaps, a cartoon character, but is not without some substance. Such individualism could no longer survive. Universities began to develop a corporate identity in response to the changing external environment. At the same time, the role of non-academic managers also began to change. The need for specialist advice, especially from accountants and registrars, began to promote the development of a new cadre of influential professional managers in an advisory role and increasingly as full members of the management team.

  As with the importance of leadership, the universities surveyed still adhere to this view. They regard 1981 as important in this development. However, they also point to some interesting differences in motivation. In 1981, the motivation was either to help in the dissemination of change within the university or to provide a political counterbalance to the vice-chancellor (and thereby help to achieve the acceptability of proposals). Today, universities point to the need for particular skills among their senior managers, in teaching or research, or in areas such as human resources or technology transfer. The priorities today have clearly changed from those existing immediately after 1981.

- The use of new computer-based models for financial forecasting, student numbers and staffing projections, very few of which existed in the 1970s, began to emerge after 1981. Whilst such techniques helped enormously in universities in planning their strategies, this was a coincidence of timing, as computing power became greater and more accessible. At the same time, whether universities would have taken up such new technology so readily in the absence of the financial pressures is an open question which cannot be answered.

  Such methods are now fundamental to university management; indeed, they are taken for granted. The growth in computing power and its accessibility has led to an explosion in management information and data analysis. This was just beginning after 1981. However, the developments which followed cannot really be said to have been caused by the events of 1981 and immediately thereafter.

- The importance of internal communications and widespread consultation with staff at all levels and with unions, both staff and student, was emphasised by all the universities surveyed after 1981. Many institutions developed newsletters in order to convey decisions or to invite feedback regarding the implications of the 1981 cuts. This initiative was primarily driven by practical considerations, but it quickly began to reinforce the emergence of the university as a corporate entity. The period after 1981 was also characterised by staff solidarity across traditional academic disciplines. In some universities, staff volunteered to take pay cuts in order to save the jobs of colleagues. Communications and consultation were clearly important in underpinning this community response. At the same time, the potential power and importance of communications as an activity to be managed in the same way as other activities began to be appreciated. Again, the role of the professional manager – the Director of Public Affairs or some similar designation – began to develop very rapidly.

Today, the universities concerned all reaffirm the importance of such communications. 1981 is still seen as something of a turning point, given the need to retain institutional solidarity in adverse circumstances. Information and communications are still important activities to be managed at the institutional level. However, there is also an interesting change in emphasis. The universities today also place a strong emphasis on the need for speed of movement and reaction in an increasingly competitive environment with the explicit recognition that such speed may preclude effective consultation. It is not clear, therefore, that the views expressed after 1981 and seen as crucial at the time retain quite the strength today as in the mid-1980s. This is reinforced by comments from universities about difficulties in securing staff involvement in the decision-making process. After 1981, 'involvement' and 'inclusivity' were encouraged and many staff responded enthusiastically; in 2003, such collegiality has been significantly eroded.

- The emergence of a real discipline of strategic planning in higher education can be dated from 1981. From the mid-1980s, compelled by the need to respond to the 1981 cuts, universities began to apply a more formal approach to planning as compared with the ad hoc approach hitherto. In 1984, universities referred to the application of a tight, step-by-step timetable, commonly a top-down, bottom-up, top-down procedure. This normally involved an extensive information gathering exercise preceding the top-down proposals, extensive consultation about the proposals and a willingness to give serious consideration to bottom-up responses, leading eventually to top-down plans for approval by senate and council.

The universities studied continue to apply this approach to planning in broad terms. Various changes have occurred, including the requirement by the funding councils in both England and Scotland for institutional plans and operating statements. However, all the institutions trace the present methodology back to the period immediately following the 1981 cuts. For many of those responding, this was one of the key developments compelled by the cuts of 1981 and a major legacy to institutional management.

The emergence of effective strategic planning was central to the implementation of the 1981 cuts. Universities were forced to review their activities and to prioritise for the future. Before 1981 universities had commonly planned their activities in isolation or in response to particular demands. After 1981, it was necessary to adopt a more corporate approach to ensure the effective integration of academic, financial, estates and human resource planning; strategic planning emerged as an ongoing, cyclical process. Moreover, planning began to reach all levels of the institutions, with planning structures to be implemented at faculty or department level as well as at institutional level. Again, professional managers began to emerge to lead and coordinate the planning procedures.

- In their replies to the 1984 survey, universities also referred to their new recognition of the need to integrate resource allocation with planning. As part of this process, the universities emphasised the need to devolve funds to 'responsibility centres', which would have some discretion over the detailed use of resources and which would be accountable for the use of funds. Historical and expenditure driven resource allocation began to be replaced by income driven models. It is apparent that the days when internal resource allocation was the preserve of the vice-chancellor and a small group of colleagues, with decisions made behind closed doors without the need for consultation and/or justification, were now over.

    The use of devolved funding models is now commonplace within universities. At the same time, there has been a continuing shift from expenditure-driven to income-driven models. The 1981 cuts marked a crucial stage in this development, but the universities point to other important factors, including the Jarratt Report in 1985 and the wider development of new approaches to public management in the late 1980s.

- After 1981, all the universities emphasised the need to make positive efforts to promote the external image of the institution and, in particular, to secure additional income from non-government sources. Many universities moved quickly to develop alternative funding. In particular, consultancy income and the sale of services were encouraged from an early date.

    To the universities studied, this is seen as the single most important change in university management arising from the 1981 cuts. In 1980–81, 64% of total income to universities came from government through the block grant. However, the scale of the cuts imposed convinced universities that not only would the 'golden age' of the early 1970s never be restored but that new sources of income were essential for institutional survival. In 2001–02, the government block grant represents 39% of the total income to universities. In 1980–81, other sources of income represented 5% of total income; by 2001–02, this had risen to 19%. The universities concerned all date this shift from 1981. Interestingly, they refer not only to a shift in thinking and priorities at institutional level, but they also point to a change in the approach and attitude of academic staff, a new appreciation of costs (both direct and indirect) and of the need to generate external income; no longer could universities or staff be dependent upon government income. In particular, they also point to the need to exploit all the university's assets, including its estate, as well as its academic resources.

Like the changes in strategic planning, the emergence of a new funding profile for UK higher education was one of the most important consequences of the 1981 cuts. Harold Thomas (2001: 20) has commented as follows:

> The way in which institutions responded to their reduced grants can be seen as marking the passing from one age to the next. Institutions with cuts approaching the 40% level were faced with devising strategies for survival. Income generating activity, reduction in costs and a fundamental refocusing of activities were all employed. Even in institutions with reductions in grants at about the average level, the dramatic nature of the cuts forced changes in approach.

The search for alternative sources of income is now deeply engrained in UK higher education, but the specific priorities have varied by institution and over time.

- In the aftermath of the 1981 cuts, universities began to recognise a new role for lay members of Council. In responding to the DES research project, many universities pointed to the role of lay members in supporting a vice-chancellor and to their responsibilities in ensuring that universities work within the resources available and identify clear priorities.

   Today, the universities retain this view of the role of lay members although the Jarratt Report of 1985 and further guidance issued by the funding councils are seen as the main factors in this change. The universities also draw attention to many other 'qualities' necessary in lay members, most notably their role in networking and fundraising.

- Finally, the universities surveyed in 1984 all refer to the importance of a financial reserve, to act as a buffer against change or to help buy time while change is implemented.

   Such attitudes are still prevalent among university managers. The same reasoning is provided, although there is a new emphasis on the use of reserves to provide investment funds. This reflects a change of attitude since 1981. At that time, universities would have looked to the UGC and to government to fund new initiatives, including capital developments; in 2003, universities are accustomed to the need to fund such initiatives from within their own resources.

5. DISCUSSION

The financial cuts imposed by the government in 1981 clearly had a profound effect on the management of universities. A new style of management began to emerge, characterised by strong executive leadership, by the vice-chancellor and by senior management teams; by an emphasis on planning, including detailed competitive analysis, scenario planning and modelling, and selectivity; by a recognition of the need to encourage, but also to control, effective communications and information flows within institutions; and to seek new sources of external income. In responding to the savings required after 1981, universities were compelled to take an overview of their activities, integrating their planning and resource allocation, and looking towards accountability and performance. Today, such procedures are taken for granted in most institutions and applied with varying levels of success; yet for most people working in universities in the early 1980s, this approach to management would have been unrecognisable. Was 1981, therefore, the crucial turning point that it may seem?

There is no simple answer. One view is that many of the changes stimulated in 1981 can actually be traced back to the 1970s; the problem was that 1981 suddenly increased the whole scale of change necessary. Interestingly, both in their response to the 1984 DES enquiry and today in responding to this project, universities look back to the 1970s as the start of this process. From that time, universities were forced to confront the need to make savings. Through the 1970s, universities were used to comparing their performance with a peer group of institutions. Whilst such analysis may have lacked the sophistication which came later with the expansion of computing power, the inter-university awareness and competitive instincts were already apparent before 1981. Similarly, an understanding of the impact of market forces was also present in the 1970s. The government began to shift funding from the block grant to fees from 1976, an early recognition of the power of the 'consumer' in the funding of higher education. The seeds for change in the management of universities, therefore, had already been planted in the 1970s and had germinated before the shock of 1981.

A second view is that many new pressures have emerged which have overtaken 1981 as a major factor in shaping institutional management. Looking back, with memories dimmed by over twenty years of change and development, there is, perhaps, a temptation to understate the importance of 1981 in shaping current arrangements in higher education. Most of those participating in this project see 1981 less as a turning point in the history of UK higher education and more as an important stage in a continuing process of change, which had begun before 1981 and which was to continue with increasing pace thereafter. Thus, the savings required in 1981 become less severe when viewed in the context of the ongoing 'efficiency gains' which were required from universities over the following twenty years. For those working in higher education today, the main factors influencing the development of institutional management are seen as the development of selectivity, especially the effect of the Research Assessment Exercise, and the pressures of external assessment, especially in teaching quality but also the informal pressures imposed by numerous 'league tables'. Most significantly, they also point to the pressure to grow. In the late 1980s this took the form of a funding model which effectively penalised those institutions which did not wish to expand. More recently, it reflects an emphasis on increasing participation in higher education. As a force for change in higher education management, this is a factor not evident in 1981 when many institutions, with UGC guidance, were looking to reduce, not expand, student numbers. Here, therefore, are several influences on management which cannot be traced back to 1981.

A third view is that there were many factors running through the period, with 1981 acting as a key point in institutional development, but not the only point in the process. Selectivity, for example, is one constant theme running through the period.

The 1981 cuts were applied by the UGC using differential quality judgments, effectively beginning the informal stratification of universities. Internally, within universities, selectivity had begun in the 1970s, refined and intensified in response to the 1981 cuts, and then accentuated by the impact of research assessment, beginning in 1986 but intensifying in the late 1980s and 1990s.

A second theme which runs through the period is one of transparency. A common response to the 1981 cuts was "why us?" or, rather, "why were we cut by x% and they were only cut by y%?" As a result, the clamour for justification began. At national level, this rapidly led to the new funding model applied from 1986–87 and to a fully transparent model from the 1990s. Within universities, management faced similar pressures. Never again would vice-chancellors and senior management enjoy the freedom to allocate resources at will as existed in the 1970s. Again, however, the impact of 1981 may be seen as part of a continuum rather than as a turning point.

The importance of effective leadership within institutions is now widely recognised. The case studies included in the DES research project show a wide range of styles, but they all show an acknowledgment of the problems facing a vice-chancellor or principal. In particular, they highlight the tension between managerial responsibility and the concept of a self-governing community of scholars. This tension, already apparent in the 1970s, became acute given the scale of savings required after 1981. The case studies show how vice-chancellors began to assert their power, fulfilling a leading role in creating the environment in which "excellence flourishes and in which mediocrity withers and dies" (Sizer, J. 1986, pers. comm.). What is significant is that these changes began to emerge in universities themselves, stimulated by the 1981 cuts; they were the result of internal debate and emerged as universities struggled to find a way forward. They predate the Jarratt Report and subsequent government pronouncements, especially the 1985 Green Paper *Development of Higher Education into the 1990s*. Universities were already developing the new style of management, based on leadership, accountability, performance and efficiency in the early 1980s. The pace and nature of change varied between institutions over time, as part of an ongoing process of change. 1981 was an important stage in this process; this importance should not be understated, but nor should it be exaggerated.

6. CONCLUSION

In their groundbreaking study of the impact of higher education reforms in Europe, Cerych and Sabatier (1986) exclude changes in management and decision-making structures from their analysis. However, they identify a three-dimensional framework for analysis: depth, functional breadth and level of change (1986: 244). Using the case studies developed in 1984 and now updated with hindsight in 2003, it is possible to assess the impact of the 1981 cuts on university management. *Depth of change* indicates the degree to which a new policy goal implies a departure from existing values and practices of higher education. As has been seen, 1981 cannot be seen in isolation, but looking at 1981 as part of a continuum of change in management practice, the depth of change is very significant indeed. Fundamental principles were eroded, in some cases beyond recognition, including self-management within the academic community, replaced by new forms of professional management; the relationship between teaching and research, replaced by selectivity and different strands of funding; and dependence on government funding to support core activities, replaced by an emphasis on alternative sources of funding. *Functional breadth of change* refers to the number of functional areas in which particular policies have an impact. Again, the changes in the 1970s and the 1980s, of which 1981 was a crucial part, have affected every facet of university life. Emerging principles of performance and accountability have had an impact on all staff and all areas of activity, both academic and non-academic. *Level of change* indicates the target of the reform: the system, the institutions or a sub-unit. What is clear from this study is that the nine universities, whilst they may differ in detail, all report very similar changes and very similar responses. To this extent, change has been system-wide. Given that change in management style has been so all-pervasive, every level within institutions has been directly affected. Management priorities and approaches have changed at the level of the university, but also at the level of faculties, departments or research groups; even at the level of the individual, the emphasis on performance and cost has had a deep impact on the academic profession.

The changes in UK university management over the last thirty years have been profound. They combine all three dimensions outlined by Cerych and Sabatier. The scale and intensity of change in how universities run themselves cannot be doubted. 1981 was a crucial year in this process. However, many changes were already happening from the 1970s and further forces for change were to emerge in later years. The changes were deep and have changed the character of higher education in the UK, but they cannot be attributed entirely to the fallout from one year and one set of events. Rather, they reflect a continuum of change, which may vary in intensity and scale, but which is ongoing.

REFERENCES

Booth, C. "DES and Treasury." In Morris, A. and J. Sizer (eds). *Resources and Higher Education*. Research in Higher Education Monograph No 51. Guildford: Society for Research into Higher Education, 1982, 25–57.

Cerych, L. and P. Sabatier. *Great Expectations and Mixed Performance: The Implementation of Higher Education Reforms in Europe*. Stoke-on-Trent: Trentham Books, 1986.

Development of Higher Education into the 1990s (Green Paper). Cmnd. 9524. London: HMSO, 1985.

Education: A Framework for Expansion (White Paper). Cmnd. 5174. London: HMSO, 1972.

Jarratt Report (Committee of Vice-Chancellors and Principals). *Report of the Steering Committee for Efficiency Studies in Universities*. London: CVCP, 1985.

Kogan, M. and S. Hanney. *Reforming Higher Education*. London: Jessica Kingsley, 2000.

(Robbins Report). *Higher Education: Report of the Committee Appointed by the Prime Minister Under the Chairmanship of Lord Robbins 1961–63*. Cmnd. 2154. London: HMSO, 1963.

Shattock, M. and G. Rigby. *Resource Allocation in British Universities*. Research in Higher Education Monograph No 56. Guildford: Society for Research into Higher Education, 1983.

Thomas, H. *Managing Financial Resources*. Buckingham: Open University Press, 2001.

HARRY F. DE BOER, JÜRGEN ENDERS
AND DON F. WESTERHEIJDEN

FROM PAPER TO PRACTICE: TWO REFORMS AND THEIR CONSEQUENCES IN DUTCH HIGHER EDUCATION

1. INTRODUCTION

1.1. Implementation Studies

The move from paper to practice – the implementation of a reform or public policy – is a real challenge, because a promising reform design can easily be devastated by poor implementation. And as the research literature on policy implementation over the last three decades shows, this happens regularly. Implementing reforms or public policies is a hard job. It is probably the most crucial and difficult step in the policy cycle, as, for instance, indicated by Bardach (1977: 3):

> It is hard enough to design public policies and programs that look good on paper. It is harder still to formulate them in words and slogans that resonate pleasingly in the ears of political leaders and the constituencies to which they are responsive. And it is excruciatingly hard to implement them in a way that pleases anyone at all, including the supposed beneficiaries or clients.

Initiating and implementing a reform or a new policy is a competitive, often hostile activity (Trader-Leigh 2002). No important changes will come without political struggle. This is no surprise since usually the stakes are high. Consequently, one usually has to overcome massive inertia, not only in the early stages of the policy cycle but in the stage of implementation as well. Most of the time the implementation phase is the last opportunity to hamper the reform, not only by those who opposed it from the start but also by those who so far did not participate in the processes of policy design and decision making at all. Opposition can have severe consequences: the reform might not be carried out at all, might be delayed, might become far more time-consuming and expensive, or might produce perverse effects. The message is clear and well known: the implementation of a reform as intended by the reformers cannot be taken for granted.

Traditionally a distinction was made between 'politics' on the one hand and 'administration' on the other. Politics concerned the formulation of policies and formal decision making, whereas administration was referred to as the

Å. Gornitzka et al. (eds.), Reform and Change in Higher Education, 97-116.

straightforward settlement of the decisions taken. The implementation of reforms, the execution of the political will, was supposed to be value free and to focus on the application of the most efficient means to accomplish the reform goals. Today a more realistic view dominates the scene.

In practice, the assertion of a strict distinction between policy design, formulation and implementation is not tenable. First, policy makers frequently design their policies with 'the implementation game in the back of their minds'. They may interact with many stakeholders trying to anticipate resistance. Second, implementation influences the earlier stages of the policy cycle by means of feedback mechanisms. Third, some policies intentionally leave ample room for local autonomy. The latter implies that in fact part of the policy is formulated during the implementation phase, for instance, by professionals or by Lipsky's street-level bureaucrats (Lipsky 1980; Prottas 1979).[1] Therefore, it makes sense to assume that policy shapes implementation *and*, at the same time, implementation shapes policy (Geul 2002). Several attempts have been made to combine the traditional top-down approach and the bottom-up approach into one, integrated approach (Gornitzka, Kyvik and Stensaker 2002; Ryan 1996).[2]

However, though an overwhelming number of implementation studies have been conducted over the last three decades, there is no general implementation theory yet. Apart from much communality in implementation analysis, researchers still disagree about approaches, concepts, theories and key variables (Ryan 1996, 1999). In other words, there is a substantial theoretical pluralism (Gornitzka, Kyvik and Stensaker 2002; Sinclair 2001). We believe that, despite progress in many respects (Sinclair 2001),[3] it remains to be seen whether we are likely to reach a generally accepted theory of implementation in the foreseeable future. One may even wonder whether the implementation analysis is best served by seeking to develop a unified theory: "Different circumstances may imply the application of different principles" (Ryan 1996: 40).

Implementation studies have contributed to the image that public policies or reforms by and large are doomed to fail (Gray and 't Hart 1998). This 'pessimism' needs a sense of perspective. First of all, many policies *have* been implemented. The lessons in the literature do not by any means lead to the conclusion that nothing works (O'Toole 1996). And sometimes this concerns policies that have had limited consensus from the start, were formulated after huge fights, or faced substantial resistance from the field.

Second, it is not always clear what 'success' and 'failure' mean. How would we rate a reform that has reached its targets to *some* extent? Or when it accomplishes its goals after ten years? Usually there is a huge grey area between the extremes of success and failure, but most of the time negative aspects get most of the attention, if not all. This issue is further complicated if we take into consideration that success may be defined and interpreted differently by different groups or cultures. Also the 'boundary issue' may complicate the assessment: what is regarded as a failure in a local community may well be a national success (Gray and 't Hart 1998).

Policies that consciously are unspecified and broad in character, in order to do justice to local situations and provide opportunities to take specific and more detailed decisions during the implementation, are hard to assess in terms of success and failure. Many policies are general in nature, sometimes deliberately, at other times from sheer necessity. Some policy problems are too complex to formulate clear goals. Other policy problems require a political compromise, which usually does not help the consistency and clearness of the policy at issue. In other words, we would like to have measurable, clear and specific goals to assess the implementation of a programme, but usually we have to cope with the opposite.

Third, frequently, large-scale innovative policies that are a clean break with the past get the spotlight, from both the public at large (by means of the media) and the research community. How realistic and fair is it to expect that precisely these of all policies be implemented without problems? It is these comprehensive reforms that deliberately create the great expectations that 'must lead to mixed, or even disappointing performances'. Reform goals can, for instance for political reasons, be highly ambitious. They:

> may produce a self-evident ... image of disastrous failure when government fails to achieve them. In political terms the very business of building and maintaining support for particular programmes sometimes requires that optimistic bright new futures are promised which can never be realized and that underachievement is dressed up as significant progress (Gray and 't Hart 1998: 10).

Fourth, reforms usually need time to be absorbed. It may take years before the 'real' consequences become visible (Sabatier 1986). A short time horizon may lead to exclude the inevitable complexity of long-term interactions and knock-on effects in policy areas with high levels of interdependence.[4] It may also render judgments more critical, particularly regarding the kind of policy which requires gradual, long-term adjustments of the attitudes and behaviour of large numbers of people or the assembling of complex implementation processes (Gray and 't Hart 1998). Thus, sometimes the conclusions about a failing policy are premature (by the way, this might also be the case with successful policies). It may take a while before people adjust to the new situation (i.e. a policy or reform is by definition meant to change the status quo). An abbreviated time span blinds us to the potential for policy-oriented learning and policy evolution (Sabatier 1986). This implies that the 'sustainability' of the policy becomes an issue.

Fifth, the rhetoric of politicians and reformers to sell their policies complicates a fair judgment (Herweyer 1987).[5] Implementation studies tended to examine the extent to which the official goals of a reasonably large reform were attained and to analyse reasons for success and failure of a formally adopted policy. The notions of 'official goals' and 'formally adopted policy' have been undermined and re-conceptualised. Statements of purpose in reform are like all formal goals: guilty of hiding the truth until proven innocent by congruence with operating goals. 'True' expectations are masked by the rhetoric necessary to build political coalitions that legitimise policy, mobilise actors and enhance morale for innovation. 'Great expectations and mixed performance' – the title of a seminal study on higher education reform in Europe (Cerych and Sabatier 1986) – might thus be due to an analysis that takes the 'missionary statements' of policy reform too literally.

Political rhetoric apart, we must also bear in mind that some policies have symbolic rather than substantive functions. These kinds of policies may require a different approach; they certainly deserve a different kind of conclusion.

1.2. Points of Departure with Respect to Two Reforms in Dutch Higher Education

In the 1980s the Dutch government changed its 'steering philosophy' with regard to higher education from a 'state control' to a 'supervisory' mode (Maassen and Van Vught 1994). In fact, the Dutch experience became an example for policy learning and borrowing across Europe. Yet the desire to reform higher education remained, and several major new policies have been promulgated since the 1980s. In the present chapter, we will describe and analyse two reform processes that originated in the mid-1980s. They stem from the same shift of governmental approach towards the higher education field; they share in that respect the same background.

From a conceptual point of view, we take up certain debates and developments in the field of policy implementation studies (see Enders, Goedegebuure and Maassen 2003). First, studies on policy implementation have called attention to the fact that policy success and failure are partly related to the specific characteristics of the regulatory field, in our case the higher education sector. Had such studies at an earlier stage concentrated on the subject of political steering (the state), an inclusion of the structure and behavioural dispositions of the higher education system and its organisational layers would have been called for (Mayntz 1998). Thus the top-down perspective of the initial paradigm of 'policy implementation' was extended to aspects related to the 'governability' of higher education systems as well as bottom-up processes at universities. Consequently, with the rise of self-steering models in public policy and the rise of the university as a 'corporate actor' more attention has been given to the other levels in higher education and their roles as a target and agent of change (Enders 2002).

The two policy reforms concern (1) the introduction of steering through quality assurance; and (2) the internal governance of higher education institutions. The underlying rationale for the present analyses of these two reforms is to trace the changes of practices associated with these policies in higher education institutions at different levels. The former, on quality assurance, will be studied at the level of faculty and institutional management, whereas the latter, concerning the internal governance of higher education institutions, will be traced down to the level of the individual professor.

In our analyses of the two reforms we take a *methodological* individualistic stand. Social phenomena should be explained in terms of the behaviours of actors. Ultimately, the actors determine the outcome of the game. They are supposed to do things differently as a result of the new policies, to relate and behave in new ways. It means that they must give up familiar behaviours and structures and actually replace these with new ones (De Vree 1982; Van der Vegt, Smyth and Vandenberghe 2000: 11). These actors are not necessarily individuals; they can be corporate actors as well (see Coleman 1990; Lieshout and De Vree 1985; Scharpf 1997). In this chapter 'individualistic' refers both to the organisational level (case 1) and to the individual level (case 2). In other words, the units of analysis differ in the two cases, though both embrace a methodological individualistic approach.

In both cases we discuss comprehensive reform in the sense that:

- It concerns changes in the core processes of the organisation;
- The initial changes – the official reform – are relatively new and radical rather than evolutionary;
- It demands significant modifications of professional activities and related organisational arrangements;
- The reform is supposed to become a permanent feature of the workplace;
- The reform is supposed to become a permanent feature of the workplace;
- It is implemented system-wide (see Van der Vegt, Smyth and Vandenberghe 2000).

2. QUALITY ASSESSMENT AND THE INSTITUTIONAL MANAGER

2.1. The Policy and the Change in 'Philosophy'

In 1985, the white paper 'Higher Education, Autonomy and Quality' (abbreviated in Dutch to 'HOAK') introduced the idea of quality assurance as a policy instrument in the 'steering philosophy' of 'government at arm's length' and 'self-regulation' (Ministerie van Onderwijs and Wetenschappen 1985). Previous developments in Dutch higher education set the stage for this major step (which space will not allow us to recount in great detail here moreover much of the actual research still needs to be done). Briefly, though, the main factors seem to be the following. At first, a relatively large retrenchment operation (known under its acronym 'TVC') had taken place early in the 1980s, in which the Minister of Education had gained cooperation from the universities in a steering group to decide upon the distribution of the budget cuts (Grondsma 1983). For instance, the steering group decided which of the dentistry faculties to close. The institutions' cooperation was gained, among others, with the promise that this would be a unique operation, never to be repeated. However, a few years later, around the middle of the decade, the same Minister of Education felt it necessary to engage in another retrenchment round (baptised 'SKG'). Faced with this lack of consistency, the universities refused to cooperate, and the budget cuts were decided upon by the Ministry on the basis of the application of a new policy instrument, namely external review committees made up of academic 'peers' that judged units' quality of education provision.[6]

Taking a more wide-angled view, the use of external peer review was not entirely new in Dutch higher education policy. A few years earlier, another part of the Ministry, which was concerned with research policy, had introduced a new policy for research funding in universities (known as 'VFO' or 'conditional funding of research'). This new policy introduced competition among universities in the first market-type coordination effort, and operated on the principle of quality judged by independent peers (Westerheijden 1997a). Initially, this was done in a paper exercise based on research output data, but when the senior civil servant engaged in VFO,

Roel in 't Veld, moved to the education part of the Ministry, he adapted the innovation to the educational process by adding interviews and possibly site visits. The threat of serious funding consequences from this research assessment proved empty, for very few reallocations in fact took place (Spaapen et al. 1988; Spaapen et al. 1986).

The relationship between the Ministry of Education and the universities seemed to be at an ebb tide after the two retrenchment operations, although the experience with VFO probably was more positive – maybe because it proved to be mainly harmless to the universities. Still the Ministry seemed to want to set the relations in a new, more positive light. In line with the then newly popular ideas of neo-liberalism, the government wanted to 'step back' from such painful retrenchment decisions; and what was easier than 'passing the buck' to the universities themselves, especially as this could be done under the guise of increasing institutional autonomy – clearly an 'honorific term' in the field? Still, neo-liberalism did not mean a return to what is popularly known as the 'old stump theory of funding', that is, autonomy *tout court*.[7] In exchange for more autonomy, more accountability was required. Hence the title of the 1985 white paper HOAK ('Higher Education, Autonomy and Quality') making explicit the change in steering philosophy that had taken place.

However, the higher education institutions had learned too from the experiences in the first half of the 1980s when the Ministry of Education published HOAK. Obviously, they were interested in more autonomy, and, although they too were under the influence of neo-liberalism, they were not interested in exchanging the 'Big Brother' Ministry for 'Little Brethren' inspectors which was in the earlier drafts of the HOAK paper. During the development of the white paper, several models for implementation were discussed among civil servants and stakeholders in the higher education community.[8] In the end, the higher education institutions gained a large degree of control over the external quality assessment scheme.

How did this ownership in the institutions' hands rather than in the government's – as is the case in most European countries even when they ostensibly followed the 'Dutch model' of quality assessment (already noted in Van Vught and Westerheijden 1993) – change the policy's aims, implementation and impact on the higher education institutions? First of all, the emphasis regarding the goals of quality assessment changed from 'accountability and quality improvement' to 'quality improvement and accountability'. From the universities' point of view this was consistent with their interest.

H. Brinkman, former president of the Free University of Amsterdam, in an interview with Don F. Westerheijden (February 2003) tells of a meeting of the association of university managers (VUBM), where representatives of the two then existing quality assessment systems were invited: John Sizer from the UK and Herb Kells from the USA.

> Sizer's hard-nosed approach with his emphasis on hard data, value for money, etc., did not go down well with the assembled *rectores magnifici*, board presidents and secretaries general. We liked the emphatic, soft approach presented by Herb Kells much more. So we invited Kells to advise us on quality assessment, and then he taught us how to do it.

The umbrella bodies of both the universities and the colleges started out to introduce this new element into the higher education landscape carefully. The name of the game in the first years seemed to be gaining acceptance in academe – no doubt from a sincere and well-founded conviction that without cooperation from academe, any quality assessment scheme would remain a paper tiger, a case of compliance (Van Vught 1989), of going through the motions without making any actual impact. At the same time, proponents of the new quality assessment schemes were convinced that if the schemes had real impact and were performed in the public domain, they would automatically also serve their accountability goal (Acherman 1988; Vroeijenstijn 1989).

2.2. Impact of the Reform on Quality Improvement

In the first years of the quality assessment reform, the emphases in the policy discussion and scholarly attention were ostensibly on consequences at the work-floor level. Learning from the early negative experience with 'conditional funding' or VFO, mentioned above, the educational assessment scheme was organised differently, and did not have such easily measurable goals as reallocation of funding. The goal of quality improvement in education was more sophisticated and 'softer', that is, more difficult for both politicians and researchers to observe.

As an intermediary and necessary variable, we studied if, how and why review reports were being used in subsequent decision making within higher education institutions (Frederiks, Westerheijden and Weusthof 1994). Note that we did not have a 'linear' assumption that visiting committees' recommendations must be implemented by the study programme. Our assumption rather was that self-evaluation would lead to new insights about strong and weak points in a study programme, leading possibly to action anticipating the visiting committee's arrival, and that the external quality assessment report would be one of several inputs to the following decision-making processes in the higher education institution, maybe leading to follow-up action, but maybe to other, unanticipated consequences.[9] While we were successful only to a very limited extent in establishing explanatory patterns based on power or contingency approaches, it became clear that non-use was very limited. More than 90% of the review reports were being used in some way in higher education institutions. If one were to use a linear approach, and look at the more detailed level of individual recommendations by visiting committees, that percentage would go down to just over half (Frederiks 1996).

The primary conclusion from the study, accordingly, was that a 'quality culture' seemed to be putting out roots in the Dutch higher education institutions. At the time, though, it was really a grass-roots level impact: central levels of higher education institutions felt that using the quality assessment outcomes was something for the study programme, rather than for management levels – in subsequent years that attitude changed radically, as we shall show presently.

In a second evaluation study (Westerheijden 1997b), emphasis was given to mid-level and top-level academic management in higher education institutions (deans of faculties and rectors, or equivalent), and to the impact of the research assessments.

In 1993, the VFO was terminated, on which occasion the VSNU[10] on behalf of institutional leadership decided to introduce its own external reviews of research, no longer limited to just the part that was funded under the VFO rules, but including all fundamental research in the universities. So on the one hand there was a shift from the first study from work-floor level to management levels, to see if impacts were 'trickling up'. On the other hand, officially, there was a change from educational reviews to research reviews.[11] One of the surprising findings in this study was that, at the management levels, both types of assessments were used quite often. Not in the first place as *the* ground upon which to make big decisions to reform education or research, but more often as one piece of information, among others, legitimising in many cases tacit knowledge about quality of units, which could be applied to many types of decisions. This is not to say that momentous decisions of internal reform were not made as a result of the review reports (in conjunction with managers' views about profile and strategy), but the pervasiveness was surprising. There were examples of, especially, deans, who had the most recent assessment reports on a bookshelf in easy reach from their desks, and who would pull them out before making almost any decision to check the standing of the professor making a proposal. Officially 'validated' information about quality differences among units in the higher education institution made it possible for academic management to make – and publicly uphold – decisions that went beyond the easy option of declaring that everyone was equal, or, in an often used metaphor fitting the flat Dutch landscape, at the same 'ground level'. In that sense, quality assessments were a lever that made other, existing management tools really usable (Westerheijden 1997b: 405), and their deepest impact may therefore well have been that they led to a change in the self-conception of university managers from ceremonial figures incapacitated by the egalitarian culture to 'doers' who could actually steer their unit (Westerheijden 1997b: 408–409). The rise of 'managerialism', of which this was an exponent, implied changing working conditions for the professoriate and other academics: as research became more programmed, they cooperated more, were in a more dependent position *vis-à-vis* management, and felt that (especially negative) quality judgments had a 'halo effect' on their (increasing) relationships with actors outside higher education (Westerheijden 1997b: 408–410).

As the research reviews were about research, that is, the prime activity in the academic ideology, and were at the level of research groups (often as small as one full professor with his – very rarely her – staff) and as they gave a feeling of precision because they used numerical scores, they were used more explicitly than the educational assessment reports. The latter were written at the level of degree programmes in which many academics cooperated, and they were written in a lucid, extremely balanced style that required highly skilled reading-between-the-lines. Maybe one can reinterpret Westerheijden's findings by saying that the educational assessments indicated which problems were to be found, that research assessments might do the same, but also showed who was to blame and who might help out.

Finally, the Netherlands Court of Accounts (*Algemene Rekenkamer*) at the turn of the century wanted to return to the main question of the impact of educational quality assessment on the quality of programmes and programme delivery. In a set of selected cases in both universities and colleges, it was found that the external educational quality assessments worked to improve the quality of programmes that were of relatively low quality – sometimes it took the additional 'call to attention' by the Inspectorate of Education, who would routinely monitor the follow-up of review reports, and was especially alert to 'worrisome cases' (Van Bruggen, Scheele and Westerheijden 1998). This was a consequence of the first evaluations of the external quality assessment (Frederiks, Westerheijden and Weusthof 1994; Inspectie Hoger Onderwijs 1992), after which the Minister of Education, aware of parliament's critical eye, wanted more assurance that at least a 'basic quality level' be reached in all programmes, and commissioned the Inspectorate to take up that task.

However, for study programmes that were clearly above the threshold, the quality assessment process after about a decade of experience was not a challenge anymore. The impact of second and (especially) third rounds of external quality assessments for them was close to zero, apart from functioning as a reminder to keep focused on maintaining quality. It was time for a new generation of quality assessment (Huitema, Jeliazkova and Westerheijden 2002; Jeliazkova and Westerheijden 2002) – which did come, but in a different way than expected, because the internal dynamics of the development of quality assessment for continued improvement were 'overruled' by external developments, to which we will now turn to round off the history of quality assessment, but only briefly as it is too early to expect any impact from the new arrangement.

2.3. Questions Not Answered and a Change of Level: Accountability Waiting for Bologna

All studies mentioned in this section were about the impact of quality assessment on quality improvement within higher education institutions. They more or less neglected the accountability question – albeit that the studies themselves were seen as an additional underpinning of the accountability function of the reviews. And indeed, the accountability side was where deficiencies began to show, around the turn of the century. Employers around the colleges wanted clearer information that a college programme was 'above threshold quality', and the HBO Council subsequently started its pilot in accreditation, with a clear 'yes, this is at least threshold quality' judgment intended, in 2000. Experiences from this pilot project (Goedegebuure et al. 2002) were among the inputs used in designing an encompassing accreditation scheme for the Netherlands in 2001–02. However, the prime driver for this new development was the impact of the Bologna Declaration on Dutch higher education which is beyond the scope of the present chapter (see e.g. Commissie-Rinnooy Kan 2000; Committee Accreditation of Dutch Higher Education 2001; Van Vught, Van der Wende and Westerheijden 2002; Van der Wende and Westerheijden 2001; Westerheijden 2001; Westerheijden and Leegwater 2003).

3. UNIVERSITIES' INTERNAL GOVERNANCE AND THE PROFESSORIATE

In 1997, the Dutch parliament passed a bill that marked the end of an era of participatory modes of internal university governance. After years of discussion, the Dutch Minister of Education had decided to fundamentally change the institutional governance and management structure of Dutch universities. The whole internal governance reform can be regarded as one of the final comprehensive institutional changes in the light of the HOAK philosophy (see previous section). In this context, one of the general thoughts behind the reform was that a shift in the position of the government towards the universities would require stronger institutional management, especially at the central and middle levels of those organisations. Another reason for trying to alter the internal governing structure of the universities was related to the constant criticisms and perceived shortcomings of the then existing structure. According to the new Act, which came into force in 1997, executive leadership would be strengthened, powers would be more concentrated, and representative bodies, where academics, non-academics and students held seats, would be stripped from their main authorities. How successful has this reform been? Has change actually been achieved or is it 'business as usual' inside the universities?

We will analyse the consequences of the new 1997 Act on University Governance at the shop level in Dutch universities. First, we will address the reform's origins and its main goals. Then we will establish our line of reasoning to discuss the effects of this institutional reform, supported by empirical data.

3.1. The Outset: The New Act on University Governance in 1997[12]

Prior to the 1970s, Dutch university governance was, by and large, comparable to the 'continental mode', where state bureaucrats and academics held the major power and dominated the internal decision-making structures and processes (Clark 1983). Authorities of academic and non-academic affairs were clearly separated in different bodies. This coexistence of a bureaucratic mode of coordination and academic self-governance was called the *duplex ordo*. At the universities, the nation state was represented by a board of curators, responsible for upholding laws and regulations, for the administration of the university finances and for personnel policies. The other pillar in this pre-1970 structure was the senate that was made up of all full professors. This senate embodied academic self-governance.

During the 1960s, there was a growing concern regarding the effectiveness and efficiency of traditional forms of internal university governance – an increasingly pressing matter caused by the unprecedented growth of participation in Dutch higher education. These concerns were overshadowed by demands for (more) democratic participation, as was happening in several Western countries (Currie et al. 2003). This democratic movement fermented turmoil in Dutch higher education resulting in a new Act on University Governance, *Wet op de Universitaire Bestuurshervorming* (WUB). The WUB-Act attracted criticism from the beginning, but it constituted the formal backbone of universities up until 1997.

In this WUB-Act of 1970 the emphasis was upon external and internal democratisation, though there were other, usually forgotten, objectives including effectiveness and efficiency. The WUB abolished both the senate and the board of curators. They were replaced by a system of functional representation through university and faculty councils. Academics (professors and other academic staff), non-academics and students were given the right to elect representatives to these legislative bodies. In addition, a limited number of lay members representing the general public were appointed to the council from outside the university (see De Boer 2003; De Boer and Denters 1999; De Boer, Denters and Goedegebuure 2000). The governance structure of the universities in the 1980s and early 1990s can be described as a system of 'mixed leadership': decision making was supposed to be on the basis of 'co-determination'. In the mid-1990s the practice in governing the universities was already slightly different from what was expected from the WUB-Act (De Boer, Denters and Goedegebuure 1998).

In the mid-1990s, interrelated problems regarding the prevailing governance system were identified by an ad hoc committee chaired by the Minister of Education, Culture and Science. These problems were: 1) the inadequacy of the governance structure pertaining to the organisation of teaching; 2) the lack of clarity regarding responsibilities (in collective decision making, individuals did not seem to accept personal responsibility); 3) the scattering of authority; 4) the dual structure of co-determination by boards and councils, particularly at the faculty level; 5) the strong orientation towards research at the expense of teaching (which may negatively impact on teaching quality); and 6) the inadequacy and incoherence of communication between the various organisational levels. These kinds of issues at the time were of concern to a wide audience. They certainly contributed to a new Act in 1997.

The introduction of the Act Modernising University's Governance Structures (MUB) in 1997 indicated substantial change, though the magnitude of change is debatable (De Boer, Denters and Goedegebuure 1998; commissie Datema 1998). The reform promoted efficiency and effectiveness in university decision making, and was in line with the overall governmental steering strategy that aimed to enhance institutional autonomy. One of the goals, though hardly (if at all) developed in detail, was the improvement of the teaching and research processes. It abolished the system of 'co-determination' by board and council and the system of power fusion. Most powers regarding academic and non-academic affairs were attributed to the executive positions at central and faculty level. In addition, the structure became less decentralised in several ways; for instance, the abolition of the organisation's third layer – that is, the powerful *vakgroepen* ('disciplinary research groups'). *Vakgroepen* consisted of one or more chairs including other academics in the same disciplinary area. From 1997 on the dean was given the authority 'to arrange the faculty's organisation'. For the purposes of our argument it is important to stress that, in the new institutional fabric, some important powers of the old *vakgroepen* have been attributed to the appointed dean. One of those powers is that in the new regime the dean ultimately decides on the research programme of the faculty – which of course is not necessarily the same as saying that the dean determines the contents of that programme. Put succinctly, from a formal point of view the role of the dean regarding the strategic aspects of the primary processes has been increased at the expense of academic authority.

Thus, Dutch universities formally acquired, at least according to the 'standards' in the academic world and compared to the past, a rather centralised structure. The new governing bodies comprise a system where executive and legislative powers are concentrated. All members of the crucial governing bodies, *Raad van Toezicht* ('Supervisory Board'), *College van Bestuur* ('Executive Board') and *decaan* ('dean'), are appointed by the body from the 'upper level'. Thus a new hierarchical management system based on appointments has replaced the old, representative system, inclusive of all interested groups based on elections.

As indicated, the reform initiated a shift in control over research from the prerogatives of individual professors to the collective setting of research agendas in line with faculty priorities and strategic plans, under the direct stewardship of the dean. In this respect and compared to its predecessors, the MUB-Act can be regarded as another attack on the professor's position regarding control over the research agenda.[13] The 1997 Act can be typified in terms of (vertical) integration, coherence, hierarchy, centralisation and concentration of powers – catchwords that are at odds with traditional values in academic governance. Since professors have a good record in resisting change,[14] the degree to which they have actually relinquished, willingly or otherwise, control of the research programme remains to be seen.

3.2. Institutional Change and Professional Autonomy

If the interest is in the effectiveness of an institutional reform, at least three questions should be asked (cf. Kiser and Ostrom 1982; Scharpf 1986). First, it is necessary to ascertain whether the institutional changes have actually been implemented. For instance, have universities initiated the new governing bodies? In other words, have universities met the formal 'requirements' of the 1997 Act? This question is not as odd as it seems. In the mid-1970s, an ad hoc committee observed that more then five years after the WUB-Act came into force, many governing bodies had not yet been installed. As has been suggested in the implementation literature, this first phase of the implementation is a battleground. It is actually a continuation of the political struggle that occurs during the earlier stages of the policy cycle; it is a process of strategic interaction among numerous special interests all pursuing their own goals (Bardach 1977). And, as mentioned in the introduction, it can lead to serious problems such as delays.

This, however, did not occur with the introduction of the MUB-Act in 1997. Several reports indicate that the universities formally altered their authority structure and by and large they did so within one year (commissie Datema 1998). Realising the comprehensiveness of the reform, one should conclude that the first hurdle in the implementation stage was in general taken easily. The opposition inside the universities has not been able to frustrate the formal introduction of the new structure. Considering the implementation literature, it is worthwhile mentioning that the new structure – imposed by the national legislator – was introduced from the 'top-down'. The legislator had not prescribed formal procedures to introduce the new governing structure. It was left to the universities to develop their own implementation scheme, of course within the boundaries of the Act. It was 'self-evident' at the universities that the central executive board was in the driver's seat, at least in its own view. Of course there was consultation with many constituencies, but the dominance of the central managers could not be denied. Apart from some exceptions, the top-down introduction passed without incident.[15]

The second question in an analysis of institutional reform is: In practice, do the new rules of the game have an impact on the actors' behaviour? Behavioural modification is a prerequisite for successful reform. And when it can be observed that behaviour has changed, the third question is: To what extent does the altered behaviour contribute to the realisation of the goals of the reform? In other words, is goal achievement realised through the changes in behaviour intended by the legislator? If these second and third question can be answered in the affirmative too, then the reform can be regarded as effective. In the remainder of this section we will focus on the second question, that is, the effects of the MUB-Act on the behaviour of individual actors.

Here we will follow a kind of 'goal attainment' model. According to the implementation literature (see section 1 of this chapter), such a model is not without problems and indeed we faced a few problems in that respect. The first question that needs to be answered concerns the goals of the reform: What are the great expectations of the legislature from the universities and its members? What should be expected from the new governing structure? According to the legislator, one of the major reform goals of the MUB-Act is to increase the quality of the research process. Immediately we run into problems. How to define, for instance, the quality of the research process? If we take this hurdle, an even bigger problem emerges: What is the expected (causal) relationship between the new governing structure and the quality of the research process? What are the causal assumptions behind the new MUB-Act? The causal assumptions ('policy theory') are a critical factor affecting the performance of the reform (Sabatier 1986). The Dutch legislator did not refer to this relationship at all. The legislator assumed, or wished, the new governing structure to enhance the quality of the research processes, but did not give a clue how that would happen.

Without solving the 'goal-attainment' issues we have chosen the following line of reasoning. Our argument is that *if* professors are not willing to play the game by the new, imposed rules in a field that has been theirs for ages, then we have to conclude that the reform cannot be fully effective.[16] For a reform can only be effective if the new rules are actually used as intended. In our study we concluded that a proportion between 15% and 30% of the Dutch professoriate did not use the new rules with respect to the organisation of research at the faculty level (see table 1). They did not go along with the rules imposed upon them by the legislature. This was a first indication that the reform could not be fully effective.

This indication was supported by the fact that about two-thirds of the professoriate said they experienced informal rules that enabled them to keep their professional autonomy. The informal rules (apparently occurring in many faculties) examined in De Boer's analysis were at odds with the formal rules, which logically

Table 1. Intentions and actual behaviours of the Dutch professoriate (%)

To what extent do professors intend to conform their research practice to the faculty's research programme and policy (N=466)								
Not at all				*To some degree*				*Completely*
10	3	15	7	20	10	26	4	5
To what extent did professors conform their research practice to the faculty's research programme and policy (N=460)								
Not at all				*To some degree*				*Completely*
11	4	15	8	22	11	23	2	5

implied that the formal rules could not be effective in these faculties. From three items covering informal research policy rules – keeping research policy intentionally vague and abstract in day-to-day practice; pursuing research that in practice is merely the summation of individual professor's interests; and conducting research in such a way that it interferes with the research domains of faculty colleagues as little as possible – a composite scale indicating the degree to which informal rules safeguard professional autonomy was constructed (see table 2). The results from table 2 indicate that faculty research policy was intentionally kept vague and broad, and that it actually was the sum of individual preferences of faculty professors who wished not to be engaged in the research of their colleagues. It is clear that such informal rules enabled professors to utilise their professional autonomy. And obviously these rules were at odds with the MUB, which meant to bring about more cohesion, cooperation and coordination of research. It can be argued that, as far as it concerns faculty research policy, the MUB-Act has far from extinguished the importance of professional autonomy. As a consequence, goal achievement becomes a mission impossible.

Table 2. Informal rules (%)

Extent to which according to Dutch professors the research policy of their faculty is characterised by informal rules that create safeguards for professional autonomy (N=442)			
Absolutely not			*Absolutely*
12	23	25	41

To support this conclusion further, we would stress that a majority of the professoriate had a negative attitude toward the MUB. Many held the view that, as a consequence of the MUB, academic freedom, the fusion of powers and democratic content had declined. A negative attitude appears to be one of the factors that explains why professors were not acting in conformity with the policy (De Boer 2003).

We have to keep in mind, however, that we have studied a policy reform *in statu nascendi*. The empirical data were gathered three years after the implementation of the new Act. The short-term pains were visible and caused restraint and resistance, but it remains to be seen what the mid-term and long-term effects of policies strengthening hierarchical leadership in higher education institutions might be, and how the professoriate responds to them when the new structures tend to sink into the system (cf. Scharpf 1986). Sabatier (1986) argued that time spans shorter than five or ten years may be misleading. In other words, it is too soon to evaluate the results.

And we have to realise that De Boer's study stresses just one aspect of the reform, that is, the effects of the MUB-Act on the research policy of faculties. The practice of science is, however, probably the most impregnable fortress of higher education. The professorial body holds absolute sway when it comes to the practice of science, at least until recently. The conclusion may have been more positive had the study focused on other aspects of the reform, such as teaching.

4. DISCUSSION: POLICY REFORMS AND THEIR CONSEQUENCES IN HIGHER EDUCATION PRACTICE

In this chapter we have presented and analysed findings of two case studies on policy reforms implemented in the Netherlands that were stimulated by the overall shift of external and internal governance of higher education towards the 'supervisory state' and managerialism. The two policy reforms at stake concerned the state-of-the-art of a reform (1) of steering through quality assurance and the introduction and further development of instruments towards quality improvement; and (2) in the internal governance of higher education institutions, namely the legal enforcement of stronger hierarchical self-steering in higher education institutions and the strengthening of the power of the deanship. From a conceptual point of view, our presentation was stimulated by developments and debates in the field of implementation studies that tend to emphasise the importance of the study of macro/micro links in the evaluation of the effects of policy reform. This comprises more attention being paid to the evaluation of policies as an evolutionary process and to the 'official' outcomes of respective policies and their unexpected consequences, as well as a closer look at the basic organisational level in higher education as the target and agent of change. The former reform concerning quality assurance was studied at the level of faculty and institutional management; the latter initiative towards the strengthening of managerialism was traced down to the level of the individual professor.

In sum, the analyses of the development and outcomes of quality assessment introduced by the white paper 'Higher Education, Autonomy and Quality' (HOAK 1985) supported the impression that a 'quality culture' had put out its roots in Dutch higher education institutions. In fact, the reform has gone through different stages that – after a certain 'trial and error' stage at the very beginning – were quite successful in selling the reform as an extension of traditional peer-review mechanisms to the academic community and in providing higher education institutions with a large degree of ownership over the external quality assessment schemes. Impacts of the reform on quality reform were consequently ascribed to the basic level of study and research programmes and their subsequent quality development. At the same time, however, attitudes changed towards the use of quality assessment reports as a tool for the rise and growing impact of managerialism in higher education institutions. The deepest impact might be seen in its function in the ongoing change in power distribution in internal governance beyond the official mission of continued quality improvement. Moreover, quality assessments seem to be in danger of being overruled in the future by the impact of the Bologna process and its emphasis on accreditation as a basic quality *control* decision instead of quality assessment as an ongoing quality *improvement* process.

Our analyses, collectively, extending over the course of more than seven years highlighted an issue of implementation necessarily overlooked in single evaluations: policies have different effects at different points in time. Two main reasons for that can be indicated. First, as actors come to learn the new rules of the game, they may start to use the policy to their own advantage, leading to a dynamic unanticipated in the official policy statements. Thus, it took several years before institutional managers (deans, rectors and their staff) sufficiently got to grips with the quality assurance outcomes to use them as a lever to enhance their steering capacity within the institution. What the professoriate thought of this and how they reacted was not researched in these evaluation projects; the MUB case gives cause to think that their attitude may have changed from initial enthusiasm for the apparent growth in academic autonomy to scepticism about increasing managerialism – with possibly a halo effect making them sceptical of any top-down initiated change. The MUB-Act may then have been a victim of the impact of the quality assurance policies.

Second, and to some extent illustrated by the hypothetical change of attitude of the professoriate, implementation of a policy may change the policy field to such an extent that the policy has different effects because it is interacting with a field where different assumptions apply than was the case initially.[17]

Both arguments are in some way in opposition to Sabatier's (1986) previously cited *caveat* that evaluation should only take place after five to ten years: a policy's effects may change over time, without any sets of effects at any one time being more 'real' than the effects at another time. Only a series of (concurrent) evaluation studies can bring this to light.

While the notion of 'quality' is an important factor in enabling managerial powers in Dutch higher education, this seems to be less true for policy reforms deliberately designed to strengthen hierarchical self-steering in higher education institutions. Respective reform attempts implemented after a new Act on University Governance in 1997 are meant to create a rather centralised structure in higher education institutions in which the professoriate is in danger of losing some of its traditional guild powers and professional autonomy. At the basic level, the position of the deanship is supposed to concentrate power and control over research programmes and their evaluation. Findings of an empirical investigation into the rules of the game among the Dutch professoriate show that many professors have a negative attitude towards the reform, resulting in non-compliance. Moreover, the empirical data tend to illustrate a case of de-coupling: changes in formal decision making are accompanied by the persistence of traditional informal rules enabling professional autonomy. It remains to be seen however what the mid-term and long-term effects of policies strengthening hierarchical leadership in higher education institutions might be, and how the professoriate responds to them when the new structures become embedded in the system.

Comparing the experiences of the big reforms devised under the regime of state control in the 1970s with those of the reforms of the 1980s and 1990s stimulated by the new steering philosophy of self-regulation and managerialism, we might conclude that they certainly share great expectations as well as mixed performance with regards to their impact on daily practices in higher education. Change seeps in less rapidly and extensively than the missionary statements of the new steering philosophy might propose. Statements of purpose in reform are usually overloaded with unrealistic statements on expected change necessary to legitimise the transaction costs of innovation. They are, like all formal goals, guilty of hiding the truth until proven innocent by congruence with operating goals. 'Great expectations and mixed performance' might thus be due to an analysis that takes the 'missionary statements' of policy reform too literally. The changing modes of governance of higher education are still at work in Dutch higher education and certainly not irrelevant for their daily practices. They are, however, still busy establishing the preconditions for the realisation of their proposed governance structures in an ongoing power game, which, as we just mentioned, may change the assumptions under which the policy theory will have to operate to such an extent, that the policy, even after obtaining some initial 'successes', will not be effective in the long run. In other words, policy makers face a devious version of the famous Red Queen principle: not only will they have to keep running to stay in the same place, and even harder if they want to get anywhere, but also by the time they get anywhere, the shape of the game board will have changed.

NOTES

[1] In fact, we would argue that reforms and public policies *always* leave room for local discretion, since even when these reforms and policies appear to be detailed they do not prescribe every single action (cf. Boudon 1981; Coleman 1994; Wippler 1983).

[2] Ryan discusses for example the 'unifying' attempts of Mazmanian and Sabatier, of Hasenfeld and Brock, and of Winter. It goes beyond the scope of this chapter to discuss these approaches.

[3] Sinclair (2001: 80) mentions four central theoretical constructs that have been emphasised in recent implementation theories: 1) policy formation; 2) intra-organisational elements; 3) inter-organisational elements; and 4) outputs or outcomes.

[4] Long time frames on the other hand are not without risk too. Policies may gradually change over time and so may the criteria that are used to assess the implementation. This makes a traditional evaluation a 'mission impossible'.

[5] Bessant (2002) provides a good example of the impact of rhetoric and metaphor in reforms in the field of higher education.

[6] The work of these review committees led to many reactions in the fields affected, for example, in sociology, political science and public administration (Nederhof 1988). Some of the review committee members became interested in the methods they had used (Van Raan, Nederhof and Moed 1989; Stokman, Popping and Missoorten 1989), and Stokman, Popping and Missoorten started to publish an annual Dutch 'top-50' of publishing professors in sociology, political science and public administration (see also Van der Meulen et al. 1991).

[7] 'You leave the money on an old stump in the forest and we promise that next morning it will be gone.'

[8] It would be an interesting project of oral historiography to interview the main participants in this crucial period of Dutch higher education policy making.

[9] This assumption was refined in the third study (Jeliazkova and Westerheijden 2000), mentioned below.

[10] The VSNU is the Association of Dutch Universities, one of the two umbrella bodies. The other is the HBO Council, the Association of Colleges (Universities of Professional Education).

11 The focus on research assessments meant that the population of this evaluation was the 13 universities in the country, excluding the, then, more than 60 colleges.
12 A lengthy discussion of the evolution of the internal governance of Dutch universities can be found in De Boer (2003).
13 Starting in the late 1960s, there have been several attempts to reduce the apparent unconditional professional autonomy of the individual professor, at least in terms of control over the research agenda. For example, since the early 1980s, research programmes and their funding have increasingly become conditional on national priorities (see also the previous section of this chapter). A more elaborate description of these 'attacks' on the dominant position of Dutch professors can be found in De Boer (2003).
14 This can be seen as a general feature of the professoriate (Altbach and Slaughter 1980) as well as a characteristic of Dutch academia in successfully countering threats to their autonomy to steer the research agenda over the last three decades (De Boer 2003).
15 'Top-down' refers to the implementation process inside universities. One might argue that system-wide the process did not have 'top-down' characteristics because the legislator gave the universities ample room to implement the new rules. On the other hand, the regulations of the new Act were imposed on the universities.
16 Which is not necessarily the same as not reaching the goals of the reform.
17 This was also stressed in Jeliazkova and Westerheijden (2002), where among others we argued that policies need to change over time to remain effective.

REFERENCES

Acherman, H.A. "Quality Assessment in a European Perspective." Paper presented at the EAIR Forum, Bergen, 15–17 August, 1988.
Altbach, P.G. and S. Slaughter (eds). *The Academic Profession*. Philadelphia: American Academy of Political and Social Science, 1980.
Bardach, E. *The Implementation Game. What Happens After a Bill Becomes a Law*. Cambridge, MA/London: The MIT Press, 1977.
Bessant, J. "Dawkins' Higher Education Reforms and How Metaphors Work in Policy Making." *Journal of Higher Education Policy and Management* 24.1 (2002): 87–99.
Boudon, R. *De logica van het sociale. Een inleiding tot het sociologisch denken*. Alphen aan den Rijn/Brussel: Samsom Uitgeverij, 1981.
Cerych, L. and P. Sabatier. *Great Expectations and Mixed Performance. Implementation of Higher Education Reforms in Europe*. Stoke-on-Trent: Trentham Books, 1986.
Clark, B.R. *The Higher Education System: Academic Organization in Cross-National Perspective*. Berkeley, CA: University of California Press, 1983.
Coleman, J.S. *Foundations of Social Theory*. Cambridge, MA: Harvard University Press, 1990.
Coleman, J.S. "A Rational Choice Perspective on Economic Sociology." In Smelser, N.J. and R. Swedberg (eds). *The Handbook of Economic Sociology*. Princeton/New York: University Press/ Russell Sage Foundation, 1994, 166–180.
Commissie Datema. *De kanteling van het universitaire bestuur (rapport van de commissie Klankbordgroep Invoering MUB)*. Zoetermeer: Ministerie van Onderwijs, Cultuur en Wetenschappen, 1998.
Commissie-Rinnooy Kan. *Advies inzake de invoering van een bachelor-master systeem in het Nederlandse hoger onderwijs* (20000417/528). 's-Gravenhage: Onderwijsraad, 2000.
Committee Accreditation of Dutch Higher Education. *Activate, Achieve and Advance: Final Report*. Amsterdam: Van de Bunt, 2001.
Currie, J., R. DeAngelis, H. de Boer, J. Huisman and C. Lacotte. *Globalizing Practices and University Responses. European and Anglo-American Differences*. Westport, CT: Praeger, 2003.
De Boer, H. "Institutionele analyse en professionele autonomie. Een empirisch-verklarende studie naar de doorwerking van de wet 'Modernisering Universitaire Bestuursorganisatie' (MUB)." (dissertatie). Enschede: CHEPS, 2003.
De Boer, H. and B. Denters. "Analysis of Institutions of University Governance: A Classification Scheme Applied to Postwar Changes in Dutch Higher Education." In Jongbloed, B., P. Maassen and

G. Neave (eds). *From the Eye of the Storm. Higher Education's Changing Institution.* Dordrecht: Kluwer Academic Publishers, 1999, 211–233.

De Boer, H., B. Denters and L. Goedegebuure. "On Boards and Councils; Shaky Balances Considered. The Governance of Dutch Universities." *Higher Education Policy* 11.2/3 (1998): 153–164.

De Boer, H., B. Denters and L. Goedegebuure. "Dutch Disease or Dutch Model? An Evaluation of the pre-1998 System of Democratic University Government in the Netherlands." In Weissberg, R. (ed.). *Democracy and the Academy.* Huntington, NY: Nova Science Publishers, 2000, 123–140.

De Vree, J.K. *Foundations of Social and Political Processes: The Dynamics of Human Behaviour, Politics, and Society.* Bilthoven, NL: Prime Press, 1982.

Enders, J. *Governing the Academic Commons. About Blurring Boundaries, Blistering Organisations, and Growing Demands.* Inaugural Lecture. Enschede: Center for Higher Education Policy Studies, University of Twente, 2002.

Enders, J., L. Goedegebuure and P. Maassen. *Governance Shifts and Policy Implementation in Higher Education: A European Bird's-Eye View.* Enschede: CHEPS, 2003.

Frederiks, M.M.H. *Beslissen over kwaliteit.* Utrecht: De tijdstroom, 1996.

Frederiks, M.M.H., D.F. Westerheijden and P.J.M. Weusthof. "Effects of Quality Assessment in Dutch Higher Education." *European Journal of Education* 29 (1994): 181–200.

Geul, A. *Beleid in uitvoering. Problemen en remedies.* Utrecht: Uitgeverij Lemma, 2002.

Goedegebuure, L.C.J., M. Jeliazkova, F. Pothof and P.J.M. Weusthof. *Alle begin is moeilijk : Evaluatie van de proefaccreditering HBO.* Enschede: CHEPS, Universiteit Twente, 2002.

Gornitzka, Å., S. Kyvik and B. Stensaker. "Implementation Analysis in Higher Education." In Smart, John C. (ed.). *Higher Education: Handbook of Theory and Research, vol. XVII.* Dordrecht: Kluwer Academic Publishers, 2002, 381–423.

Gray, P. and P. 't Hart. *Public Policy Disasters in Western Europe.* London/New York: Routledge, 1998.

Grondsma, T. *TVC-proces en speltheorie.* Delft: Technische Hogeschool Delft, 1983.

Herweyer, M. "De dynamiek an doelstellend gedrag: een struikelblok voor evaluatieonderzoek." In Lehning, P.B. and J.B.D. Simonis (eds). *Handboek beleidswetenschap.* Meppel/Amsterdam: Boom, 1987, 177–195.

Huitema, D., M. Jeliazkova and D.F. Westerheijden. "Phases, Levels and Circles in Policy Development: The Cases of Higher Education and Environmental Quality Assurance." *Higher Education Policy* 15.2 (2002): 197–215.

Inspectie Hoger Onderwijs. *De bestuurlijke hantering van de externe kwaliteitszorg 1989 in het wetenschappelijk onderwijs.* De Meern: Inspectie Hoger Onderwijs, 1992.

Jeliazkova, M. and D.F. Westerheijden. *Het zichtbare eindresultaat.* Den Haag: Algemene Rekenkamer, 2000.

Jeliazkova, M. and D.F. Westerheijden. "Systemic Adaptation to a Changing Environment: Towards a Next Generation of Quality Assurance Models." *Higher Education* 44.3/4 (2002): 433–448.

Kiser, L.L. and E. Ostrom. "The Three Worlds of Action." In Ostrom, E. (ed.). *Strategies of Political Inquiry.* Beverly Hills: Sage Publications, 1982, 179–222.

Lieshout, R.H. and J.K. de Vree. "How Organisations Decide." *Acta Politica* XX (1985): 129–155.

Lipsky, M. *Street-level Bureaucracy. Dilemmas of the Individual in Public Services.* New York: Russell Sage Foundation, 1980.

Maassen, P.A.M. and F.A. van Vught. "Alternative Models of Governmental Steering in Higher Education." In Goedegebuure, L.C.J. and F.A. van Vught (eds). *Comparative Policy Studies in Higher Education.* Enschede/Utrecht: CHEPS and LEMMA, 1994, 35–64.

Mayntz, R. *New Challenges to Governance Theory. European University Institute.* Jean Monet Chair Paper, RSC No. 98/50, 1998.

Ministerie van Onderwijs and Wetenschappen. *Hoger Onderwijs: Autonomie en Kwaliteit.* Tweede Kamer, vergaderjaar 1985–1986, 19253, nr. 2, 1985.

Nederhof, A.J. "The Validity and Reliability of Evaluation of Scholarly Performance." In Van Raan, A.F.J. (ed.). *Handbook of Quantitative Studies of Science and Technology.* Amsterdam: Elsevier, 1988, 193–228.

O'Toole, L.J. "Implementing Public Programs." In Perry, J.L. (ed.). *Handbook of Public Administration.* 2nd edn. San Francisco: Jossey-Bass Publishers, 1996, 250–262.

Prottas, J.M. *People-processing. The Street-level Bureaucrat in Public Service Bureaucracies.* Toronto: Lexington, 1979.

Ryan, N. "A Comparison of Three Approaches to Programme Implementation." *International Journal of Public Sector Management* 9.4 (1996): 34–41.

Ryan, N. "Rationality and Implementation Analysis." *Journal of Management History* 5.1 (1999): 36–52.

Sabatier, P. "What Can We Learn From Implementation Research?" In Kaufmann, F.X., G. Majone and V. Ostrom (eds). *Guidance, Control, and Evaluation in the Public Sector.* Berlin/New York: Walter de Gruyter, 1986, 313–325.

Scharpf, F.W. "Policy Failure and Institutional Reform: Why Should Form Follow Function?" *International Social Science Journal* 108 (1986): 179–190.

Scharpf, F.W. *Games Real Actors Play. Actor-centered Institutionalism in Policy Research.* Boulder, CO: Westview Press, 1997.

Sinclair, T.A.P. "Implementation Theory and Practice: Uncovering Policy and Administration Linkages in the 1990s." *International Journal of Public Administration* 24.1 (2001): 77–94.

Spaapen, J.B., A.A.M. Prins, C.A.M. van Suyt and S.S. Blume. *De Voorwaardelijke Financiering de maat genomen.* Amsterdam: UvA, 1986.

Spaapen, J.B., C.A.M. van Suyt, A.A.M. Prins and S.S. Blume. *De moeizame relatie tussen beleid en onderzoek: Evaluatie van vijf jaar Voorwaardelijke Financiering.* Zoetermeer: Ministerie van Onderwijs and Wetenschappen, 1988.

Stokman, F.N., R. Popping and R. Missoorten. "Een relationele database voor wetenschappelijke productie." *U and H* 35 (1989): 231–245.

Trader-Leigh, K.E. "Case Study: Identifying Resistance in Managing Change." *Journal of Organizational Change Management* 15.2 (2002): 138–155.

Van Bruggen, J.C., J.P. Scheele and D.F. Westerheijden. "To be continued ... Syntheses and trends." In Scheele, J.P., P.A.M. Maassen and D.F. Westerheijden (eds). *To Be Continued ...: Follow-Up of Quality Assurance in Higher Education.* Maarssen: Elsevier/De Tijdstroom, 1998, 87–99.

Van der Meulen, B.R., D.F. Westerheijden, A. Rip and F.A. van Vught. *Verkenningscommissies tussen veld en overheid.* Zoetermeer: Ministerie van Onderwijs and Wetenschappen, 1991.

Van der Vegt, R., L.F. Smyth and R. Vandenberghe. "Implementing Educational Policy at the School Level. Organization Dynamics and Teacher Concerns." *Journal of Educational Administration* 39.1 (2000): 8–23.

Van der Wende, M.C. and D.F. Westerheijden. "International Aspects of Quality Assurance With a Special Focus on European Higher Education." *Quality in Higher Education* 7.3 (2001): 233–245.

Van Raan, A.F.J., A.J. Nederhof and H.F. Moed. *Science and Technology Indicators: Their Use in Science Policy and Their Role in Scientific Studies – Select Proceedings.* Leiden: LISBON, 1989.

Van Vught, F.A. (ed.). *Governmental Strategies and Innovation in Higher Education.* London: Jessica Kingsley, 1989.

Van Vught, F.A., M.C. van der Wende and D.F. Westerheijden. "Globalization and Internationalization: Policy Agendas Compared." In Fulton, O. and J. Enders (eds). *Higher Education in a Globalizing World. International Trends and Mutual Observations.* Dordrecht: Kluwer, 2002, 103–120.

Van Vught, F.A. and D.F. Westerheijden. *Quality Management and Quality Assurance in European Higher Education: Methods and Mechanisms.* Luxembourg: Office for Official Publications of the Commission of the European Communities, 1993.

Vroeijenstijn, A.I. "Autonomy and Assurance of Quality: Two Sides of One Coin." Paper presented at the International Conference on Assessing Quality in Higher Education, Cambridge, 1989.

Westerheijden, D.F. "Quality Assessment in Dutch Higher Education: Balancing Improvement and Accountability." *European Journal for Education Law and Policy* 1 (1997a): 81–90.

Westerheijden, D.F. "A Solid Base for Decisions: Use of the VSNU Research Evaluations in Dutch Universities." *Higher Education* 33.4 (1997b): 397–413.

Westerheijden, D.F. "*Ex oriente lux?* National and Multiple Accreditation in Europe After the Fall of the Wall and After Bologna." *Quality in Higher Education* 7.1 (2001): 65–75.

Westerheijden, D.F. and M. Leegwater (eds). *Working on the European Dimension of Quality: Report of the Conference on Quality Assurance in Higher Education as Part of the Bologna Process, Amsterdam, 12–13 March 2002.* Zoetermeer: Ministerie van Onderwijs, Cultuur en Wetenschappen, 2003.

Wippler, R. "De plaats van roltheoretische ideeën in de sociologie." In Visser, A.P., E. van der Vliert, E.J.H. ter Heine and J.A.M. Winnubst (eds). *Rollen; Persoonlijke en sociale invloeden op het gedrag.* Amsterdam/Meppel: Boom, 1983, 61–82.

ALBERTO AMARAL AND ANTÓNIO MAGALHÃES

IMPLEMENTATION OF HIGHER EDUCATION POLICIES: A PORTUGUESE EXAMPLE

1. INTRODUCTION

In this chapter we present the Portuguese national case by analysing at the macro level some higher education policies and the effects of their implementation on the higher education system, over the period 1974 to the present. The first part of the chapter presents the historical context in which the reforms were implemented, and this is very relevant as Portugal went through a revolutionary process that overthrew the previous dictatorship. The 1974 Revolution initiated a transformation of Portuguese society and its political organisation that impinged strongly on education policies.

After the revolution, increasing the rate of participation to European standards became one major aim of education policies in Portugal. In this chapter we use Cerych and Sabatier's (1986) framework, together with the three aspects of higher education policy mentioned by Bleiklie, Høstaker and Vabø (2000), namely the ideological aspect, the organisational aspect and the educational and research policy aspects, to examine the Portuguese policies aimed at increasing access to higher education, with special reference to the development of private higher education and the implementation of a binary system.

2. THE HISTORICAL CONTEXT

At the time of the 1974 Revolution, Portugal was a rather backward country due to more than half a century of right wing narrow-minded policies of the former dictator Salazar. The higher education system was elitist with a participation rate below 7% of the relevant age cohort, and minute participation of students from the lower classes. In the early 1970s, the former dictatorial regime had become aware of these shortcomings, but it did too little, too late to solve the problem before being overthrown. It was only in 1973 that the National Assembly (the parliament) passed Act 5/73, of 25 July, reforming the higher education system. This Reform Act formally created for the first time in Portugal a *binary system*. Inspired, on the one hand, by 'human capital' theories, and, on the other hand, legitimated by OECD reports and recommendations, the Minister of Education expanded and diversified the higher education system. New universities and the first polytechnic institutes

Å. Gornitzka et al. (eds.), Reform and Change in Higher Education, 117-134.

were established. This set of reforms aimed at expanding the higher education system within a new binary structure. However, the 1974 Revolution suspended the implementation of this reform, and many new higher education institutions, such as the new polytechnics, were to remain as mere 'political statements' for some years.

The 1974 Revolution caused a dramatic turn from a right wing conservative authoritarian regime to a radical left wing socialist regime. Higher education institutions were quickly submerged in political turmoil, the traditional governance bodies being disbanded as they were viewed as fascist, authoritarian and undemocratic.

The loss of all forms of authority faced by higher education institutions combined with a substantial increase in demand for access to higher education and a dramatic change to socialism led to a crisis that was met with 'revolutionary' measures. Decree-Law 61/75, of 18 February, suspended all first-year classes, as well as access to new students. Students ready to enter higher education were instead admitted to one year of 'civic service' – not very different from the system of brigades of young university students in communist Cuba – to increase the integration of the university into the Portuguese society and to develop the freshmen's awareness of national issues and the problems of active life. This had the double advantage of promoting the new revolutionary values while allowing the government some time for reorganisation of the higher education sector.

In the days following the revolution, all policies were aimed at the construction of a socialist country in reaction to the former dark times of the authoritarian regime. 'Medium level' schools were promoted to higher education institutions in order to redress what was considered an unjust situation which mainly penalised the less favoured classes. Intermediate level education institutions were upgraded and transformed into the Industrial and Commercial Institutes of Lisbon, Porto and Coimbra (Decree-Law 830/74, of 31 December). The preamble of the law read:

> The democratisation of education demands a reform of the present educational structures, which reflect a hierarchical, antidemocratic and stagnated situation. Medium level schools are a telling example of this reality, as their enrolled students in general come from less favoured social classes than those entering universities. At those schools, education is intentionally aimed at keeping their graduates throughout their professional life, in a situation of disadvantage or subaltern to the graduates from higher education institutions.

The Decree-Law 363/75, of 11 July, passed by the Council of Revolution was very explicit as to the aims of the new policies:

> ... as the Portuguese people move towards socialism, it becomes evident the need of democratic 'control' to force all the material and cultural production system to harmoniously function at the service of the socialist revolution.
> This democratic control is achieved by participation of representatives of the working people in the decision-making bodies ... This direct presence of representatives of workers' organisations and of national and regional interests in the governing bodies of universities is especially important while it is not possible to significantly change the composition of the student population, today still originating from the most privileged classes.

Universities were asked to help in the search for answers to national problems while making their technical and scientific capacity available to other public services. On the one hand, higher education was supposed to expand and provide training or retraining courses, and to increase its offer of specialised services to the community. On the other hand, it was supposed to diversify either by creating new schools and new courses or by differentiation of some already established courses. Another important political goal was to regionalise some universities in order to serve the economic and social needs of the population (Programa do Governo Provisório 1975).

The Decree-Law 363/75 established a new 'senior grade year'[1] in between the conclusion of secondary education (11th grade) and higher education. The senior grade year was a combination of the 'civic service' revolutionary type activities – in order to impart socially productive working habits to the new 'socialist' students – with preparatory courses aimed at initiating students in the general methodology of advanced intellectual work and in those scientific areas most relevant to the study programmes in which they planned to enrol.

However, despite all the socialist fervour, human nature did not change much and many students took advantage of the new freedom to enter the schools of medicine, seen to offer better prospects of upward social mobility. The answer from the government was swift and radical. The Decree-Law 601/76, of 23 July, established a system of *numerus clausus* for medicine and the Decree-Law 701/76, of 28 September, established a system of *numerus clausus* for veterinary medicine, as it became obvious that students not entering medicine would inundate veterinary medicine. This did not solve the problem, as those students unable to enter either medicine or veterinary medicine enrolled in areas such as pharmacy or biological sciences and forced the government to pass the Decree-Law 397/77, of 17 September, that extended the *numerus clausus* system to all higher education study programmes.

The establishment of the *numerus clausus* system was necessary because following the revolution public higher education institutions could not cope with the large increase in demand without serious disruption. And due to the difficult economic situation, no resources were available to invest in expanding the system. Indeed, the *numerus clausus* system was in general determined by the institutions' capacity in terms of physical infrastructure and academic staff rather than by market demands. This policy has protected higher education institutions from an excessive increase in enrolments but has generated very strong social tensions because many candidates have been left outside the system without any alternative. This has brought about the development of a large private system.

The *numerus clausus* system also received support from the World Bank (Teixeira, Amaral and Rosa 2003: 186), which recommended that:

> ... the efforts of the educational authorities should be devoted more to rationalising the supply of higher education and improving the management of the system, namely in terms of mechanisms of accountability, coordination, and efficiency. Future expansions should be better planned taking into account manpower needs, and demographic and enrolment trends.

The new 1976 Constitution recognised the right of all Portuguese to education. But by sanctioning the freedom to learn and teach as a fundamental right, the Constitution opened the way for the development of private higher education.

It is against this historical background – a sharp increase in the demand for higher education, a generalised *numerus clausus* system, the constitutional guarantee of the freedom to learn and to teach – that the implementation of some major higher education policies will now be examined.

3. POLICY 1: THE DEVELOPMENT OF THE PRIVATE SECTOR

At the time of the revolution, the international educational indices placed Portugal among the less developed countries. Consequently, all governments after the 1974 Revolution considered that education was a priority area. Most of the initial efforts were mainly devoted to the basic and secondary education systems, as a large number of young people, especially those from the lower classes, did not complete secondary education, or even basic education. Educational priorities determined policies aimed at answering the most pressing demands for universal basic education (6 years at the time, later 9 years), for reduction of the illiteracy rate (still high), and for increased access to secondary education (2 years at the time, later 3 years) while developing the vocational component of education to increase the students' employment prospects.

Higher education initially attracted neither the full attention of governments nor the level of investment needed to redress its weak development. However, the sharp increase in demand for higher education after the 1974 Revolution combined with the *numerus clausus* restrictive access policies caused an increasing number of young people to be excluded from higher education, without any adequate alternative, thus creating an acute social and political problem. This situation gave rise to a very favourable environment for the emergence of the private sector, which allowed for the easing of the access problem without further demands on the public purse.

The development of private institutions was initially rather slow, probably due to the lack of legislation and/or tradition. In January 1979, the Minister of Education authorised the first private higher education institution by granting the 'Free University (Universidade Livre) Cooperative for Education' a temporary permit to initiate operations. Many associates of the cooperative were former university professors expelled from public institutions due to their close connections to the deposed regime. The Decree-Law 426/80, of 30 September, formally recognised the Universidade Livre, and the Decree-Law 59/83, of 11 July, allowed the institution to offer study programmes in the two main cities, Lisbon and Porto. However, the existence of the Universidade Livre was short. Internal strife between its members, and fights between the cooperative – the owner of the university – and the university itself created an impossible situation that forced the government to take drastic action. On 21 June 1986, the Minister of Education recognised two new private institutions, one in Lisbon (Universidade Autónoma Luís de Camões) and the other in Porto (Universidade Portucalense), owned by a new cooperative (University

Higher Education Cooperative) set up by dissidents from the Universidade Livre. On 16 September 1986, the Minister made public that the Universidade Livre was no longer officially recognised.

Enrolments in private institutions in 1982–83 (including the Catholic University established in 1971) were only about 11% of total enrolments. But the pace of implementation accelerated after the mid-1980s. In 1986, Minister Deus Pinheiro recognised two new private universities (Lusíada and International) and several polytechnic-type institutions, some of them resulting from upgrading already existing medium level institutions which until then were not allowed to confer higher education degrees. The new institutions concentrated their offer of study programmes in areas of low investment/low running costs, such as languages and administration, management, journalism, training of secretaries and interpreters, and informatics.

However, it was Minister Roberto Carneiro (1987–91) who created the conditions for the explosive development of the private sector. Not only did he approve a large number of new institutions but he also decided to lower the requirements for access to higher education. In 1989 the Minister determined that entrance examinations were only to be used for ranking students in the national tender for vacancies, without any minimum required marks. Figure 1 shows that in 1989 there was an increase of over 20,000 candidates (more than 60%) from the previous year, which the public sector could not enrol thus creating very favourable market conditions for the private sector. Many students who until 1989 were unable to enter higher education because of their low marks suddenly were offered a unique opportunity. Students could now enter higher education – and many did – even with a zero in the entrance examinations, provided there were vacancies.

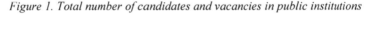

Figure 1. Total number of candidates and vacancies in public institutions

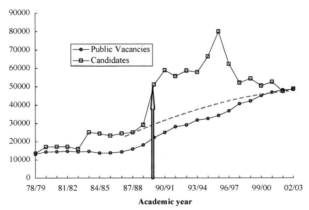

Political agency artificially created this new important market for higher education that allowed private institutions to prosper and proliferate. This was made easier as the government did not exert any visible control over quality while passing legislation allowing the private sector to take full advantage of the moonlighting activities of public sector academics. The development of the private sector was so fast that in the academic year 1991–92 the number of vacancies at private institutions exceeded those at public institutions (see figure 2).

The private share of student enrolments jumped from 11% in 1982–83 to 21.6% in 1989–90, and to 34.7% in 1996–97, and it is evident that no higher education sector could develop so fast while at the same time caring for quality. The number of candidates remained stable until 1994 when a new increase was observed. The Ministry of Education had implemented a new reform of secondary education and decided to discontinue the enrolments of those students who had stalled in grades 10 to 12 because they failed their examinations. In that it was inconvenient to maintain the old reform (for failed students) in parallel with the new reform, the Ministry created special conditions allowing the old reform students to complete their studies, thus increasing the number of candidates aspiring to higher education. This episode had dramatic consequences as it gave a false impression. All private institutions assumed that the number of candidates would go on increasing when in reality the number was already starting to consistently[2] decrease (Amaral and Teixeira 1999, 2000) due to demographic factors, and instead of adapting to this new situation they initiated new study programmes and made additional investments.

Figure 2. Vacancies offered by public and private higher education sectors

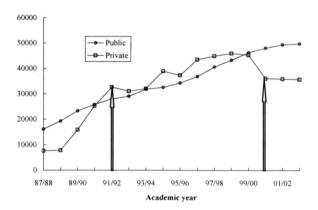

At the same time, large investments were being made in the public sector, allowing the number of vacancies at public institutions to increase steadily over the years (see figure 2). Students enrolled in public higher education institutions pay only nominal tuition fees (around €400 annually) while students at private institutions pay full costs, and in general it is considered that public institutions offer better quality than private ones. This explains why students show a preference for public institutions.

The consistent decline in the number of candidates combined with the preference of students for the public sector have created a very difficult situation for the private sector. From the academic year 1995–96 to 1997–98 the number of new students entering private institutions decreased 31.3% while it increased 19.4% in public institutions (Amaral and Teixeira 2000). Presently, the number of vacancies in public institutions accommodates most candidates.

This has led the government to change its policy from uncontrolled expansion to increased quality. The Minister of Education, Marçal Grilo, implemented legislation passed in 1993 by Minister Couto dos Santos (pass examinations at the end of the 10th and 11th grades, and national examinations for each subject at the end of the 12th grade) which again imposed national examinations at the end of secondary education. Marçal Grilo reversed the access rules established by Roberto Carneiro by allowing higher education institutions to set minimum marks in the access examinations to higher education, thus putting an end to the ludicrous situation of allowing students to enter higher education even with zero marks.

This decision exposed to public scrutiny those institutions that could not attract students. While the best institutions had no problems in setting minimum marks, this was carefully avoided by less reputable institutions which tried to fill as many vacancies as possible by using lower entrance standards. However, lowering standards did not help much, and in 1997–98 many private institutions filled less than 50% of their vacancies (some of them could not fill more than 30% of the available vacancies). In 2000–01 the Ministry decided to penalise those institutions which did not set minimum entry marks by reducing their *numeri clausi* and from the academic year 2000–01 the number of vacancies in private institutions fell below the number of public vacancies (see figure 2).

Today the crisis is being felt by public institutions, particularly the polytechnics (due to their lower social standing *vis-à-vis* the universities) and some universities located in the less populated regions (inland), as well as some study programmes which do not offer reasonable employment prospects. In the academic year 2002–03 about 200 study programmes of public institutions had less than 50% of available vacancies filled, and 16 study programmes had no candidates.

More recently (2002) a new minister initiated legislation enforcing minimum marks in the national access examinations for all candidates in all sectors of higher education the effects of which will be felt in two years time. This legislation will have significant consequences, as it will further decrease the number of candidates. For the academic year 2003–04 the Minister decided to close down some 35 study programmes because of low student enrolment and reduced about 3200 vacancies in the public sector in areas of low student demand, in an attempt to increase the percentage of students in priority areas such as health and technologies, and to force some students to move inland thus protecting universities and polytechnics located away from the more populated areas.

4. POLICY 2: THE DEVELOPMENT OF THE POLYTECHNICS

In 1977, the Decree-Law 427-B/77 instituted polytechnic higher education as "short duration higher education, aiming at training technicians and professionals of education at an intermediate level of higher education".[3] The explicit political intention was both "to diversify higher education, and to satisfy urgent needs in several socio-economic sectors through the training of qualified technicians". In 1979, the expression 'short duration higher education' was formally replaced by 'polytechnic higher education' and the professional scope of polytechnic education was emphasised (Decree-Law 513-T/79) against the 'more conceptual and theoretical characteristics' of university education.

The World Bank played an important role in the development of the polytechnic subsystem, being responsible for several projects implemented in the period between the 1974 Revolution and the integration of Portugal in the EU. At the time, the World Bank policies for higher education were influenced by the planning and forecasting of manpower needs and the direct link between the offer of study programmes and the needs of the economy. The World Bank thought of Portugal as a less developed country that would need fewer high-skilled graduates, and thought that the focus should be on training middle-level graduates and technicians (Teixeira, Amaral and Rosa 2003).

Successive ministers of education regarded the development of the polytechnics as a priority of the higher education system. Access policies were combined with large investments in new buildings and equipment and an academic career progression more attractive (less demanding) than a university one to promote the development of the polytechnic sector. The regional character of the polytechnics was stressed by allowing the institutions to reserve a percentage of vacancies for students living in the region.

Although there are still more students enrolled in public universities than in public polytechnics, the development of the public polytechnic sector was impressive (see figure 3 where the number of annual vacancies for public universities and public polytechnics are compared).

From 1983–84 to 2001–02 the share of enrolments changed from 76.2% in public universities, 12.6% in public polytechnics, 7.9% in private universities and 3.3% in private polytechnics to 43.6%, 27.9%, 13.1% and 15.4% respectively. The available data also show that over the period 1980–98 vacancies in the public university sector increased at a yearly average rate of 5.21% compared to 17.17% for public polytechnics. This demonstrates that the government policies were effective in increasing the enrolments in polytechnics.

*Figure 3. Number of new places offered by higher education
public institutions*

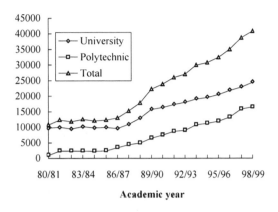

Source: Correia, Amaral and Magalhães 2002: 127

Despite this apparent quantitative success, the polytechnic sector has not been able to emerge as an attractive option for many students, and its present situation is rather fragile. The first problem for polytechnics lies in the lack of a clear definition of their mission. Polytechnics are to provide a good match between education and the demands of the economy by producing technicians who are able to act at the intermediate level of industrial, service and educational organisations. Decree-Law 513-1/79 states that polytechnic higher education should provide study programmes with strong applied and technical emphasis and marked vocational orientation, adapted to regional needs.

However, instead of defining a distinctive profile aimed at gaining a strong position in the market of intermediate level human resources training, most polytechnics have chosen to copy the model of the new universities, which had also adopted a style of discourse that addressed closer connections with local communities. And the fact that the higher schools of education were in many cases the initial core of the new polytechnics created problems in defining the mission and the role of the new institutions. Therefore polytechnics are in a disadvantageous position, both in terms of quality and social standing.

The Comprehensive Law of the Educational System (CLES-Law 48/86) helped to consolidate the new polytechnic network. Besides the declaration of intentions regarding the technical and cultural educational tasks allocated to this subsystem, together with the new mission of developing capacities of innovation and criticism, the law reasserts the polytechnics' task to train human resources for professional activities through teaching based on scientific knowledge transmission. But the legislator did not have the courage to draw a clear distinction between polytechnics and universities. For example, commenting on the Comprehensive Law, Simão and Costa (2000: 24–25) argue that the law:

> ... shows great embarrassment in drawing the distinction that it intends to make, almost limiting itself to a mere semantic exercise, expressing similar ideas in non-coincidental times and modes. With visible effort and a desire to find some differences, maybe one can register at least two impressive notes: a) first, to keep the development of the capacity of 'creation' within university higher education; b) second, to provide an orientation, apparently more specific in polytechnic higher education, of 'scientific knowledge of a theoretical and practical type' and its application to the 'exercise of professional activities'.

This ambiguity is particularly visible in the field of research, for the polytechnics were not kept out of research, but instead were expected to explore less traditional fields, such as applied research, areas of experimental technologies and education, in articulation with regional and local needs. The emphasis was on the professional and technical characteristics of the polytechnics along with the regional and national economic role of their mission, embodying the political assumption that economic development is a more or less direct consequence of an adequate educational system. However,

> In reality, most polytechnics instead of following a strategy of differentiation addressed at the take-over of a space in the intermediate levels of human resources training have made the choice of identifying themselves with the university model which was extensively mimed to their obvious disadvantage, both in terms of quality as of social standing (Amaral et al. 2000: 25).

The second problem lies in the low capacity of polytechnics to attract students, which places them in a difficult situation, as there is increasing competition for students. To understand this situation one must not ignore the positional character (Hirsh 1976) of higher education.[4] Diversification via the binary system is tainted by a political suspicion: the elitism implicit within the university subsystem. In Portugal – and the same appears to be valid for the majority of OECD countries (OECD 1987: 35) – according to Seixas, "polytechnic higher education is characterised by a larger number of students coming from the working classes in comparison to students coming from the upper classes" (1991: 110). This class feature has led researchers to ask, at least in the Portuguese case, if polytechnic higher education corresponds to "a form of social promotion or to a form of differed elimination" (Vargas 1996).

The recent decision of the Ministry to increase the academic qualifications of the candidates to higher education will exacerbate this problem. As students in general see polytechnics as a second choice, most students entering the polytechnics are those who could not compete for a place in a university because of their lower academic marks. A simulation of the new access criterion for the academic year 2002–03 (table 1) shows an average decrease of 26.8% of filled vacancies, with some polytechnics facing a dramatic situation, thus revealing a very difficult situation for the sector.

Table 1. Simulation of the new access system for the academic year 2002–03

Polytechnic	Total vacancies	Filled vacancies (old system)	Filled vacancies (new system)	Loss %
Beja	815	509	376	-26.1
Coimbra	1 650	1 057	640	-39.5
Lisboa	1 635	1 411	768	-45.6
Porto	2 122	1 638	911	-44.4
Setúbal	1 288	942	597	-36.6
Viseu	1 525	1 190	809	-32.0
Total Polytechnic	19 392	14 244	10 431	-26.8

5. ANALYSIS OF ASPECTS OF HIGHER EDUCATION POLICY AND DEGREE OF ATTAINMENT OF OBJECTIVES

We applied Cerych and Sabatier's (1986) analytical framework to the access policies implemented in Portugal assuming that their goals were:

1. to widen access to higher education;
2. to increase the diversity of the system;
3. to stimulate the regional relevance of higher education;
4. to promote social equity.

Widening access was the first priority when those policies were first implemented.

5.1. Aspects of Higher Education Policy

5.1.1. The Ideological Dimension

The reasons behind the development of the private sector were both pragmatic and ideological. On the one hand, private higher education could be seen as a necessary evil to solve the dramatic problem of increasing demand for higher education that could not be met by the public sector, especially in the years of severe economic stringency following the revolution. On the other hand, Minister Roberto Carneiro (1994) edited a book entitled *Free Education – A Frontier of State Hegemony* that contains a passionate apology for private higher education and leaves no doubt about his ideological commitment to the private sector. In a chapter entitled "Manifesto Against State Hegemony" he (p. 9) writes:

> The situation of free education [free education meaning private education] is one of the most accurate barometers of the healthy condition of a society's fundamental freedoms and of the degree of maturity of its institutions ...
>
> A developed nation is thus the one that unites a State aware of its subsidiary role and a society endowed with self-regulation mechanisms sufficient to cherish the development

of fundamental freedoms and this includes without any shade of doubt the freedom of education.

The book contains contributions from a number of authors, including several former ministers and high-level employees of the Ministry of Education. This demonstrates that private higher education clearly was assumed by leading political actors as an important ideological instrument for strengthening Portuguese democracy, and as a tool for its social and economic development.

However, trust in private education was not widespread and other ministers of education had a more critical view of this sector. This is more in accord with the European tradition. Quite recently, the European ministers of education signed the Prague declaration supporting the "idea that higher education should be considered a public good and is and will remain a public responsibility" (Communiqué of the Meeting of European Ministers in Charge of Higher Education in Prague, 19 May 2001: 1).

This lack of trust in the private sector was so visible that the APESP[5] wrote a letter to the Minister complaining about the situation:

> How is it possible, under these conditions of instability, insecurity and lack of future prospects, for private institutions to consolidate their educational projects? How is it possible to give credibility to the system if the Government systematically makes public new decisions capable of developing in public opinion a generalised feeling of mistrust of the private higher education subsystem? (1998).

As in other countries, the Portuguese government has not yet been able to:

> ... attain a satisfactory balance between intervention in, and co-ordination of, the private sector and the autonomy of private institutions. Governments have either controlled too much, because of their mistrust towards private initiative in education, or they have assumed an over-relaxed position, which has allowed the mushrooming of private institutions that possess no sound academic and financial criteria (Teixeira and Amaral 2001: 391).

The first attempt to create a binary system dates from 1973 and it was strongly influenced by OECD reports. The political justification for the reform was mainly economic and it aimed at using manpower resources as a tool for convergence with the development patterns of other European countries. This attempt did not succeed due to the 1974 Revolution, and the project was restarted in 1977 under the influence of the World Bank.

The World Bank's approach was also economic and supported by two key ideas. The first idea emphasised the improvement of the system's level of economic efficiency by containing long duration university degrees while promoting shorter technical degrees (shorter teacher training degrees, higher student/staff ratios, etc.). The second idea took on a perspective of a world division of labour viewing Portugal as a provider of specialised manpower for manufacturing industries, services and agriculture (Teixeira, Amaral and Rosa 2003).

The World Bank was very critical of the fast expansion of university higher education and recommended instead the development of a system of short-cycle higher education to match closely the manpower demands of the Portuguese economy. The World Bank was also aware that short-cycle higher education would be socially discredited vis-à-vis university education and praised the fact that the "...

government severely restricted enrolments in engineering as well as in other university faculties ..." thus endorsing the policy of establishing the *numerus clausus* system. This supports our hypothesis that access policies to higher education have played a major role in the state's regulation of the system.

5.1.2. The Organisational Dimension

The relationship between the government and the private sector has been ambiguous. It is true that initially the government created the conditions for the rapid development of the private sector. However, the government kept close bureaucratic control over private institutions that were conferred less pedagogical autonomy than the public universities. This is a question raised by APESP (1998):

> ... the State has been exceeding the limits of its right of surveillance conferred by constitution by exercising over private institutions a direct and suffocating tutelage thus completely eliminating their scientific and pedagogical autonomy, obstructing the institutional development and creating large difficulties to the implementation of new projects due to the need of a priori Ministerial permission for almost any kind of scholarly activity.

Despite those difficulties, private institutions (or at least some of them) had strong lobbying capacity (Amaral and Teixeira 2000), which allowed them to expand despite the proclaimed government policy goals of increasing student enrolments in fields that were of economic importance to the country. Private institutions were indeed able to impose their own agenda, as widening access was initially the dominant priority.

During the years of uncontrolled expansion, private institutions used their strong lobbying capacity to force the approval of new institutions and new study programmes without close scrutiny of legal conditions or quality. Now that there is a serious crises threatening the survival of many institutions, the private sector has started to blame the government for its lack of capacity to regulate the system, and for allowing the public sector to increase its number of student vacancies:

> ... we are witnessing a sustained approval of more study programs and a continuous increase of vacancies offered by the public network, in areas of competition against private education, without any regard for already available projects and placing in danger the viability of those institutions which are better provided with facilities and human resources (APESP 1998).

The polytechnic sector was supposed to define its offer of study programmes on the basis of the needs of industry, services and education at the national, regional or local levels. Without denying that in some cases there was success, the overall result was that both institutional and local objectives seemed to be missed, with the role of institutions being characterised more by the unexpected consequences produced (e.g. a mismatch between the quantity of graduates and their qualifications and the real needs of local and regional industry and commerce) than by the original political steering objectives.

The obvious disadvantage of polytechnics *vis-à-vis* universities resulted in pressure to change the legal framework to allow them to imitate universities. In 1997, the Minister of Education proposed an alteration to the 1986 Comprehensive

Law of the Educational System. The Law (115/97) was passed by parliament entitling polytechnics to award the 'licenciado' degree which, until then, was a prerogative of universities. Some researchers recognise traces of undesirable academic drift in this measure. More recently polytechnics have started a public campaign to be allowed to confer postgraduate degrees and to increase their autonomy to the level of the autonomy of public universities. With around 120,000 students, the polytechnic subsystem is presently trying to redefine its specificity, arguing that this redefinition implies "legal reforms that will necessarily involve the Comprehensive Law of the Educational System, the Law of University Autonomy, and the Higher Education Career Statutes and other legislation relevant to polytechnic higher education" (CCISP 2000: 6). In the latter document it is of interest to note that the presidents of the polytechnics argue that the polytechnics are not mocking the universities, but rather that the opposite is happening,[6] thus justifying the need for legal reforms based precisely on "the identical status" (CCISP 2000: 13) that both types of institutions apparently have.

5.1.3. The Educational and Research Policy Aspects

The private sector developed at an extremely fast pace, without proper attention being paid to quality. Amaral and Teixeira (2000: 254–255) state: "it has become common knowledge that in general most private institutions are of rather low quality". This was the result of a shortsighted strategy of most private institutions, aiming more at immediate profit than at long-term survival.

The polytechnics were not able to define a distinctive profile allowing them to overcome the handicap of lower social standing relative to universities. This has resulted in considerable academic drift, and the present strategy of public polytechnics concentrates on using political pressure to change the legal framework with the purpose of being conferred the same level of autonomy and prerogatives as that of public universities.

Neither the private sector nor the public polytechnics contributes substantially to research. Private institutions are in general teaching-only schools. And the initial expectation that public polytechnics might develop specific activities of applied research and experimental development in applied areas with regional relevance was not fulfilled. Despite some research activity, this is still a rather weak area that the recent policy of allocating research funds on a competitive basis did not help to strengthen.

5.2. Degree of Attainment of Objectives

5.2.1. To Widen Access to Higher Education

This objective was very successfully fulfilled. Today there are many more vacancies than candidates thus allowing for every student with adequate qualifications to enter higher education.

5.2.2. To Increase the Diversity of the System

Private institutions did not contribute strongly to programmatic diversity of the system. They have concentrated their education provision in a narrow range of scientific and disciplinary areas, generally, those requiring less investment in educational and research infrastructure, such as management and humanities: 60% of the students in the private sector are concentrated in the areas of the social and behavioural sciences, management and law, compared to 25% in the public sector (Correia, Amaral and Magalhães 2002).

There are mixed feelings about the contribution of the polytechnics to the system's diversity. It is true that polytechnics offer a vast number of new study programmes, some of them looking for market niches at the regional level. However, polytechnics have copied to some extent the profile of the new universities, and the emergence of academic drift has reduced the contribution of polytechnics to diversity.

5.2.3. To Stimulate the Regional Relevance of Higher Education

The available data show that private higher education institutions are mainly concentrated in the most populated areas of the districts of Lisbon and Setúbal (49.3% of all vacancies) and Porto (27.2% of all vacancies). The element of profit present in the market's logic explains why private institutions avoid less developed regions or regions with lower population density (Correia, Amaral and Magalhães 2002).

The public sector presents a much more even distribution of vacancies across the country than does the private sector. The network of 16 public polytechnics with an institution in every district strongly contributes to this more balanced distribution.

5.2.4. To Promote Social Equity

Data from a report published in 1997 (CNASES/CEOS) show that the social stratification of the students' families does not differ significantly with regard to the higher education subsystem (public or private, universities or polytechnics). However, in general, students from families of administrators, managers and qualified technicians (those with higher cultural capital) enrol preferably in public universities while students from families of employers (on average they do not possess a very high cultural capital, but they can possess a significant economic capital) prefer private universities (the cultural background of the family is a handicap for their academic success). Students from families of the lower classes show more preference for local polytechnics (the economic factor has more influence). Therefore we cannot say that the private sector plays a decisive role in promoting social equity.

Most students see polytechnic education as having less prestige than university education, especially when compared to public university education. This explains why the polytechnic subsystem has low attraction capacity for students.

The class origin of the students also correlates with this choice. A larger proportion from the lower classes are enrolled in polytechnics. We can say that polytechnics play an important role for students originating from families without previous traditions in higher education and not holding a large economic capital.

6. CONCLUSIONS: FACTORS AFFECTING POLICY IMPLEMENTATION

The main objective – increasing access to higher education – was clearly and consistently defined, and it aimed to substantially change the system. However, there were also some secondary objectives, which, while also quite important, were not so clearly spelled out or were not consistently pursued. Objectives such as giving priority to areas relevant to the national economy or the pursuit of quality were many times sacrificed to the dominant objective of improving participation in higher education at any cost.

It is obvious that the theory underlying the reforms was seriously flawed or at least some of its basic assumptions were wrong. The idea that free private initiative associated with market regulation would provide a diversified higher education system more responsive to the needs of the regions and the demands of the more disadvantaged population sectors (Franco 1994) was mere wishful thinking.

And the political decision of implementing the polytechnic network "was not underpinned by any credible forecasts of general or sectoral labour demands which were likely to result from the development dynamics of the Portuguese economy" (Amaral el al. 2000: 21). The World Bank's recommendation to limit access to university education in favour of shorter degrees, based on a perspective of a world division of labour, was not adequately implemented, and later the World Bank recognised that it had led to a scarcity of engineers (Teixeira, Amaral and Rosa 2003).

The fact that successive ministers of education had different ideological commitments to the development of the private sector, as well as some distrust of private higher education, also played a negative role in the implementation of this policy. On the other hand, although the initial definition of the role and objectives of the polytechnics was quite clear, they have become increasingly blurred due to academic drift. Several changes of the legal framework have made less distinct the differences between polytechnics and universities without reinforcing the social standing of polytechnics.

It is evident that different actors had different degrees of commitment to the various objectives of the reforms. Sometimes the objectives of different actors were even quite different from those of the government.

The private sector was "characterised mostly by its low-risk behaviour, and its peculiar responsiveness in terms of market *stimuli* that favoured concentration in low-cost and/or *safer* initiatives" and "it was more frequent to observe either a duplication of public supply, or a rapid expansion (but not its launching) of low-cost disciplines, in both cases in areas with a strong demand" (Teixeira and Amaral 2001: 390–391). This resulted in the expansion of the private sector in areas that were not a priority of the government.

Not all actors shared a common idea of the role and objectives of polytechnics. After 1986, governments began to emphasise the need of polytechnics to "develop professional knowledge which was better adapted to production" in opposition to the "more theoretical and abstract knowledge imparted by the universities ..." (Amaral et al. 2000: 24). However, most polytechnics proclaimed their role as "providers of local services, connected through their curricula to local realities" as a rhetorical device while in reality offering study programmes covering "an array of disciplinary and technological areas of knowledge which were identical to the initial training programmes of the new universities, or of the schools of engineering and management/economics of the more traditional universities" (Amaral et al. 2000: 23).

As one of the objectives of the implementation of the private sector was increasing enrolments without additional public costs, no significant public funds were provided for the development of private institutions. This placed the private sector at a serious disadvantage in relation to the public sector because of the difference in tuition fees. One may say that the private sector could only develop as it did because at the time students had no alternative. On the other hand, the government provided adequate financial resources for public polytechnics, both for investment in physical infrastructure as well as for running expenses. Public polytechnics were provided with new buildings properly equipped, and with a large number of scholarships for the upgrading of the academic qualifications of their staff.

Recently there has been a drastic change in social conditions. A constant decrease in the number of candidates to higher education has led to a situation where the number of vacancies clearly exceeds the number of candidates. Economic conditions have changed from a relatively comfortable economic situation to one of economic recession which has strongly influenced governmental priorities from unfettered expansion to a decrease in enrolments and strong emphasis on quality, thus creating additional problems for a private sector already under stress. Like the private sector, polytechnics were also strongly affected by the recent change in governmental priorities. Being seen as 'second choice institutions' their low capacity to attract students will place them in a difficult situation as competition for students increases.

Finally, we may say that both policies have presented mixed results, one of the major problems being the difficulty of consistently implementing the policies because different actors and successive ministers did not share the same values and ideology, and because social and economic reality has changed over the years.

NOTES

[1] Known in Portuguese as the 'Vestibular' year.

[2] Figure 1 illustrates quite well that without the new secondary education reform the number of candidates would follow approximately the broken line, thus warning institutions two years in advance that the number of candidates was starting to decrease.

[3] Decree-Law 61/78, of 28 July, further clarified this expression stating that the goal was to train "high level technicians and professionals of education" (see also Simão and Costa 2000: 20).

[4] Following Marginson (1998), positional goods are social positional goods that tend to be monopolised by those social groups in a better situation to compete.

[5] APESP is an association of owners of private higher education institutions.

[6] "In fact, the need to guarantee the competitiveness of university graduates vis-à-vis polytechnic graduates motivated the universities to increase the preparation of their students for entry onto the labour market" (CCISP 2000: 13).

REFERENCES

Amaral, A., F. Correia, A. Magalhães, M.J. Rosa, R. Santiago and P. Teixeira. *O Ensino Superior pela Mão da Economia*. Porto: CIPES, 2000.

Amaral, A. and P. Teixeira. *Previsão da evolução do número de alunos e do financiamento. Ensino superior, 1995 a 2005*. Porto: CIPES, 1999.

Amaral, A. and P. Teixeira. "The Rise and Fall of the Private Sector in Portuguese Higher Education?" *Higher Education Policy* 13.3 (2000): 245–266.

APESP. Letter to the Minister of Education. 26 November, 1998.

Bleiklie, I., R. Høstaker and A. Vabø. *Policy and Practice in Higher Education. Reforming Norwegian Universities*. London: Jessica Kingsley Publishers, 2000.

Carneiro, R. (ed.). *Free Education – A Frontier of State Hegemony*. Porto: Edições Asa, 1994.

CCISP (Conselho Coordenador dos Institutos Superiores Politécnicos). *Ensino Superior Politécnico: Algumas Reflexões*. Lisbon: CCISP, 2000.

Cerych, L. and P. Sabatier. *Great Expectations and Mixed Performance. The Implementation of Higher Education Reforms in Europe*. Stoke-on-Trent: Trentham Books, 1986.

CNASES/CEOS. *O perfil sócio-económico dos estudantes do ensino superior*. Lisbon: CNASES, 2000.

Correia, F., A. Amaral and A. Magalhães. *Diversificação e diversidade dos sistemas de ensino superior. O caso Português*. Lisbon: CNE, 2002.

Franco, A.S. "Liberdade de Aprender e de Ensinar no Âmbito das Liberdades Fundamentais: Fundamentação da Liberdade de Ensino" ("The Freedom to Learn and to Teach"). In Carneiro, R. (ed.). *Ensino Livre: Uma Fronteira da Hegemonia Estatal*. Porto: Edições Asa, 1994, 17–42.

Hirsch, F. *Social Limits to Growth*. Cambridge: Harvard University Press, 1976.

Marginson, S. "Competition and Diversity in the Reformed Australian Higher Education System." In Meek, V. Lynn and Fiona Q. Wood (eds). *Managing Higher Education Diversity in a Climate of Public Sector Reform*. Higher Education Division. Canberra: Department of Employment, Education, Training and Youth Affairs, 1998, 81–96.

OECD. *Universities Under Scrutiny*. Paris: OECD, 1987.

Programa do Governo Provisório. Lisboa, 1975, 137–144.

Seixas, Ana Maria. "'Escolas Modelo' ou 'Escolas Refúgio': Política Educativa e Representações Sociais dos Estudantes do Ensino Superior." Coimbra: Master Thesis, 1991.

Simão, J. Veiga and A. Almeida Costa. *O Ensino Politécnico em Portugal*. Report. Lisbon, 2000.

Teixeira, P. and A. Amaral. "Private Higher Education and Diversity: An Exploratory Survey." *Higher Education Quarterly* 55.4 (2001): 359–395.

Teixeira, P., A. Amaral and M.J. Rosa. "Mediating the Economic Pulses: The International Connection in Portuguese Higher Education." *Higher Education Quarterly* 57.2 (2003): 181–203.

Vargas, José Pires. "Ensino Politécnico: Via de Promoção Social ou Forma de Eliminação Diferida." University of Porto: Master Thesis, 1996.

JOSÉ-GINÉS MORA AND JAVIER VIDAL

TWO DECADES OF CHANGE IN SPANISH UNIVERSITIES: LEARNING THE HARD WAY

1. IMPLEMENTING CHANGE IN SPANISH HIGHER EDUCATION

Over the last two decades Spain has experienced a period of profound change affecting its social and economic systems. Political and economic changes have affected the higher education system considerably. These changes have taken place over a short period of time creating a dynamic situation. Two main legal reforms have been implemented (1983 and 2001) and both have had an important impact on the whole system. These reforms are not isolated from other policies, and have been affected by the political context or the so-called *external events* (see Sabatier in this volume). For the organisation of higher education, the most important influence was the transition to democracy and the new concept of the state in Spain. The top-down culture of Spanish implementation policies has undergone an important change: regionalisation. This new model of state organisation is still being established. The change is not a move from the top-down perspective to the bottom-up one, but a change in the role of actors and in the definition of where is 'the top'.

Using the revised Advocacy Coalition Framework of Sabatier (this volume), it can be said that there has been a strong top-down implementation approach with few coalitions; that the context has been very dynamic with few stable exogenous variables; and that the role of academics has been a key factor, introducing both the collective perspective and the distortion of the individual perspective mentioned by Sabatier.

The two main issues in higher education policy affected by this change are university governance and regionalisation discussed below in sections 3 and 4 respectively. Another important factor has been the remarkable increase in resources for higher education, examined in section 5, but it seems this has been inadequate. In addition to these more general issues, some specific topics in higher education have been selected for analyses in this chapter. First, in section 6, the chapter looks at the human resources: the role, selection and promotion of academic staff. Second, curriculum design and the impact of the Bologna process are discussed in section 7 followed by an examination of quality assurance and accreditation in section 8. But before beginning these discussions, the chapter presents a brief historical outline.

Å. Gornitzka et al. (eds.), Reform and Change in Higher Education, 135-152.

2. RECENT HISTORY: FROM THE LRU (1983) TO THE LOU (2001)

Under the influence of the Catholic Church, Spanish universities, the oldest of which was founded in the Middle Ages, remained relatively unchanged until the eighteenth century. At the beginning of the nineteenth century, liberalism stemming from the French Revolution changed the structure of the state. Under the 'Napoleonic' system of higher education adopted by Spain, the universities were state agencies, totally regulated by laws and norms issued by the state. Everything in the daily functioning of a higher education institution was controlled by the application of external rules, applicable to all educational institutions. Until very recently, academic programmes were identical in all institutions: they had the same curricula and there were no differences even in the syllabi. Universities had no specific budgets and expenditure was regulated by the state down to the smallest detail.

This strictly regulated higher education system was also an elitist system whose main goal was to prepare the ruling elite of the modern state, especially the civil servants. Spanish universities had a strong professional orientation. The teaching process was focused on the transmission of skills essential to the development of professions, many of which were in the state structure.

The situation described above began to change during the 1970s, when the system started to shift from an elite system to mass higher education. Legal changes helped trigger a complete transformation of the higher education system. After the restoration of democracy and the promulgation of the new Constitution in 1978, the transformation of the universities was one of the main political objectives of both academics and politicians. The first major change in the educational system was the reform of higher education. In 1983 the *University Reform Act* (*Ley de Reforma Universitaria*, hereafter referred to as LRU) was passed, resulting in a profound transformation of the Spanish higher education system. The LRU formed the basis for the process of emancipation of higher education from the control of the state, as occurred in other European countries during this decade (Neave and Van Vught 1991). The main changes introduced by this Act were (García-Garrido 1992; Mora 1997a; Sanchez-Ferrer 1997):

- universities became autonomous entities with the capacity to establish their own programmes and curricula;
- professors were no longer part of a national body and began to 'belong' to each university;
- responsibility for universities was transferred to regional governments;
- institutions began to receive public appropriations as a lump sum, and to have wide-ranging capabilities in allocating funds internally.

It is worthwhile to point out that there was not only a shift of formal control from the government to the institutions, as happened in other countries (Woodhouse 1996), but also a movement from the central government to the regional governments.

More recently, three factors have led Spanish universities to face new circumstances:

- a new legal framework drawn up by the central government towards the end of 2001 (*Ley de Ordenación Universitaria*, hereafter referred to as LOU);
- the Bologna Declaration, affecting all European higher education systems;
- the decrease in the number of students as a consequence of the dramatic fall in the birthrate.

The LOU made certain changes to the legal structure of higher education. Among the most noteworthy features of the Act were: a) the incorporation of some lay persons (always a minority group) into the running of the university; b) election of the rector by direct vote (as opposed to being appointed indirectly by the senate); c) an increase in academic staff representation in the collegial bodies (reducing the former high representation of students); d) the requirement that academic staff obtain national qualifications before being appointed by universities; and e) the obligatory post hoc accreditation of study programmes by the new National Agency for Quality Assessment and Accreditation (ANECA).

In general, the Act gives both universities and autonomous regions more independence to organise themselves as they wish. This is a positive feature because it allows both universities and regions to develop their own legal regulations and adapt them to the new situation. Perhaps this could have been done without the LOU, but the Act has created the need to rethink the new situation. Many university statutes will improve if they are adapted to the new situation, which is very different from that which existed at the end of the Franco dictatorship 20 years ago. Moreover, the autonomous regions are starting to draw up their own university laws and regulations in addition to setting up their own agencies to assess the quality of teaching and institutions. This new situation is interesting insofar as it will allow the differentiation and improvement of those universities which fulfil two conditions: their heads must be interested in promoting change and they must be located in autonomous regions whose governors are also concerned about the competitiveness of their universities. It is still too soon to assess the initial results, but it can already be seen that some regions are doing more than others.

Despite the process of decentralisation and autonomy carried out over the last two decades, problems have not been fully resolved and conflicts are relatively frequent. Below, some of the crucial factors behind these conflicts are analysed.

3. UNIVERSITY GOVERNANCE: THE ENDLESS DEBATE

3.1. A Peculiar Concept of Autonomy

The 1978 Spanish Constitution allowed for the autonomy of universities contained in the LRU. Following the LRU, universities were no longer dependent on the state and became collegial structures. Decision-making power was transferred to collegiate bodies in which non-academic staff and students constituted a considerable proportion (roughly, one third). The university senate also had considerable power, including the election of the rector. Boards, with large numbers of members, make decisions in faculties and departments, and elect deans and heads of departments. The Social Council (based on the pattern of boards of trustees in other university systems) was established as an external body to represent the wider interests of society in the university. Nevertheless, the real influence of this body is quite limited, due to a lack of tradition and to an unclear legal definition of its role. According to the criteria used by McDaniel (1996), Spanish universities have a similar level of autonomy to those of the Netherlands and Sweden, less than Anglo-Saxon countries, but higher than that of most European continental countries.

As a consequence of an action against the LRU by a regional government, a judgment of the Constitutional Court interpreted that autonomy was a prerogative of the 'university community' (i.e. staff and students) instead of a privilege of the 'institution' itself. This interpretation of the Constitutional Court (incidentally, mostly composed of university professors at that time) has had at least two perverse effects. First, it has prevented external bodies, such as the Social Council, from representing the interests of the community – external influence goes against this peculiar idea of autonomy. Second, it has given excessive power to academics in the full control of institutions.

In addition to governing universities, the main responsibility for managing institutions also rests with academics. Although some institutions hire professional managers for some managerial positions, they are always in dependent positions. Most of the decision-making power rests with academics temporarily occupying a managerial post. There is no evidence that academics have sufficient managerial knowledge or training. On the contrary, in general, they have no experience in the management of any type of large organisation. The results are usually far from being a model of good practice.

The democratic development of Spanish universities at the beginning of the 1980s was necessary to shake off old bureaucratic structures and reduce direct interference from the state. Nevertheless, in this new scheme, academics act in many cases as a guild which is more concerned with how to defend its own interests than with serving the community and students. As McDaniel (1997) points out, the move from direct state intervention to institutional autonomy should be accompanied by other factors, such as competitiveness (for students, staff, funds and reputation), diversification of resources and increasing client power and social responsibility of institutions. These factors have not been sufficiently adopted by Spanish universities for two reasons: first, there is a lack of tradition of serving the community. Coming from a bureaucratic model, universities and staff (mostly civil servants) consider themselves more as belonging to a branch of the public administration than as part of an institution serving the community; second, there is a lack of governmental policies on higher education. Regional governments, with few exceptions, have not been able to define higher education policies, establish goals for public institutions or require universities to achieve specific objectives.

3.2. A New Model for the New Millennium?

By the end of the 1990s, all academic analysts and politicians were aware of the need for change in the legal structure of higher education. After two decades of change, the situation was analysed in numerous seminars all over the country and in a wide variety of publications. Proposals were put forward to reform the legal structure of Spanish universities. The Conference of Spanish University Rectors (CRUE) commissioned a study on the situation and the need for reform, which resulted in the Bricall Report (Bricall 2001). The report gathered the opinions of administrators and managers, and funding, quality and teaching experts. The report was highly acclaimed by experts, but it was subtly rejected by university heads who considered its proposals too revolutionary. They were particularly against the report's proposal to set up a governing body for universities with a considerable proportion (49%) of lay persons. Before its publication (when the content of the report was known only to those who commissioned it, i.e., the rectors), there were student demonstrations protesting against it. The reasons for such a reaction were clear to see: the leaders of some universities regarded this report as a danger to the status quo of their universities.

On the other hand, politicians running for election in 2000 had an agenda which included the reform of the LRU. All parties considered it to be a politically essential requirement. The Socialist Party candidate even stated that the Bricall Report would form the basis of his higher education policy. However, the Conservative Party won the election and put forward its own proposals for a new law.

The new LOU made only slight changes in the legal structure of universities: a) the incorporation of three lay persons in the Governing Board of the university; b) election of the rector by direct vote (as opposed to being appointed indirectly by the senate); and c) an increase in academic staff representation, which created a slight reduction in student representation. Although these were not major changes, they were not well received by most university and student leaders, who considered them to be an attack on university autonomy and university democracy. In that the Act contained such minor aspects and unambitious reforms, it did not attract the support of those most interested in change. The debate was reduced to markedly political, simplistic wrangling in the press along with some street demonstrations. The Act was eventually passed but all experts considered that it did not go far enough. They believed that the Act would only bring about a few major improvements, coupled with some negative effects. The overall impression was that it would make very little difference to the Spanish higher education system.

The conflict over university governance in Spanish universities raises several questions: What is the meaning of university autonomy? What should be the role of government in steering higher education? What should be the role of academics in governing and managing universities? Public debate on these questions only started recently in Spain and experts agree that finding correct answers is one of the most important problems facing Spanish universities. Nevertheless, this debate is extremely complicated and associated with a number of political and sociological factors. It comes as no surprise that there is tension as Neave (1997a: 9) envisaged:

> ... from 1983 onwards reform in Spanish higher education has successively tackled issues which, elsewhere in Western Europe, were spaced out, and dealt with, over a quarter century ... I am suggesting that the move from reform justified in the name of

participant democracy to the rigours of competition and economic efficiency is likely to
be a source of considerable tension, and not only in academia.

Six years after the establishment of the LRU, the Spanish government asked an
international team of experts to assess the reform. This team's report (ISCED 1989)
presented an extraordinary insight into the potential dangers of the reform. Though
at the time they only identified potential dangers, their warnings have proven
prophetic indeed.

4. REGIONALISATION: A POSITIVE MOVE?

4.1. The Increase in the 'Political Value' of Universities

Higher education has always had a substantial regional dimension, especially in
recruiting students (Neave 1994). Nevertheless, the importance of regions in
European policy making is relatively recent. Generally speaking, to adapt
universities to regional needs may be a positive step but may also create problems.
The Spanish case, in which regionalisation of universities has been a very fast and
far-reaching process, provides a good example of some of the dangers of
regionalisation.

In Spain, there are fifty public universities distributed in seventeen regions. In
the smallest regions, universities are the most important institution after the regional
government. Universities have become highly valued by politicians due to their
social relevance. Governments and politicians tend to influence the internal
government of institutions, including the election of rectors. On the other hand,
rectors sometimes use their position to develop a political career. Under the current
system for electing rectors, the actual political ability of the candidate is the basic
requirement needed to win an election. Political conflicts are more frequent than
what is desirable. In the largest regions, where there are several universities, these
problems are perhaps less relevant, but still present.

The excessive political pressure on universities is in itself serious, mainly
because it impedes a reasonable solution to the problem of the excessive power of
academics as previously mentioned. The reluctance of academics to relinquish full
institutional control can be explained, in part, by a reasonable fear of an excessive
and direct role by politicians in university affairs. It is necessary to find a sensible
way of combining an increase in the community's influence on the governing of
universities with a reduction in partisan political interest.

Universities depend on eighteen authorities (one central and seventeen regional
governments) with different political ideologies and irregular knowledge of what
higher education is and what it should be. Although universities need not be closely
coordinated under a single competitive system, common goals for the whole public
higher education sector should be stated and developed. The correct functioning of
the system, especially in the context of growing internationalisation, requires
coordination of many aspects such as student aid, mobility of students and
academics, quality assessment procedures and many other areas that are more
efficiently managed across institutions and regions. Currently, the Council of

University Coordination (formerly Council of Universities), where rectors and regional representatives meet, is the coordinating body. Nevertheless, its real decision capacity is very weak due to the conflicts among the excessive number and type of stakeholders. Political confrontations are hindering many initiatives and are impeding the development of higher education policies. Ironically, regionalisation has increased the political value of universities but has weakened the capacity of government to steer public higher education not only in terms of a 'supervisory state' (in the sense of Neave and Van Vught 1991), but also as a 'facilitator state'.

4.2. Institutional Differentiation or Competition?

Mass higher education has been achieved by geographical expansion of the higher education system throughout the country: from fourteen universities in the late 1960s (mostly in the big cities) to the current almost seventy public and private institutions spread over the country. This process has reduced the direct costs of higher education for students, making universities more economically accessible, but has also reduced student mobility. New universities, which are clones of the old ones, tend to offer the same programmes and services. Moreover, all universities are research oriented, something that is both inefficient and ineffective in a mass higher education system, particularly when there is no alternative to universities. It seems that most of the stakeholders in Spanish higher education do not realise that mass higher education necessarily implies differentiation (Meek et al. 1996). Consequently, nobody is promoting differentiation, increasing competitiveness or taking whatever action necessary to make the whole system more oriented to the diversity of social needs.

There is little student mobility because of cultural traditions and the lack of an efficient student aid programme. Universities have a 'captive student audience' because young people always attend the closest university irrespective of the quality of its academic programmes. Consequently, most universities are not interested in differentiation and in student mobility because these would result in undesirable competition.

In principle, it is reasonable to assume that regionalisation will increase differentiation (Neave 1997b). Ironically, regionalisation is not promoting differentiation in Spain. On the contrary, each region, and in many cases each university, wants to have a complete range of teaching programmes and research activities. When each region is considered as a higher education system (irrespective of the size and number of universities), differentiation among universities is unlikely.

A final danger of regionalisation is the possibility of increasing parochialism. Universality is at the core of the concept of the university, but when regions finance and monitor universities there is a danger that this concept is damaged. When regions want a university system based entirely on students and academics from the region, and when they promote research mostly on regional issues, parochialism may be the result. It is difficult to evaluate to what extent this problem is affecting regional universities, but intuition supports the idea that this phenomenon is rather more frequent than what is desirable. Certainly, some university activity must be regionally oriented, and universities should be an economic engine in their regions. Nevertheless, a reasonable balance between these duties and the consubstantial goal of universities to look for universal knowledge and a broad perspective must be found.

5. THE FINANCIAL SYSTEM: INADEQUATE GROWTH

Before the LRU, expenditure in public universities was merely an item in the central government budget. The LRU instigated a profound financial change. Under the current financial model, regional governments grant funds to universities as a lump sum. Universities are free as to how they allocate these funds internally. However, universities control neither the main expenditure item (salaries, which are determined by the central government) nor the main sources of income (public allocations and tuition fees, which are established by regional governments).

In general, the total amount of funds allocated to universities has increased enormously. In 1985 the total expenditure on higher education was only 0.54 per cent of GDP; in 2000 it reached 1.2 per cent of GDP (OECD 2003). However, there are special features that need clarification in order to understand how the budget is distributed. Firstly, there is the relative importance of resources set aside to fund new teaching and research infrastructure. During the 1990s, greater efforts were made to invest in the higher education system in order to solve one of its key problems: the shortage of buildings and equipment. In 2000, Spain allocated to capital investment 20.6 per cent of total expenditure on higher education, which was quite higher than the average in OECD countries (11.6 per cent).

Secondly, most of the current expenditure in Spanish higher education institutions is on staff salaries. As mentioned above, this is one aspect of expenditure which universities have little control over since salaries are set by central government and, to a lesser extent, by regional governments. This is an important factor because it means that only a small percentage of recurrent resources can be set aside for expenses other than staff salaries, in particular, funds to purchase goods and services.

Thirdly, the role of private sector funding has increased during the 1990s. In 1991, approximately 20 per cent of funding came from the private sector. This percentage increased to 25.8 per cent in 1999. It is important to mention that during this period of growth in Spain, private funding in other EU countries fell. In 1995 average private sector funding in EU countries was 15.6 per cent of total expenditure, in 1999 the figure had fallen to 13.8 per cent.

Finally, an important and controversial feature of higher education funding in Spain is the lack of resources set aside to provide financial aid to students. Student grant expenditure in 1999 was only $436 per student (corrected by Purchasing Power Parity), which is only 0.08 per cent relative to GDP. Such scant funding of grants to students is due both to the nature of the financial aid system itself and the inadequacy of funds provided to students who gain access to higher education. The grant system is still administered by the central government.

6. ACADEMIC STAFF: (CIVIL) SERVANTS OF MANY MASTERS

Before the LRU, the internal organisation of universities was extremely hierarchical. Departments did not exist and the basic unit was the chair. The LRU significantly changed the situation. The main structural changes were as follows:

- Departments, with several professors working together and sharing teaching and research activities, replaced the former individual chairs.
- Professors became members of a university, and could only move to other institutions through open competition.
- An increase in academic staff salaries, making an academic career more competitive from an economic point of view.

The legal changes implemented during the 1980s have profoundly shaped the current structure of the Spanish academic profession. The hierarchical system, based on the individual power of the chairholder and the excessive influence of the national guild of chairholders, collapsed. Old academics claim that the profession has lost prestige and social recognition. This is probably true but it is mostly due to the simple fact that the number of professors has grown enormously as a result of the move towards a mass higher education system.

6.1. Too Many Masters

Nevertheless, the LRU did not change the legal status of academics. Academics, at least those in stable positions, are still civil servants and members of national bodies. There is a deep contradiction between the determination of the employment status of academics and university autonomy. For instance, candidates for tenured positions in one university are selected by a committee consisting of members of the national body of professors, that is, by members of other (perhaps competing) universities. Hence, the selection of personnel in one autonomous and independent university is dependent on decisions undertaken by members of other universities.

Personnel matters are a perfect example of the conflicts among intervening institutions. On the one hand, the central government decides on general personnel policies (basic structure, workload and salaries) while regional governments are responsible for financing universities and indirectly for the payroll in public universities. Yet the employees in universities are mostly civil servants with salaries and working conditions defined by the central government. In addition, universities can establish their own personnel policies, such as the number of staff allocations by category or staff workload. In fact, decisions taken by universities are made by the staff through their collegiate boards. Eventually, decisions on staff numbers made by universities and decisions on salaries made by the central government have direct ramifications for costs that regional governments have to meet. It is obvious that such a complex, four-level structure of decision making on university personnel issues is inevitably a permanent source of conflict and discord. Fortunately, though these conflicts are permanent, they are less virulent than one might expect of such a potentially volatile structure.

There is also another relevant consequence of retaining civil servant status for academics. Salaries and working conditions of academics are fixed at the national level for all members of the national body of professors (with differences according to appointment level). Commitment to work, higher productivity or superior outputs cannot be negotiated and rewarded at the individual level because inclusion in the national body means the same rules for all members. How to reward the different levels of performance? In Spain, the solution adopted by the LRU was to allow academics to carry out 'external' activities in addition to their 'civil servant' activities. Academics are allowed to engage in extramural activities such as teaching a continuing education course (sometimes in another university), contracting for applied research services or consultancy, or organising any other activity that is more or less related to the profession. There are rules establishing limits to these activities but they are not very restrictive. This mix between 'civil servant activities' and 'market activities' of Spanish academics has contradictory consequences. On the one hand, it has been a stimulus for most active academics to engage in many diverse entrepreneurial activities, satisfying social demands that institutions by themselves are not able to meet, at least not with enough flexibility. Also, engaging in such activities substantially increases academics' salaries. On the other hand, the system has several shortcomings. Firstly, institutions do not receive (at least, not as much as they should) the benefits of academics' extramural activities. Although academics may have to pay a small overhead to their host institution, their extramural activities may be carried out in other institutions competing with their own institution. Secondly, in many cases this system compels academics to look for earnings external to their core academic duties. There is a potential danger in having academics too involved in externally paid 'market' activities, for these commitments may overshadow their main research and teaching duties.

As expected, the LOU has maintained the civil servant structure, although it allows regional governments to create new positions for academics without civil servant status. However, so far, the regional governments that have introduced these positions have only created middle-ranking posts with the exception of the Catalonian and Castilla-Leon governments which have created a contract position at the level of full professor. This limitation inevitably makes this new employment avenue a second-class, less desirable, option for academics.

6.2. Selection and Promotion: Another Endless Debate

The way in which teaching staff are selected and promoted is one of the most substantial changes brought in under the LOU. It is therefore worth examining the old and the new selection and promotion systems in order to analyse the differences between them.

According to the LRU, the basic system for obtaining a civil servant position was (and still is) similar for all types of professors. When there was a vacancy in a tenured position, or a university decided to create a new position, a public call for applicants ensued. The advertised position would be open to anyone who satisfied the academic requirements. A selection committee composed of five members would be established to select the candidate. The university would appoint two members to this committee, following the recommendation of the relevant department. The other three members would be appointed through a random process in which only professors in the same field from other public universities were eligible. The committee would hold a public session where candidates presented their case. After closed discussions, the committee would make its recommendations.

Universities created new positions following departmental requests. In many cases, departments only made this request when they had a 'suitable internal candidate' who fulfilled the academic requirements and who had a reasonable chance of success. If there were no internal disputes, the local candidate (i.e. the favourite of the department) had a better chance (around 95 per cent of the positions are obtained by the 'favourite local' candidate). It is obvious that this selection procedure concealed a dangerous trend towards endogamy. What is the reason for this trend towards endogamy in Spanish universities? Departments are run by their staff who decide when and how to promote members. If no external control is exerted and/or there are no incentives to maintain the high standard of the department, there is a logical trend towards promoting close colleagues instead of bringing in new people who may destabilise the internal status quo. The quality of academic staff has suffered as a result of this system since good internal relations have been the main criteria for selection and promotion, above professional values relating to teaching and research abilities.

The most significant change in the selection and promotion of academic staff, and that which has caused the greatest uproar under the new Act, is the national *habilitation* of academic staff (to some extent, the system is similar to the model used in France). Applicants for professorships must undergo a test conducted by a seven-member national committee. Only those who pass the test (and numbers are limited to the number of university vacancies) can be selected by a university. This new system has had two immediate effects which highlight the corrupt nature of the previous system. Before the Act came into effect (in December 2001), universities announced around 10,000 vacant posts for new professors (out of a total of 50,000 established positions). The scale and speed with which this endogamic mechanism was set in motion to guarantee that the 'candidates with contacts' managed to pull strings and get jobs before the new Act came into effect are a clear sign of just how corrupt the old system was. Only 200 new positions have been announced since the Act came into effect (at the end of 2001). Although the first examinations have not yet taken place, for some positions more than 100 people have applied for a habilitation. This may be because all the applicants who were sufficiently well qualified but who were rejected by the previous system because they lacked the internal, extra-professional support required to be considered for the post, have now begun to apply. Now, universities will fill their vacant teaching posts by choosing who they consider to be the most suitable candidate for the post from those applicants who are 'habilitated'.

The new selection system may avoid some of the problems of the previous one, but it will create others. One negative effect is that it will do away with multidisciplinarity. The new national habilitation committees are made up of professors from each area of knowledge. It is unlikely that these committees will select people from outside the core subject field. Although it is still too soon to judge, the new system does not appear to have any advantage over other selection systems successfully used elsewhere, such as in Anglo-Saxon countries.

7. CURRICULA REFORMS: THE DISGRACE OF STARTING TOO EARLY

7.1. First Round: The Early 1990s

After the LRU, all types of higher education institutions became part of universities. There are three basic types of university degrees: three-year degree courses (*diplomatura*) which are more vocationally oriented; five- and six-year degree courses (*licenciatura* and *engineering*); and doctoral programmes which contain two years of coursework and require the preparation of a research-oriented thesis. The traditional organisation of coursework in Spanish universities was a consequence of the centralised system which existed before the LRU. Curricula were fixed, were almost identical in every university, and contained a very limited number of options. Courses were also strongly based on theory, to the detriment of practical aspects. The rigidity of this system was evident. Adaptability to society's needs, to students' curricular demands and to the variability of labour market demands necessitated substantial reform of the curriculum. This process of reform began in the late eighties when basic national criteria for new curricula were established. The aim of the curricula reform was to adapt the system to the new situation, introducing a new teaching and learning style which was to be more focused on practical lectures and tutorials, more flexible, and more suited to social needs. Consequently, the new curricula have a modular structure, courses are mostly delivered in semesters, the proportion of optional courses has increased and practical content has been extended in every course.

The main guidelines of the reform were designed by national committees of experts in each field who set the bases for the new curricula. These committees did a reasonable job in establishing the bases for the new curricula. Universities were given extensive freedom to develop detailed curricula based on their own objectives. Ad hoc committees for each degree in each university developed these guidelines. However, conflict arose in these committees over what was in the interests of academics (keeping and developing courses related to their field of expertise, personal interests or merely their routines), and the necessity to adapt curricula to new requirements. In most cases, academics eventually imposed their own interests. In addition, when the new curricula started to be implemented most academics did not fully realise that the old model of teaching and learning was obsolete. They considered the reform as a mere reorganisation of old programmes. The result of the process is that new curricula are still too 'theoretical and knowledge oriented', practical sessions are in many cases just a prolongation of theoretical lectures, semester courses are just the compression of a longer course, courses are sometimes more related to teachers' expertise than to the real needs of students, students have too many hours of lectures, and so on. In brief, the interests of academics (most of whom did not have a thorough understanding of the goals of the reform) were excessively favoured. In the late 1990s, a counter-reform took place in the hope of correcting the more obvious failings of the previous one, but precious time has been wasted due to a lack of understanding of the mass higher education system and the excessive power of academics in universities.

7.2. Second Round: The Bologna Process

One of the negative effects of the LOU (although in this case unintentional) has been that it has halted the Bologna process in Spain. During 2001 and 2002, universities devoted a large proportion of their time and energy to debating and adapting to the LOU. During this period the Bologna process was taken off the agenda of Spanish universities while most European countries began to make changes. Although the LOU makes general references to the Bologna process, it has only recently been 'discovered' by Spanish universities. The draft document for adapting the Spanish university system to the European space for higher education has been recently published by the government (MECD 2003). The document outlines the general guidelines and sets out the issues to be discussed in the University Coordination Council (made up of university rectors and regional education ministers). Universities are starting to introduce internal programmes to explain and discuss the new initiatives involved in this process.

Following the relative failure to implement the new syllabi as a result of the academic staff's refusal to adopt the aims of the reform, adaptation to the new European common space for higher education is considered to be an excellent opportunity to point the system in the right direction. However, two problems threaten the success of this adaptation process. Firstly, academic staff are tired of curricular reform. This is in fact a serious problem. The last decade has been one of constant curricular change. Many courses have appeared and disappeared over a short period of time, which, in turn, means that professors have been moved from one course to another. In addition, syllabi and a wide range of activities have had to be reorganised, and, in such a 'democratic' system, this involves a great many meetings and discussions. At present, adapting to the Bologna process represents a radical change in the organisation of academic life, which will once again require a similar process experienced in the last decade. It is doubtful whether academic staff will be in the right frame of mind to implement the new reform. The other problem is whether those who implement the reform fully understand it. One of the basic aims is to change the educational model from a teaching- to a learning-based model. However, the new European Credit Transfer System may simply become a different way of counting credits based on teaching hours, instead of representing a new approach to teaching. As stated previously, the reforms carried out in the early 1990s were well designed but badly implemented because academic staff were not fully aware of the objectives. Something similar could happen now unless there is an awareness campaign to illustrate the need for and the aims of the reform.

8. QUALITY ASSURANCE: A STORY WITH AN UNHAPPY ENDING

The LRU made a general statement on the necessity to incorporate some formal system of quality assessment for universities. Nevertheless, several years passed before this principle was implemented. Generalised assessment of individuals and institutions began in the early 1990s. Teaching and research activities of academics are evaluated on a regular basis. Promotion and some salary increases depend on performance assessments (Mora 2001).

Nevertheless, several years passed before quality assurance was implemented with respect to study programmes. In the early 1990s, The Experimental Program for Assessment of the Quality in the University System was launched. The programme evaluated teaching, research and institutional management in several universities. As an experimental project, the primary purpose was to try various methods and make proposals for change based on the experiences gained (García et al. 1995; Mora 1997b; Mora and Vidal 1998).

Immediately after the Experimental Program, the European Union launched the European Pilot Project for Evaluating Quality in Higher Education. This was also a pilot project for testing a common methodology among European universities. The most important result of the project was probably the recommendation made by the European Commission in 1998 (EC 1998) to establish a relatively common system of quality assessment in European universities based on the methodology of self-study and external visits. Each country could change the process in light of national characteristics. This European initiative had an important impact in Spain as it convinced some sceptical people, especially politicians from central and regional governments, to support quality assessment in universities.

Following these pilot projects, the Council of Universities established the National Program for Assessment of Quality in Universities in 1995 (Mora 1997b; Mora and Vidal 1998) with the aim of introducing a systematic assessment of universities. This programme inculcated the culture of quality among Spanish universities. In the space of only a few years, Spanish universities have set up new offices to support quality assurance programmes and thousands of people are participating in self-assessment activities and external visits around the country. Regional governments are also involved in these programmes, and have created their own quality agencies. The overall impact of these activities has been irregular: some universities and regions are very active in these matters (e.g. Catalan universities with the support of the very active Catalan Agency for Quality); in others, the impact has been lower because neither the university leaders nor the regional governments have shown any special interest in quality assurance.

In light of previous experience, the Second Plan for Quality of Universities was established in 2001 in order to continue improving the assessment process. The general objectives of the plan were to develop and improve systems for quality assessment of Spanish universities. These included the need for transparency and relevant information on the standards reached by each university which could serve as a basis for programme accreditation.

The LOU established that programmes must undergo assessment, certification and accreditation. The management of quality assurance may be carried out by the newly created ANECA or by regional agencies in their own territories. The LOU also obliges study programmes to undergo a process of accreditation in order for them to be recognised as official qualifications. This represents an important innovation in the regulation of Spanish higher education. Requirements have always had to be met in order to obtain official course approval, but no further checks followed. The accreditation of study programmes is currently in an experimental design phase and it will be at least several years before it is implemented.

Our main conclusion is that the move towards quality assurance in Spanish universities is recent but positive. In just a few years quality has been formally implemented in the higher education system and in the daily dealings of a growing number of institutions. Nevertheless, there are many weak points that should be emphasised (Mora and Vidal 2000). Quality assessment for all its success is threatened by two dangers: bureaucratisation and frustration.

A centrally organised process of this nature could be considered by some people as an additional, formal, and perhaps unnecessary, requirement. The danger is that the process may become too bureaucratic. The capacity of the ANECA and other regional agencies to develop a dynamic structure to overcome these problems is crucial to circumventing this threat. The first moves of the ANECA are not optimistic. Those responsible for the ANECA, recently appointed by the minister with a strong political bias, do not seem to cover the needs required of a reliable leadership that will develop a sound and credible accreditation system. On the contrary, the first actions of this agency and the rush to implement new activities (including accreditation) are provoking a negative reaction to the culture of quality that can spoil the previous ten years of improvements.

Implementation of recommendations and process follow-up are also essential. If people involved in the assessment and the university community in general do not feel that this is a worthwhile activity, with substantial consequences and rewards, growing feelings of frustration with the process could be a real danger.

9. CONCLUSIONS ... FOR FURTHER DEBATE

Within a specific environmental context, a system can be defined by a set of components and the interrelationships within it. In this respect, it can be said that the higher education system in Spain has changed in several ways.

Firstly, new actors and new components have arisen. The regional governments have emerged based on the fundamental principles of the new democratic Spanish Constitution (1978). Nearly all the competencies in education were transferred from the central government to the regional governments. That was not a specific educational reform, but a reorganisation of the whole state. In addition to the decentralisation of administration, the quality and accreditation agencies have emerged within the new organisation of the state, but with an unclear distribution of power and responsibility between the national and the regional governments. In this case, the reform has been a specific educational reform.

Secondly, the environment has changed. The new environment includes Europe as a whole. This is not the result of a Spanish educational initiative, but a consequence of the much desired entrance of Spain into the international political context. The most important aspects of the change are yet to come.

Thirdly, the most important change involves relations among old and new actors within the old and new environment. And, from our point of view, here rests the most important problems that the Spanish higher education system faces. There has been a decentralisation process where the relations among all the actors have changed. Despite a recent reform (LOU), it can be said that there is still not a very efficient distribution of responsibilities. Some examples of this imbalance are the selection of academic staff, the design of study programmes and the quality assurance processes. The three have a great impact on the whole system.

With respect to the selection of academic staff, the central government controls the process for the two main groups (civil servants and non-civil servants). In both cases, a previous positive evaluation is needed in order to apply for a position in a university. Tension arises because regional governments have no control over the criteria for those evaluations, but they pay the bill for all university personnel. This is the most important debate in Spanish higher education policy, with significant social consequences.

In terms of study programmes, the national government designs around 70% of the total curriculum. Hence, most of the curriculum is compulsory for all the students at Spanish universities. The universities design the rest. Regional governments have nothing to do with curriculum design. They can decide whether or not to approve a programme but, once they do, they have to pay the consequences of what has been decided by the national government and universities.

Since 1996, Spanish universities have been developing the Plan for the Quality of Universities. The main aim of this plan was the implementation of the improvement proposals. Now, a new concept has arisen: accreditation of programmes. And universities are very aware (and worried) of the consequences of the accreditation process, as might be expected. The ANECA is in charge of accreditation, but quality assurance is the responsibility of regional quality agencies too. The role of accreditation and quality assurance in the improvement of quality of higher education is not yet clear. In this case, unresolved overlap is creating many difficulties.

In the implementation of most of these policies, academics have had an excessive influence on the role of the higher education system. This excessive influence is a consequence of the limited influence of other agents. On the one hand, there has been a lack of a resolute introduction of market forces into the higher education system. On the other hand, there has been a lack of consistent public policy on higher education due to the fragmentation of the public system. This situation has not stimulated universities to be more responsive to social needs. On the contrary, universities have been concerned about maintaining their privileges.

The problem for our policy implementation analysis is not to find whether there is a top-down or a bottom-up approach. The debate is about where is '*the top*'; is it at the national, the regional or the institutional level? In the decentralisation process the central government has attempted to recoup some of its lost power using legal reforms, rather than consensus. This strategy is not an isolated case – it is not only a problem for higher education, but is an aspect of a larger debate concerning the organisation of the new decentralised state. In the end, most of the conflict comes from an unresolved tension among the three main groups of actors: universities, regional governments and central government.

REFERENCES

Bricall, J.M. *Universidad 2000*. Madrid: CRUE, 2001.
Clark, B.R. *The Higher Education System: Academic Organisation in Cross-National Perspective*, Berkeley: University of California Press, 1983.
Clark, B.R. "Diversification, Competitive Autonomy, and Institutional Initiative in Higher Education Systems." In Herbst, M., G. Latzel and L. Lutz (eds). *Wandel im tertiären Bildungs-sektor*. VDF Hochschulverlag AG an der ETH Zürich, 1997, 37–42.
EC. "Recommendation." 1998, http://europa.eu.int/eur-lex/es/archive/.
García, P., J.G. Mora, J.J. Pérez and S. Rodríguez. "Experimenting with Institutional Evaluation in Spain." *Higher Education Management* 7.1 (1995): 111–118.
García-Garrido, J.L. "Spain." In Clark, Burton R. and Guy Neave (eds). *The Encyclopedia of Higher Education, vol. 1, National Systems of Higher Education*. Oxford: Pergamon Press, 1992, 663–675.
ISCED. *The Spanish University Reform: An Assessment Report*. Madrid: Consejo de Universidades, 1989.
McDaniel, O.C. "The Paradigms of Governance in Higher Education Systems." *Higher Education Policy* 9.2 (1996): 137–158.
McDaniel, O.C. "Les établissements d'enseignement superieur peuvent-ils se passer de l'intervention de l'Etat?" *Gestion de l'enseignement superieur* 9.2 (1997): 129–149.
MECD. 2003, http://www.univ.mecd.es/.
Meek, V.L., L. Goedegebuure, O. Kivinen and R. Rinne (eds). *The Mockers and Mocked: Comparative Perspectives on Diversity, Differentiation and Convergence in Higher Education*. Oxford: Pergamon, 1996.
Mora, J.G. "Market Trends in Spanish Higher Education." *Higher Education Policy* 10.3/4 (1997a): 187–198.
Mora, J.G. "Institutional Evaluation in Spain: An On-going Process." *Higher Education Management* 9.1 (1997b): 59–70.
Mora, J.G. "La situación del profesorado universitario en una perspectiva internacional: algunas conclusiones." In Mora, J.G. (ed.). *El profesorado universitario: la situación en España y las tendencias internacionales*. Madrid: Consejo de Universidades, 2000, 207–213.
Mora, J.G. "The Academic Profession in Spain: Between the Civil Service and the Market." *Higher Education* 41.1/2 (2001): 131–155.
Mora, J.G. and J. Vidal. "Introducing Quality Assurance in Spanish University." In Gaither, J. (ed.). *Quality Assurance in Higher Education, New Directions on Institutional Research*. San Francisco: Jossey-Bass, 1998, 29–38.
Mora, J.G. and J. Vidal. "Lifelong Learning in Spanish Universities: The Market Inside a Public System." *European Journal of Education* 35.3 (2000): 317–327.
Neave, G. "Redutio ad Regionem: The Swings and Roundabouts on a Side Show." Paper presented at the 12th General Conference of the IMHE Programme, Paris, 11–13 September, 1994.
Neave, G. "The Rise of the Evaluative State: The State of the Art." Paper presented at the Seminar *Retos presentes y futuros de la Universidad*. Consejo de Universidades and IVIE, Valencia, 1997a.
Neave, G. "The European Dimension in Higher Education. An Historical Analysis." Paper presented at the Conference *The Relationship Between Higher Education and the Nation-State*, Enschede, 1997b.

Neave, G. and F.A. van Vught (eds). *Prometheus Bound. The Changing Relationship Between Government and Higher Education in Western Europe*. Oxford: Pergamon Press, 1991.

OECD. *Education at a Glance*. Paris: OECD, 2003.

Sanchez-Ferrer, L. "From Bureaucratic Centralism to Self-regulation: The Reforms of Higher Education in Spain." *West European Politics* 20.3 (1997): 166–184.

Woodhouse, D. "Quality Assurance: International Trends, Preoccupations and Features." *Assessment and Evaluation in Higher Education* 21.4 (1996): 347–356.

GIUNIO LUZZATTO AND ROBERTO MOSCATI

UNIVERSITY REFORM IN ITALY: FEARS, EXPECTATIONS AND CONTRADICTIONS

1. THE CONTENTS OF THE REFORM

1.1. The Starting Point

During the last third of the past century, higher education in all developed countries, including Italy, experienced a dramatic increase in student numbers. From 1965 to 1995, enrolments in Italian higher education went from 298,000 students to 1,116,000 – nearly a fourfold increase.

However, there was no significant change in the structure of the higher education system. During the 1960s and 1970s, various reform laws were proposed, but never came to a final vote in Parliament; this was due not only to governmental instability, but also to strong academic political connections and conservatism.

Of course, minor adjustments were implemented in order to meet new needs. The number of professors substantially increased, and in 1980 their status was reorganised according to three positions: full professor, associate professor and researcher. In the same year, PhD programmes started. In 1990 a short-cycle course (*Diploma universitario*, 3 years) was added to the traditional long-cycle one (*Laurea*, 4 or 5 years). Elements of autonomy were introduced into a system traditionally highly centralised and bureaucratic: universities obtained a certain amount of freedom in defining their statutes (in 1989) and in managing their budgets (in 1993).

However, there was no autonomy at all as far as degrees and curricula were concerned. A decree by the Minister was required to establish or to change any degree. The decree covered every detail concerning the curriculum leading to the degree. The system was quite rigid.

Two indicators demonstrate the inadequacy of this system. From 1965 to 1995, the students *fuori corso*, that is, those not graduating in standard time but still enrolled at university, increased from 105,000 (one-third of regular students) to 569,000 (more than a half). This reduced the numbers graduating, with the average age at the time of graduation being between 25 and 26 years old. The proportion of drop-outs reached more than 65% in 1997.

Diplomas (short-cycle courses) brought no meaningful improvement: less than 10% of students followed diploma programmes. Their lack of attractiveness was due

153

Å. Gornitzka et al. (eds.), Reform and Change in Higher Education, 153-168.

both to the fact that diplomas were not a 'first-cycle' *Laurea* programme, and to their lack of recognition by the labour market.

Also due to unsuccessful experimentation with short-cycle courses, there has been no political effort to establish a non-university sector in higher education, except for the particular field of Arts (*Accademia* for visual arts, *Conservatorio* for music). There are experiments with postsecondary programmes (*Istruzione e Formazione Tecnica Superiore*, IFTS), and a possible expansion of IFTS is indicated in a very recent reform law of the secondary school system. However, at the moment, IFTS has very low student numbers, is present in only a few cities and has no institutional status.

1.2. The Reform Law (1997) and the following Decrees (1999–2000)

In 1997, a general higher education Reform Law was adopted. Its goal was to enable the system – whose structures still corresponded to an obsolete idea of an elite university – to fulfil new functions, and be more widely open to a dynamic world. A first objective was to overcome the negative situation outlined above. This required both a differentiation of the degrees, in order to meet different needs, and a student-centred teaching organisation, in order to lower the number of drop-outs and *fuori corso* and to have a graduation age comparable to that in the rest of Europe.

Thus, there were clear political goals to be achieved. A necessary instrument to reach them was flexibility of programmes and curricula; and flexibility required increased university autonomy. Consequently, autonomy had to be interpreted as a valuable tool, not as an end in itself.

The general objectives provided by the 1997 Law had to be specified by ministerial decrees. A committee of experts, led by Guido Martinotti, vice-rector of the University of Milano-Bicocca, was appointed to elaborate proposals for those decrees. After a few months, a report was submitted, and a debate about it started throughout the university world in Italy. While almost every academic senate, every faculty, every professor had always complained about the absence of reforms, many diverging opinions immediately came to the fore once a concrete project was put on the table.

Minister Luigi Berlinguer thought that aligning the reforms with European trends in higher education could help in overcoming internal resistance. Thus, together with French Minister Claude Allègre he seized the opportunity of a Sorbonne centennial celebration (in 1998) in order to draw up a joint statement by the Ministers of France, Germany, Italy and the United Kingdom about a common orientation in their university policies; that statement, together with the following Bologna declaration (1999), became a cornerstone on the way towards implementing the Italian reform.

A change of minister (quite frequent in Italy) brought some delay. However, continuity was ensured by Under Secretary of State Luciano Guerzoni, who was in charge of the ministerial action concerning the Reform, and finally Decree Number 509, *Regolamento recante norme concernenti l'autonomia didattica degli*

Atenei, was adopted in November 1999. The Decree organises university degrees and programmes along the following lines:

- The first degree (*Laurea*) is a prerequisite for the second degree (*Laurea specialistica*),[1] and a qualification for the labour market. Curricula may be partly differentiated, in order to orient students more towards further study or towards employability, by varying the mix of basic foundations of disciplines and of applied activities (laboratory or extramural).

- Credits, to be defined according to ECTS (European Credit Transfer System), are now part of an accumulation system, not just a transfer system, as was the case with respect to the European programmes for student mobility. The credits connected with each course are the bricks on which a 'modular' curriculum is built. Programmes are defined in terms of credits, not by their length: *Laurea* is a 180-credit programme, *Laurea specialistica* is a 300-credit programme. The specification of three, or five, years of study merely indicates the time usually required by regular full-time students to complete those programmes.

- Normally, 180 of the 300 credits needed for *Laurea specialistica* are obtained through recognition of credits acquired in a *Laurea* programme. For the same *Laurea specialistica*, more than one *Laurea* may have an entirely recognised curriculum; the 120 credits to be added are going to be different for students coming from different *Lauree*, in order to complement the ones already acquired. Access to a *Laurea specialistica* may also be allowed from a *Laurea* curriculum only partly recognised; in this case, more than 120 credits have to be added.

- For both *Lauree* and *Lauree specialistiche*, *Classes of study programmes* are determined at the national level; a Class is the framework for the study programmes offered by universities in the same disciplinary field.[2] The legal value of a degree (e.g. for access to regulated professions or to the civil service) is the one attributed to the Class to which the degree belongs.

- Each Class is characterised through a description of its general cultural and professional objectives, and through prescriptions concerning no more than two-thirds of the credits required for the degree; those prescriptions assign a certain number of credits to sets of subjects, not to individual subjects, leaving in any case at least 5% of the credits as electives for each student. The determination of the Classes, and their characterisation, may be revised every three years.

- Within any Class, each university may build up one or more study programmes. For each programme, the university: (i) determines precise cultural and professional objectives, in the frame of the general ones indicated for the Class; (ii) defines the exact title of the degree awarded at the end of the programme; (iii) assigns a part of the credits by choosing one or several subjects within each set as defined by the national prescriptions; (iv) is completely free in assigning the remaining number of credits (at least one-third).

- In each programme more than one curriculum may be offered, and this enhances flexibility. Moreover, students may propose a do-it-yourself curriculum, combining credits according to their own interests. Such a proposal has to be submitted to the Council in charge of the programme, and the Council may either approve it, or reject it, or ask for modifications.
- To guarantee transparency, the study programmes of all universities are listed on a national web site; furthermore, it is compulsory to add to any degree the 'Diploma Supplement', formulated according to European agreements.
- The PhD is the third degree which has legal recognition. No *Classes* are defined in this case; the only national prescription is that *Laurea specialistica* is necessary to be admitted, and that the PhD programme has to last at least three years.
- Programmes not leading to a recognised degree (e.g. programmes for further education, or specialisation courses) may be offered by universities on a completely autonomous basis. A programme of 60 credits at least, requiring a degree for admission, may use the name of *Master universitario* ('*di primo livello*' if it follows *Laurea*, '*di secondo livello*' if it follows *Laurea specialistica*).
- Generally, there are no restrictions (*numerus clausus*) to entering university programmes, except for the cases where rules are given by the EU. Universities are allowed to place some restriction on individual programmes, due to restrictions in existing facilities (e.g. classrooms, laboratories).

Having given the general rules through the Decree Number 509, the next step for the government was the determination of the various *Classes* and their characterisation. This was accomplished in 2000, through a decree defining 42 Classes for *Lauree* and another one defining 104 Classes for *Lauree specialistiche*. To give an idea of what a Class means, here are some examples: for '*Laurea*' there is a Class 1 *Biotechnologies*, a Class 25 *Physical Sciences and Technologies* and a Class 38 *Historical Sciences*; for '*Laurea specialistica*' a Class 7/S *Agricultural biotechnologies*, a Class 85/S *Geophysical Sciences* and a Class 98/S *Modern History*.

Inside each Class, there are prescriptions concerning sets of subjects and corresponding credits. In order to avoid programmes constituting a very narrow group of disciplines, for all Classes not only subjects belonging to the most specific area characterising the Class are indicated, but also subjects belonging to related areas, and some space is guaranteed for interdisciplinary connections and extramural work (Luzzatto 2001).

Within the framework described above, the universities had to reorganise their whole teaching programme. Almost all programmes for the new *Laurea* started in 2001; for *Laurea specialistica*, the first programmes started in 2002.

2. PROBLEMS IN THE REFORM IMPLEMENTATION

All educational reforms have a number of obstacles to overcome. In its implementation, the Italian University Reform had to face (and is still facing) a number of difficulties that can be differentiated into two domains:

- The absence of the consideration of a number of prerequisites as crucial for the success of the Reform and its 'philosophy'.
- The attitudes of the main actors involved in the change process, particularly academics.

2.1. Weaknesses in the Framework

Basically, the idea of the Reform originated with a small number of members of the government and the professoriate. Government supporters feared Parliament would endlessly debate all the details and possibly impose delaying strategies. The result was an unusually rapid process of elaboration, presentation and approval of the project. This speediness – although useful to the Reform's approval – left the core of the project deprived of a number of structural supports of crucial relevance for its complete success.

First of all, a redefinition of the academic profession in terms of rights and duties of this peculiar category of civil servants, making it more in line with the new rules the Reform was introducing, did not become a political issue. Consequently, there is no clear definition of the distribution of teaching loads, which the Reform has increased together with a new involvement in administrative matters, tutoring and organisational business. In addition, academics remain linked to their disciplinary fields, hindering identification with their university as an institution. Thus institutional collegiality is made less appealing and more difficult to achieve.

Secondly, the government did not provide an additional financial allocation in the budget to support the Reform. The Reform, if nothing else, created a substantial increase in teaching. This created a shortage of teachers and, in many cases, of classrooms, which will become more and more evident when the second level of courses is completely activated.

Lack of financial resources prevented significant incentives for academic staff to be willing to give more time to teaching activities and prevented the part-time engagement of school teachers. This was one of the reasons why the proposed comprehensive orientation programme for secondary school students in their final years was not implemented. This created a serious mismatch between the cultural background of prospective university students and the requirements of the new courses, that could be measured in terms of debts of credits. The problem is that, due to a number of organisational reasons, it is very difficult for universities to provide a large number of remedial courses before or during the first year of study for students who may have chosen a field of study without any serious consideration of their background and inclinations.

Another consequence of the weakly supported start to the Reform is the delay in the implementation of the evaluation policy which remains undeveloped. This is particularly unfortunate for the complete development of the autonomy that is supposed to characterise the system. Without evaluation the autonomy of the universities will not create a real system of higher education.

The same governmental attitude (which became less and less favourable with the change of Minister of the University and Scientific Research, and later when the entire government changed following the 2001 election) did not help the presentation of the main points of the reform project. Besides a few minor initiatives in some universities, the rather complex structure of the Reform was not publicly debated. The government was supposed to hold a number of conferences throughout the country, but they were constantly postponed. Thus, the implications of the Reform were not at all clear to the large majority of academic staff, and in many cases they were misunderstood. Even now there are many different interpretations of the Reform in the university system.

Finally, with respect to autonomy, there is the further issue of the adaptation of university governance to the new needs of individual universities and of the system as a whole. The way of leading a self-governing university in competition with other universities has been left to the traditional leadership (rector, academic senate and administrative council), which is tailored to a centralised system where power in the individual university is based on the balance among different disciplinary fields. At the system level, the Ministry did not reshape its structure (or develop its culture) in order to provide the general framework for the working of university networks and to verify and reword individual performances. Consequently, the old structure (and culture) retain power and control.

2.2. The Attitude of the Academic World

The lack of an appropriate framework able to facilitate the success of the reform project presents only one side of the picture – a side where the predominant role is played by the government and the world of politics in general. However, in the analysis of the implementation process a crucial role is also played by other actors, mainly the professoriate.

The attitude of the university professors towards the Reform has been far from homogeneous. Opposing positions have been taken with differences arising among disciplinary fields and divisions within the same area, faculty or department. Generally, academic staff in the Hard Sciences (pure and applied) seem to be more in favour of the Reform, perhaps thanks to their tradition of being more in touch with the European dimension and thus more aware of the needs to reduce the gap with other European systems of higher education. On the other hand, groups of professors from the Humanities and Law developed a sometimes strong resistance toward the innovations sponsored by the Reform. Besides a general resistance towards innovations and change processes, the attitude of this part of academia is an example of a traditional way of interpreting the role of the university, and academic staff, which is very much diffused among Italian university professors (Moscati 1997). Simply, this attitude conceives of the university as an institution for the formation of an elite and, accordingly, the role of the university professor is dedicated to the accomplishment of this purpose. This attitude, while producing a rather vertical and authoritarian structure of internal relations inside academia, well described by Clark (1977), can be explained by the self-reliance of the academic world and its relative marginality in Italian society. The transformation of the system from elite to mass higher education (which began in Italy in the early 1960s) conflicted with the traditional attitude of a relevant part of the academic staff who wanted to maintain strong selection of students. On the one hand, the government's open-door policy supported the growing social demand for higher education, while on the other, a substantial proportion of academics continued selecting students through a very severe evaluation of their performance based on elite standards. This elitist attitude explains the resistance of part of the academic staff to the reform project since it made very clear the difference between the task of the first level of courses (the heightening of the country social capital) and that of the second level (the training of the elite) (Trow 1974; Capano 1998, 2002). For the academic 'traditionalist', the introduction of the first level simply meant the cultural decline of the university.

At the same time, a large number of university professors, even inside the Humanities and Social and Political Sciences, accepted the idea of the Reform. Support came first from the academic leadership, namely, rectors (through their National Conference: the CRUI), deans and heads of departments; also, professors responsible for individual study programmes were heavily involved. Due to their roles of collective responsibility these members of academia were more than others aware of the need for a modernisation of the higher education system, and thus started to work for the Reform's implementation. The traditional vertical academic power structure helped to engender a positive attitude toward the Reform. As a result, a good number of academic staff became involved in the hard work of transforming the structure of study courses and curricula. Through this collective effort the new configuration of courses (at least for the first level) was ready earlier than expected (Luzzatto 2001).

Problems arose with respect to the contents of the curricula. As we recalled in section 1.2, national rules defining Classes of study programmes were not extremely compelling. In implementing the rules the ministerial bureaucracy tried to increase the compulsory components, based on the excuse of preserving the legal validity of the degrees. Nevertheless, a high degree of autonomy was left to universities.

The faculties were compelled to structure their curricula and organise courses. The traditional habit of leaving professors free to teach courses in their discipline without requiring any shift among topics or to coordinate the content of their courses with those of others was a barrier to innovation in structure and content of curricula. Thus, in some cases the need to reduce traditional four- or five-year programmes into three-year ones, required by the Reform, created a concentration of the existing curricula into smaller units: that is, the same number of courses with abridged content. Someone called it 'the bonsai phenomenon' (Pontremoli and Luzzatto 2002).

In addition, the traditional culture of conceiving university studies as the final period in the life span devoted to training and organised learning prevented the rethinking of course content where some aspects could be completed through future lifelong learning activities.

Lack of collegiality has been mentioned already as a problem in the building of coherent curricula. An individualistic attitude hindered collective debate on difficulties related to the first experimentation of the Reform, and made academic staff resentful of the 'excessive waste of time' produced by frequent meetings at the faculty or department level. Also, examination of the basic content of the legal aspects of the reform project were often insufficiently pursued because of the scattered attendance of faculty members at meetings.

To sum up, it seems fair to say that Italian academics, not accustomed to the collective design of the curricula and study programmes, were, on the one hand, overwhelmed by the new freedom to elaborate courses of study in different ways while, on the other hand, they found it easier and more convenient not to intrude into the autonomy and independence of their colleagues justifying this under the 'sacred' label of 'academic freedom'. Thus, very often a number of new opportunities were not taken into consideration, particularly with respect to curricula differentiation. For example, we can emphasise the debate on the apparently contradictory characteristics of the first three-year level, leading to the labour market or to the second level of studies. There was criticism about the possibility of combining professional courses with courses of basic theory. However, the problem did not eventuate.

The weak understanding of the 'philosophy' of the reform project and its implications left in many cases under-utilised other possibilities made available in the building of the curricula. For example, in the majority of cases credits have been assigned in each study programme only to those subjects which had already been indicated as compulsory, at the national level, for the corresponding Class. Thus, most faculties demonstrated little creativity and relinquished the possibility of relating their programmes to specific cultural and professional needs. This gap *vis-à-vis* the evolution of the culture outside the university domain seems particularly evident in the Humanities (in the Faculty of Letters, to be more precise), where criticism toward the Reform has been sharper (Detti and Guastella 2002). Furthermore, the creation of individual paths was opposed by the authoritarian tradition of providing de facto compulsory tracks, while professors ignored the new possibilities offered to students.

Another consequence has been the lack of interdisciplinarity due to the tradition of non-cooperation among disciplinary fields. Each faculty defined programmes through the almost exclusive utilisation of its own academic staff. As mentioned above, the way professors are 'aligned' to the disciplines in each scientific field allows them to refuse any involvement in other sections where knowledge has been academically divided. While the Reform has expanded access to an entire disciplinary field, few know it and even less take advantage of it. The combination of a field's separation with the unawareness of the appropriate utilisation of the university degrees in the labour market explains the unrealistic building of curricula leading to unlikely professional role models. This is characteristic of some of the new second-level study programmes (Luzzatto 2002).

Another opportunity provided by the reform project and not seized upon by the university community has been a new kind of diversified relationship with external 'stakeholders'. As stated already, the academic world has traditionally relied on itself, keeping to the Humboldtian model in terms of absence of relationships between collective academic entities while allowing individual academics to provide their expertise to external 'buyers'. This academic isolation has been reinforced by a society which has failed to understand the relevance of higher education from social and political points of view. From an economic perspective, it can be noted that large Italian industrial companies have developed a policy of hiring people at lower levels and then providing internal training for career advancement. Also, the majority of firms are traditionally very small and thus not in a position to establish any serious relationship with the world of higher education. Both characteristics help to explain the limited relevance given to higher education and research by the Italian industrial sector. In other domains (services) middle-level degrees have resulted in being more useful for companies very often having handicraft origins. Only very recently are there signs that these trends are changing (Frey and Ghignoni 2000).

From the university perspective this lack of external demand has reinforced the tendency of self-reliance, with a number of consequences that the Reform is making more and more evident. The Reform has been resisted by a number of academic staff who have ignored what has been going on in other European systems of higher education. In addition, the establishment of relations with the external environment has been resisted due to the fear of interference in the independence of researchers and the decline of pure research in favour of applied research for the benefit of private interests. If nothing else, this fear appears outdated and inconsistent with the reality of the Italian situation where there is a traditional weakness of private interest and support of university teaching and research. This attitude suggests a fear of accepting the challenge of an open confrontation with the external world, in favour of maintaining the status quo which offers a 'stable revenue'.

Finally, the Reform promotes the increased relevance of teaching activities. This is a phenomenon which is in general related to the transition from elite to mass higher education, but in Italy it was only through the Reform that it became clear to all. The new two-level structure (plus the masters programmes and the doctoral programme) provides a substantial increase in the number of courses each university has to offer. Further, counselling programmes to advise students have had to be provided, together with a number of remedial programmes. For the last three years, a large group of academic staff has been involved in building new courses. The academic world resents the increasing amount of time and energy devoted to teaching activities (and to the related organisational and administrative duties) to the detriment of research activities. Yet, universities are compelled to promote teaching, since a larger number of students results in more financial subsidies from the Ministry, more resources to hire new academic and administrative staff, and more money from student fees. It seems that also among Italian universities the competition for students is ready to start.

3. THE PRESENT SITUATION

3.1. The Monitoring

As the Reform radically changed the whole structure of Italian universities, systemic monitoring of its implementation was essential. However, monitoring was only partial.

Detailed quantitative analyses of the first outcomes have been conducted by a specialised committee: the *Comitato Nazionale per la Valutazione del Sistema Universitario* (CNVSU). We refer to two of the committee's results.

First, the new system of university degrees has attracted strong appeal. The number of first-year students (*immatricolati*), which had been stable for some time, increased from 310,924 in 2000–01 (the year before the Reform) to 331,368 in 2001–02 (+6.6%) and to 346,894 in 2002–03 (+4.7%).

Second, there has been a small improvement in one of the major problems of Italian universities, namely the drop-out phenomenon. Eighty-four per cent of the students who first enrolled in 2001–02 have reached the second year in 2002–03, whereas two years earlier the proportion continuing was 80%. This should bring about an increase in the number of graduates.

No national analysis has been done concerning qualitative aspects. Preliminary studies, by some universities, of their implementation of the new programmes exist, but are insufficient for a meaningful general understanding.

The following items deserve further investigation:

- Did the rules for Classes of study programmes leave adequate space for local choices?
- Did the universities completely utilise those spaces which were at their disposal?
- Are interdisciplinary programmes present or, at least, how much relevance has been given, in the various programmes, to disciplines different from the ones most directly characterising specific programmes?
- Flexibility was supposed to become a cornerstone of a system: but to what extent is it really present? Examples: alternative choices inside the curricula; possibility of entering the same *Laurea specialistica* coming from different first-level *Lauree* etc.

As can be seen, both national and local decisions should be under scrutiny. The main objective would be to identify the precise cause of each unsatisfactory result with respect to: what can be ascribed to the framework (our point in section 2.1), what can be ascribed to the rules, and what can be ascribed to the way the rules have been applied.

Even in the absence of systematic monitoring, some statements can be made. Without models to guide the correct way to proceed with the Reform, and not being supported by efficient systems of evaluation to rectify wrong policies, the universities revealed a serious weakness in the mechanism of governance. The large majority of universities could not rely on governing structures which were able to deal with the basic problems of administration, especially in terms of coordinating the didactic supply and the research activities among different faculties. Further, university administrations had no model to refer to in the process of adopting policies of fund-raising from different sources (other than the traditional ministerial ones) and offering various services in order to balance the budget.

Nevertheless, the Reform did not collapse. On the contrary, it was able to take off and to develop the three-year first level and later the two-year second level in all universities. The reason for this success is based on the positive response that the top (the Reform promoters) received from the bottom (namely the academics). It seems fair to say that a consistent part of the academic staff either felt that the old system of higher education had to change or, as we have already suggested, accepted the reform because it was coming from the local academic authority (rector, dean, head of the department, and the like).

Without a detailed inquiry into the successes and weaknesses of the Reform implementation, there is a serious danger that new decisions to modify the Reform will be taken in the absence of sufficient and objective data. In fact, a 'reform of the Reform' based on prejudices could destroy elements which are (at least potentially) satisfactory, without correcting mistakes and insufficiencies.

3.2. An Overall Analysis

Almost all the components of the situation outlined above can be explained in the framework of the traditional relationship between the university and society in Italy. An unwritten agreement of reciprocal non-interference has regulated this relationship which has been at least partially functional as long as the university was devoted to elite formation in a country whose economy was not based on scientific innovation. Small groups of scientists could modernise their departments (in Hard Sciences) here and there without affecting the higher education system which produced individuals of high quality but a poor level of education on average. The centralised structure of the system could not be changed from the inside, being too dependent on the political domain, and it could resist changes imposed from the outside. This was the case when a minister, coming from the university community (the former rector of the University of Rome, Ruberti), tried to modernise the system in the 1980s. The Parliament approved his proposals but the laws were not implemented.

With respect to the Reform debated here the situation was somewhat different. On the one hand, a part of the academic community was convinced that the situation (the role and functions of the university) had to change and the majority of these academics included most of the rectors and many of the faculty deans who trusted the minister in charge (again a former rector: Berlinguer). On the other hand, the aims of the Reform were presented in advance to the academic community while the Law was passed in the Parliament almost without debate. Unfortunately, the Minister changed immediately after the approval of the Reform and a few months later the entire government changed. The connection between the politicians who introduced the Reform and the innovators inside academia first weakened and then was clearly broken. Using Cerych and Sabatier's words, the 'fixers' of the reform lost the political support from outside the academic community and the push for change began to lose power. Nevertheless, the Reform was diluted but not cancelled thanks basically to the growing awareness among academics of the need for a new kind of higher education (Cerych and Sabatier 1986: 251).

In terms of authority distribution, we can refer to the traditional 'continental mode' described by Burton Clark by saying that in Italy (i) the power of allocation of funds has partially shifted from the government to the individual university thanks to the introduction of administrative and financial autonomy in the 1990s, while (ii) the combination of faculty guild and state bureaucracy has largely lost its impact. In fact, the growing complexity of the system has given room to "strong rectorial power at university level ... [as well as] to stronger deanships at the faculty level" (Clark 1983: 127). This development allows the seesawing between innovators (rectors basically supporting the reform) and forces opposing the reform: the rank and file of academia who otherwise – with the not-so-hidden support of government – would have easily maintained the status quo.

The purpose of widening access to higher education has been included as one of the main goals of the Reform through the shortening of the first cycle and the programme of orientation, guidance and introductory remedial courses. As has been said, while the drop-out rate is declining, the programmes for supporting first-year students have not been developed as expected. Still, we have to wait to evaluate the complete results of the Reform.

The contribution of higher education to regional development was included in the goals of the Reform but largely has not been realised. Reasons are possibly related to the resistance to the general idea of mass higher education and the university meeting social demands. Only the three polytechnics developed a policy that took into account the local environment, being based on faculties (architecture and engineering) traditionally devoted to applied research. The Reform included a coordination of rectors at the regional level, aiming for a better connection of the universities with the social and economic environment but so far there are no examples of productive coordination. Universities still have to clarify for themselves the new tasks of cooperation and competition that the Reform implies.

As mentioned, there have been examples of vocational and short-cycle higher education in Italy. Their failure has to do basically with the lack of corresponding professional role models in the labour market and with the low level of prestige attributed to vocational courses even if provided by universities. This last point is due to a cultural attitude that is hard to overcome. This is also one of the reasons why the Reform attempted to combine in the first level the two aims of providing a professional background for those who wanted to enter the labour market and a preliminary cultural background for those who intended to pursue studies at the second level (*Laurea specialistica*). The general difficulty is the resistance to introducing elements of vocationalisation inside the university.

But the real general problem – using the Cerych and Sabatier scheme – is the attempt to realise a comprehensive reform affecting, in one hit, curriculum, system structure and the distribution of power. In this respect the Italian reform is reminiscent of the 1968 French one. Perhaps, from one perspective, the attempt involved too many radical changes all at once. But, on the other hand, another change (the redefinition of the academic staff role) is missing. In a system which had resisted change for so long, revealing its bottom-heavy, weak attitude toward innovation, the attempt to introduce a general reform could have been the best way to obtain, in the end, a reduced but still effective transformation.

4. FURTHER PERSPECTIVES

4.1. The Attitude of the New Government Toward the Reform Implementation

The process of implementation started to face difficulties when the government changed. The new government did not have the same positive attitude toward the reform project as the previous one.

Reasons for this are not very clear, neither in theoretical nor ideological terms. The present government of centre-right quickly demonstrated (as in other political fields) a need to differentiate itself from the former government of left-left. Therefore, it cancelled the School Reform at elementary and secondary level, but could not do the same at the university level since, as we have seen, the Reform had already started, and academic support was also relevant from a political point of view. So far, the government has produced some decrees on minor points and has proposed some 'adjustments' through a committee of university professors. Basically, all these moves can be interpreted according to three factors.

4.1.1. Distrust of Academia

The Ministry of the University has produced a decree introducing the so-called 'minimal prerequisites' (*requisiti minimi*) for the creation of any new study programme. Some dimension of spaces, number of structures and technical resources have been listed but especially a minimum number of academic staff has been established, specifying how many full professors, associate professors and researchers are needed to start a new course, no matter which kind of disciplinary field and which kind of university are involved. Now, it is fair to say that in some cases the way new courses have been established gives ground to the ministerial reaction since it is possible to suspect the basic underlying reasons were related to the personal interests of individual academics (or of small groups of them) to the detriment of minimal scientific standards. However, the rigidity of the established rules, disregarding the specificity of the local situation, belongs to the old bureaucratic attitude of the centralised system.

The same attitude is revealed by the attempt the government has recently made to abolish the financial autonomy of the universities (introduced by another government some ten years ago). Taking advantage of the difficulties many universities are now facing in balancing their budgets – thanks to the reduction of financial support from the government itself, but also because of their weakness in dealing with this aspect of the autonomy – the government indicated its willingness to directly administer the financial part of the higher education system (De Maio 2002).

4.1.2. Managerial Attitude

The measures presented above may also derive from the managerial origin of some of the leading members of the present government (the Prime Minister and the Minister of Education, University and Research among others). A new proposal recently circulated would reform the first level of studies providing a common first year for all students and then a division into two tracks of two years: one for those who want to pursue studies at the second level and one for those who want to enter the labour market after the first degree (*Laurea*). This modification – redesigning the first three-year level in a 'Y' shape – has been presented as a way of cancelling the overlap between the two goals included in the first level of courses, which the Reform conceived either as leading to the second level or to the labour market, but within the same track. The separation of tracks clearly is a way of simplifying the alternatives, assuming there are jobs in the labour market, following the first university level, which require only technicians and others (at higher level) which require 'knowledge of methods' (meaning that the 'how' can be separated from the 'why'). No one can avoid noticing that the 'philosophy' underlying this proposal belongs to a now defunct cultural and economic period. This reminds one of the long debate in recent years about the German *Fachhochschulen*. In addition it is worth remembering that a parallel professional postsecondary track already exists in the School Reform and operates at the regional level. The new proposal, not even requested by the Italian economic world, seems a gift to that part of academia that fears the cultural decline of the first level of university instruction: the brilliant students will be separated from the average ones.

4.1.3. Political Support From Pressure Groups

As is understandable, the new government, not being in favour of the current Reform, has to rely on groups who, for different reasons, resist it.

Take for example the exception proposed for the Faculty of Law. Some prominent law representatives have asked to have a long-cycle (five years) course, without a first level, for the legal profession. Needless to say, this exception may be the beginning of a number of similar requests by several professional organisations and other groups in the professoriate.

Another case in point is represented by the curricula content in teacher education programmes, where conservative academic forces are trying to enforce the disciplinary components to the detriment of educational sciences, didactics and teacher training activities.

A third example is the proposal to make the 120 credits of the second level independent from those of the first level. The idea of the Reform was to consider all the 300 credits together (180 at the first level + 120 at the second) in order to allow students coming from different disciplinary first levels to enrol in the same second level (with different debts in terms of credits to cover). The separation of the two sets of credits would prevent de facto this possibility and in practical terms would compel students to stick to their original disciplinary field. Again a rigidity, which would reduce the innovative impact of the Reform to the benefit of those sectors of the academic community who are opposing the transformation of the status quo.

Finally, there is a sympathetic attitude towards pressures by the powerful leaders of *Ordini professionali* (the organisations of engineers, lawyers etc.), who want the reduction of the rights of first-level graduates. This converges with the interests of those professors who still consider only long cycles as meaningful.

We can say that in terms of the interest group perspective (as suggested by Burton Clark), the present situation can be seen as reproducing the unstable seesawing between reform supporting groups and reform opposing groups where the former include the modernising forces inside academia as well as the economic and political domains, while the latter include conservatives from the three sectors of society with the support of the present national government (Clark 1986: 265).

4.2. The Present Debate

As we have seen, the implementation of the Reform seems to risk the progressive dwindling of its strength because of the unofficial opposition of one of the key implementing institutions: namely, the government. Consequently, if no other interest group (stakeholders) supports the Reform, all the burden will remain on that part of academia that in the first period has been directly involved in the implementation of the Reform.

Thus, it is not surprising that firm opposition to proposals of hasty changes came, first of all, from university rectors, through their National Conference (CRUI). Traditionally, Italian professors, and even more their leadership, are rather conformist. This time, they resisted government's proposals.

As mentioned earlier, financial autonomy of universities is under attack, together with important elements of the reform of didactical activities. Many universities have real problems in managing their budgets, due to the reduction in state funding. However, they refuse to give up their administrative autonomy, only recently acquired.

As far as the Reform is concerned, the main objections to drastically altering its structure are based on the need of waiting for its first results. At the national level, not only rectors, but also a usually conservative institution representing the various disciplinary areas, CUN (*Consiglio Universitario Nazionale*), expressed this need. At the local level, all those who three years ago (for *Lauree*) and one year ago (for *Lauree specialistiche*) worked hard in building up new curricula were frightened by the idea of starting all over again.

According to recent statements by the Minister, the government could partly modify its attitude: no new rules would be imposed, whereas some changes would be allowed, on an optional basis, to those universities, or those academic sectors, willing to adopt them. The debate is still going on, and at the moment no final official decision has been taken.

To conclude, we can only repeat that an exhaustive monitoring of successes and failures should precede any substantial revision of the Reform; otherwise, there is the danger of a mere revival of obsolete schemes. In this chapter, we have expressed a number of criticisms concerning weaknesses in the framework of the Reform and insufficiencies in its implementation. In our opinion, they should stimulate further progress; surely, it would be disastrous to go back.

NOTES

[1]   There is an exception to this 'serial' structure of short cycle and long cycle (a central point in the Bologna Declaration). In a few cases (e.g. medicine and pharmacy), where prescriptions about degrees and curricula are given by the EU, there are study programmes leading directly to *Laurea specialistica*.

[2]   To better understand the meaning of Classes, below we provide a few examples of Classes of *Laurea* and Classes of *Laurea specialistica*.

REFERENCES

Capano, G. *La politica universitaria*. Bologna: Il Mulino, 1998.
Capano, G. "La riforma universitaria: l'anarchica attuazione di un sistema tecnocratico." *Il Mulino* 6 (2002): 1154–1163.
Cerych, L. and P. Sabatier. *Great Expectations and Mixed Performance: The Implementation of Higher Education Reforms in Europe*. Stoke-on-Trent: Trentham Books, 1986.
Clark, B.R. *Academic Power in Italy: Bureaucracy and Oligarchy in a National University System*. Chicago: Chicago University Press, 1977.
Clark, B.R. *The Higher Education System: Academic Organization in Cross-National Perspective*. Berkeley: University of California Press, 1983.
Clark, B.R. "Annex – Implementation in the United States: A Comparison with European Higher Education Reforms." In Cerych, L. and P. Sabatier. *Great Expectations and Mixed Performance: The Implementation of Higher Education Reforms in Europe*. Stoke-on-Trent: Trentham Books, 1986, 259–267.
De Maio, A. *Una svolta per l'Università. Riforme per costruire una formazione europea*. Milano: Il Sole 24 Ore, 2002.
Detti, T. and G. Guastella. "La riforma fenice. La didattica universitaria nel settore umanistico." *Il Mulino* 6 (2002): 1175–1181.
Frey, L. and E. Ghignoni (eds). *Trasformazioni del sistema formativo e qualificazione dell'offerta di lavoro per generazioni*. Milano: Franco Angeli, 2000.
Luzzatto, G. *2001: l'Odissea dell'Università nuova*. Milano: La Nuova Italia, 2001.
Luzzatto, G. "La 'nuova' università. Contesto e contenuti della riforma." *Il Mulino* 6 (2002): 1164–1174.
Moscati, R. (ed.). *Chi governa l'università? Il mondo accademico italiano tra conservazione e mutamento*. Napoli: Liguori, 1997.
Pontremoli, S. and G. Luzzatto (eds). *Università, la riforma è iniziata*. Milano: La Nuova Italia, 2002.
Trow, M. *Problems in the Transition from Elite to Mass Higher Education*. Paris: OECD, 1974.

GRANT HARMAN

IMPLEMENTING COMPREHENSIVE NATIONAL HIGHER EDUCATION REFORMS: THE AUSTRALIAN REFORMS OF EDUCATION MINISTER JOHN DAWKINS, 1987–90

1. INTRODUCTION

This chapter reviews implementation of major national reforms in the Australian higher education sector initiated by Education Minister John Dawkins over the period 1987–90. In doing so, it employs the theoretical framework developed by Cerych and Sabatier (1986) in their landmark comparative study of implementation of major European higher education reforms of the 1960s and 1970s. A supplementary aim of the chapter is to assess the utility of the Cerych and Sabatier framework in explaining the Australian reforms, and to do so in the light of more recent theoretical work on public policy implementation and higher education policy change.

The reforms initiated by Minister Dawkins were dramatic and extensive, and far more ambitious than any single set of reforms initiated previously or since then in the Australian higher education system. Further, they were far more extensive and substantial than any of the European reforms discussed by Cerych and Sabatier. They thus pose the intriguing question as to how a single minister and the government of which he was a member could have so fundamentally changed a large national higher education system over the space of about three years.

In essence, the reforms of John Dawkins substantially restructured the Australian higher education system, abolishing the binary line between universities and polytechnic-type institutions known as colleges of advanced education (CAEs), combining separate universities and colleges through mergers to form larger and more comprehensive institutions, introducing new resource allocation arrangements, reintroducing student tuition fees through an income contingent loan system, substantially changing university management and governance, and placing a much stronger emphasis on research but with more selectivity in research funding (Harman 1989; Marginson and Considine 2000).

At the time the reforms were initiated in 1987, Australian higher education was almost entirely a public sector system, with about 390,000 students located in 19 universities and some 44 CAEs. While almost all these institutions had been created by state governments, since 1974 all regular government operating funding had come from the Commonwealth government, giving the Commonwealth considerable powers in policy direction.

Å. Gornitzka et al. (eds.), Reform and Change in Higher Education, 169-186.

In contrast, today the Australian higher education system is distinctively different, with over 900,000 students located in 37 public universities and another 30,000 students located in two private universities and a large number of smaller private colleges. Australian higher education is now much more entrepreneurial, with public universities generating a substantial proportion of their own income, largely from tuition fees from international and domestic students, and the sale of a variety of educational services. By 2002, there were 185,000 international students studying in public universities and this group constituted 20.6 per cent of total student enrolments. To a substantial extent, the reforms led by John Dawkins provided the policy and institutional base that made these impressive developments possible, creating a public higher education sector much better fitted to operate in a more competitive international environment (Sharpham and Harman 1997; Gallagher 2000).

Although the reforms of John Dawkins took place more than a decade ago, they remain controversial within universities and the wider community. Many academics who worked in universities and CAEs during the period of reform continue to blame Dawkins for a wide range of ills affecting higher education today, while some prominent former Labor colleagues of Minister Dawkins are still highly critical of his abolition of the binary line between universities and CAEs. On the other hand, many university leaders and higher education bureaucrats consider that Dawkins laid the basis for a more efficient, more confident and more competitive higher education system. But whatever the various perspectives, there is a degree of puzzlement about how, in such a short space of time, a single minister could have initiated and achieved such a high degree of policy change.

The chapter will first comment briefly on the theoretical framework developed by Cerych and Sabatier since it is necessary to explain the author's particular interpretation of the theoretical framework that contains a number of ambiguities. The reforms initiated by Minister Dawkins will then be outlined, addressing the following questions:

- How did the reforms originate and what were the official goals?
- To what extent have those objectives been attained over time? What other politically significant impacts have they had? Have additional objectives emerged and, if so, with what effects?
- What principal factors influenced those objectives?

Later sections discuss the utility of the framework to help understand the Australian higher education reforms of 1987 to 1990, and attempt an overall evaluation in the light of more recent research and writing.

2. THE CERYCH-SABATIER FRAMEWORK

Influenced by a growing public policy literature at the time on policy implementation (e.g. Pressman and Wildavsky 1973; Bardach 1977; Majone and Wildavsky 1978), Cerych and Sabatier undertook the ambitious task of evaluating the implementation and success of a number of major national European higher education reforms initiated in the 1960s and 1970s. They were well aware that a popular view at the time was that in many cases the high expectations of the reforms had not been achieved and that the degree of change achieved in implementation was far less than that hoped for.

The theoretical framework they developed following extensive case study work was set within the idea of public policy generally following a number of sequential stages, with their interest being on the implementation stage, particularly the extent and significance of goal achievement, and reasons for programme success or failure. The following factors were identified as being of crucial importance in explaining success or failure:

1. Legal: clarity and consistency, and degree of system change envisaged.
2. Adequacy of causal theory underlying the reform.
3. Adequacy of financial resources provided to implementing institutions.
4. Degree of commitment to various programme objectives of those charged with implementation within institutions.
5. Degree of commitment to various programme objectives among legislative and executive officials outside the implementing agencies.
6. Change in social and economic conditions affecting goal priorities or the programme's causal assumptions.

All these factors were seen as being important, but Cerych and Sabatier placed special emphasis on the adequacy of the causal theory and the degree of commitment to the reforms by both ministry officials and those within higher education institutions.

Later in their main theoretical chapter the authors summed up their theory by emphasising particularly the importance of the following factors:

- The amount of system change envisaged and the extent of support and resistance from ministry and higher education officials.
- The adequacy of causal theory, that is, the extent to which the means of reaching the objectives were understood and in which supportive officials were given jurisdiction over critical levers.
- The amount of active, informed support mobilised in favour of the reform by parliament, high officials, interest groups and university faculty.
- The extent to which a specific objective was affected over time by change in socio-economic conditions that gave rise to conflicting public policies or that undermined or fostered its causal theory or political support.

In a concluding chapter, the theoretical framework was further discussed with some minor adjustments being suggested. While goal clarity and consistency continued to be viewed as important, Cerych and Sabatier recognised that these conditions often cannot be fulfilled since vague goals are frequently the price for consensus in the formulation stage. Analysis of the case studies also led the authors to suggest a more complex conceptualisation of the scope of change within a three dimensional framework of depth of change (extent to which a new policy implies departure from existing values and practices), functional breadth (the number of functional areas in which the given policy is expected to introduce more or less profound modifications) and the level of change (indicating the target of reform, such as a whole system or a particular sector).

Final comments in the concluding chapter somewhat surprisingly related to the importance of power processes and complexity, with the authors expressing their attraction to a perspective that focused almost exclusively on groups of political actors and the power they bring to the process. This comment was significant since the original framework did not explicitly address issues of power and influence.

3. THE AUSTRALIAN REFORMS OF MINISTER JOHN DAWKINS

The following overview of the Australian reforms is organised around the three key questions that guided the first stage of the research by Cerych and Sabatier, with some efforts to apply elements of the theoretical framework.

3.1. How the Reforms Originated and Reform Goals

The significant changes of the reforms in the Australian higher education system were driven by a number of influences but by far the most important driver was macro- and micro-economic reform. The Labor government of Bob Hawke was returned to office in the general elections of July 1987 committed to major structural reform of the Australian economy. In the past, Australia had depended largely for its export income on a relatively small number of rural commodities, and on minerals and coal. International fluctuations in major commodity prices in the mid-1980s resulted in a number of commodities simultaneously experiencing major price declines. This prompted a major review of economic policy, resulting in the development and articulation of new strategies aimed to enlarge the export base and, in particular, to encourage the export of specialised manufacturing and services. It also led to further reductions in tariffs and micro-economic reform in order that Australian manufacturers should be better placed to compete internationally. In such a new economic order, higher education was seen to have a much enhanced role in producing more and better qualified graduates, and in supporting economic growth with a stronger R&D base (Harman 1989).

Other factors operated to support the general directions of reform. Increasing student retention rates in secondary schools and labour market changes contributed significantly to stronger demand for student places, both from school leavers and adults. Another important influence was structural changes in public sector management with the application of new ideas about competition and the use of market mechanisms to guide the allocation of resources and management of public sector organisations (Harman 2001). Further, within the government, there was a strong view that universities in particular had been slow to change and that major reforms were needed to jolt them from their complacency.

Minister John Dawkins, who previously had been Minister of Finance, took on the newly created mega Department of Employment, Education and Training after the Hawke government was returned to office in 1987 and immediately began planning reform of the higher education system. With a background in law and economics, Dawkins had proved to be particularly successful as a tough and energetic finance minister. With his higher education reform agenda he moved with considerable speed, assisted by a loose group of senior advisers that included both selected government officials and sympathetic senior university vice-chancellors. By late 1987, Dawkins had published a green paper (Dawkins 1987) that set out the proposed reform agenda and, following wide consultation, by July 1988 had confirmed the detailed policy directions in a white paper (Dawkins 1988). These cleverly crafted documents, written largely for a wider community audience, outlined both the broad directions and key details of the reform, but they also provided explanations why rapid and fundamental change was seen to be essential.

In summary, the higher education reforms of Minister Dawkins aimed to achieve:

- replacement of the binary system made up of separate university and polytechnic sectors by a Unified National System of Higher Education;
- reduction in the number of separate higher education institutions to form larger institutional units through institutional mergers;
- a more competitive approach to funding, with more emphasis on institutional performance and monitoring;
- increased research funding but with a more selective approach with greater emphasis on national research priorities and competitive funding;
- changed management practices within institutions, giving vice-chancellors considerably more authority and giving universities more autonomy in charting their own directions;
- more flexible policies for academic employment and academic work;
- increased government funding to facilitate major increases in student enrolments, with substantial new financial contributions from students who from 1974 had not been required to pay tuition fees;
- replacement of the Commonwealth Tertiary Education Commission (CTEC) by a higher education division within the Department of Employment, Education and Training (Harman 1991).

To these original reform objectives others were soon added. Universities were given approval to charge full-cost fees to international students, and to charge tuition fees for domestic students enrolled in postgraduate courses other than research higher degrees. The new arrangements for overseas students together with additional government support mechanisms, especially more effective marketing, facilitated major growth in international student enrolments in public universities from 24,998 in 1990 to 95,605 in 2000. Developments with both domestic and international fee-paying students and other initiatives have resulted in universities themselves generating an increasing proportion of their income, with only about 50 per cent of university revenue today coming from regular federal government grants (Nelson 2002).

3.2. Extent to Which the Reform Goals Were Achieved and Their Impact

Overall, Minister Dawkins was highly successful and his reform package was substantially achieved. The binary system was abolished simply by ministerial fiat and confirmed later in legislation enacted by the Commonwealth Parliament, while the plan to reduce the number of separate institutions was far more successful than even the Minister anticipated. By the early 1990s, the number of separate higher education institutions had been reduced from 44 CAEs and 19 universities to 36 relatively large and more comprehensive universities (Harman 2000). More competitive approaches to funding were introduced and some funding was removed from universities and allocated to the new Australian Research Council for competitive allocation. Vice-chancellors were encouraged to exercise more authority and take a stronger role in planning and priority setting within their institutions while state and territory governments were pressed to review the composition of university governing bodies and strengthen the strategic planning and monitoring capacities of universities. Although the Labor government of Gough Whitlam in 1973 had abolished student tuition fees to enhance access, student contributions were re-introduced through the Higher Education Contribution Scheme (HECS), which was essentially an income contingent deferred graduate loan scheme. From the start, the HECS scheme operated successfully with a surprisingly small degree of student opposition. Minister Dawkins cleverly managed the decision on HECS by giving responsibility for devising the new scheme to a high-level prestigious committee, chaired by a former Labor Party Premier of the State of New South Wales. Substantial additional funds were found by the Hawke government to facilitate expansion, with the result that total student enrolments grew quickly from 393,734 in 1987 to 485,075 in 1990 and then on to 722,816 by 2000.

On the other hand, it must be admitted that a small number of items in the original reform agenda were not implemented. The idea of consolidating distance education into a small number of special distance education centres in selected universities was soon abandoned as being impractical, while the attempts to achieve greater flexibility in staffing proved less successful than anticipated, largely because of the strong role of academic unions and the operation of national industrial relations machinery. However, this demonstrates a willingness by Dawkins to compromise on items of secondary importance in his plans.

3.3. Explaining Implementation Success

The high degree of success that was achieved can be attributed to a range of factors but particularly important were the following:

- The energy, political skills and commitment of Minister Dawkins to the reform package, his ability to clearly articulate his objectives and details of the reforms, and his ongoing role of chief advocate for the reform process.
- The high degree of support that Minister Dawkins had within the cabinet and government, and his ability to attract additional public financial resources for the higher education sector.

- A high level of influential community support for the reforms, especially from business, the media and particular university vice-chancellors.
- Replacement of the existing bureaucratic agency for higher education coordination (CTEC) by a new administrative division within the Department of Employment, Education and Training that was responsible for implementation of the reforms, and staffed by sympathetic senior staff.
- The use by Minister Dawkins and his department of a variety of policy instruments, particularly persuasion, financial incentives, performance funding, and ongoing support from ad hoc advisory groups.
- The difficulty for opponents to deal with such a large and comprehensive reform package, combined with the speed of change employed by the Minister.

Since the Dawkins reforms, the Australian higher education system has been remarkably stable. Only one merged institution has failed while the total number of public universities has increased by only one. The main policy initiatives of successive governments since then have focused mainly on further developments along the policy directions set in the period 1987 to 1990. Particularly important have been the increased use of competition and market mechanisms in funding allocations and policy steering, the introduction of stronger quality assurance and monitoring mechanisms, further reforms in increased targeting of research funding, and new efforts in R&D and research commercialisation. Unfortunately, more recently, first the Labor government led by Paul Keating and then the coalition government led by John Howard, have substantially reduced public funding levels per student unit. This reduction, combined with the effects of salary increases awarded separately by individual universities through enterprise bargaining, have resulted in substantial deterioration in staff: student ratios from 14:1 in 1990 to 20:1 in 2002 (Nelson 2002).

4. THE AUSTRALIAN CASE AND THE CERYCH-SABATIER FRAMEWORK

The Cerych-Sabatier framework, as already noted, focuses particularly on two major elements in analysis of implementation: the extent and significance of goal achievement, and reasons for programme success or failure. The following sections attempt to relate the Australian case more directly to the key elements of the framework.

4.1. Programme Goals

Cerych and Sabatier saw success or failure of policy implementation being significantly influenced by two aspects of the goals themselves: the amount of change envisaged, and the clarity and consistency of the goals themselves. They saw the amount of change envisaged as being highly important, especially with regard to how far such change departs from the values and procedures of the existing order, with major changes being more likely to be resisted than minor ones. They suggested analysis of the degree of system change in terms of the number of institutions affected, the proportion of individuals in institutions whose behaviour would have to change, and the amount of behavioural change expected of each.

The Australian reforms run counter in a number of respects to the European cases discussed by Cerych and Sabatier and to the conclusions drawn. They involved major change from the existing order and constituted a dramatic and extensive departure from traditional values about institutional autonomy, collegiality and the desirability of incremental change being initiated by the universities themselves. A large number of institutions were affected – in fact, all public higher education institutions, and significant behavioural change was expected by each including a formal application to join the new Unified National System of Higher Education and accept its key guiding principles in order to qualify for Commonwealth government funding. All this raises questions about some of the conclusions drawn by Cerych and Sabatier from their European cases. For example, in discussing the British Open University, they draw the conclusion that "radical departures can be implemented [only] if they are limited to one or very few functional areas of the institution or the higher education system" (Cerych and Sabatier 1986: 245).

Why did the Australian reforms succeed so well despite the degree of change envisaged? A number of factors appeared to operate. First, while academics generally and some individual institutional heads were strongly opposed to important elements of the package, at the same time there was considerable support amongst influential sections within the higher education sector. A 1989 study of governing body chairs and registrars of university and CAE and senior executives in charge of government agencies concerned with the management of the higher education sector reported that 70 per cent of respondents thought that elimination of the binary line was desirable while 80 per cent favoured increased competition between institutions and 90 per cent felt that institutional management should be strengthened (Meek and Goedegebuure 1989). Some individual senior academics were attracted to the possibility of rapid future growth in student enrolments and increased research funding. Vice-chancellors generally were in favour of a stronger role for university leadership and increased autonomy for universities, although many publicly voiced criticisms of the reform agenda, possibly mainly to placate their staff. Many CAE staff enthusiastically supported ending the binary line and gaining parity of esteem with university academics, even though they may have strongly opposed mergers affecting their own institutions. Second, substantial increases in funding facilitated rapid growth in student enrolments and increases in research funding and so quickly offset to some extent particular less desirable aspects of the reform package while implementation of the reforms soon provided energetic and well-qualified academics with opportunities to take new academic and research initiatives. Third, since the reforms sprang from major economic restructuring, they carried a stronger degree of government endorsement while the higher education reforms themselves attracted wide-based business, professional and media support. Fourth, the fact that the reform package was extensive and made up of various separate elements made the task of opponents extremely difficult, as did the relatively rapid speed with which the reform process moved.

Clarity and consistency of goals were seen by Cerych and Sabatier to be particularly important. Overall, the main stated objectives of the reforms were clear and consistent, although at the same time there was scope in the early stages for variations of interpretation on particular details. For example, with regard to institutional mergers, the green paper used the word 'consolidation' rather than 'merger' or 'amalgamation'. While most institutions interpreted consolidation to mean mergers, some institutions thought the Minister would be satisfied with loose associations between institutions. However, the white paper clarified this issue and clearly spelt our institutional merger requirements. This suggests that while clarity and consistency may not be essential for a reform package in its early stages, certainly final documentation needs such clarity and precision in order to facilitate implementation.

Another factor that proved important was the role of the Minister as chief advocate of his reforms, giving numerous speeches on university campuses and to public bodies. On numerous occasions, he faced noisy student and staff demonstrations on university campuses. Clearly advocacy and persuasion proved powerful policy instruments.

4.2. Goal Achievement

Cerych and Sabatier identified six key factors that affected the implementation process and for each, distinguished between those that offered the potential for intervention at the policy formulation stage in order to structure the implementation stage, and those where policy makers actually did so. Each of the six factors will be discussed briefly.

4.2.1. Legal-clarity and Consistency; and Degree of System Change Envisaged

According to the Australian constitution, powers over education are reserved for the states. However, at the time of the reforms, for four decades the Commonwealth government had played a major role in education largely on the basis of a constitutional provision that allowed the Commonwealth Parliament to provide grants to the states on whatever conditions that it set. This 'power of the purse' was greatly strengthened for higher education in 1974 when the Commonwealth accepted full responsibility for funding higher education. Minister Dawkins in 1987 was well aware that many of the key elements of his reforms could be achieved only through the use of financially based power. This power was used effectively in a number of respects, such as requiring all public higher education institutions to formally apply for membership of the new Unified National System of Higher Education, which required giving guarantees to abide by the guiding principles specified by the Minister. Some reforms such as institutional mergers, however, required amendment to state or territory legislation. By various means, Dawkins successfully persuaded state governments as well as the government of the Northern Territory to take appropriate administrative and legislative action.

4.2.2. Adequacy of Causal Theory Underlying the Reform

Cerych and Sabatier placed special emphasis on the adequacy of the causal theory and the degree of commitment to the reforms by both ministry officials and those within higher education institutions. Every reform, according to Cerych and Sabatier, is based on a set of assumptions about the exact causal process by which goals are attained. Particularly important is the extent to which the means of reaching the objectives are understood and in which supportive officials are given jurisdiction over critical levers.

Minister Dawkins was a superb political operator who had a clear vision of what he hoped to achieve, a well-developed strategy in mind to achieve his objectives, and was highly successful in ensuring that the reform goals and causal theory were well understood by key Commonwealth officials as well as by ministers and officials at state level. Since Dawkins doubted the capacity of the CTEC to effectively implement his reforms, he quickly replaced the Commission with a new major administrative unit within his new department, staffed by new and highly experienced senior officials sympathetic to the reform goals. In fact, a number of these officials had been part of the loose group called 'the purple circle' who worked personally with the Minister in planning the reforms and in drafting the green paper. During the implementation process, the Minister himself kept tight personal control over the process, using his officials and an Amalgamation Task Force to work directly with state governments and with universities and CAEs. Some key university vice-chancellors were coopted early to his efforts, as were most state education ministers over time. Further, as already noted, Minister Dawkins was well aware of federal and state powers with regard to higher education and so proceeded carefully to assure maximum federal-state cooperation. So successful was he in gaining the cooperation of state governments that in a number of states including New South Wales non-Labor governments became some of his most enthusiastic partners.

A major factor in explaining the success of Minister Dawkins lies with his strong political position in cabinet and his ability to attract loyal and enthusiastic support from the Prime Minister and cabinet colleagues. The Dawkins' reform plan received unequivocal cabinet support before it was publicly released, although it was many months before any enabling legislation was passed. But there was never any doubt that the key elements of the reform package would be translated in law, although in the case of the Australian Capital Territory a major institutional merger involving the Australian National University eventually was blocked by members of minor political parties who held the balance of power in the upper house of the Commonwealth Parliament.

4.2.3. Adequacy of Financial Resources Provided to Implementing Institutions
Adequate financial resources were provided to facilitate implementation. Despite the strong opposition of staff and academic staff groups to reintroducing student tuition fees, a cleverly designed new fee system was successfully introduced. Moreover, the Minister was successful in persuading the government to allocate sufficient additional funding to facilitate major expansion in student enrolments, significant increases in research funding, additional capital funding (which went to cooperating higher education institutions) and incentive funding to assist institutions willing to enter mergers.

4.2.4. Degree of Commitment to Various Programme Objectives of Those Charged With its Implementation Within the Education Ministry and Affected Institutions

This factor proved to be of great importance. As already noted, the Minister used the strategy of agency replacement to ensure that implementation was handled by highly competent and committed officials. Moreover, during the early planning stage the Minister drew around him a loose group of university vice-chancellors and Commonwealth officials, highly sympathetic to the reform package.

With regard to higher education institutions likely to be adversely affected by the reforms, the Minister already had a group of vice-chancellors strongly committed to the reforms, with others soon joining, attracted by the overall package or particular elements in it, or by the possibility of attracting additional funding by being cooperative. This was important in helping neutralise the impact of those vice-chancellors opposed to the reforms, many of whom over time saw the wisdom of linking themselves with the Minister's cause, or giving up overt opposition.

While publicly many university vice-chancellors criticised the Minister's reform package, privately many moved quickly within their own institutions to implement key elements. Vice-chancellors of leading research universities, for example, soon became involved in merger discussions with one or more colleges, perceiving that in the new Unified National System of Higher Education institutional size would be an important determinant for attracting additional financial resources. Vice-chancellors and governing bodies also quickly embarked on reforms to enhance the authority of senior management and their capacity to undertake more effective strategic planning.

4.2.5. Degree of Commitment to Various Programme Objectives Among Legislative and Executive Officials Outside Implementing Agencies

Minister Dawkins retained strong support within the cabinet and support was forthcoming from other Commonwealth government departments, particularly the Department of Prime Minister and Cabinet and the Department of Finance. However, much of the early stages of implementation were achieved without enabling legislation.

4.2.6. Change in Social and Economic Conditions Affecting Goal Priorities or the Programme's Causal Assumptions

Implementation was clearly facilitated by continuing business and elite support for both economic reform and reform of higher education. While there was strong opposition from academic staff unions to particular elements of the reform package, as already noted, academic union leaders found great difficulty in simultaneously opposing large numbers of separate reform measures, while individually many academic staff supported particular elements of the reform package. Further, as implementation proceeded, many vice-chancellors, state education ministers and state government officials to a large extent were coopted to assist with implementation.

In their concluding chapter, Cerych and Sabatier commented on the attractiveness of using interest group analysis in explaining national higher education reform efforts. Interest group analysis has a clear utility in understanding implementation of the Australian reforms. Basically, Minister Dawkins and his allies formed a broad coalition of interests, and were successful largely because of their clear objectives, the considerable political power they had available to them, their political skills in advocacy and attracting others to their cause, and their willingness to use their available power and skills to maximum advantage. Dawkins' period as education minister worked to his advantage and he was soon rewarded with the more senior portfolio of treasurer.

5. ASSESSMENT OF THE CERYCH AND SABATIER FRAMEWORK MODEL

The theoretical framework developed by Cerych and Sabatier worked reasonably well in analysis of their case studies of European higher education reforms and in providing the final comparative overview. It should be noted, however, that in their analysis the researchers showed surprising flexibility in use of the framework, introducing additional elements or elaboration where necessary. In discussing the British Open University, for example, particular emphasis under goal structure was given to the efforts of the founders, particularly Minister Jenny Lee and the planning committee, while under implementation major emphasis was given to the role and strong commitment of key implementing officials especially the foundation vice-chancellor, Walter Perry (Cerych and Sabatier 1986: 50–55). Yet the original framework did not provide explicit reference to the political skills or roles of individual key actors.

The analysis in this chapter of the Australian reforms demonstrates the utility of the Cerych and Sabatier framework for studying more recent reforms and in a country located in the Asia Pacific region rather than in Europe. In particular, the framework's major headings directing attention to goal structure and goal achievement proved useful in identifying major items for analysis.

With regard to goal structure, the emphasis on the degree of change envisaged and the clarity and consistency of goals proved helpful especially in raising issues about the clarity and goal consistency of the Australian reforms. With regard to goal achievement, the six elements of the framework were useful in identifying major contributing factors. However, the element on legal aspects was somewhat repetitious since it also included reference to causal theory. Adequacy of financial resources, commitment amongst legislators and officials in related agencies and whether or not there were significant changes in social and economic conditions affecting goal priorities all proved highly useful categories. But more powerful items were the adequacy of the causal theory underlying the reform and the degree of commitment to the reform by ministry officials and affected higher education institutions.

What appears lacking in the framework, however, from the perspective of the Australian case study are items related specifically to power and politics, and to political resources and their effective use in implementation. There is also little, if any, emphasis on the range of different political instruments that reformers can use and how more subtle and indirect instruments sometimes better suit some situations.

One reason for the remarkable success of John Dawkins was his political power as a highly experienced minister with high standing in the cabinet, well-developed advocacy and persuasive skills, and ability to use a surprisingly varied number of different political instruments, including persuasion and advocacy, consultation, financial incentives, threats and sanctions, legislation and regulations.

In their theoretical framework, Cerych and Sabatier pay no attention to simultaneous policy developments in other policy domains of government, or the possible impact that other problems being tackled by government at the same time might have on higher education reform. Neither is there attention to where higher education reforms fitted in a government's overall policy agenda, or the possible effects of there being a number of administrative steps between implementers and higher education institutions. On the last point, Dawkins and his officials were fortunate in that they could relate directly on a personal basis to state ministers and officials, as well as to heads of higher education institutions.

At the same time, the framework was a bold and ambitious attempt in comprehensive theory building that has stood the test of time well, and still has the potential to provide considerable help in conceptualising and understanding national higher education reform, particularly at system level. Few other studies of higher education reform have come up with such a comprehensive framework.

In the period of almost three decades since Cerych and Sabatier completed their manuscript, there has been considerable research internationally on public policy research and some important work on higher education policy studies. Yet, to a large extent, the achievements of this period have been disappointing in the sense that they have failed to come up with alternative comprehensive theoretical constructs.

The public policy research efforts since the early 1980s have produced a considerable body of literature as demonstrated by recent reviews by public policy and public administration scholars (e.g. Sabatier 1999; Cline 2000; O'Toole 2000; Wilson 2000; Sinclair 2001; Blair 2002; De Leon and De Leon 2002). But, as two of these scholars comment:

> Starting with the seminal work of Jeffrey Pressman and Aaron Wildavsky, policy implementation has burgeoned from a largely overlooked interest to perhaps the policy analysis growth industry over the last thirty years. However, even though an enormous set of books and articles deals with implementation, it has been described by some as an intellectual dead end because of its problematic relationship to a generalised theory of policy implementation (De Leon and De Leon 2002: 467).

While this view might overstate the situation, at the same time the contributions of three decades of work appear not to have provided as much in terms of significant new approaches for studying the implementation of national higher education reform as might have been expected.

Some work points to possibilities for gaining a better understanding of problems related particularly to why sometimes national reform gains a central place in higher education agendas and why sometimes substantial reform is achieved after long periods of continuity and incremental change. For example, Sabatier (1999) has reviewed a range of theoretical work, including institutional rational choice, the multiple streams framework, the punctuated equilibrium framework, the advocacy coalition framework, the policy diffusion framework and the funnel of causality framework. Of these, the multiple streams framework and the punctuated equilibrium framework appear to offer the best prospects in studies of national higher education reforms. The multiple streams framework views the policy process as being composed of three streams of actors and processes: a problem stream consisting of data about problems, a policy stream involving proponents of policy solutions to policy problems, and a politics stream consisting of elected officials. These three streams normally operate independently of each other, except when a window of opportunity permits policy entrepreneurs to couple the various streams together. This framework could be useful in helping explain how particular policy reforms gain a place on national government agendas and possibly could be linked to earlier work of scholars such as Cobb and Elder (1972).

The punctuated equilibrium framework sees policy making as being characterised by long periods of incremental change punctuated by brief periods of major policy change. Policy change comes about when opponents manage to fashion new policy images and exploit the multiple policy venues characteristic of countries such as the United States. A similar approach is that of Wilson (2000) who suggests a policy regime model with particular attention on stressors (such as catastrophic events), economic crises, demographic changes and shifts in production impacting on policy regimes and creating pressures for change. Such theory could be useful in the case of the Australian higher education reforms where an economic crisis prompted major economic reform that in turn impacted on higher education. Much of the political leverage employed effectively by Minister Dawkins was based on perceptions of both politicians and the business, professional and media elites that national reform was urgent in order to address issues of export income, and macro- and micro-economic blockages.

Other possibilities relate to work on policy tools and implementation networks (Blair 2002). Since the late 1980s, one line of policy implementation research took a different path by focusing on policy instruments rather than policy actors. As explained by Maitland (1995), this approach views public policy delivery in terms of specific government actions. Policy tools include grants, subsidies, regulations, tax incentives, persuasion, authority and direct provision. This approach would be useful in more detailed analysis of the Australian case study since one of the reasons for a high degree of success was the variety of suitable policy instruments used by Minister Dawkins and his implementing officials.

Network analysis has potential for dealing with situations when public service delivery no longer remains the exclusive and direct responsibility of employees on government payrolls. Rather implementation takes place indirectly involving intricate administrative links among public, government and non-profit organisations. Hence in some situations it is important to consider in programme implementation the role of networks and various organisational linkages. Of particular relevance is the work of O'Toole (1997) who sees service delivery depending on network linkages that in many cases may be informal with administrative direction being often dispersed. While in the case of the Australian reforms there were clear lines of bureaucratic and political authority, at the same time loose networks played an important role in building support.

The higher education policy studies literature is more limited, especially in terms of work with a strong focus on implementation of substantial and comprehensive national higher education reforms. Some of the most interesting literature has come from team projects working on comparative studies of Swedish, Norwegian and British higher education reforms. In their comparative study of *Reforming Higher Education*, Kogan and Hanney (2000) concentrate particularly on theoretical issues concerning changes in the role of the state and universities within it, the extent to which contexts or individual actors cause change, modes of higher education policy making including the role of elites and interest groups, and continuity and discontinuity in policy. In elaborating on each of these issues, they draw on a considerable body of social science research. Particularly relevant in terms of higher education policy development and implementation is the extent to which higher education policy was determined as a matter of public policy as opposed to how far it was created in the higher education system itself.

To take another example, in their study of Swedish university reforms, Bauer et al. (1999) considered policy formulation processes and reform decisions by state authorities concerning the higher education system. They took particular interest in how government reform policy and goals corresponded with reform outcomes, although this effort was not primarily an investigation into reform implementation. In explaining change and continuity, they looked particularly at elements including the content and values of the reform policy and policy formation processes at national level, the instruments of reform, the impact of reform on higher education institutions and their responsibilities, obligations and internal distribution of authority as well as the response and action by institutional leadership, the demands on basic units affecting academic working conditions and professional roles, and academic values and professional identities influencing the reception of and reactions to the reform by faculty. Various theoretical work from other scholars informed different issue areas, but an important element was development of a two-dimensional model of change forming a matrix based on purpose (intrinsic and extrinsic elements) and authority (centralisation and decentralisation). They also used a frame/process model, based on the idea that educational processes and outcomes are often influenced by circumstances and preconditions at various levels in an educational system. Such framing factors are not always taken into account when reform goals are formulated. On the issue of implementation, they developed an arena model based on the twin concepts of space of action and capacity for action. The key point in this conception is "that the actor's autonomy is dependent upon the extent to which [they] succeed in exploiting [their] space of action and ... capacity for action in order to realise [their] own preferences" (Bauer et al. 1999: 35).

6. CONCLUSIONS

We return to the central question that this chapter has addressed. How was a single education minister able to change a national higher education system so fundamentally in a short space of three years? Why was Minister Dawkins so successful in the implementation of his reform package? His success was particularly significant when it is remembered that Dawkins was Commonwealth education minister and within the Australian federal system of government the Commonwealth has never had constitutional powers for higher education, although for the past half century it has achieved significant leverage over higher education through its 'power of the purse'.

In terms of the Cerych and Sabatier framework, despite the substantial change envisaged, Dawkins was successful because of the clarity and consistency of the reform goals that were an integral part of major national economic reform and were strongly supported by leading business and professional groups, and influential media. There was a clear underlying causal theory with a well-developed plan of implementation, particularly concerning political and administrative processes and how key reform elements might be achieved. The latter related particularly to achievement of substantial increases in student enrolments and graduate completions, increased research activity and university contributions to national R&D, increased institutional efficiency achieved and an effective return to a form of student tuition fees. Attracting substantial additional Commonwealth financial resources to facilitate rapid expansion in student enrolments and in research proved relatively easy because of the high standing of Dawkins in cabinet, and especially after he gained agreement on the new mechanism for student financial contributions. Although the bulk of additional financial resources were employed to facilitate expansion in student numbers and research, significant resources also were employed as incentives to assist institutional mergers and reward cooperating universities. A high degree of commitment from officials was ensured by replacing the CTEC with a new higher education division and from the start Dawkins was strongly supported by an influential group of university vice-chancellors. With few exceptions, the passage of enabling legislation in Commonwealth and State Parliaments provided no major problems, while social and economic conditions worked to the Minister's advantage, generating on-going strong support from higher education sector leaders and from community elites and the serious press.

Apart from all this, of vital importance were political factors and political alliances, particularly the political skills and commitment of the Minister, and his ability to attract support, persuade, publicly confront opponents, bargain and personally steer the implementation process. Significantly, the Minister used a surprisingly large range of different policy instruments while the speed with which he moved and the breadth of the reform package provided difficulty for opponents to mount effective and timely opposition. This was especially the case with the academic unions and student associations.

REFERENCES

Bardach, E. *The Implementation Game: What Happens After a Bill Becomes a Law.* Cambridge: MIT Press, 1977.

Bauer, M., B. Askling, S.G. Marton and F. Marton. *Transforming Universities: Changing Patterns of Governance, Structure and Learning in Swedish Higher Education*. London: Jessica Kingsley, 1999.

Blair, R. "Policy Tools Theory and Implementation Networks: Understanding State Enterprise Zone Partnerships." *Journal of Public Administration Research and Theory* 12.2 (2002): 161–190.

Cerych, L. and P. Sabatier. *Great Expectations and Mixed Performance: The Implementation of Higher Education Reforms in Europe*. Stoke-on-Trent: Trentham Books, 1986.

Cline, K.D. "Defining the Implementation Problem: Organization Management versus Cooperation." *Journal of Public Administration Research and Theory* 10.3 (2000): 551–571.

Cobb, R.W. and C.D. Elder. *Participation in American Politics: The Dynamics of Agenda Building*. Baltimore: Johns Hopkins Press, 1972.

Dawkins, The Hon. J.S. *Higher Education: A Policy Discussion Paper* (Green Paper). Canberra: Australian Government Publishing Service, 1987.

Dawkins, J. *Higher Education: A Policy Statement* (White Paper). Canberra: Australian Government Publishing Service, 1988.

De Leon, P. and L. de Leon. "What Ever Happened to Policy Implementation? An Alternative Approach." *Journal of Public Administration Research and Theory* 12.4 (2002): 467–492.

Gallagher, M. "The Emergence of Entrepreneurial Public Universities in Australia." Paper presented at the IMHE General Conference, Paris, 11–13 September, 2000.

Harman, G. "The Dawkins Reconstruction of Australian Higher Education." *Higher Education Policy* 2.2 (1989): 25–30.

Harman, G. "Institutional Amalgamations and Abolition of the Binary System in Australian Higher Education under John Dawkins." *Higher Education Quarterly* 45.1 (1991): 176–198.

Harman, G. "Institutional Mergers in Australian Higher Education." *Higher Education Quarterly* 54.4 (2000): 343–366.

Harman, G. "The Impact of New Public Management on Higher Education Reform in Australia." In Nolan, Brendan C. (ed.). *Public Sector Reform: An International Perspective*. London: Palgrave (formerly Macmillan), 2001, 151–166.

Kogan, M. and S. Hanney. *Reforming Higher Education*. London: Jessica Kingsley Publishers, 2000.

Maitland, R.E. "Synthesizing the Implementation Literature: The Ambiguity-Conflict Model of Policy Implementation." *Journal of Public Administration Research and Theory* 5.2 (1995): 145–175.

Majone, G. and A. Wildavsky. "Implementation as Evolution." In Freeman, H. (ed.). *Policy Studies Review Annual*. Beverly Hills: Sage, 1978.

Marginson, S. and M. Considine. *The Enterprise University: Power, Governance and Reinvention in Australia*. Melbourne: Cambridge University Press, 2000.

Meek, V.L. and L.C.J. Goedegebuure. *Higher Education: A Report*. Armidale: Department of Administrative and Higher Education Studies, University of New England, 1989.

Nelson, B. *Higher Education at the Crossroads: An Overview Paper*. Canberra: Department of Education, Science and Training, 2002.

O'Toole, L.J. Jr. "Treating Networks Seriously: Practical and Research-Based Agendas in Public Administration." *Public Administration Review* 57.1 (1997): 45–52.

O'Toole, L.J. Jr. "Research on Policy Implementation: Assessment and Prospects." *Journal of Public Administration Research and Theory* 10.2 (2000): 263–288.

Pressman, J.L. and A. Wildavsky. *Implementation*. Berkeley and Los Angeles: University of California Press, 1973.

Sabatier, P.A. (ed.). *Theories of the Policy Process*. Boulder: Westview Press, 1999.

Sharpham, J and G. Harman (eds). *Australia's Future Universities*. Armidale: University of New England Press, 1997.

Sinclair, T.P. "Implementation Theory and Practice: Uncovering Policy and Administration Linkages in the 1990s." *International Journal of Public Administration* 24.1 (2001): 77–94.

Wilson, C.A. "Policy Regimes and Policy Change." *Journal of Public Policy* 20.3 (2000): 247–274.

ROLLIN KENT

THE CHANGING ROLE OF THE STATE IN MEXICAN HIGHER EDUCATION: FROM THE CRISIS OF INEFFECTUAL POPULISM TO NEW FORMS OF SYSTEM COORDINATION

1. INTRODUCTION

This chapter[1] examines policy change in Mexican higher education throughout the 1990s and draws on a comparative research project[2] on higher education policy change in North America to which I am a contributor. In exploring these changes Clark Kerr's insistence on the word *change* rather than *reform* seems pertinent – it will be necessary to describe how the organisational and institutional aggregate that is called the *system* of higher education has been altered in the context of rather significant political and cultural shifts. In the concluding section, these emerging issues and patterns will be discussed using Cerych and Sabatier's analysis in *Great Expectations and Mixed Performance* as well as parts of Sabatier and Jenkins-Smith's (1999) later work on the *Advocacy Coalition Framework*.

2. EXAMINING POLICY: CULTURAL AND POLITICAL SHIFTS SURROUNDING HIGHER EDUCATION

Cerych and Sabatier's title *Great Expectations and Mixed Performance* says it all. Expectations – high and low – are crucial to policy change and to the evaluation of policy. In his foreword to *Great Expectations*, Clark Kerr rightly points to the importance of the social and cultural climate surrounding higher education policy. In periods of social optimism, great things are expected of higher education. In the current pessimistic climate, expectations tend to be more circumscribed by realistic assessments of what is possible and by cynical views of the intentions of policy makers and institutional leaders. The word *performance* is also heavily laden with values and premises that usually go unsaid. Consequently, how performance is judged cannot be value-neutral. Moreover, we should not forget Elaine El-Khawas' (2001) well-taken point that all too often judgments are made on the basis of insufficient evidence developed from skewed questions. Inevitably, tacit judgments are present in the following analysis, as it is directly influenced by the author's involvement in the ongoing academic and political debate surrounding higher education policy in Mexico.

Å. Gornitzka et al. (eds.), Reform and Change in Higher Education, 187-206.

This chapter will argue that the ongoing undeclared judgments by policy makers influenced the evolution of policy decisions. These ongoing assessments were usually not the object of public debate, either in the legislative arena or through the circulation of policy papers. But, at the same time, this technocratic style of policy making was usually receptive to ongoing controversy in the media and to input from academics and specialists. If policy formulation and implementation are not merely a rational technical exercise – as they surely are not – we must expect the political and cultural texture of policy making to be important and we must assume it will vary across national contexts. The policy environment in Mexican higher education has been undergoing significant change. The political system and the structures of public administration have been in flux for a decade and a half. Thus, uncertainty about changing rules was part of the landscape in the early 1990s. But it also provided new opportunities for political, academic and institutional entrepreneurs who thrive in situations of changing resource levels and porous boundaries.

This chapter will examine how policy produced new system behaviours and roles. Today, the higher education system in Mexico includes various types of functionaries, planners, evaluators, financial managers and consultants, who bring their networks, values, discourses and varying modes of access to resources and influence. These roles, practices and values were absent a decade ago. The dynamics of specialisation, professionalisation and division of labour in the policy-making establishment are a visible symptom of new forms of system coordination and regulation. They are partly explained by shifts in the belief systems of the various agents and their emerging forms of interaction. As a result, over a period of a decade and a half, the role of the state in higher education has been transformed: in the 1980s the federal government had become virtually a captive financial supporter of institutions politicised by unions, political parties and student movements; today, various levels of government at the national and local level seek to regulate public and private institutions that must inevitably play the game of financial incentives and strategic planning according to government rules.

3. AN OVERVIEW OF THE SYSTEM CHANGE IN THE 1990s

Retrospectively, one may imagine a fictitious conversation back in 1989 with the rector of a public university in Mexico. The question might be:

> What would you say if I predicted that ten years from now we will have an accreditation system, public universities will be doing strategic planning, there will be 40 new two-year technical institutes, more than 160 four-year technical colleges, 10 new polytechnic universities, a rapidly growing postgraduate level and a booming private sector with a growing interest in online programmes?

The rector would naturally respond:

> I'd say you're crazy. That would imply a major reform. And anyway our Association of Rectors would just not let the government do that.

Well, it did happen. And the Rectors' Association did not do much about it, except for some resistance at first. It is noteworthy that these changes occurred without a major reform movement in the political sense. There has been public debate, of course, but it certainly lacked the intensity that one would have expected, given the ideological climate of the 1980s. With the exception of student opposition at the National University (UNAM) to various attempts at raising fees, almost every other public university in Mexico has raised fees moderately without much ado – a significant ideological shift in itself. The media pounced on the exception of UNAM and downplayed the larger picture.

Nor have these transformations been the result of widely debated legislative decisions. They have been undertaken without legal reforms of any significance. The executive branch of government used its considerable authority and the power of the purse to push through policies that clearly went against the grain. For financially starved universities, the economic incentives offered by the federal Secretary of Education were irresistible (see table 1 for a succinct view of funding trends).

Table 1. Public expenditures on higher education

	1989	2001
Public (federal + state) expenditure on education/GDP	3.7%	5.2%
Federal expenditure on higher education/GDP	0.4%	0.7%
Federal expenditure on higher education/Total Federal Budget	1.2%	3.1%
Federal expenditure on higher education (millions of US$)	$1409.7	$3992.1

Source: Fox 2001

A closer look at the figures would reveal a less significant increase in terms of per student expenditures. It is also important to note that the 1995 financial collapse in Mexico brought a decrease in public funding for higher education. The decline ended four years later when pre-1995 funding levels were once more attained. Complaints by state university rectors are a constant, especially when they (rightly) point out that enormous federal institutions with great political clout like UNAM get an unfairly large share of public funding. Overall, however, federal and state spending for education generally, with an emphasis on basic education, has remained a priority throughout the decade. Most certainly the initial burst of spending in the early 1990s contributed to bringing the Rectors' Association on board with policy changes that they had originally resisted.

These figures tell only part of the funding story. Private expenditures in higher education have also grown over the past decade. Data from household income surveys show that the percentage of total family income spent on higher education has doubled since 1992 (INEGI 2002). Figures for corporate donations are not available, but many large private universities depend more and more on this type of funding, as evidenced by the growing number of private foundations. If this data were available, they would certainly reveal a significant increment in private funding for higher education overall.

3.1. Social Participation and Equity Issues

The trends in funding mentioned here are manifestations of the growing social demand and willingness to pay for higher education that were the driving forces behind enrolment expansion. As can be seen from table 2, national enrolments increased by 70% between 1985 and 2001. Women and private sector enrolments took up much of this growth. Also notable is the relative growth outside the capital city: regional expansion of higher education is a very important part of the changes underway.

Table 2. Enrolment growth and social participation

	1985	1990	2001
Total enrolments in higher education	960,000	1,078,000	1,700,000
Women/total	35%	40%	48%
Private sector enrolments/total	15.7%	17.4%	31.5%
Decentralisation: Enrolments in Mexico City/total	30%	23.3%	19.5%
Participation rate 19–23 yr olds		12.6%	17.5%
Population over 18 yrs with higher education		7.4%	10.9%
Population with higher education/1000 inhabitants		12.8	18

Source: ANUIES (Rectors' Association) 2000

Nonetheless, the participation rate of 19 to 23 year olds in higher education is still quite low, compared to other Latin American countries that have also reformed their systems, such as Argentina or Chile. This means that while most of the middle and upper strata are sending their young people to higher education, this is not so for lower income families. In spite of its growth, Mexican higher education remains very inequitable. National data on the socio-economic status of students are not collected as a matter of course (a notable policy failure), but analyses of household income surveys show that public subsidies favour middle and upper income groups over lower income students (Post 2001; SEP 1999). Local surveys at some public universities also show that few incoming students come from families with less than upper secondary schooling. Expansion does not necessarily lead to social mobility, if poor students lack financial aid or if institutions are not within reach of the rural population. The opportunity costs of higher education for poor rural students in a transition economy such as Mexico's can also be very high (Lewis and Dundar 2002): many young people between 15 and 20 years from the poorer rural areas in Southern Mexico decide to emigrate illegally to the United States rather than continue studies beyond secondary school. The growth of private establishments, all based in large cities and charging fees, does little to offset social inequality.

Persistent inequity is thus a crucial issue for higher education policy, but it was not recognised as such when the reforms were initiated in the early 1990s. At that time, quality was the main concern and it remained so throughout the decade. However, by the mid-1990s the single-minded emphasis on quality was criticised by the OECD examiners of higher education, who pointed out that quality improvement policies would not overcome severe social inequities (OECD 1996). Since that moment and continuing into the Fox administration (SEP 2001), there has been a greater emphasis on providing higher education to poor students and young people from rural areas and indigenous groups.

3.2. Institutional Diversification (1): New Public Institutions

A notable trait of this expansion has been institutional diversification, as shown in table 3. The public sector has developed a whole range of two-year and four-year technical institutes. All of the establishments are part of the push for decentralisation: they are partly funded by the federal government but it is up to state governments to carry out the planning, partial funding and coordination of these institutes, most of which are set in small cities and rural areas. The goals of this policy are twofold: on the one hand, to provide opportunities to preparatory school graduates in poor urban and rural settings; and, on the other hand, to strengthen technical capacity and links with firms at the local level. An implicit goal is also evident: involving state and local governments in the funding and coordination of higher education, thus changing and diversifying the interactions between higher education and the state.

Table 3. Institutional diversification

	1990	2001
Public Sector		
Federal and state universities	43	46
Federal technical institutes	96	111
State technical institutes	0	80
Two-year technical institutes	0	38
Polytechnics	0	3
Research institutes	3	26
Private Sector		
Universities	50	100
Institutes, academies, colleges	162	545
Total number of establishments	354	946

Source: ANUIES 2000

A new sector of research and postgraduate institutes has received consistent support as part of federal policy for research and development. These centres tend to specialise in certain areas, such as applied mathematics, optics, metallurgy, biotechnology and marine sciences. They are mostly staffed by young PhDs led by a small group of senior scientists, and their facilities are usually well equipped. Their mission is to develop strong links with firms and to train new generations of scientists.

These institutions – generically called CONACYT centres – are not strictly universities in the sense that their teaching role is limited to postgraduate students and because their overarching function is research and development. As such, CONACYT centres are coordinated directly by the National Science Council,

CONACYT, rather than by the Assistant Secretary for Higher Education in the Ministry of Education who is responsible for the university sector. Implicit in this design is the realistic assessment by policy makers of the weak scientific capacity of state universities. Recent studies have shown that public and private universities are responding quite feebly to federal incentives for strengthening research capacity (Kent et al. 2003; Chavoya 2002). The unspoken understanding is that most universities[3] have a deeply ingrained culture oriented toward the teaching function, with research usually playing a minor role often beset by internal bureaucratic tensions. As a result of this undeclared assumption, federal research policy has focused not only on strengthening existing groups of scientists within universities but also on creating non-university settings in which new scientific research may flourish. There is a general policy leitmotiv here that deserves to be brought forward. As the 1990s progressed, policy makers seem to have experienced growing dissatisfaction with meagre results in research productivity and quality of teaching in the university sector. In addition to partially sidestepping state universities in research policy, we will have occasion to argue that this critical ongoing assessment had other consequences for policy reformulation.

3.3. Institutional Diversification (2): The Growing Private Sector

Most notable in this story of institutional diversification, of course, is the expansion of the private sector. In Mexico, the number of private establishments tripled in eleven years. Although most of the new ones are small academies with feeble infrastructure and part-time faculty who do not normally hold masters or PhD degrees, there is a growing number of academically respected private universities as well.

Similar trends are evident in other developing countries, such as South Africa, the Philippines and Brazil (Kruss and Kraak 2003; Altbach 1999). But then perhaps this is not exclusively a developing country phenomenon either: except for differences in time, geographical reach and level of funding, these trends may not be unlike the growth of private higher education in the United States in the twentieth century, as described by Burton R. Clark (1987: 14):

> the private sectors, with only one-fifth of the students and one-fourth of the faculty, [are] enormously varied: the research-centered university ... the secular urban-service university ... the Catholic municipal university ... the secular elite liberal arts colleges ... the rear-guard denominational schools ... and institutions at the tail end of the academic procession, inferior to the best high schools [which] are, as put by David Riesman, 'colleges only by the grace of semantic generosity' (Riesman 1956).

In Mexico today, certain conditions prevail that provide fertile ground for private expansion in higher education. There are profits to be made in a market with conditions such as the following:

- Demand for higher education diplomas is on the rise.
- Barriers to entry are low: relatively small investments in facilities and infrastructure are required if academic offerings are limited to the

administrative professions; technology costs could be high but this is optional if the establishment is surrounded by internet cafés.

- Official requirements for quality control are not stringent, although this has become an important issue and will probably change.
- There is a qualified workforce seeking jobs in a buyer's market: higher education graduates are having trouble finding work and often accept low wages for part-time employment as teachers in private establishments.
- No legal distinction exists between for-profit and non-profit establishments of higher education; in such a lax legal environment private entrepreneurs are under no pressure to distinguish themselves from bona fide educational institutions.
- Accreditation systems are in their infancy and good information for the consumer of educational services is not easily obtained.

In some ways, this higher education market differs little from that of the informal sector of the economy, which has expanded so briskly in countries experiencing deep economic dislocations such as Mexico. That is, the dynamics of supply and demand are so brisk that they overwhelm state capacity to regulate or coordinate. From the entrepreneurial perspective, this market is vigorous and healthy; but opinion leaders in the public sector fret over the chaos and low quality, calling for government intervention. However, it must be pointed out that the current state of private higher education in Mexico is not merely the result of unplanned change. There is a tacit policy goal being realised here as well. Public officials declare that government resources are insufficient to create sufficient student places in public institutions to meet demand, recognising implicitly that private sector expansion is in the public interest. This should be the case if publicly funded institutions exclusively served economically needy students without subsidising higher income students; but recent studies show that this is not the case, as noted above.

There has been significant growth in the academically consolidated universities, which doubled in number over the decade. Some of these universities evolved entrepreneurially: having started out as small establishments, they matured over the years into more established academic institutions or specialised technical colleges as a result of academic entrepreneurship.

Other academically consolidated universities are actually spin-offs from previously well-established academic institutions, taking any of the following routes:

- *Expansion through franchising*: This is the model followed by the Monterrey Technical Institute, which today has large campuses in more than 20 states throughout Mexico. The franchise is sought out by business and/or academic leaders in a region that lacks a good private university; they approach Monterrey Tech, pool the financial resources and usually lobby the state government to donate the land. Once these conditions have been met, the Institute provides the academic and business model for the new establishment and also usually hires the senior academics, who then hire the rest of the staff locally as well as recruit Tech graduates from other regions. The new campus is then extensively advertised locally in the media and on urban billboards, signing up students in advance who pay up front and help finance the new installations, which can be up and running within a year. A national council led by the central campus in Monterrey brings regional managers together regularly and sets guidelines for the national network.

- *Entrepreneurial growth with support from a religious order*: This route goes from single to multi-campus establishments. The political and business clout of the religious order help in lobbying local authorities for land donations. Churches and lay groups associated with the order spread the word through social networks that a new type of humanist and value-centred curriculum is coming to town. The Universidad Iberoamericana, the largest Jesuit higher education establishment in Mexico, has followed this route in establishing large campuses in five cities. Its example is being followed by other Catholic orders.
- *Expansion through buyouts*: An example of this route is, in 2000, Sylvan Learning Systems in the United States bought into Universidad del Valle de México, a private establishment with campuses in several cities. Their publicity offers online programmes and opportunities for international study. The Mexican buyout by Sylvan seems to be part of a more ambitious business plan for internationalisation, since Sylvan has also bought into a private university in Chile.[4]
- *Online programmes*: Monterrey Technical Institute, for example, has developed a Virtual University that offers online programmes to clients throughout Mexico and other Spanish speaking countries. Online programmes from other countries, mostly the United States, are also on offer.

4. THE CRISIS OF THE 1980s: SETTING THE STAGE FOR *MODERNISATION* IN THE 1990s

Fifteen years ago no mechanism of quality assurance existed in Mexican higher education, except for peer review and other traditional mechanisms in the scientific community. Decisions over hiring academics, creation of new programmes and funding allocations within and across institutions were generally made on the basis of political calculation and resource availability. The then powerful federal executive was the primordial focus for policy decisions, to the exclusion of state governments and the legislature (which usually approved executive budgets after nominal debate). Public universities were in the habit of mobilising unions, friendly political parties and student groups to exert pressure on a yearly basis for the approval of budgetary allocations. A paradox resulted: rather than setting the agenda and making policy, the powerful executive branch was actually captive to political forces within the university community and their partners throughout the political system. As long as funds were available to the government, this state of affairs was able to continue. That this situation was clearly detrimental to academic quality and institutional efficiency was a concern to federal officials in the education ministry, but the federal government had a national economic and financial emergency on its hands and thus lacked the political and financial resources to set things aright in higher education.[5] For the social and economic elites another option was available through the creation of private institutions of higher education for their offspring, thus exercising the *exit* option to situations of economic, political and organisational decline, to use Albert O. Hirschman's classic formulation (Hirschman 1970).

In 1988, the political balance was radically upset by the financial devastation resulting from the debt crisis, the collapse in international oil prices and the fiscal breakdown of the state. It became clear to all actors concerned that a new policy framework was required. Beginning with the Salinas administration in that year, a deeply critical assessment of the prevailing situation led to a series of policy formulations by federal officials, which today come under the term *modernisation of higher education*. The term *modernisation* was taken from the overall policy discourse of the period that focused on the need to reform the economy and the social institutions in the context of globalisation. Thus, modernisation refers to improving quality and efficiency of public and private organisations, amending public administration to increase national competitiveness and adapt social norms and values accordingly. The basic policy framework for higher education that emerged at that time has been sustained, with some reformulations, throughout three federal administrations to the present.[6]

5. SYSTEMIC REFORM THROUGH QUALITY IMPROVEMENT AND ASSURANCE AND INSTITUTIONAL DIVERSIFICATION

This section presents a summary of the priorities and programmes set forth by federal officials throughout the 1990s. Since broader description is precluded by the limits of this chapter, this list of policy initiatives attempts to present their general evolution over time.

First wave of reforms 1989–94

- Institutional self-evaluation by universities
- Quality improvement through investment in academic infrastructure and institutional facilities
- Focused competitive funding for development projects presented by universities
- Fee increase in public universities
- Upgrading faculty through support for postgraduate study by in-service professors
- Non-contractual performance incentives for faculty, raising income selectively on a competitive basis

---

- R&D policy: expand research capacity through new PhD programmes, competitive funding for research, investment in infrastructure and incentives to reverse the brain drain[7]
- *Laissez faire* policy toward rapid expansion of the private sector

---

Second wave 1995–2000

The financial crisis of 1995 resulted in funding cutbacks in higher education, although funding levels for elementary education were sustained. It took four years for higher education funding to recover to pre-1995 levels.

OECD Report on higher education:
- Strong critique of inequity, lack of responsiveness to economy
- The need for institutional diversification
- The need to create a single federal policy-making structure for all types of public institutions of higher education[8]
- The need to provide short-cycle postsecondary offerings

The federal response:
- Expand specialised research institutes throughout the country
- Increase funding for new short-cycle technical institutes
- Create a new subsector of four-year technical institutes under the coordination of state governments. Federal Undersecretary for Technical Education loses its centralised control over all new technical institutes

A critical federal reappraisal of policy results: public institutions are not responding as expected to quality assurance and improvement through benevolent input policy. Thus, a shift in causal theory behind reform leading to:
- Stricter evaluation procedures
- Creation of an accreditation system
- Financial control and audit
- Stronger faculty development programme

2000 to the present

Fox's policy document for higher education stresses:

- New definition of quality: learning, student mobility, curricular flexibility
- Greater emphasis on equity and access

- Accelerating links with business
- Strategic planning in public institutions: detailed three-year planning documents with performance targets to be monitored, programme accreditation is required
- Extension of the operations of the new National Council for Higher Education Accreditation to all public and private universities
- Greater push for internationalisation

2000 to the present (cont.)

- R&D policy: partnerships with industry; partial decentralisation of federal policy agency (CONACYT) to the state level
- Creation of a new public sector: regional polytechnic universities under coordination of state governments
- Financial aid for poor students (a first)
- New focus on regulating the private sector: greater stringency and control over official licencing procedures for new institutions and programmes; greater federal-state coordination over licencing; information on private institutions made available to the public

---

6. CHANGES IN THE STRUCTURE OF POLICY FORMULATION AND IMPLEMENTATION: THE STATE IS DEFINITELY BACK IN THE PICTURE (IN COMBINATION WITH THE MARKET)

Of principal concern to policy makers in the 1980s was the lack of state capacity to set priorities, to establish funding criteria, to promote quality control and improvement, to arbitrate disputes, and to involve institutions and social actors in developing higher education. Today, in contrast, the presence of the federal government as the effective public authority over higher education is very evident. There is a new role, which has been instigated at the federal level, for state and municipal governments to participate in funding and coordination. The balance of power at the federal and state levels has shifted as well: the loss of power in 2000 by the PRI after 70 years of one-party government has led to a more active role by legislatures and the judiciary over specific policy issues. Although there has been no constitutional change in higher education legislation, policy definition and enactment today are more complex processes influenced by a diverse array of forces. The budget is highly contested in the legislature, which is also lobbied directly by rectors (a practice unheard of in the *ancien régime*). The Rectors' Association plays an increasingly important and diverse set of roles as intermediary, lobbyist, implementer and mouthpiece. The growing influence of the association of private universities is evident in its participation in the National Council for Higher

Education Accreditation. Business associations publish position papers on higher education policy and participate in the establishment of private institutions locally.

This is an emergent process that has developed over recent years, and can be depicted as a complex dialectic among various forces, such as the following:

- Greater activism by federal government and closer management of more diverse public sectors of higher education, alongside a *laissez faire* stance toward the private sector.
- Federal consultation with the Rectors' Association on policy, but decision making and policy design carried out *en petit comité* by small technical groups.
- Vigorous entrepreneurial responses by the various agents in the private sector, including foreign institutions selling services online and establishing partnerships with Mexican universities.
- Growing involvement of other government actors, such as state and municipal governments, in promoting and regulating higher education.
- Increased attention by the media to public and private higher education, especially the issue of *educational fraud* and accountability.[9]
- Greater presence of multilateral organisations (OECD, World Bank, IADB) in policy orientations and public debate.

But this should not be interpreted as the reconstruction of *statism*, in which the market would be subordinated or controlled by political command centres. On the contrary, just as the state has enhanced and diversified its role, so too has the market. Put another way, there is a more active state that is openly experimenting with market mechanisms in the public sector, on the one hand, and engaging the private sector directly, on the other. Private institutions are no longer considered the enemy of the state but partners that contribute to higher education.[10]

Although there is an emerging consensus among the main actors in higher education along these lines, this did not happen quickly or easily (Kent and Ramírez 1999; Mendoza 2000). In the 1980s and early 1990s, government officials seemed to turn a blind eye to the expansion of the private sector, partly because they saw a positive trade-off between private growth and the obvious quality problems in the *demand-absorbing* institutions (Daniel Levy's term for diploma mills). Moreover, the priority at that point was dealing with grave problems in the public sector. But there was also an ideological taboo on public policy engaging the private sector directly. More recently, the incoming Fox administration attempted to abolish that taboo by naming the President of Monterrey Technical Institute, the largest and most successful private university in Mexico, as Secretary of Education. The taboo may not have been abolished but this attempted designation certainly was: the usually staid Rectors' Association rose up in rebellion along with the national teachers' union; the President backtracked, and then named a non-threatening state university rector as Secretary of Education.

Today, government officials openly talk of 'using' the market as a lever for change. For example, in a recent interview with our research team a state official acknowledged that the best way to manage the private sector, from the government standpoint, is to promote competition; therefore his boss the Governor openly lobbied the prestigious Monterrey Technical Institute to set up shop in his state in order to force the lesser institutions to improve. His office is also pushing these demand-absorbing institutions to become accredited and to introduce ISO recognition of their administrative processes. Thus, regulating the role of the private sector is on the agenda, and diverse options are being explored by policy makers. A far cry from a decade ago.

7. DISCUSSION AND CONCLUSIONS

Before proceeding with a more specific analysis of this process, it is useful to briefly consider the general characteristics of the political and economic context in the Mexican case. First, higher education reforms were launched within a centralised but paradoxically fragmented and ineffective policy subsystem. The central government, that is, the executive branch (with minor participation by the legislature, except to authorise funding), made the principal decisions, but its authority was fragmented at the top into two public sectors; and its decisions were constantly subjected to political negotiations with the universities and their mobilised constituents. With hindsight, it is reasonable to state that reforming this subsystem in order to rebuild state capacity was itself a major priority of higher education policy.

Second, the wider structure of public administration has been changing as it moves toward decentralisation, that is, devolution of powers and attributions from the federal to the state and municipal levels of government.

Third, the national political setting has undergone important changes toward pluralism, competition, democratisation and greater separation of powers. Today, higher education policy must be made and implemented in the context of divided governments, where one party controls the executive and another party or coalition may control the legislature. The judiciary has woken up from a prolonged slumber and is intervening in policy decisions as well.

Finally, but crucially, the economic context has shifted radically away from being closed and politically controlled toward international competition and the uncertainty that comes with it. The economic boost of the first post-NAFTA years has been overshadowed by other new competitors (such as China) which are today displacing Mexico because of the latter's decreasing national competitiveness in wages, technology, innovation and efficiency. These emerging problems have played an important role in the ongoing critical assessment of results obtained by higher education reforms.

From the perspective of Cerych and Sabatier's formulation, the structure of decision making and implementation of higher education policy has been affected by a number of important changes which are evident in various stages of the policy process:

- policy initiation and consultation with a more diverse policy community;
- budget approval;
- specific policy design and funding allocations;
- implementation;
- evaluation and reformulation.[11] In general terms for the Mexican case, the concept of consecutive stages has less explanatory power than the concept of ongoing interaction between formulation, implementation and reformulation in an evolutionary process. In general, therefore, the critique of the *stages heuristic* as recognised and developed by Sabatier and Jenkins-Smith (1999) is relevant here.

Using both Cerych and Sabatier's framework for higher education policy and the later position expressed by Sabatier and Jenkins-Smith, the analysis below will examine the following aspects: programme goals, the factors affecting implementation and changes in the belief system.

7.1. Analysis of Programme Goals

According to Cerych and Sabatier, success of reforms is critically dependent on two aspects of the goals themselves: clarity and consistency of goal formulation and the amount of change envisaged.

With regard to the first aspect, policy documents for Mexican higher education tend to use general goal statements followed by quite precise formulations of policy instruments. For example, quality improvement was obviously a high priority, but specific goals for quality improvement were not defined. The means to attain these goals were, however, clearly specified in terms of investing in inputs (infrastructure, salaries) and creating evaluation systems. The same may be said of goals pertaining to access and equity, which were formulated in rather general terms but lacking specific standards to be met. Throughout the policy documentation, there is a clearer formulation of and emphasis on policy instruments, whereas the ends themselves received a broader treatment. This strategy – whether it reflects actual ambivalence about goals or not – in effect served the purposes of policy makers who were not under specific constraints to develop policy programmes and could therefore adapt and modify them as the need arose. It also reflects the characteristics of the policy formulation process in the federal government in Mexico at the end of the 1980s: a powerful executive in a one-party system without major constraints from the legislature or the judiciary is a natural setting for a technocratic decision-making process.

As for the depth of the reforms envisaged by policy makers, it is useful to recall Cerych and Sabatier's words: "... the difficulty a reform encounters is likely to be crucially dependent upon its departure from the values and procedures of the existing order" (1986: 12). Now, there is no doubt that the goals set forth in a clear policy statement by Mexican officials in 1989 represented a break with tradition and with values deeply embedded in the higher education system. With its emphasis on quality improvement and assurance, accountability, institutional diversification and competition for funds, the new policy discourse embodied a drastic shift in values and expectations. Public universities and technical institutes were accustomed to competing politically for funds, not on the basis of academic performance but on the basis of influence and pressure. Quality had been subsumed under a longstanding push for unregulated expansion. Initial resistance by university rectors and unions was nonetheless overcome by the federal government's use of financial incentives to bring the rectors on board and by public debate which clearly favoured a change in policy.

In terms of *scope*, policy attempted to have an effect on all public sectors (normal schools, universities, technical institutes). Policy affected the private sector only indirectly at first, nonetheless creating significant opportunities for private sector expansion. As the consequences of this unregulated expansion became problematical, policy makers began concerning themselves with more direct regulation of private institutions.

7.2. Factors Affecting Implementation

7.2.1. The First Factor: Adequacy of Causal Theory
With hindsight, it is possible to say the understanding of causal theory was relatively vague in the first wave of policy change in Mexican higher education. Clarity actually emerged and improved over time, as different strategies were attempted and assessed in succeeding efforts to raise quality. At the beginning, it was thought that injecting fresh resources and establishing evaluation mechanisms would lead to quality improvement. When this proved to be too simple a formulation, a new element was added to the quality improvement equation: if faculty were upgraded in their disciplines (by attaining masters and doctoral degrees), quality of teaching and learning would improve. Later, another component was added to the equation, as it became clear that governance and management needed to be reformed as well through specific strategic planning mechanisms imposed on institutions.

As for jurisdiction by policy makers over critical linkages in the higher education system, it was clear from the beginning that academic institutions, especially legally autonomous ones, would not respond to a command strategy, particularly in view of the recent history of politicisation and mobilisation in public universities. In this respect, the role of the Rectors' Association in mediating between the government and institutional leaders became crucial. Additionally, federal policy makers learned that financial incentives are very useful tools in implementing policy in higher education.

7.2.2. The Second Factor: Adequacy of Financial Resources
In general, and over a period of a decade, new financial resources were injected into the higher education system. Fresh funds provided through competitive bidding for institutional development projects clearly contributed to weakening opposition to the reforms, although the rectors' complaint of insufficient resources has never been fully addressed. Additionally, the financial crisis of 1995 brought about serious cutbacks in public expenditures, which took three years to recover the levels reached

in 1994. This uncertainty in year-to-year funding levels has tended to undermine the effectiveness of federal policy toward public universities and technical institutes. Financial constrictions are especially detrimental to technical institutes which operate within a centralised bureaucratic structure and therefore lack the political room to manoeuvre enjoyed by autonomous universities. On the other hand, financial support for the newly created two-year technical institutes is widely deemed to be sufficient (based on reports by institute officials and on complaints by universities of what they perceive as over-generous funding for this new institutional sector).

7.2.3. The Third Factor: Commitment to Objectives by Implementing Agents and Veto/Clearance Points

In the creation of a new sector, the two-year technical institutes, these issues were overcome rather easily. But in the public university sector, implementation by rectors and department heads was uneven and often unenthusiastic at best. The principal instrument applied in overcoming these veto points were financial inducements. The result has been simulation games that produce uneven implementation. This means that as one examines different institutions (and different departments within them), quality improvement and assurance policies are perceived and developed in different ways and with differing intensity.

7.2.4. The Fourth Factor: Interest Group Support

Nonetheless, there has been notable continuity in objectives and programmes across three federal administrations, from 1989 to 2003. This is all the more interesting since this period has not been politically stable: it covers two PRI administrations and the first non-PRI administration in modern Mexican history; it also covers important episodes such as the signing of the North American Free Trade Agreement and the 1995 financial crisis as well as the Zapatista uprising in late 1994.

There are several reasons for this policy resilience throughout a period of great socio-economic change. One explanation has to do with a basic ideological legitimacy for *modernisation* in higher education: in spite of resistance by some rectors and other interest groups, federal policy discourse was able to express a widely felt critique of the crisis reached by higher education in the late 1980s as well as a consensus among elites in academe, policy and business around the need to upgrade and modernise higher education.

Another reason for continuity is that federal policy makers formed an *esprit de corps* and a commitment to policy objectives, in part as a result of their common academic origins. Most policy makers are recruited from highly regarded academic programmes in universities that are friendly to policy objectives. There has been relatively little turnover within a given administration, and policy leaders have been successful in recruiting and training younger policy experts who later develop careers within public administration.

Third, and most significantly, federal policy makers were able very early in the game to neutralise a very important political actor in higher education: university unions. The implementation of merit pay based on individual productivity assessments for academics successfully sidelined the historic role of unions in the battle for pay rises. The new discourse on productivity and quality brought about a process of *individualisation* in academic identity and behaviour, resulting in the abandonment by academics of union participation as a means of economic advancement. Professors thus concentrated on upgrading through obtaining postgraduate degrees and researchers on intensifying productivity through publications.

A fourth explanation for policy continuity is the supportive role of the Rectors' Association (ANUIES) which evolved relatively rapidly from a dissenting pressure group in the early 1990s to represent a positive force for implementation. The Association occupies a singular place as an intermediary in the higher education policy system: on the one hand, it is an association that represents university rectors; but, on the other hand, it receives most of its funding from the federal government, rather than from members' dues. ANUIES carries out an important role in aggregating and expressing the interests of public universities before legislative committees when federal budgets are debated. At the same time, federal officials know they may communicate regularly through ANUIES with rectors as a group.

7.3. Changes in the Belief System

A slight shift in theoretical focus is useful here, taking up the *Advocacy Coalition Framework* presented by Sabatier and Jenkins-Smith (1999) developed after Cerych and Sabatier's earlier study (1986) on higher education policy in Europe. Sabatier and Jenkins-Smith point out that "On major controversies within a *mature* policy subsystem, when policy core beliefs are in dispute, the lineup of allies and opponents tends to be rather stable over periods of a decade or so" (1999: 129).

In contrast, the episodes of change in Mexican higher education policy reveal shifting systemic sands, rather than a mature and stable coalition. This was especially so during the first half of the 1990s when longstanding beliefs were questioned by the collapse of traditional university-state relationships during the turbulent 1980s. To Sabatier and Jenkins-Smith's terminology, this would seem to qualify as a significant *external perturbation* that shook core beliefs. Since that time, however, the dust has settled somewhat, and a relatively stable policy subsystem seems to have developed. In this new context, *secondary beliefs* about the higher education system are in a process of change through experience and learning.

Throughout this period, the levels of government that interact with higher education have multiplied: from a single interaction with a centralist federal government to a multi-level interaction with federal, state and municipal governments; increasingly, international involvements are playing a role in higher education policy as well.

Once again, using the Advocacy Coalition Framework, one important result of policy change in Mexican higher education over the past decade and a half is the emergence of a policy subsystem with a new set of actors and rules. One notable trait of this scenario is the increased capacity of the state to coordinate higher education. In retrospect, it is probable that achieving this shift in the relationships between the state and higher education has been a central policy goal throughout the 1990s. Put another way, a crucial goal has been accomplishing greater *system coordination*, in order to align higher education with economic reforms and to facilitate international integration of higher education. This implies legitimating system-wide values that align with the public interest, rather than with specific institutional interests.

NOTES

[1]   I wish to express my thanks to Don Westerheijden from CHEPS for making available a copy of Cerych and Sabatier and to the anonymous reviewer of the first version of this chapter, whose critique was so useful.

[2]   Alliance for International Higher Education Policy Studies, headed by Richard C. Richardson, NYU, with the participation of Canadian colleagues coordinated by Donald Fisher and Kjell Rubinson, UBC. The project web site is at: http://www.nyu.edu/iesp/aiheps.

[3]   By design, technical institutes in Mexico do not have a research function, with minor exceptions.

[4]   According to a vice rector of the Chilean establishment, "Sylvan has left the academic side of the university largely in the hands of the original administration; the main changes Sylvan has introduced are mandatory English lessons and a greater emphasis on the use of computer technology in education. Our graduates in law, for example, know how to use Excel and make PowerPoint presentations" (Bollag 2003: A23). In effect, teaching English and the use of Microsoft *Office* seems to be the substance of this innovative academic offering.

[5]   Social and educational policy in general suffered neglect for the same reason: for several years the federal government's full attention was focused on negotiating the national debt and bringing about macro-economic adjustment.

[6]   Carlos Salinas (PRI) was President from 1988 to 1994, Ernesto Zedillo (PRI) to 2000, and Vicente Fox (PAN) to the present.

[7]   R&D policy was funded through a World Bank loan. All other higher education programmes were funded from fiscal resources.

[8]   The federal Ministry of Education contains two undersecretaries for higher education: one for autonomous universities and one (the Undersecretary for Technical Education) for the highly centralised subsystem of federal technical institutes.

[9]   *Reader's Digest* in its Spanish language version in Mexico has initiated the publication of a ranking of public and private higher education institutions. The methodology is based partly on indicators and partly on opinions solicited from experts, business people and academics.

[10]   Actually, the conceptual dichotomy of market vs. state in regard to forms of coordination loses explanatory relevance in the current context. It is increasingly clear that intermediate solutions are being attempted in various European nations. One conceptual perspective on these experiments is expressed by the proponents of the *new managerialism in public administration* (see Merrien 2000).

[11]   This chapter has expressed special interest in a point brought forth by Cerych and Sabatier: "Of particular interest is the reaction of implementing officials and the government to evidence of programme failure and success. For example, under what circumstances does failure lead to suppression of the evidence, a search for more effective means to attain the same goal, or a change in goals or goal priorities?" (1986: 11).

REFERENCES

Altbach, Philip G. (ed.). *Private Prometheus: Private Higher Education and Development in the 21ˢᵗ Century*. Boston: Center for International Higher Education, 1999.

ANUIES. *La Educación Superior en el Siglo XXI: Líneas Estratégicas para su Desarrollo*. México: ANUIES, 2000.

Bollag, B. "In Chile, a Fast-Growing University, Owned by Sylvan, Produces Profits and Scorn." *Chronicle of Higher Education* 49.42 (2003): A23.

Cerych, L. and P. Sabatier. *Great Expectations and Mixed Performance: The Implementation of Higher Education Reforms in Europe*. Stoke-on-Trent: Trentham Books, 1986.

Chavoya, María Luisa. "La institucionalización de la investigación en ciencias sociales en la Universidad de Guadalajara." *Revista de la Educación Superior*. México: ANUIES, vol. XXXI, 1.121 (2002): 7–26.

Clark, Burton R. *The Academic Life: Small Worlds, Different Worlds*. Princeton, NJ: Carnegie Foundation for the Advancement of Teaching, 1987.

El-Khawas, Elaine. "Today's Universities: Responsive, Resilient, or Rigid?" *Higher Education Policy* 14.3 (2001): 241–248.

Fox, Vicente. *First Annual Report by the Executive (Primer Informe de Gobierno)*. México: Presidencia de la República, 2001.

Friedman, Thomas. *The Lexus and the Olive Tree: Understanding Globalization*. New York: Random House, 2000.

Hirschman, Albert O. *Exit, Voice and Loyalty: Response to Decline in Firms, Organizations and States*. Cambridge, MA: Harvard University Press, 1970.

Instituto Nacional de Estadística, Geografía e Informática (INEGI). *Encuesta Nacional de Ingresos y Gastos de los Hogares*. 2002, http://www.inegi.gob.mx.

Kent, Rollin, G. Alvarez, M. González, R. Ramírez and W. de Vries. *Cambio organizacional y disciplinario en las ciencias sociales en México*. México: DIE-CINVESTAV y Plaza y Valdés Editores, 2003.

Kent, Rollin and Rosalba Ramírez. "Private Higher Education in Mexico in the 1990s: Growth and Differentiation." In Altbach, Philip G. (ed.). *Private Prometheus: Private Higher Education and Development in the 21st Century*. Boston: Center for International Higher Education, 1999, 95–112.

Kruss, Glenda and André Kraak. *A Contested Good? Understanding Private Higher Education in South Africa*. Boston: Center for International Higher Education, Boston College and PROPHE, 2003.

Lewis, Darrell R. and Halil Dundar. "Equity Effects of Higher Education in Developing Countries: Access, Choice and Persistence." In Chapman, David W. and Ann E. Austin (eds). *Higher Education in the Developing World. Changing Contexts and Institutional Responses*. Westport, CT: Greenwood Press, 2002, 169–193.

Mendoza, Javier. "La educación superior privada." In Latapí, Pablo (ed.). *Un siglo de educación en México*, vol. II. México: CONACULTA/Fondo de Cultura Económica, 2000, 325–354.

Merrien, François-Xavier. "Reforming Higher Education in Europe: From State Regulation Towards a New Managerialism?" Working Paper, Washington, DC: IADB, INDES, 2000.

OECD. *National Reviews of Policies for Higher Education: Mexico*. Paris: OECD, 1996.

Post, David. "Student Movements, User Fees, and Access to Mexican Higher Education: Trends in the Effect of Social Background and Family Income, 1984–1996." *Mexican Studies/Estudios Mexicanos*. Palo Alto, CA: Center for Latin American Studies, Stanford University, January, 2001, 8–20.

Riesman, David. *Constraint and Variety in American Higher Education*. Lincoln: University of Nebraska Press, 1956.

Sabatier, P.A. and H.C. Jenkins-Smith. "The Advocacy Coalition Framework: An Assessment." In Sabatier, P.A. (ed.). *Theories of the Policy Process*. Boulder, CO: Westview Press, 1999, 117–168.

Secretaría de Educación Pública (SEP). *Perfil de la educación en México*. 2nd edn. México: SEP, 1999.

Secretaría de Educación Pública (SEP). *Programa Nacional de Educación, 2001–2006*. México: SEP, 2001.

Vite, Norma. "Knowledge Based Development in Mexico: Is There a Role for the University?" Unpublished Working Paper, New York: New School University, 2003.

NICO CLOETE, PETER MAASSEN AND JOE MULLER

GREAT EXPECTATIONS, MIXED GOVERNANCE APPROACHES AND UNINTENDED OUTCOMES: THE POST-1994 REFORM OF SOUTH AFRICAN HIGHER EDUCATION

1. INTRODUCTION

The title of Cerych and Sabatier's seminal book on higher education policy implementation, *Great Expectations and Mixed Performance*, reflects also in many respects the feelings of a considerable proportion of the actors involved in the South African higher education reforms since 1994. The transition from a closed state ideology with higher education as part of the state structure, to a more open, democratic society has seen remarkably little dissent over both the new vision on higher education and the implementation of the higher education reforms. Nevertheless, the outcomes of the reforms are in many ways not in line with the reform aims. Very characteristically, this gap between expectations and performance has been characterised by the South African Minister of Education as being the result of an 'implementation vacuum' (Department of Education 2001).

In this chapter we will examine some of the underlying dimensions of this so-called implementation vacuum. We will do so by discussing the higher education reforms implemented since 1994 from the perspective of the shifts in governance introduced by the new, democratic South African government. We have decided to focus on the new governance approach because it provides the framework within which the higher education reforms had to be implemented. The starting point for our examination is the governance approach that the new government inherited from the apartheid era. We will discuss how the new government 'distanced itself' from this governance approach, amongst other things, by formulating policies that were intended to 'redress' some of the injustices of the apartheid regime.

2. FIRST REFLECTIONS ON GOVERNANCE

Cloete et al. (2002) developed a network approach to the higher education policy process in which three main groups of actors were identified, namely state-related actors, higher education actors and societal actors. The interactions between these actors were conceptualised and presented in the form of an analytical triangle (Cloete et al. 2002: 5–6; Maassen and Cloete 2002: 19–29). This triangle was used for describing and discussing policy developments in a number of areas, such as

Å. Gornitzka et al. (eds.), Reform and Change in Higher Education, 207-226.

staff and students, research and teaching, and funding. However, the triangle did not allow for an examination of the underlying nature of the changes taking place in the state–higher education relationship. One of the main reasons for this is that it focused exclusively on the policy dimension of the relationship, without making an effort to place this in a broader conceptual framework. In this chapter we will attempt to apply such a framework by taking the concept of governance as our 'analytical umbrella'. In our view, governance includes, in addition to the policy dimension, also the way a social sector such as higher education is organised and structured, as well as the way in which the management functions and decision-making structures in the sector are arranged. Instead of focusing solely on the policy dimension we will attempt to analyse policy processes as part of the governance shifts that have taken place in South Africa since the early 1990s.

As such, governance refers here to the efforts of a government to affect (regulate, steer, coordinate, control) the behaviour of citizens and organisations in the society for which it has been given responsibility. Governance arrangements are the set of institutions (Scott 1995: 33) and the 'steering capacity' used to influence the behaviour of individuals and organisations in society (Peters 2001: 1). We will start our analysis by introducing a conceptual scheme for considering shifts in governance.

3. NEW MODES OF GOVERNANCE

The renewed academic interest in the concept of governance has to do with the development of alternatives to hierarchical government control, that is, to the traditional mode of state-dominated coordination (Mayntz 1998). This traditional governance model was based on the following common principles (Peters 2001: 4–13). First, the civil service was apolitical, in other words 'neutrally competent' (Kaufman 1956). In addition politics and administration were seen as separate elements of governance. Second, public management was based on hierarchical principles and rule-boundedness. Third, the governmental organisations were permanent[1] and stable. Fourth, the civil service was institutionalised and governed as a corporate body. Fifth, the civil service was strictly controlled and regulated in detail. Finally, equality was an important principle in governance, with respect to outcomes as well as to organisation.

The importance and appropriateness of these principles for modern day governance have been questioned if not rejected. As a consequence, over the last few decades many countries around the world have undergone changes in the forms and mechanisms of governance, in the location of governance, in governing capabilities, and in styles of governance (Van Kersbergen and Van Waarden 2001; Peters 2001). For example, when it comes to the location of governance with respect to higher education, vertical shifts can be observed from national to supranational public bodies such as the European Union, or from national to regional authorities, such as in France, South Africa and Spain. Horizontally, shifts have taken place from public to semi-public or private forms of governance, for example, in the area of student support systems. Finally, an example of a mixed horizontal-vertical shift is the rise of international semi-public or private accreditation agencies in areas such as business administration.

Many authors have identified possible causes for the decrease in the effectiveness of traditional governance arrangements and hence the rationale for introducing new governance modes. A cause referred to by many authors is the economisation of societies. It is argued that the economic crises of the 1980s and early 1990s have forced governments to adapt their governance arrangements and to put economic considerations at the forefront of their governance approach (Savoie 1995). However, other authors have suggested that this explanation alone cannot account for the fundamental and far-reaching nature of the shifts in governance. Peters (2001: 14–15), for example, points to changing demographics and the decreasing social and political homogeneity among individuals and groups in society. In addition, traditionally stable governance arrangements and organisations have become destabilised making it more complicated for government to intervene in society (Cohen and Rogers 1994). These general developments can be observed worldwide, even though many smaller and larger variations can be found at the national level.

Since the late 1980s, a number of higher education scholars have used the concept of 'steering' to analyse changes in the relationship between the state and higher education. Van Vught (1989) introduced, for example, state control and state supervision models of government steering (Neave and Van Vught 1991; Maassen and Van Vught 1994; Maassen 1996). The implicit assumption underlying these models was that a development from state control to state supervision was to be promoted, because a supervising role of the state would lead to a better performance of higher education than a controlling role. State 'steering' was thus, from this perspective, the preferred alternative to the traditional 'top-down' form of coordination.

In the 1990s, a number of European higher education researchers (see e.g. Van Heffen, Verhoeven and De Wit 1999; Gornitzka and Maassen 2000) became interested in the four so-called state models introduced by Olsen (1988): the sovereign (or unicentric) state, the institutional state, the segmented (or corporatist) state, and the market state. Of these four models the first two, the sovereign state model and the institutional state model, can be regarded as variations of the traditional governance model discussed above. The other two models are alternatives to the traditional models. Unlike the models introduced by Van Vught, these four models are not necessarily mutually exclusive. They represent different ways of organising the relationship between the state and society, namely, state dominance and control, state protection of specific social values and norms, the state as one of the involved interest groups, and a minimal state. Mixed forms, far from being unusual, were common, as indicated by Gornitzka and Maassen (2000) who speak of 'hybrid' forms of governmental steering with respect to higher education. We will elaborate this notion of 'hybridism' later in this chapter.

The steering models introduced by Van Vught (1989) and the state models developed by Olsen (1988) reflect the governance shifts of the 1980s. They represent the transition period in which new governance approaches were studied without the old ones having been rejected completely. Maassen and Van Vught

(1988, 1989) talk in this period about the *Janus-head* character of state governance with respect to higher education (see also Amaral and Magelhães 2001).

Fifteen years later, it can be concluded that the transition period has in many ways reached its final stage. The traditional governance model in its basic form has been abandoned everywhere, even though in South Africa much of the governance debate is still cast in dichotomous terms of control versus steering. As a consequence, in discussing the nature of alternative governance models and the assumptions they have with respect to policy processes, a different approach is chosen compared to the approaches included in the above-mentioned studies. Instead of comparing 'old' and 'new' models it is assumed that the traditional model is, as such, no longer used and that various alternatives have been developed to replace the traditional model in practice.

We will start our analysis with a general discussion of shifts in governance. The purpose of this discussion is to "examine the ideas that motivate reform and that provide a diagnosis of the problems in the public sector as well as the basis for prescriptions to remedy the problems" (Peters 2001: 2). Peters makes a distinction between the first waves of reform of the traditional approach to governance that took place in the 1980s and early 1990s and were ideologically driven, and a recent, more pragmatic, development that combines further 'repair work' of the traditional model with attempts to deal with some of the flaws of the ideological reforms. In the first wave, four alternative approaches to governance emerged as alternatives to the traditional governance model, namely, governance through applying market mechanisms, through increased participation, through more flexibility, or through deregulation (see table 1).[2] The ideological nature of the reforms was especially clear in the case of the market approach that was introduced in many countries as an unquestioned improvement to the traditional governance approach.

Table 1. Summary of four alternative governance approaches

	Market	Participation	Flexibility	Deregulation
Principal diagnosis	Monopoly	Hierarchy	Permanence	Internal regulation
Structure	Decentralization	Flatter organizations	Virtual organizations	Power hierarchy
Management	Pay for performance; other private sector techniques	Management teams	Managing temporary personnel	Greater managerial freedom
Policy making	Internal markets; market incentives	Consultation; negotiation	Experimentation	Active bureaucracy
Public interest	Low cost	Involvement; consultation	Low cost; coordination	Creativity; activism

Source: Peters 2001: 21

Even though there is some overlap between the four approaches they can be distinguished on the basis of their different problem diagnosis with respect to the functioning of the traditional governance model and their ideas about the nature of the reforms necessary to address the problems.

This analysis of the introduction of alternatives to the traditional governance (steering, or state) model made in the late 1990s, early 2000s is more detailed and empirically better informed than the discussions of state steering to be found in the field of higher education studies at the end of the 1980s. Therefore we assume that this analysis is also of relevance for our examination of the governance changes in South Africa, and the policy processes with respect to higher education in particular.

4. GOVERNANCE APPROACH WITH RESPECT TO SOUTH AFRICAN HIGHER EDUCATION

4.1. Governance During Apartheid

While the apartheid period is commonly perceived to be massively repressive, allowing little or no autonomy, the apartheid state produced contradictory effects in interacting with higher education. In certain areas, some universities acquired a remarkable degree of autonomy and freedom whilst in other areas racist legislation and the use of the state security apparatus turned some of the universities into ideological and physical battlefields (Moja, Muller and Cloete 1996).

The apartheid regime's governance model for black institutions had certain features of what was described above as the traditional model, that is, control by legislation backed up by hierarchical central government administrative and executive powers with respect to administrative and academic structures, access, student affairs and funding, as well as the appointment of senior members of staff.

In contrast, the historically white institutions achieved an unprecedented degree of autonomy in the 1980s. However, this autonomy was relative given that these institutions were part of and had to operate within the apartheid regime's state structure. As a consequence there were episodic examples of state interference, targeting particularly individual students and staff. This situation can be interpreted by referring to Olsen's institutional state model (Olsen 1988). This model represents a variation of the traditional governance model in which a state wants to protect specific social values and norms. The historically white universities were seen as important instruments of the apartheid state in its efforts to protect certain values and norms linked intrinsically to its basic ideology, therefore the state 'protected' the white universities against certain external trends and influences. The combination of protection from the government side and the accompanying autonomy on the institutional side would only be maintained as long as the historically white institutions respected the 'pact' and cooperated in protecting certain values and norms.

4.2. Initial Governance Changes From 1994

What governance reforms with respect to higher education were introduced by the new democratic government from 1994? We will discuss these reforms in terms of the dimensions in the Peters (2001) typology, namely how the problems in the previous system were diagnosed, as well as structural, management and policy principles. As we will see, there were two phases to the reforms, involving quite different sets of assumptions and hence governance arrangements.

4.2.1. Diagnosis

The apartheid higher education system was regarded as discriminatory, non-participative, unaccountable, divisive, inequitable and undemocratic (NCHE 1996). As was the case in Eastern Europe, the rejection of the entire regime and its ideology over-determined the rejection of the governance arrangements, tarring all the arrangements, good and bad, with the same brush. Therefore developing a new governance approach could not be based on a straightforward analysis of what was wrong with the previous governance arrangements. The entire ensemble was to be rejected, at least rhetorically.

The new government consequently had to start with a policy statement of how it differed, especially ideologically and politically, from the previous one. The content of the policy statement as such was not the first priority. When a new government, in principle, has to distance itself politically from a continuation in governance arrangements (institutions and civil service, including staff) it cannot build upon what worked and change only what did not work in the past. As a consequence, the process of governance reform becomes more complicated than in countries where governments can ground reforms on stable and continuous governance structures. In other words, at the onset of reform in the mid-1990s, South Africa did not have the luxury of policy incrementalism available to it.

Influenced by the history of the problematic relationship between the government and higher education institutions, and taking into account international debates of the early 1990s, the National Commission on Higher Education (NCHE), appointed by President Mandela in 1994, proposed a model of 'cooperative governance' (NCHE 1996). Cooperative governance as conceptualised in the NCHE was a prescriptive, politically influenced schema derived from a reading of the new governance literature (Kooiman 1993; Maassen and Van Vught 1994) and of governance relationships in Africa. This governance proposal, though modelled on new governance approaches, was provided with no content beyond process statements on how to make decisions.

'Cooperative governance' accepted academic freedom as guaranteed by the South African Constitution and accepted that institutional autonomy would be exercised within a framework of government leadership through funding and planning. The government accepted the framework of the NCHE and the 1997 White Paper (Department of Education 1997a: section 3.6) states that:

> Recognising the need to transcend the adversarial relations between state and civil society arising from the apartheid era, the Ministry of Education adopts a model of co-operative governance for higher education in South Africa based on the principle of autonomous institutions working co-operatively with a proactive government and in a range of partnerships.

One of the central assumptions of this governance approach was that participation and cooperation would lead to greater equity and democracy, and thereby, it was tacitly assumed, to better higher education. To ensure this, all possible stakeholders had to participate in as many decisions as possible. The democratically elected government would have a 'proactive' role through developing national policy, thereby 'supervising' the system towards the desired democratic ideals.

4.2.2. Structural Reforms

According to the White Paper, higher education should be planned, governed and funded as a single national coordinated system in order to overcome the fragmentation, inequality and inefficiency which were the legacy of the past (Department of Education 1997a: section 2.1). The national Ministry of Education would drive the transformation of the higher education system through policies and strategies that would give effect to the transformation of higher education in the spirit of the cooperative governance approach. The Ministry would enhance the capacity of the newly established Higher Education Branch of the Department of Education, and establish a Council on Higher Education (CHE) with an affiliated Higher Education Quality Committee (HEQC) (Department of Education 1997a: sections 3.9, 3.10). Other structures introduced as part of the development towards a single coordinated system were the South African Qualifications Authority (SAQA) and the National Student Financial Aid Scheme (NSFAS). The advisory body for universities and technikons (AUT), which approved until then new academic programmes, was disbanded. Its functions were to be taken over by the SAQA and the CHE.

The White Paper also declared that the national government would 'enable reform of the governing structures of higher education institutions' (Department of Education 1997a: section 3.10). At the institutional level, the 1997 Higher Education Act made the Council the highest decision-making body with responsibility for the good order and governance of institutions and for their mission, financial policy, performance, quality and reputation. Meaningful involvement of students and staff in all permanent governance was encouraged through the establishment of an Institutional Forum, and the powers of the senate were circumscribed to dealing with academic and curriculum matters.

In addition to dealing with transformation at the institutional level, in the post-1994 period institutional leadership had to deal with an infinitely more complex national environment with a vastly increased and more complex institutional and legislative environment created to undo apartheid and promote equity and democracy.

The institutional landscape in 1994 consisted of 36 institutions: 21 universities and 15 technikons. This landscape was, in the words of the current Minister of Education, "the product of the geo-political imagination of apartheid planners" (Department of Education 2001: i) and it consisted of what the widely accepted critical diagnosis called 'historically black' and 'historically white' institutions, analytically referred to as 'advantaged' and 'disadvantaged'. With race and advantage being largely, but not completely, overlapping, the way to create a 'single coordinated system' was thought to be by the hopeful, but vague, notion of 'institutional redress'.

The debate about institutional redress started before the elections of 1994 (NEPI 1992) as a demand that all institutions must be 'equal' and shifted to a basis of 'differentiated functionality', meaning that it was acknowledged that institutions could have different missions and emphases, but redress would ensure that all institutions would have the minimum resources and capacity to function as effective higher education institutions. In the 1997 White Paper and the Higher Education Act, redress and the creation of a coordinated system were emphasised. However, this never materialised in a satisfactory way; as a consequence, the continued and increasing inequality in resources and academic and management capacity within the same system was to drive some of the post-1999 reforms.

4.2.3. Management Reforms

The White Paper at least tacitly acknowledged that all the new functions associated with steering would require additional capacity by noting that "the [higher education] Branch will augment its resources by contracting out as well as by the use of secondments from the higher education sector" (Department of Education 1997a: section 3.30). In practice this rarely happened.

Governance shifts entail management capacity for implementing the intended changes. In 'mature democracies' this mainly means building management capacity qualitatively, that is, by informing and, if necessary, (re)training the existing managers, while in South Africa, management capacity was a qualitative and quantitative requirement. Many of the existing managers, who had been part of the apartheid governance structure, had to be replaced, while the discontinuity in governance arrangements meant an introduction of new organisations and structures with the accompanying need for new managers with new capacities. In addition, in mature democracies, governance shifts hardly have a direct consequence for the composition of the civil service. Civil servants simply have to adapt to their new role. In South Africa, the intention was to replace the civil servants who were closely connected with the apartheid regime. Also, here was the need to build new structures/institutions with the accompanying managerial capacity, for instance, the need to reorganise the national Ministries of Education, the abolition of the 'homeland' Ministries of Education, and the building of education civil service capacities in the provinces. Throughout this phase, then, the dominant new ethos was that of 'cooperative' (democratic) management, which in the main meant cooperative decision making within a system of traditional hierarchies.

4.2.4. Policy Reforms

Apartheid was a comprehensive, state driven system that consisted of government formulated policy, implemented by the different government departments and state institutions. It was a fairly typical central planning approach to coordinating society; an approach that the apartheid planners shared with their great enemy, communist East Europe. What put it apart from 'normal' policy regimes was its comprehensiveness. It could be argued that its cessation was partially caused by poor or faulty evaluation, because the evaluation feedback loop did not lead the policy formulators to review the goals and objectives till it reached such a stage that it had to be abandoned, the frequent fate of ideologically driven policy regimes.

Policy formulators preparing for a new democratic state started from the assumption that apartheid had been such a pervasive, central state driven system that its undoing would likewise require a state driven, planned policy process, with the key differences being that the goals and processes would be progressive and participative. Thus, in addition to having different goals, the process would be democratised, but still with a strong central planning component. There was widespread belief that the market would not correct the injustices and imbalances caused by apartheid, and that individual institutional transformation would not result in an equitable and efficient system. Thus, despite the radically different goals and processes, what the two systems shared was a belief in the 'making', and 'remaking' of society, and the belief that a key instrument would be policy, formulated at the national level.

This approach to reform assumes that the collective will can be realised via a linear process that starts with identifying a problem, collectively formulating new policies to address the problem, and an implementation strategy to deliver the redemptive change. Unsurprisingly, such policy approaches usually founder in unintended consequences and disappointment, as will be discussed in the next section.

5. UNINTENDED CONSEQUENCES

Unintended consequences are inherent in all policy processes, but in South Africa, the emerging new higher education system did not look at all like the one described in the White Paper and the Higher Education Act of 1997. The following unintended outcomes have been described in Cloete and Bunting (2002), CHE (2000), Department of Education (2001) and Cloete et al. (2002):

1. Black student enrolment in the universities rose as a percentage of total enrolment from 32% in 1990 to 60% in 2000, while in the technikons it rose from 32% to 72%. Female student enrolment increased from 42% in 1990 to 53% in 2000. However, this equity revolution, undeniably impressive, was skewed because the enrolments of black and female students were still mainly in the less prestigious fields of study and overall throughput rates decreased.

2. At the historically black universities the number of students fell by 35,600 between 1995 and 2000 while, in comparison, the historically white Afrikaans-medium institutions gained 54,200 students over the same period. The historically black universities did not manage to attract white students (they are still more than 99% black) and retention rates as well as graduation rates at these institutions declined. The research output of the historically black universities as a group in percentage of the total output of the system decreased from 11% in 1995 to 10.2% in 2000. In rand terms,

the government appropriation to the historically black universities dropped by R102 million over the 1999–2001 budget cycle while the historically white Afrikaans-medium universities gained more than R230 million (22%) in subsidies because of increased black student enrolments.

3. A survey of 273 of South Africa's major employers reported in 1999 that 76% of them were experiencing a shortage of professional workers (Kraak 1999). This survey predicted that in the period 1998–2003 the job opportunities at this professional level would grow by between 16% and 18%, in other words, by far more than the current graduation rate.

4. Despite standardisation of subsidy criteria across the system, the result was increased differentiation and fragmentation, not the desired unified system. The vice-chancellor of the University of Cape Town, Njabulo Ndebele, had the following to say in 2001: "The expression 'single coordinated system' carried the same declarative and mobilising effect as the expression of South Africa being 'non-racial, non-sexist' and so on. In reality it will be a while before we have such a system" (Cloete et al. 2002: 441).

5. At an annual higher education stakeholder meeting (November 2002), the CEO of the Council on Higher Education spoke forcibly to a subdued audience permeated with pessimism, about the widening credibility gap between higher education and society, with the ruling government, in particular, perceiving higher education to be inefficient, crisis ridden and failing to produce the graduates and knowledge required for societal transformation. The policy process that started in the early 1990s may inadvertently have contributed to this gap by systematically, and publicly, identifying weaknesses and failures in the system that required transformation. The effect has been to demoralise a large section of the higher education community and to contribute to a negative public perception of the whole system (Cloete and Kulati 2003).

5.1. Accounting for Unintended Outcomes

It has been argued that a major achievement of the post-1994 democratic government was the development, in a participative, cooperative manner, of a comprehensive new policy framework. However, when it came to implementation, there were major problems about developing instruments that could give effect to the new policy framework. Particularly problematic, so this account runs, was the lack of a new integrated funding and planning system that would allow government to steer different aspects of the system.

In the National Plan for Higher Education (NPHE), the Ministry of Education offers the following explanation for this 'uncontrolled' situation:

> It is arguable whether a more robust and timely implementation of key policy instruments would have been possible, given the capacity constraints at both the national and institutional levels. However, it is clear that the implementation vacuum has given rise to a number of significant developments, including unintended and unanticipated consequences which, if left unchecked, threaten the development of a

single, national, co-ordinated but diverse higher education system (Department of Education 2001: 8).

The NPHE explains the implementation vacuum as being partly the consequence of an incremental approach that

> ... was adopted for three reasons. First, the lack of systemic capacity in terms of both person-power and technical skills, in particular statistical modelling and analytical skills, to implement the comprehensive and wide-ranging planning agenda outlined in the White Paper. Second, the absence of an adequate information base, in particular analyses and understanding of systemic and institutional trends. Third, the need to develop a consultative and interactive planning process through dialogue between the Ministry and higher education institutions to underpin the principle of co-operation and partnership (Department of Education 2001: 8).

In the NPHE the Minister raises three issues that should be addressed. The first is a "rampant and even destructive competition" (Department of Education 2001: 9) that is in direct contradiction to the cooperative governance approach promoted by the White Paper which aimed at a more systematic and coherent approach. According to the Minister, the "point to emphasise is that the long term future of individual public institutions and their restructuring must be determined by national policy and needs not by the vagarics of the market and competitive pressures" (p. 9).

Secondly, the Minister appears to put the policy of institutional redress to the sword with the rhetorical question: "Redress for what?" (Department of Education 2001: 11). He goes on to say that the continued instability and state of crises of a small number of historically black institutions cannot be countenanced any longer (p. 11). The prescription of how this is to be remedied is through institutional audits, and an "agreed delineation of the roles of different institutions linked to the overall restructuring of the higher education system" (p. 12).

Thirdly, by linking planning with funding, through the approval of 'rolling three year plans' for each institution, the Ministry will "ensure that targets and goals of the National Plan are met" (Department of Education 2001: 12). Together, these mark a shift from input based funding to output and target related funding. In other words, the Minister here seems to move from a social interest in equity and redress to one of functionality and efficiency.

The inauguration of the new centralised National Student Financial Aid Scheme (NSFAS) offered for the first time financial support to students at the institution of their choice. The effect – a major diversion of enrolments from the historically black to the historically white universities and technikons – was completely unanticipated, though quite understandable in retrospect. What this scheme did was to create a large internal market for students who, for the first time, chose institutions as consumers rather than as ethnic affiliates. These student-consumers based their choices on a combination of perceived status, cultural compatibility and available public information (Cosser 2002). That the Afrikaans speaking institutions with good public relations departments were the main beneficiaries is thus not as surprising as it seems at first sight. This 'market' mechanism was well complemented by the SAPSE based funding system, which likewise is a 'market' based mechanism that rewards enrolments, throughput and research output (Bunting 2003). Finally, closing down the AUT without immediately putting into place a new programme regulating mechanism, together with partially deregulating private higher education, created further entrepreneurial opportunities for institutions seeking a market niche and with capacity to pursue it effectively (Muller 2003). Closely associated with these 'marketising' forces in higher education, was a discernible shift in espoused public interest from equity and democracy to efficiency and sustainability.

The discursive shift can also, with hindsight, be traced in the policy documents. The National Commission on Higher Education Report (NCHE 1996) and the 1997 White Paper (Department of Education 1997a) both started with equity as the first transformation principle. The Council on Higher Education Report (CHE 2000) started with effectiveness and efficiency challenges before mentioning equity. Most recently, the National Plan for Higher Education (Department of Education 2001) starts its discussion on the challenges facing higher education with human resource development.

Together, these reinterpretations make it necessary to examine closer the government's diagnosis of apparent policy failure as due to an 'implementation vacuum'. At first glance we can see that the emerging governance practice after 1996 had a number of characteristics of a market model. However, the emerging student and institutional markets were not the result of deliberate efforts by the Ministry of Education to introduce a market-driven governance approach. Consequently what is meant here by 'implementation vacuum' was the inability of the Ministry of Education to prevent market forces to 'push' the higher education system in another direction than the one intended by the Ministry. The annual, systematic application of the SAPSE based funding formula, with its market effects, the increased funding support for NSFAS, and the abolition of controls on new programmes all contributed to a substantial increase in market conditions, aided by the massive increase in research and consultancy money made available by other government departments and the international donor agencies and companies. At the University of Pretoria, the amount of contract income between 1995 and 2000 increased by 480% and at the University of Natal by 300%.

In diagnosing the nature and unintended outcomes of the emerging market elements in the governance approach with respect to higher education, the Ministry points to the problematic implementation dimension of the reform process as the main reason for the gap between the high expectations and the unintended outcomes. It thereby suggests that 'if only' it would have had the right instruments, the right people and the right information, the outcomes of the reform process would have been much more in line with the intentions. This diagnosis is on the one hand understandable, and refers at least to a part of the explanation for the gap between reform intentions and outcomes. However, on the other hand a more fundamental understanding of 'what went wrong' in the reform process with respect to higher education in South Africa after 1994 can be provided by pointing to the inconsistencies in the new governance approach. From a governance perspective it was not in the first place an implementation vacuum that led to the unintended outcomes. Rather it was the participation approach to governance that allowed the new schemes (NSFAS) and old institutions (the SAPSE based funding system) to stimulate market behaviour of individual students and universities/technikons, without this market behaviour being regulated by the Ministry. While the Ministry was trying to reform the higher education system through consultation and negotiation, amongst other things, the introduction of NSFAS and the continuation of the use of the SAPSE based funding system led to changes in the system that were unintended, and unwanted. As is indicated by Peters (2001: 71) "participation can be a great strength, but it is also a weakness when flexibility and rapid adaptation to a changing environment become important".

The discursive shift from a participatory governance vision to a de facto market one can be captured in terms of Peters' typology presented in table 2.

Table 2. Charting the path to governance reform using the Peters typology

	DoE's 1ˢᵗ version (NCHE 1996; White Paper 1997)	DoE's revised version (NPHE 2001)
Diagnosis of what's wrong in the previous model	• wholly tainted because of association with apartheid • too centralised ('top-down'); not 'democratic'	• lack of managerial capacity and 'expertise' • inadvertent 'destructive competition' (market forces)
Most valued public interest	• democracy • equity • redress	• efficiency and accountability • rational allocation and distribution of resources
Structure	Unitary-coordinated system (decentralised)	• rationalised institutional landscape (mergers) • institutional differentiation
Management	Cooperative governance (team-based democratic decision making)	Professional management and output based performance management
Policy making	• consultation and negotiation • comprehensive policy, vision based	• policy by commissioned expert review • target based allocation by the DoE

5.2. Hybridism, Consistency and Compatibility With Respect to Governance Approaches

In discussing the unintended outcomes of the governance shifts with respect to South African higher education we have pointed to the ineffectiveness of the combined market and participative elements in governance practice. This combination of elements can be seen as an example of a hybrid governance approach with respect to higher education (Gornitzka and Maassen 2000). The fact that most governments will use elements of more than one state model in their steering approach with respect to higher education is in line with Olsen's (1988) point that his state models will not be found in the form in which he conceptualised them in practice, neither with respect to higher education nor to another sector. Also Peters (2001) refers to the fact that the models he identified will not be found in a pure form in practice. These models are analytical tools for examining developments in the relationship between the state and society. The issue is not whether governance approaches used by a government matches Peters', Olsen's or any other model in a 100% fashion, but rather what can be learned from using theoretical models as 'measuring devices' for studying the successes and failures of a government's governance approach with respect to a certain public sector, such as higher education. In addition to hybridism, the notions of compatibility and consistency are of relevance here.

Hybridism refers to the use of elements from more than one theoretical model in a governance approach in practice. Hybridism is in itself not negative or positive, since the latter characterisation is not dependent on the extent to which a governance approach is hybrid or not, but on the effects of its application in practice by a government. This can be analysed by relating the effectiveness (success or failure) of a governance approach in practice to the consistency and compatibility of the elements in the governance approach. While some 'hybrids' might be consistent with elements that are compatible with each other, others might be less consistent, containing elements that are not compatible. Peters, for example, argues that the market governance model appears to be compatible with the flexible government approach, just as the participation approach is compatible with the deregulation approach (Peters 2001: 95).

The latter is of interest when we look at the South African case. What does the South African Ministry of Education see as the basic future governance principle(s) through which the intended outcomes are expected to be reached: more competition, more involvement of a larger number of stakeholders, less permanence, or less rules and regulations? As indicated it is certainly not more competition, rather the contrary. Also less permanence is not the basic governance principle in which the Ministry believes. This leaves the principles of participation and deregulation. How do these relate to the statements in the NPHE? The Ministry wants to use targets for a more diversified higher education system. It can be argued that ideally, according to the above governance principles, these targets should be agreed upon with all stakeholders involved, especially representatives of each institution individually. Once there is agreement on the targets, it should be left to the institutions themselves how they want to achieve them. The agreed upon targets can be included in a 'contract' between Ministry and individual institution, as can the principle of non-interference of government. Combining the two governance principles in this way results in a hybrid that is consistent and uses various elements that are compatible.

However, the targets and goals included in the NPHE are not necessarily the result of an agreement between the Ministry and each individual institution, nor is the way in which these targets are to be achieved left to the individual institution – the planning framework requires that every course be approved by the national government. Concerning the latter there is a crucial difference between linking public funding directly to targets and measuring the extent to which each institution has met national targets, as included in the NPHE, and agreeing with an institution on what it wants to achieve in the next three years, and on the public budget it will get in that period, after which the institution will be allowed, within the stable budget limits, to achieve without direct external interference the agreed upon outcomes.

According to the new funding framework:

> The Minister of Education formulates policies and plans for the higher education system, approves plans for individual institutions, and implements these through the funding framework. The Minister's powers for doing this arise from within a democratic environment ... The new funding framework in the 1997 White Paper reconceptualises the relationship between institutional costs and government expenditure on higher education. The new funding framework has to be seen as a distributive mechanism, ie as a way of allocating government funds to individual institutions in accordance both with the budget made available by government and with government's policy priorities. The crucial feature of the new framework is that it operates in a top-down way ... and [is] intended to pay institutions for delivering the teaching-related and research-related services specified by government-approved plans (Ministry of Education 2003: 2–3).

In a response to this new framework, the South African Vice-Chancellors Association (SAUVCA) asserts that:

> The new funding framework, as outlined in the funding framework document will give the minister unprecedented freedom to manipulate and direct the funding of higher education institutions in future ... the Minister will be given almost complete freedom to change the values assigned to the framework's different components. No parameters within which the Minister may exercise his discretion are given (SAUVCA 2003: 2).

The vice-chancellors further argue that:

> No clearly articulated basis is provided for the proposed new funding framework. Although in some respects, it is orientated towards the market model, particularly in its emphasis on outputs, i.e. the graduates needed by the economy; in other respects it is simply a mechanism for dividing the pool of funds that the Treasury has found it expedient to provide ... former notions of university autonomy, requiring 'arm's length' treatment of higher education, will cease and higher education will be treated as part of the civil service (SAUVCA 2003: 3).

It can be expected that after the 'implementation vacuum' of the post-1996 period, which was due to the incompatibility of a participative governance approach with market-oriented policy instruments, the new phase will consist of a mixture of a market model and a top-down steering approach, which will also be characterised by unintended policy and implementation outcomes.

6. CONCLUSION

The South African case provides a fascinating example of a government that is trying to reorganise the governance arrangements with respect to its higher education system within different and largely incompatible reform frameworks. The first framework was determined by the transition from the apartheid regime to the democratic government. In this framework the new governance approach had to be based on the political and ideological principles underlying the new democratic government, that is, equality, democracy and redress. It was crucial in the transition period that the new government distance itself from the political principles and the accompanying governance approach of the apartheid era. Consequently the Ministry of Education proposed a governance approach that had many features in common with the participatory governance model conceptualised by Peters (2001: 50–77).

The second framework was provided by international experience in developing alternatives to the traditional governance model. In this framework the market concept features prominently in the new governance approaches with respect to higher education in most countries at the end of the 1980s, early 1990s. This framework entered South Africa not through the Ministry of Education, but through other ministries and government agencies.

The third framework is an attempt to re-regulate the system through strong 'top-down' steering, driven by a central government planning and funding regime.

It could be argued that the international reform agenda as well as shortcomings in the governance approach chosen caught up rapidly with the reform intentions of the Ministry of Education. Nationally, the Ministry of Education did not sufficiently recognise the importance of de-institutionalising the core institutions, such as the funding mechanism, of the old regime, and creating a new institutional infrastructure, in other words re-institutionalising the arrangements needed to fit the governance approach used in the transition period. As a result, while the Ministry was consulting and negotiating with representatives of the field about implementing the redress and equality agenda, many actors in the same field were using the opportunities provided by the same Ministry of Education to conduct themselves in ways contrary to the formal reform agenda being negotiated. Internationally, the ideologies that were pushing a different reform agenda to that of the Ministry of Education by emphasising responsiveness and efficiency were embraced by the South African government and operationalised in its macro-economic approach. Consequently, the Ministry of Education had to abandon its participatory governance approach in favour of an approach that would, at least theoretically, improve the chances that the reform efforts of the Ministry became more successful.

One might have expected that the Ministry of Education would change its governance approach in order to implement its specific reform agenda focusing on democracy, equality and redress. Instead, the Ministry of Education seemed to have changed course along the lines of the reform and policy trajectory of the rest of the government in all respects but its governance approach. In the second half of the 1990s, the emphasis on democracy, redress, and equality was gradually replaced by an emphasis on efficiency and responsiveness (see e.g. Department of Education 2001). At the same time however, the Minister strongly rejected, and continues to reject, a market approach to the governance of higher education. Instead of formally following a market approach, with all the consequences this entails, the new governance approach of the Ministry of Education strongly emphasised control, accountability and performance.

At first sight this development is not unlike general developments with respect to governance in other countries. Also in developed countries, where governance shifts took place in a single reform framework and not in two as in South Africa, the experiences of the first wave of reforms were used by many governments to adapt their governance approach on the basis of principles such as control, accountability and performance (Peters 2001: 120). In these countries there was the feeling that the first round of mainly ideological governance reforms had created a number of difficulties that had to be addressed. In the second wave of governance reforms the identified problems and difficulties with respect to the first round of reforms were firstly that the reforms had led to an unacceptable disaggregation of certain sectors, making it necessary to reconsider the notion of coordination through markets. Secondly, the reforms had led to a loosening of the control possibilities for governments. The politically, socially or economically undesirable developments that resulted made it necessary to re-introduce or strengthen external control mechanisms. Thirdly, deregulation had led to excessive autonomy for certain sectors, making it necessary, for example, to use output measures. Fourthly, the reforms had led to a deterioration in the quality of certain services, making it necessary to assess quality and focus on performance (Peters 2001: 120–121). One might thus be tempted to conclude that the South African Minister of Education seems to be fully in line with international governance trends. Such a conclusion must be approached with care.

The international trends in governance do not represent a break with the first round of reforms, but an adaptation of it. In other words, it does not mean a re-introduction of the traditional 'strong government' governance model, but a careful continuation and adaptation of the patterns of change introduced in the first reform round (Peters 2001: 124). This implies, for example, developing external control mechanisms within a market, participatory, flexible or deregulation approach to governance instead of replacing the approach in question with a control model.

In the South African case, the Minister of Education does not seem to intend to continue and adapt the participatory governance model. Instead, partly due to its manifest failings and partly due to the Cabinet's reform trajectory, he is making a move to greater government control. It is somewhat early to formulate a definitive conclusion about this, but the NPHE (Department of Education 2001) and the new funding framework signals the direction of a Minister who does not believe in participation as the basic governance principle anymore, nor in a market approach as an acceptable alternative. Instead the Minister seems to believe that the implementation of the higher education reforms can be made more successful by strengthening the grip of the government on higher education through control mechanisms, through performance measures, and through other instruments. He clearly expects that these will allow him to steer the higher education sector in the direction he prefers.

Contrary to the international trends in governance referred to above, these mechanisms, measures and instruments are not developed and used within a market governance or participatory governance approach, nor in a flexible or deregulatory governance approach. In terms of the Peters (2001) typology, the Minister is trying to combine a de facto market (deregulation) model, with a strong re-regulation approach. He is thus mixing a de facto market model that requires deregulation and weak steering, with a re-regulation or, in the terms of Olsen's (1988) typology, an institutional state model. As a consequence there is the danger of inconsistency and incompatibility of the mechanisms, measures and instruments chosen. Equally important, implementation of reforms is to a large extent dependent on the decisions and actions of the actors involved. Being confronted by a government that does not seriously consult with them anymore, and instead tries to prescribe the way in which the higher education system has to change, the actors' reaction is most likely be one of deflection, if not rejection of the intended reforms. It can be expected that this tension could be exacerbated in a situation where the government subsidy currently forms 50% or less of the total income of the institutions.

It is too early to arrive at definite conclusions, but using governance arrangements without having a framework within which to use them, will almost inevitably lead to contradictions, inconsistencies and incompatibilities of the measures, mechanisms and instruments used. Deploying these arrangements without involving the main actors in serious negotiation can also be expected to undermine the reform implementation effort. If this is indeed the outcome, the Minister of Education might take comfort from the fact that he is not alone in this uncomfortable position, as the following quote from Peters (2001: 16–17) makes clear:

> ... the results of reforms have tended to disappoint so many of their advocates. What has often happened is that governments have selected 'off the shelf' reforms derived from one set of assumptions (implicit or explicit) at the same time that they selected others based on quite different, or even directly contradictory, premises. The political and administrative leaders made these selections, expecting all the changes to work well together. It is therefore little wonder perhaps that in practice the sets of reforms have not worked together in a large number of instances and also at times the interactions have proven to be negative.

NOTES

1   In higher education this principle forms the basis under the 'tenure' phenomenon.
2   For a detailed discussion of the nature of these approaches see Peters (2001: 23–118). For an application in the area of higher education, with an emphasis on the management function in governance approaches, see Maassen (2003).

REFERENCES

Amaral, A. and A. Magelhães. "On Markets, Autonomy and Regulation. The Janus Head Revisited." *Higher Education Policy* 14 (2001): 1–14.

Bunting, I. "Memorandum." Pretoria: Department of Education, 2003.

Cerych, L. and P. Sabatier. *Great Expectations and Mixed Performance: The Implementation of Higher Education Reforms in Europe.* Stoke-on-Trent: Trentham Books, 1986.

CHE (Council on Higher Education). *Towards a New Higher Education Landscape: Meeting the Equity, Quality and Social Development Imperatives of South Africa in the 21st Century.* Pretoria: CHE, 2000.

Cloete, N. and I. Bunting. *Transformation Indicators: Case Studies of the University of Port Elizabeth and Peninsula Technikon.* Pretoria: CHET, 2002, http://www.chet.org.za/transformation.html.

Cloete, N., R. Fehnel, P. Maassen, T. Moja, H. Perold and T. Gibbon (eds). *Transformation in Higher Education. Global Pressures and Local Realities in South Africa.* Lansdowne, SA: Juta and Company, 2002.

Cloete, N. and T. Kulati. "Managerialism Within a Framework of Cooperative Governance?" In Amaral, A., V.L. Meek and I.M. Larsen (eds). *The Higher Education Managerial Revolution?* Dordrecht: Kluwer Academic Publishers, 2003, 229–251.

Cohen, J. and J. Rogers. "Solidarity, Democracy, Association." *Politische Vierteiljahrschrift* Sonderheft 25 (1994): 136–159.

Cosser, M. (with J. du Toit). *From School to Higher Education? Factors Affecting the Choices of Grade 12 Learners.* Pretoria: Human Sciences Research Council Publishers, 2002.

Department of Education. *Education White Paper 3: A Programme for the Transformation of Higher Education.* Pretoria: Department of Education, 1997a.

Department of Education. *Higher Education Act of the Republic of South Africa*. No. 101 of 1997. Pretoria: Department of Education, 1997b.

Department of Education. *National Plan for Higher Education*. Pretoria: Department of Education, 2001.

Gornitzka, Å. and P. Maassen. "Hybrid Steering Approaches With Respect to European Higher Education." *Higher Education Policy* 13 (2000): 267–285.

Kaufman, H. "Emerging Doctrines of Public Administration." *American Political Science Review* 50 (1956): 1059–1073.

Kooiman, J. "Findings, Speculations and Recommendations." In Kooiman, J. (ed.). *Modern Governance: New Government Society Interactions*. London: Sage, 1993, 249–262.

Kraak, A. *Human Resources Development Planning for the New Millennium*. Pretoria: HSRC, 1999.

Maassen, P. *Governmental Steering and the Academic Culture. The Intangibility of the Human Factor in Dutch and German Universities*. Utrecht: De Tijdstroom, 1996.

Maassen, P. "Shifts in Governance Arrangements: An Interpretation of the Introduction of New Management Structures in Higher Education." In Amaral, A., V.L. Meek and I.M. Larsen (eds). *The Higher Education Managerial Revolution?* Dordrecht: Kluwer Academic Publishers, 2003, 229–251.

Maassen, P. and N. Cloete. "Global Reform Trends in Higher Education." In Cloete, N., R. Fehnel, P. Maassen, T. Moja, H. Perold and T. Gibbon (eds). *Transformation in Higher Education. Global Pressures and Local Realities in South Africa*. Lansdowne, SA: Juta and Company, 2002: 13–58.

Maassen, P. and F. van Vught. "An Intriguing Janus-head. The Two Faces of the New Governmental Strategy for Higher Education in the Netherlands." *European Journal of Education* 23 (1988): 65–76.

Maassen, P. and F. van Vught. *Dutch Higher Education in Transition*. Culemborg: LEMMA, 1989.

Maassen, P. and F. van Vught. "Alternative Models of Governmental Steering in Higher Education. An Analysis of Steering Models and Policy-Instruments in Five Countries." In Goedegebuure, L. and F. van Vught (eds). *Comparative Policy Studies in Higher Education*. Utrecht: LEMMA, 1994, 35–65.

Mayntz, R. *New Challenges to Governance Theory*. Jean Monnet Chair Paper RSC No. 98/50. Florence: European University Institute, 1998.

Ministry of Education. *Funding of Public Higher Education: A New Framework*. Pretoria: Ministry of Education, 2003.

Moja, T., J. Muller and N. Cloete. "Towards New Forms of Regulation in Higher Education: The Case of South Africa." *Higher Education* 32 (1996): 129–155.

Muller, J. "Knowledge and the Limits to Institutional Restructuring: The Case of South African Higher Education." *Journal of Education* 30 (2003): 101–126.

NCHE (National Commission on Higher Education). *A Framework for Transformation*. Pretoria: Department of Education, 1996.

Neave, G. and F. van Vught. *Prometheus Bound. The Changing Relationship Between Government and Higher Education in Western Europe*. Oxford: Pergamon Press, 1991.

NEPI (National Education Policy Investigation). *Post Secondary Education Report*. Cape Town: Oxford University Press, 1992.

Olsen, J.P. "Administrative Reform and Theories of Organization." In Campbell, C. and B.G. Peters (eds). *Organizing Governance, Governing Organizations*. Pittsburgh: University of Pittsburgh Press, 1988, 233–254.

Peters, B.G. *The Future of Governing*. 2nd edn, revised. Lawrence, KS: University Press of Kansas, 2001.

SAUVCA (South African Vice-Chancellors Association). "Comments on the Proposed New Funding Subsidy Framework for Higher Education Institutions." Pretoria, 2003.

Savoie, D.J. "What is Wrong with the New Public Management?" *Canadian Public Administration* 38 (1995): 112–121.

Scott, W.R. *Institutions and Organizations*. Thousand Oaks: Sage Publications, 1995.

Van Heffen, O., J. Verhoeven and K. de Wit. "Higher Education Policies and Institutional Response in Flanders: Instrumental Analysis and Cultural Theory." In Jongbloed, B., P. Maassen and G. Neave (eds). *From the Eye of the Storm. Higher Education's Changing Institution*. Dordrecht: Kluwer Academic Publishers, 1999, 263–295.

Van Kersbergen, K. and F. van Waarden. "Shifts in Governance: Problems of Legitimacy and Accountability." Paper on the theme 'Shifts in Governance' as part of the Strategic Plan 2002–05 of the Netherlands Organization for Scientific Research (NWO). The Hague: NWO, 2001.

Van Vught, F. (ed.). *Governmental Strategies and Innovation in Higher Education.* London: Jessica Kingsley, 1989.

RICHARD JAMES AND CRAIG MCINNIS

EQUITY POLICY IN AUSTRALIAN HIGHER EDUCATION: A CASE OF POLICY STASIS[1]

1. INTRODUCTION

The formulation of equity policy and its change from a radical to a conservative position provides an illuminating case study of policy development in Australian higher education. Improving the higher education participation of under-represented community groups became a major government objective in Australia during the mid-1980s. The principal target at the time was the significant under-representation of students from certain social backgrounds, especially in the elite professional degree courses. By the early 1990s, a detailed equity policy framework designed to reduce inequities and imbalances in higher education participation was finalised and in operation. Yet after a decade of policy implementation, the overall effects of the policy on improving the participation of the most significantly disadvantaged groups, including people from lower socio-economic backgrounds and from rural or isolated regions, are arguably negligible. Despite the apparent ineffectiveness of policy, the basic policy framework has remained largely fixed, if not inherently immutable. This chapter examines the particular difficulties the issue of widening access to higher education creates for policy formulation and implementation. We begin by tracing the social and political origins of the Australian equity agenda and outlining the core features of equity policy, before presenting a critical analysis of the policy outcomes.

2. THE GENESIS OF HIGHER EDUCATION EQUITY POLICIES

The concept of social equity is firmly embedded in Australian culture. Australians like to think of their nation as an egalitarian society that is dismissive of class differences, one in which the principle of a 'fair go' underpins social relationships and opportunities. Despite this ethos, unease about the narrow social backgrounds of university students took some time to emerge. Prior to the Second World War, and even for some time afterwards, there was little explicit attention given to the effects of family background, gender, geographical location or schooling on the likelihood of enrolment in higher education and relatively little research had been undertaken to map the social backgrounds of higher education students (Anderson and Vervoorn 1983: 5). The focus instead was on occupational outcomes from schooling. It was not until the first wave of expansion towards mass higher education in the 1960s that

Å. Gornitzka et al. (eds.), Reform and Change in Higher Education, 227-244.

university access became the subject of discussion. Even so, the establishment of new universities during this period was driven not by notions of equity but by the need to meet greater demand, broad economic goals and concern for 'the waste of human capital' expressed in the Martin Report (Committee on the Future of Tertiary Education in Australia 1964).

Research into the participation and academic performance of females and students from rural areas increased considerably during the 1970s, as did studies into the educational aspirations and participation in higher education of people from the various waves of immigrant groups which had settled in Australia following the Second World War. The early studies showed that students from some migrant groups, including students from working class families, had higher educational aspirations than did Australian-born students and were at least as likely to enter a higher education institution (Anderson and Vervoorn 1983: 11).

By the early 1970s, the federal government began to show concern regarding the elite social backgrounds of students entering the higher status professional programmes in universities. The first major reforms were system-wide and structural, in response to the pressure of the demographic bulge of the baby-boom generation reaching school completion age. In 1974, the left-wing federal Labor government assumed principal responsibility for higher education, which was previously in the hands of the states, and overhauled the university system, abolishing tuition fees and introducing a means-tested Tertiary Education Allowance System for eligible full-time students with the goal of improving access for a wider cross-section of the Australian community. These changes precipitated an increase in the participation of older students, especially women.

During the 1980s, the concepts of participation and equity emerged in the federal government's policy for schools, Technical and Further Education (TAFE) and higher education. The social justice policy in the mid-1980s can be broadly summarised as directed at improving the low participation rates of disadvantaged groups by increasing opportunities for all through a 'program of growth' (CTEC 1984: 1). The general thrust of the Commonwealth Tertiary Education Commission's (CTEC) programme in 1984 for promoting equity, defined largely as opportunity, was to increase the size of the cake: "... the best means of redressing the imbalances and inequities of past provision is to increase opportunities for the whole community" (CTEC 1984: 1).

Through the allocation of additional resources to the areas where access to higher education had been low, it was expected that the specified disadvantaged groups would be picked up in the educational net. The government established the Aboriginal Participation Initiative and the Higher Education Equity Programme (HEEP), providing universities with funding for pilot programmes to increase the diversity of students in higher education. However, there was a considerable lack of detail as to how these might be implemented.

The major pressure within the left-wing Australian Labor Party towards equity in education during the 1970s and 1980s came from a strongly anti-meritocratic movement that sought to shift the social composition of the student body to counter the perceived self-perpetuating nature of the elite. By 1987, the universities which had not made obvious inroads into reducing social imbalances were being openly criticised, specifically those offering highly selective professional courses such as law and medicine. The term 'equity' became a shorthand way of referring to equality of opportunity rather than outcomes, that is, "'equity' may not necessarily result in equality of outcomes, in the sense of numbers participating in or graduating from certain courses or types of activity" (CTEC 1987: 92).

The massification of the Australian higher education system progressed rapidly from 1987 with a series of major policy changes (Dawkins 1988). Once again, many of the reforms involved system-wide restructuring. The binary divide between universities and colleges of advanced education was removed, creating a Unified National System (UNS) through a series of amalgamations and mergers. The Dawkin's White Paper (1988) cited growth and efficiency as prerequisites for access and equity, establishing as a priority an increase in the skill base of the population. References to changing the social composition of the student body were more subdued, compared with previous policy rhetoric, and considerably more localised at the institutional level:

> The equity goals of institutions should be based on an analysis of the nature and level of disadvantage experienced in an institution's student population and wider catchment area (Dawkins 1988: 55).

The government of the time was committed to making equity objectives a central concern of higher education management, planning and review, as reflected in the emphasis on social justice set out in *Towards a Fairer Australia: Social Justice Under Labor* (ALP 1988). It was anticipated that the Dawkins expansion of higher education would in itself broaden access and resolve many of the existing imbalances in higher education participation. In other words, there was continuing faith that merely by expanding the size of the cake there would be greater shares for all. Specific initiatives at the time included the introduction of AUSTUDY to provide income support for students – designed to make study a more attractive option for students from low income families than unemployment benefits – and the creation of the innovative Higher Education Contribution Scheme.

The Higher Education Contribution Scheme (HECS) was the centrepiece of Labor Party policy in the later 1980s. HECS offered students the opportunity to make an interest-free repayment of the partial cost of their tuition through the federal taxation system once their annual income after graduation reached a threshold level. Not only was HECS a mechanism for financing the expansion of the system, but it also complemented equity goals by eliminating the potential barrier of upfront payment of fees to access for lower income students and families.

3. THE CREATION OF A COMPREHENSIVE POLICY FRAMEWORK FOR EQUITY

By the late 1980s, the demographic composition of the university student population had changed somewhat since the 1960s, however it was apparent that sizeable imbalances remained between certain social groups in their likelihood of gaining a university education. Indeed, for some groups the reforms throughout the 1970s and 1980s had done little to improve their participation share in universities. New steps were taken to establish a stronger framework for monitoring and acting on equity, one that located responsibility for monitoring system performance with government while devolving the responsibility for programmes to reduce imbalances to individual institutions. From the outset, it was expected that the net national result would be the accumulation of universities' individual achievements in reducing local participation imbalances.

The present equity policy framework in Australia had its origins in a discussion paper prepared by the National Board of Employment, Education and Training (NBEET), which, after extensive consultation, was released under the title *A Fair Chance for All* (NBEET 1990). This paper established the government's new goals for equitable participation in higher education, articulating and giving substance to the Dawkins (1988) objectives which were based on the underlying principle that the higher education student population should more closely reflect the wider Australian population. At the time, *A Fair Chance for All* was somewhat overshadowed by the attention focused on a series of complex institutional mergers. However, the paper was later recognised as a landmark in the development of equity policy in Australia and lauded, despite the limitations of policy implementation that we later describe, as "the most comprehensive overarching framework for educational equity for any national higher education sector in the world" (Postle et al. 1995: 2) and recommended as required reading for governments "looking to use the funding mechanism to encourage universities and colleges to broaden the social base of their courses" (Parry 1998).

A Fair Chance for All was based on the assumption that the key to achieving equitable participation would lie in measurement, targets and linked funding. The paper proposed a strategy that included:

- improved data collection on participation patterns, to allow evidence-based decision making;
- the articulation of performance indicators;
- greater financial inducements for universities.

Six equity groups were identified as requiring particular assistance: people from lower socio-economic backgrounds; people from rural and isolated areas; people with a disability; people from non-English speaking backgrounds; women (especially in non-traditional areas of study and higher degrees); and Indigenous people. These groups largely reflected the disadvantaged groups defined in the government's social justice agenda of the 1970s for the school sector. *A Fair Chance for All* foreshadowed the development of processes to monitor institutional performance through performance indicators and the linking of funding to the performance of the equity groups.

A Fair Chance for All launched an optimistic agenda to approach equity issues through a set of integrated, rational policy measures, though the reaction across the sector to the policy was initially muted and somewhat indifferent. While the objectives for each equity group were carefully described in *A Fair Chance for All*, performance measures were outlined in only general terms and further technical work on the development of performance indicators was needed before the policy would have a significant influence on institutional activity.

In 1991, Linke identified 27 performance indicators for higher education that included certain participation and equity indicators. Based in part on Linke's work, data collection at the time of student enrolment each academic year was expanded. Institutions were required to ask students to respond to certain standard demographic questions and then to report these data to the government using a standard format. Further work by Martin (1994), reported in *Equity and General Performance Indicators in Higher Education,* clarified the operational definitions of the six equity groups identified in *A Fair Chance for All,* and set out detailed definitions of performance indicators. This work finally consolidated the data collection and reporting framework that was initiated in 1991. The main features of the equity policy framework are summarised below.

3.1. Summary of the Australian Equity Framework

3.1.1. Equity Groups
The current equity target groups were first designated in 1990 in *A Fair Chance For All,* broadly following the disadvantaged social groups identified during the mid-1970s. Data collected from students at enrolment are used for classification of group membership. The equity groups are:

- *people from lower socio-economic backgrounds* (student socio-economic background is measured by the postcode of their permanent home address – the 4-digit code used to identify urban and rural districts for mail delivery. All Australian postcode districts are classified using an index of low, medium and high socio-economic status derived from national census data);
- *people from rural and isolated areas* (student location is measured by postcode of student permanent home address and classified with an index of urban, rural and isolated postcode districts derived from population density data and proximity to large cities);
- *people with a disability* (self-identified by students on enrolment, through responses to the question "Do you have a disability that may affect your studies?");
- *people from a non-English speaking background* (defined as people who were born overseas, who arrived in Australia within the previous ten years and who speak a language other than English at home);
- *women in non-traditional areas of study and higher degrees*;
- *Indigenous people* (self-identified on enrolment).

3.1.2. Performance Indicators
The performance of the equity groups is measured by five indicators:

- *Access* (proportion of the equity group among commencing domestic students).
- *Participation* (proportion of the equity group among domestic students overall).
- *Retention* (the proportion of equity group students who re-enrol at an institution in a given year compared with the students who were enrolled in the previous year, less those students who have completed their course).
- *Success* (the mean *student progress rate* for the previous year for the equity group, this being the proportion of units passed within a year to the total units enrolled).
- *Completion* (the proportion of students completing all the academic requirements of a course).

3.1.3. Monitoring and Reporting

To monitor performance, the access and participation indicators are generally referenced against the proportion of people in the equity group within Australia overall. Retention, success and completion are referenced against all other students. Indicators are reported as percentages or ratios as appropriate. Universities are required annually to report the performance of the six equity groups and to have an equity plan. HEEP provides universities with funds to assist the equity groups, with the exception of Indigenous students who are supported through the separate Indigenous Support Funding programme.

4. THE IMPACT OF EQUITY POLICY

As a direct result of the federal equity policy framework, equity considerations influence many university activities. Soon after the creation of the framework in the early 1990s, universities established administrative infrastructures to respond to the policy's expectations. Within a short period of time, equity units or similarly titled units became commonplace in university administration, new equity officer positions were created, and access and equity committees proliferated. Equity programmes of various kinds were established, some with significant influence over student recruitment and selection activities, and extensive data collection and analysis commenced, as required by the government. Administrative units, personnel and programmes associated with equity are now firmly and often prominently located within the administrative structures and processes of Australian universities.

What have been the outcomes of this activity for the designated equity groups? A number of analyses of the trends in the performance of the groups have been conducted since 1991 (e.g. NBEET 1996; Andrews 1999; Birrell et al. 2000; Dobson 2003). It is not the purpose of this chapter to repeat these. However, the participation patterns for one group, people from lower socio-economic backgrounds, are sufficient to illustrate the apparently limited impact of the equity policy framework.

Table 1 and figure 1 present time series data drawn from federal government statistics for participation shares in higher education according to students' socio-economic background or socio-economic status (SES). To comprehend the significance of the data, a brief explanation of the technique for definition of socio-economic status is helpful. The equity policy framework utilises a national index of socio-economic status in which individual socio-economic status is classified according to the postcode district in which people live. By definition, 25 per cent of Australians are classified as lower SES, 50 per cent are classified as medium SES and 25 per cent are classified as higher SES. These fixed national proportions provide reference points against which to compare the composition of the university population using the postcode of students' permanent home address as the measurement device.

The absence of change in the participation shares of the three socio-economic subgroups, as revealed in table 1 and figure 1, is remarkable. Despite the considerable expansion in overall higher education participation between 1991 and 2002, the relative proportions of the three designated socio-economic groups have remained virtually unchanged. People from lower socio-economic backgrounds (i.e. people living in postcode areas classified as lower SES) are significantly under-represented in aggregate terms, with a share of university places consistently below 15 per cent, well short of the population reference value of 25 per cent. Furthermore, people from medium socio-economic backgrounds are also under-represented, albeit less substantially so. In contrast, higher socio-economic background students occupy 15 per cent more places than would be predicted solely on the basis of their population share. This group consistently out-performed the other two groups over the past decade, not only in access but also in mean success rates and retention rates.

Table 1. Higher education participation share by socio-economic background, 1991–2002 (%)

	Higher SES (Population reference point of 25%)	Medium SES (Population reference point of 50%)	Lower SES (Population reference point of 25%)
1991	39.52	44.12	14.70
1992	39.22	44.60	14.62
1993	39.33	44.85	14.41
1994	38.97	44.88	14.38
1995	38.44	45.21	14.48
1996	38.11	45.18	14.49
1997	37.94	45.67	14.61
1998	37.62	45.70	14.68
1999	37.62	45.70	14.68
2000	37.30	46.64	14.93
2001	39.11	44.72	14.79
2002	39.14	44.67	14.72

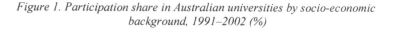

Figure 1. Participation share in Australian universities by socio-economic background, 1991–2002 (%)

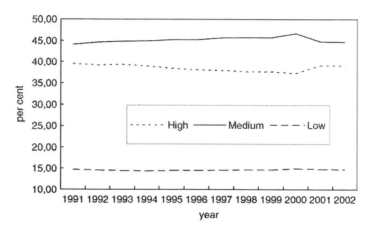

Though the imbalances in the aggregate participation rates presented in table 1 and figure 1 are sobering enough, they mask further inequalities in regard to the universities, fields of study and levels of awards in which students are enrolled. Higher SES students are most well represented in the higher status 'Group of Eight' research-intensive universities, with the proportion increasing from 50.4 per cent in 1991 to 53.8 per cent in 2002. In contrast, lower SES students are most highly represented in regional universities. Lower SES students have been consistently least well represented in the fields of medicine, law, architecture and creative arts, but less under-represented in the lower status fields of teacher education and agriculture. Students from higher socio-economic backgrounds consistently comprise the largest proportion – over half – of all students enrolled in masters degrees and doctorates by research and coursework. Though people classified as lower SES make up 25 per cent of the Australian population, lower SES students made up under nine per cent of the total enrolment in higher degrees in 2001.

This sketch of the performance trends for the lower SES equity group highlights the absence of inroads into one area of educational disadvantage during over a decade of policy implementation. For people from lower socio-economic backgrounds, the gaps in higher education participation are large and extraordinarily consistent over time given the overall expansion of the system. Furthermore, close inspection of enrolment patterns suggests even greater inequities may have emerged in the types of institutions and courses in which students are enrolled. In the context of the origins of equity policy in the desire of successive Labor governments to loosen the grip of a social elite on the most prestigious universities and courses, these figures are particularly galling for they suggest that the overall participation rates for the lower SES group are bolstered by expansion in the less competitive areas of the higher education system.

Similar data could be presented for rural and isolated people, however a single example is sufficient for the purposes of this chapter. It is not our intention to examine the persistent underlying causes of participation imbalances, though the Centre for the Study of Higher Education has recently conducted such research (James 2002; James et al. 1999), nor do we intend to discuss the many definitional and measurement issues associated with monitoring access to university according to social class – the bluntness and inadequacy of using postcode of home address for individual classification are acknowledged. Our interest here is in the policy response, or rather absence of a policy response, to data such as we have presented.

Granted, some equity groups have fared better than the lower SES group, some considerably better. However, in these cases the link between improved participation and equity policy is tenuous and problematic. The participation of women in non-traditional areas, and overall, has improved dramatically. Women comprised 56 per cent of higher education entrants in 2002, though there were a few areas (for example information technology) where they remained significantly under-represented. People from non-English speaking backgrounds do very well and have done so for some time. However, the relationship between the gains made by these two groups and equity policy is uncertain. The other equity groups have shown negligible gains, if any. The participation share of rural and isolated people is much lower than their population share and may have declined slightly during the past decade. Isolated people in particular continue to have very low higher education access rates. People with disabilities are also under-represented, though there have been some apparent gains in access overall. The participation share of Indigenous students has improved, not to the point of equivalence with population share, but enrolment is often in lower level courses and in lower status fields and institutions. The retention and completion rates for Indigenous students are very low compared with other students (Encel 2000; DEST 2002).

5. POLICY STASIS

The framework for equity policy initiated with *A Fair Chance for All* and enhanced with *Equity and General Performance Indicators in Higher Education* remains unchanged, by and large, over a decade later. Subsequent analyses and reviews have done little to question or alter the basic premises on which policy is built. However, signs of growing concern about the adequacy and impact of the framework have gradually emerged. In 1996, the NBEET report, *Equality, Diversity and Excellence: Advancing the National Higher Education Equity Framework* examined progress since A *Fair Chance for All* and noted that while there appeared to be some progress with certain equity groups, people from socio-economically disadvantaged backgrounds and from rural and isolated regions continued to be highly under-represented, an observation that is now an annual reporting ritual in government documents. The NBEET report called for a deeper examination of the reasons for inequalities in participation and outcomes and for "more complex solutions to be devised". The justification for seeking equitable participation now became couched in terms of national vitality as well as social justice.

More recent federal policy statements on higher education have reiterated a commitment to equity but have done little to introduce new thinking or to modify the fundamental framework. *Learning for Life* (West 1998), the report of the Review of Higher Education Financing and Policy, was the first major review of higher education since the late 1980s. The report contributed to the growing rhetoric of 'expanding individual choice', emphasising flexibility of provision and the need to respond to student needs and choices. Equity considerations were not a major focus of the report, however in regard to the equity groups it was noted that Indigenous students, those from rural or isolated areas, and those with a disability had increased in numbers but remained under-represented, despite the efforts of universities since the introduction of equity policy.

The Ministerial Statement, *Higher Education at the Crossroads* (Nelson 2002), which launched the most recent review of Australian higher education by the right-wing Liberal Coalition government, once again identified an equitable system as one of the underlying goals for the higher education system in Australia, doing so in the following terms:

> There must be equality of opportunity in higher education to allow individuals to fulfil their potential, regardless of their personal circumstances and backgrounds. There should be no systematic barriers to participation. There should be provision for the varying needs of students from different backgrounds. Special intervention measures may be needed to encourage participation from groups that are under-represented in certain areas, or to sustain their success, including 'second chance' opportunities and dedicated support (Nelson 2002: 2).

The 'Crossroads' review led to significant new proposals relating to equity, though the substantive detail is not clear at the time of writing. These proposals included new Commonwealth Education Costs Scholarships (CECS) to be awarded to selected students from lower socio-economic and/or Indigenous backgrounds, Commonwealth Accommodation Scholarships (CAS) to be awarded on the basis of merit to selected students from rural/isolated regions, a number of new initiatives for Indigenous students, and a change in the HEEP funding arrangements that will remove the present partial block funding so that all funding is performance-based. At the time of writing, the formula for the latter is yet to be developed, however it has been indicated that for eligibility for HEEP allocations universities will be required to "run an outreach programme to attract equity groups students to higher education" and "offer specialised support for equity group members to assist their progression through higher education" (Nelson 2003: 36).

6. THE PROBLEMS IN FORMULATING AND IMPLEMENTING POLICY FOR EQUITY

Higher education researchers and analysts have become increasingly critical of the equity policy framework. At one extreme, there have been suggestions that the policy "is in disarray" (Birrell et al. 2000). Despite such concerns and the apparent ineffectiveness of policy, the proposals emerging from the Crossroads review were among the first signs of the possibility of a reconsideration of policy. In this section we offer an explanation for the stasis or ossification in equity policy in Australia in recent years by arguing that at least four interrelated factors associated with policy formulation have inhibited the effectiveness of equity policy and stifled policy development. In summary, these are:

- the inconclusive evidence on the effects of policy on participation trends;
- the inadequacy of the implicit theoretical assumptions regarding the nature of educational disadvantage that underpin policy;
- the tendency for equity policy to be formulated in isolation from, or without reference to, other higher education policies and relevant public policies;
- the limited financial incentives for universities to address participation inequities.

6.1. Inconclusive Evidence on the Effects of Policy on Participation Trends

A major reason for the equity policy stasis is the ambiguity in assessing the performance of the equity groups over time. Evidence of the impact of policy is far from conclusive due to at least two factors. First, the rapid expansion of higher education during the past decade has conflated the influence of equity policy, if any, with the effects of wider social changes, including rising overall participation rates in higher education. Second, there are significant methodological difficulties in the definition and measurement of the equity groups and the calculation of appropriate reference values against which to judge equity group performance. Both of these factors limit the confidence with which conclusions can be drawn from the performance trends for individual equity groups.

Equity policy implementation has coincided with a period of significant expansion in Australian higher education, with substantial growth in the overall number of students. This expansion, together with social trends unrelated to equity policy, obscures the potential impact of policy. This can be once again illustrated with the example of the participation trends for people from lower socio-economic backgrounds. In 1991, there were 74,309 students from lower socio-economic backgrounds in Australian universities, representing 14.70 per cent of the domestic student population, a proportion well below the population reference point of 25 per cent for people of lower SES as noted earlier. By 2002, the number of lower socio-economic background students had climbed to 97,156, however the population share for this group remained virtually unchanged at 14.72 per cent due to the corresponding growth in student numbers overall. By one interpretation of this situation, policy could be depicted as highly successful, for close to 23,000 more students from lower socio-economic backgrounds were participating in higher education. Equally, however, it could be argued that equity policy had been strikingly unsuccessful, for despite a decade of intervention, people from lower socio-economic backgrounds made no ground at all in securing a larger share of places within a greatly expanded system – in fact, they may have become slightly less successful in gaining a share of the available places. For the authors, the lack of success in budging the percentage share is reasonably conclusive, although it could be argued that but for the presence of equity policy during this period the participation shares for lower SES students might have worsened.

The main point to be emphasised here is that quantitative analysis of the equity dataset is unlikely to unequivocally settle the question of the impact of policy. Making matters even more complex, there are also significant measurement difficulties in the collection and interpretation of data that also prevail against definitive interpretation of the findings. There is widespread acknowledgement that socio-economic disadvantage, rurality and isolation are the most difficult categories to define (Western, McMillan and Durrington 1998). In 1996, NBEET concluded that "socio-economic status is a dominant factor in predicting students' likelihood of participation in higher education", however they added that "identification of this characteristic remains one of the more contentious aspects of the definitional and indicator work ..." (NBEET 1996: 63). Equally, there are many problems with group membership based on student self-report, in particularly for people with a disability that might affect their studies. While the equity groupings may be useful for the purposes of broad monitoring, they are far from adequate for identifying individual disadvantage. In fact, diversity within groups is likely to be greater than the diversity between groups.

The inconclusiveness of the Australian equity dataset, despite its careful design and the effort devoted to data collection, points to the caution with which empirical data should be treated for the purposes of informing policy formulation and policy implementation. The interpretation of the Australian equity dataset is inescapably value-laden and the various analyses conducted over the years have rarely been politically neutral. In a sense, what is revealed in the data depends very much on what one chooses to look for.

6.2. The Inadequacy of the Implicit Theoretical Assumptions Regarding the Causes of Educational Disadvantage

A second factor inhibiting policy formulation has been the rather shallow theoretical underpinnings of policy. Ramsay (1999), for example, has argued that while there is much activity around equity policy and a remarkable level of compliance from institutions, the policy is focused on numerical outcomes and accountability rather than on critical consideration of the causes of disadvantage:

> In begging the question of what it is that has caused the inequalities of access and participation, the framework provided little guidance regarding what needs to occur at an institutional level to eliminate these causes nor to counteract their effects in the longer term (Ramsay 1999: 178).

Policy formulation has emphasised objectives, measurement and targets without the articulation of an underlying theory of the reasons for educational disadvantage as a basis for developing plausible corrective strategies. As a result, misleading stereotypes are implicit in policy formation, such as the persistent equating of socio-economic disadvantage solely with financial disadvantage or hardship. Admittedly, there is limited consensus on the underlying causes of educational disadvantage among policy makers and academics alike. Birrell et al. (2000) suggest that, broadly, there are two frameworks for explaining the persistent under-representation of persons from socio-economically disadvantaged backgrounds. First, a considerable body of research points to attitudinal and aspirational factors in socio-economically disadvantaged families and young people. Second, there is also evidence that lack of family financial resources contributes to the under-representation. Both explanations pose problems for government, the first pointing to the need for complex social and cultural change to raise aspirations and attainability, the second with implications for the levels of student financial support needed if financial barriers are to be reduced or removed.

Much policy thinking has been based on the implicit assumptions of barriers to participation and the belief that membership of certain social groups, due to particular social, cultural, economic or geographic circumstances, increases the likelihood of experiencing such barriers. However, the concept of barriers has significant shortcomings, particularly if applied to the current gender imbalances in particular fields of study. While women remain highly under-represented in fields such as engineering and information technology, there are no apparent barriers to the participation of women in these areas of study, for women attain the necessary levels of academic achievement for the often highly selective courses, the course costs are no more prohibitive than for other fields, and there are no systematic biases that favour males in university selection procedures. These gender imbalances, like the under-representation of males in teacher education and nursing courses, have their origins in differing perceptions of personal relevance and social status. If the concept of barriers is relevant here, then it must be broadened to embrace attitudinal social inhibitors as well as obstacles which might be inherent in the design of education systems. The policy question, if gender imbalances are believed to be a social issue, is whether they are reduced by an equity policy framework in which the dominant assumption informing programmes is one of removing or reducing explicit barriers.

6.3. The Formulation of Equity Policy in Isolation From Other Policies

The third factor constraining the achievement of equity objectives is the tendency for equity policy to be formulated in isolation from related policies both within and outside the higher education portfolio. In part, this is a result of the creation of designated equity units within the federal ministry responsible for higher education, which has balkanised policy making within the portfolio. But the problem is wider than this, for equity problems and their possible solutions run across a number of federal policy areas and are likely to require whole-of-government consensus and coordinated policies.

There are well-known difficulties in creating a whole-of-government policy-making environment with which to tackle the more persistent, complex and seemingly intractable social problems. In Australian higher education, there are numerous examples of tensions between policy priorities within the higher education portfolio and of equity policy being undermined by other higher education policies. Examples include the gradual fee deregulation during recent years, which has allowed universities to offer places for full-fee paying domestic students at fee levels substantially above HECS levels and well out of the reach of most disadvantaged students, and the direct support for the international marketing of Australian higher education, which, during a period of reduced public funding, has encouraged universities to pursue international students with far more intensity than disadvantaged domestic students. In 2003, a new example of the challenges of policy coordination across portfolios surfaced. Soon after the Crossroads reform package proposed a new means-tested scholarship scheme for financially disadvantaged students, the Department of Family and Community Services indicated that if a university awarded a scholarship, waived fees or exempted a student from HECS, this amount would be treated as income for social security purposes and thus would jeopardise eligibility for the Youth Allowance on which many financially disadvantaged students rely.

Discord of this kind between government departments is hardly unusual. However, this is a timely example of how the effectiveness of equity policy in higher education is contingent on policies that are formulated and managed outside the higher education policy arena. Needless to say, educational equity is an intricate social issue that extends beyond the reach of higher education policy. In 1996, NBEET called for more 'complex solutions' to equity problems that would require difficult and challenging political decisions, especially in regard to socio-economic disadvantage. To achieve this would require a significant cultural shift in Australian politics to permit the creation of coordinated employment policies, family policies and regional development policies, among other things.

6.4. The Limited Financial Incentives for Universities to Address Participation Inequities

The final reason for the failure of equity policy is simply that the federal funding for universities associated with equity has provided insufficient financial incentives. As Bacchi (2001: 122) expressed it, "the rhetoric of equity has never been matched by a funding commitment". Policy has failed to provide sufficient financial incentives for improvement in university performance to stimulate serious action. Universities have been rewarded through HEEP for complying with the ritualised reporting of institutional equity plans – which were described by NBEET in 1996 as largely open-ended and very variable in quality. The poor alignment between funding levels and demonstrable improvement in meeting equity targets has significantly limited the commitment of universities to equity, especially during a period of dwindling public resource allocation that has compelled universities to vigorously pursue alternative revenue sources. Achieving equity objectives is costly. Notwithstanding the commitment of universities and university staff to the broad objective of equity, maintaining a resource allocation to equity programmes above a token level has been difficult, even for the universities for which equity is a prominent element in their mission.

7. THE FAILURE OF EQUITY POLICY: AN UNEXCEPTIONAL CASE?

The four factors we have identified, together with others, make equity an especially difficult arena for policy. Our analysis has barely touched upon the grassroots issues involved in creating effective equity programmes at institutional level, where policy implementation works within tight constraints. Dilemmas are caused, for example, by the incompatibility of equity goals and the core values of excellence and merit that are characteristic of the culture of universities. Even though around half of each age cohort are now expected to enter university at some stage during their lives, there remain strong associations between higher education and the 'best and brightest'. For the research-led universities, attracting the most capable students is an overt objective. In such circumstances, student selection processes put the commitment to equity to a serious test, particularly for the institutions and courses which have the highest demand from prospective students. The tensions between values at the critical point of student admission have received virtually no recognition in policy.

The recent history of equity policy in Australian higher education highlights the triumph of complexity over aspirations. After well over a decade of equity policy, the likelihood that an individual will go to university in Australia is still significantly determined by social class and geography. Yet despite the apparent failure of policy to remedy the problem, there has been little or no drift in the fundamental objective of equity and the strategies for achieving this goal have remained largely unchanged.

The Australian experience provided in this case study is, in essence, unremarkable. In the 1980s social justice programmes involving government intervention through education appeared especially susceptible to failure. Higher education was no exception. The consistency of apparent policy failures was perhaps made remarkable by the persistence of governments in pursuing social justice goals in the face of well-documented cases of little change (Cerych and Sabatier 1986). Much of the analysis of the failure to change was limited, as Cerych pointed out, to the stereotyping of academics and universities as inherently resistant:

> ... we do not explain the dynamics of academic change and, in particular, the limited successes of reforms when we turn to simple answers as 'universities are conservative', 'academics resist change', and 'only gradual and slow change of higher education is possible'. Rather, complex systems require varied and complex answers (Cerych 1984: 253).

Beyond this mix of anecdote and conventional wisdom, the analysis of implementation failure has tended to be based on excessively rational, goal-directed and linear notions of the policy process in general.

> Discussion of policy implementation was bogged down in the mid-1980s with a myriad of idiosyncratic case studies, competing and incompatible models, an exponentially growing list of variables, and few coherent theories. The analysis and model-building lost sight of the policy itself; indeed, implementation threatened to become the sole benchmark by which success or failure of the policy could be judged (McInnis 1996: 101).

Most analysts agreed with Wittrock and De Leon (1986) that the policy drift was typical over long time periods and that eventually the relationship between the policy and the implementation process became 'asymmetrical'. While this is not entirely true of the case study presented here, it is clear that the various permutations of equity policy and the interpretation of policy through the target group mechanisms seemed to have separate and at times not necessarily complementary rationales.

In everyday usage and certainly in the policy arena, equity remains as broad and loose a concept now as it was in the early 1980s when it first emerged in the Australian context. The term has been embraced and reinterpreted by successive governments of differing ideological persuasions over the last two decades and it is precisely because the concept of equity is so elastic that it is an especially interesting example of the policy idea as a 'moving target' (Wittrock and De Leon 1986).

The freezing or ossification of equity policy, as we have described it, is partially because equity has become politically untouchable. Social equity is now a value shared across the political spectrum, though perhaps not with equal intensity, and governments are unlikely to contemplate an overt dismantling of equity policy. The aspiration of equity has potent appeal, lobby groups are well organised (especially in rural communities) and most Australians identify strongly with the 'battler'. Equity policy has significant symbolic political purposes, even if the effectiveness of policy, when put to scrutiny, might be quite limited. However, many of the assumptions on which equity policy has been built are being indirectly challenged. Increasingly, equity policy in Australian higher education is awkwardly juxtaposed with the new ideology of the market, student choices and diversity. The discourse in higher education policy is now redolent with the terminology and the philosophy of the free market, in which students are depicted as consumers with diverse opinions, wants and desires. The objective for the system overall is now increasingly construed as catering for diversity of this kind.

Australian higher education is at the threshold of a testing time for equity policy. The projected growth of fee-paying places and limits on the number of government funded places will put pressure on universities to rethink their distribution of opportunities for students from disadvantaged backgrounds. Federally, there is a pressing need to re-invigorate equity policy and to challenge a dominant and entrenched mode of thinking. As a first step, work needs to be done to re-assess whether the current equity groups best reflect those students who are disadvantaged in higher education. More importantly, the effectiveness of the current policy for re-energising and supporting equity initiatives at institutional level should be seriously questioned.

NOTES

[1] The authors are grateful for the assistance of Robyn Hartley in the preparation of this chapter.

REFERENCES

ALP. *Towards a Fairer Australia: Social Justice under Labor* (Platform of the Australian Labor Party). Canberra: Australian Government Publishing Service, 1988.

Anderson, D. and A. Vervoorn. *Access to Privilege: Patterns of Participation in Australian Post-Secondary Education.* Canberra: Australian National University Press, 1983.

Andrews, L. *Does HECS Deter?* Higher Education Division, DETYA. Canberra: Australian Government Publishing Service, 1999.

Bacchi, C. "Managing Equity: Mainstreaming and 'Diversity' in Australian Universities." In Brooks, A. and A. Mackinnon (eds). *Gender and the Restructured University.* Buckingham, UK: Society for Research into Higher Education and Open University Press, 2001, 119–135.

Birrell, B., A. Calderon, I. Dobson and T. Smith. "Equity in Access to Higher Education Revisited." *People and Place* 8.1 (2000): 50–61.

Cerych, L. "The Policy Perspective." In Clark, B. (ed.). *Perspectives on Higher Education: Eight Disciplinary and Comparative Views.* Berkeley, CA: University of California Press, 1984, 233–255.

Cerych, L. and P. Sabatier. *Great Expectations and Mixed Performance. The Implementation of Higher Education Reforms in Europe.* Stoke-on-Trent: Trentham Books, 1986.

Committee on the Future of Tertiary Education in Australia. *Tertiary Education in Australia: Report of the Committee on the Future of Tertiary Education in Australia to the Australian Universities Commission* (Martin Report). Melbourne: Government Printer, 1964.

CTEC (Commonwealth Tertiary Education Commission). *Report for 1985–87 Triennium.* Canberra: Australian Government Publishing Service, 1984.

CTEC (Commonwealth Tertiary Education Commission). *Report for 1988–90 Triennium.* Canberra: Australian Government Publishing Service, 1987.

Dawkins, The Hon. J.S. *Higher Education: A Policy Statement* (White Paper). Canberra: Australian Government Publishing Service, 1988.

DEST (Department of Education, Science and Training). *Achieving Equitable and Appropriate Outcomes: Indigenous Australians in Higher Education.* Canberra: Australian Government Publishing Service, 2002.

Dobson, I. "Access to University in Australia: Who Misses Out?" In Tight, M. (ed.). *Access and Exclusion.* London: JAI Elsevier Science, 2003, 29–58.

Encel, J. *Indigenous Participation in Higher Education.* Higher Education Division, DETYA, Canberra: Australian Government Publishing Service, 2000.

James, R. *Socioeconomic Background and Higher Education Participation: An Analysis of School Students' Aspirations and Expectations.* Canberra: Australian Government Publishing Service, 2002.

James, R., J. Wyn, G. Baldwin, G. Hepworth, C. McInnis and A. Stephanou. *Rural and Isolated Students and Their Higher Education Choices: A Re-Examination of Student Location, Socioeconomic Background, and Educational Advantage and Disadvantage.* Canberra: Australian Government Publishing Service, 1999.

Linke, R. *Performance Indicators in Higher Education: Report of a Trial Evaluation Study.* Canberra: Australian Government Publishing Service, 1991.

Martin, L. *Equity and General Performance Indicators in Higher Education, vol. 1: Equity Indicators.* Canberra: Australian Government Publishing Service, 1994.

McInnis, C. "Academic Cultures and Their Role in the Implementation of Government Policy in Higher Education." In Brennan, J., M. Kogan and U. Teichler (eds). *Higher Education and Work.* London: Jessica Kingsley, 1996, 99–118.

NBEET (National Board of Employment, Education and Training). *A Fair Chance for All: National and Institutional Planning for Equity in Higher Education, A Discussion Paper*. Canberra: Australian Government Publishing Service, 1990.

NBEET (National Board of Employment, Education and Training). *Equality, Diversity and Excellence: Advancing the National Higher Education Equity Framework*. Canberra: Australian Government Publishing Service, 1996.

Nelson, B. *Higher Education at the Crossroads: An Overview Paper*. Ministerial Statement. The Honourable Dr Brendan Nelson, MP, Minister for Education, Science and Training, Canberra, 2002.

Nelson, B. *Our Universities: Backing Australia's Future*. Ministerial Statement. The Honourable Dr Brendan Nelson, MP, Minister for Education, Science and Training, Canberra, 2003.

Parry, G. "Review of *Towards Excellence in Diversity: Educational Equity in the Australian Higher Education Sector in 1995*, G.D. Postle et al." *Studies in Higher Education* 23.3 (1998): 362–364.

Postle, G.D., J.R. Clarke, E. Skuja, D.D. Bull, B. Batorowicz and H.A. McCann. *Towards Excellence in Diversity. Educational Equity in the Australian Higher Education Sector in 1995*. Toowoomba: University of Southern Queensland Press, 1995.

Ramsay, E. "The National Framework for Australian Higher Education Equity: Its Origins, Evolution and Current Status." *Higher Education Quarterly* 53.2 (1999): 173–189.

West, R. *Learning for Life: Review of Higher Education Financing and Policy* ('The West Review'). Canberra: Australian Government Publishing Service, 1998.

Western, J., J. McMillan and D. Durrington. *Differential Access to Higher Education: The Measurement of Socioeconomic Status, Rurality and Isolation*. Canberra: Australian Government Publishing Service, 1998.

Wittrock, B. and P. de Leon. "Policy as a Moving Target: A Call for Conceptual Realism." *Policy Studies Review* 6.1 (1986): 44–60.

JUSSI VÄLIMAA

SOCIAL DYNAMICS OF HIGHER EDUCATION REFORMS: THE CASE OF FINLAND

1. INTRODUCTION

1.1. The Objectives of the Study

The main objective of this study is to analyse the social dynamics of Finnish higher education reforms. Finnish higher education reforms may be defined as a social field where various actors struggle for power, status and influence (on field of social action see Kogan et al. 2000; Bourdieu 1984). 'Field' should not, however, be understood as a mechanical machine which will automatically lead to the right analysis but, rather, as an intellectual device which helps to see relationships and social dynamics between different actors when they seek to influence each other during higher education reforms.

The field of Finnish higher education reforms should be analysed historically in the context of the expansion of Finnish higher education. The field of higher education reforms is also a political field in two senses. On the one hand, the attempt to change Finnish higher education is an attempt to use power to make things different. On the other hand, views of how to use power have changed in the history of Finnish higher education. According to Kivinen, Rinne and Ketonen (1993), it is possible to distinguish in Finland, after the Second World War, three periods influenced by different doctrines of higher education policy making. The first was the period of academic and traditional doctrine characterised by strong traditional values based on Humboldtian ideas of a university and a weak Ministry of Education. This period lasted till the beginning of the 1960s. It was followed by a period characterised by the systematic development of the Finnish higher education system on the basis of higher education development acts as will be discussed below. It was under their influence that the Finnish higher education system reached the level of mass higher education. This doctrine came to an end in the middle of the 1980s. The world was developing into a place where it was more difficult to predict the future than during the previous decades. It was also evident that the previous higher education policy, based on rational planning, did not work very well anymore. As a solution to the new situation, the Ministry of Education reformulated the national policy goals. The Higher Education Development Act of 1986 emphasised efficiency and institutional autonomy. The present Development Act

Å. Gornitzka et al. (eds.), Reform and Change in Higher Education, 245-268.

continues with this tradition by emphasising higher education as a part of the national innovation system.

A historical analysis of the field of higher education reforms should begin with the assumption that social dynamics may also vary during each of these periods. For this reason the main *aim of this study is to identify the underlying principles, or causal regularities, in the reforms of Finnish higher education.* The concept of causal regularities was borrowed from Skocpol (1984) through Kogan et al. (2000) to focus attention on the fact that historical events are always specific processes which take place in specific historical contexts. At the same time, however, it is possible to look for patterns that are repeated in various historical contexts. Therefore, this study *not only analyses the 'general social dynamics' of Finnish higher education policy making but also asks whether it is possible to discern historical changes in the social dynamics of Finnish higher education reforms: What are the causal regularities underlying Finnish higher education reforms?*

However, for two main reasons, the purpose of this study is not to rush through the history of all Finnish higher education reforms. First, the relevant analyses can be found in several Finnish books and articles (see e.g. Ahola 1993; Aittola and Määttä 1998; Eskola 2000; Hölttä 1988; Kivinen, Rinne and Ketonen 1993; Lahtinen 1988; Lampinen 2003; Liljander 2002; Salminen 2001; Välimaa 1993, 1994). For the same reason, the following study is based mainly on current research literature on Finnish higher education. The focus of the study is on the level of the national higher education system. Analytical categories to classify higher education reforms will be developed followed by a more detailed analysis of three reforms: the degrees reform in the 1970s, the free allocation of teaching resources reform which began in the 1980s and the polytechnics reform which took place in the 1990s. The second main reason for this approach is the difficulty to make an analytical distinction between a particular reform of Finnish higher education and a policy change. Both reforms and policy changes may change the functioning of Finnish higher education when the aim is to bring about 'an official change in the way something is done or organised', as the *Oxford Advanced Learner's Dictionary* defines the word 'reform'.

Change, in turn, remains one of the most popular and permanent topics in higher education research. It is easy to agree with Clark who argues that much of academic change is invisible. Reforms and innovations usually creep into the academic world quietly "by small steps instead of far-reaching reforms" (Clark 1983: 235–236). According to Clark "in academic systems, it is difficult to perceive from on high or from the outside, or indeed from within, what is constant and especially what is changing" (p. 236). This, in turn, means that in the study of higher education systems we cannot separate "the study of changes from the study of structure and tradition" (Clark 1983: 237).

In higher education research literature, the concepts of innovation, reform and change are very often confused with each other. It seems that change is a passive phenomenon more closely related to the functioning of the world, whereas innovation and reform are active processes or products. They are seen as outcomes of human actions. Contrasting active and passive thinking in this way can be found in Becher and Kogan (1992: 133–135) who separate the phenomenon of innovation into organic change (evolution of thinking) and radical change (a rapid switch from previous practice). Gradual change has been defined as a third category (Kogan et al. 2000).[1]

In this chapter the concept of reform will be used to describe any intentional change to the higher education system emanating from government policy. The concept of change refers to a process where you can see a difference between the beginning and the end of the process. All these concepts are also related to perceptions of policy, which consist of all the attempts and measures that public authorities and various social actors undertake to influence the development of higher education (see Lampinen 1998, 2003).

2. MAKING HIGHER EDUCATION POLICIES IN FINLAND: THE HISTORICAL CONTEXT

University and higher education have been considered important aspects in the development of the Finnish nation as a nation state. Traditionally, universities have been defined as national cultural institutions rooted in the Humboldtian ideals of the university. Training civil servants has always been an important social function of Finnish higher education, also because the majority of university students have been and are employed by the public sector. The high social prestige of universities and university degrees (and academics) remains a social reality in Finland (Välimaa 2001).

In 2003 Finnish universities admitted 21,031 students and the polytechnics 25,806 students. A comparison of these numbers with the size of the relevant age cohort reveals that about 70 per cent were offered a starting place in higher education (Välimaa 2001, in press). The expansion of Finnish higher education was closely linked with, and at the same time one of the results of, a welfare state agenda supported by all major political parties. Creating equal educational opportunities – including equal access to higher education – became one of the most important objectives on this agenda, implemented over a period extending from the 1960s to the 1990s. The expansion of higher education was supported by a regional policy principle. All major provinces were allowed to establish a university of their own in the 1960s, the 1970s and the 1980s (see Välimaa 2001). There are 20 universities and 32 polytechnics in Finland at the beginning of the 21st century, which equates to one higher education institution for each 100,000 inhabitants.

Simultaneously, however, the history of Finnish higher education is the history of making higher education policies in Finland in certain historical contexts. These historical contexts constitute the present landscape of Finnish higher education like archaeological layers influencing not only the present structures but also how higher education is perceived in Finland (see Välimaa in press). The Finnish field of higher education reforms is therefore a field with many layers and many actors who have not only emerged and gained their positions over time but who are "part of our historical presence because they still exercise their effects" as Bourdieu (1984: 34) puts it.

A Finnish higher education policy in the modern sense emerged in the 1960s after which the development of Finnish higher education has been guided by higher education development acts. The first Higher Education Development Act covered the years from 1967 to 1986. One of the main purposes of the Act was to foster social and geographic equality by increasing access to the universities and to mobilise reserves of talent in the rural areas to reach the level of development in the other industrialised countries (Kivinen, Rinne and Ketonen 1993). This first Higher Education Development Act was accompanied by the Council of State's expectations concerning the measures to be taken by higher education institutions, which is another essential element related to the implementation of the Development Act. It may be said that the Higher Education Development Act and the government decisions connected with it opened a new space for higher education policy making. Increased university funding legitimised the government's endeavour to reform universities, or, to put it in other words: to interfere with the internal life of universities in ways that had not been seen before. The centrally planned aims of the Development Act promoted the practices of a centrally steered system preparing the political basis for reforms of university administration and degrees.

The new Higher Education Development Act of 1986 and the government decisions connected with this law introduced a new development strategy which followed the principles of the strategy of self-regulation as described by Van Vught (1989). The government's 'expectations' focused attention on the following higher education policy-making objectives: the autonomy of the universities will be expanded by combining budget sub-items; teachers' duties will be made more flexible; and the authority and powers of university rectors and deans will be strengthened. Both the ideas about how a university should be managed and how its activities should be developed implied changes: effective planning and cooperation were emphasised in research activities; productivity was paid more attention when allocating resources; and university evaluation was developed (Välimaa 1994).

Finnish universities supported this Act as much as they had opposed the first Act, because the Act of 1986 ensured universities (for the time being) their basic resources and a 15 per cent annual growth in appropriations. Towards the end of the 1980s, this was an exceptional trend in Western Europe. Even though the promised increase failed to fully materialise, funding rose steadily until 1990. After a change of government in 1991, growth started to slow and in 1992 the budget was frozen to the level of 1991 when Finland was hit by a severe economic recession. Because of budget cuts made in 1993, the Higher Education Development Act was eventually repealed. The newest Higher Education Act was launched in 1999 covering the years 1999–2004.

3. ANALYSING FINNISH HIGHER EDUCATION REFORMS

There are alternative ways to categorise and analyse reforms. For example, in a European study (Eurydice Studies 2000) the analysis of reforms was based on six thematically oriented categories.[2] These categories fail, however, to concentrate attention on the social dynamics of reforms; the focus is, rather, on various aspects of European policy making. The analysis of Finnish higher education reforms should take into account the dimensions essential for the social dynamics of higher education reforms. Therefore, the analysis of Finnish reforms should begin with the creation of categories which are unified by their scope in the system of higher education.

The first category, *reforms of academic degrees and curricula*, includes the degrees reform carried out in the 1970s, which was one of the largest reform measures in the history of Finnish higher education (see below). In addition to changes brought by the reform, revising curricula is part of the annual routine of higher education institutions. However, these changes in curricula are not defined as reforms but as a part of the organic and gradual changes taking place in higher education institutions. This category also includes numerous pedagogical innovations implemented in Finnish higher education institutions (see e.g. Honkimäki 1999; Välimaa 1994; Välimaa and Vuorinen 1991).

The second category, *reforms of institutional structures and practices*, includes the attempts to change the decision-making practices of Finnish universities at the turn of the 1970s, known as the reform of university administration *(yliopistojen hallinnonuudistus)* (Kivinen, Rinne and Ketonen 1993). This category also covers the gradual changes initiated by a new doctrine adopted in Finnish higher education policy making in the 1980s. The aim of the Higher Education Development Act of 1986 was to enhance leadership and management in Finnish higher education institutions and introduce accountability and quality assessment into Finnish higher education (Välimaa 1994). This category also includes the free allocation of teaching resources reform, which changed the definition of academic work (see below). However, these changes have not necessarily been seen as reforms but rather as consequences of policy changes. The Finnish experience thus suggests that the difference between a policy change and a reform is this: reforms are understood as rapid changes, whereas changes in higher education policies are a part of the organic development of policy making.

The third category, *reforms of the structure of the Finnish higher education system*, consists of two types of reforms. The first type includes the establishment of a new sector of higher education. The establishment of a modern open university in the 1970s provides the first example (see Lampinen 2003). However, the establishment of a higher vocational education sector (polytechnics) offers the best example of structural reform of this type (see below). The second type of these reforms consists of the reorganisation of existing structures or processes. The best example is provided by the reform of doctoral education implemented in the 1990s, which established the system of graduate schools in Finland (see Määttä 2001).

The fourth category, *reforms of the mechanisms used to steer Finnish higher education*, covers the introduction of both the 1967 and 1986 Higher Education Development Acts which have promoted the expansion and development of Finnish higher education by providing a framework for higher education policies and policy making. The introduction of management by results in the 1990s changed the mechanisms used to steer Finnish higher education while the establishment of the Finnish Higher Education Evaluation Council in 1995 linked evaluation activities more closely to the steering of higher education (Välimaa in press).

In order to analyse higher education reforms in more detail, three reforms which represent three different reform categories will be focused upon. The first case study analyses the degrees reform which took place in the 1970s. It was implemented during a period when the ideas of rational planning and the central steering of higher education were seen as efficient. The second case study describes an alternative reform strategy based on the idea of self-regulation and institutional autonomy: the free allocation of teaching resources reform was launched in the 1980s and finished in the 1990s. The third case study analyses a major reform of the higher education system: the establishment of polytechnics in Finland in the 1990s. This reform represents an effort to restructure the system of higher education in the context of globalising higher education.

4. CASE STUDIES OF HIGHER EDUCATION REFORMS

4.1. The Ideal of Rational Planning: The Degrees Reform

4.1.1. Historical Context of the Reform

The social and political context of the reform of Finnish university degrees was provided by the reform of decision-making processes in universities and university administration. The government's aim was to introduce democratic decision-making practices into all university councils by the end of the 1960s. The goal was to establish universal suffrage in university and abolish the traditional authority of professors in the decision-making bodies.

The reform of the university administration was initiated following normal Finnish procedure, appointing, in 1968, a committee given the brief to 'suggest various models for the administrative organisation of the higher education institutions'. During this crazy year in European universities, Finnish university students joined the European student movement by seizing one of the symbolically important buildings close to the University of Helsinki and demanding the democratisation of the university's decision-making structures. The National Union of Students in Finland (NUSF) supported their demands, whereas the rectors of the universities established the Finnish Council of University Rectors 'to promote the common interests of higher education institutions', in other words: to resist the reform. In this heated political context, the administrative reform committee found it difficult to agree on models of university administration. Following a suggestion made by the committee, the Council of State prepared a draft law. According to the proposal, university councils would be elected by universal suffrage, whereas in lower decision-making bodies there should be quotas for professors, other staff and students. The suggestion was vigorously resisted inside universities mainly by professors who established their trade union in 1969 to fight against the reform, whereas the students supported it. In the general election of 1970 the reform of university administration became one of the most important political issues. The reform was supported by the government (consisting of the Centre Party and the

Social Democrats) and resisted by the opposition, mainly the right-wing parties. The draft law did not pass the parliament (Kivinen, Rinne and Ketonen 1993: 80–106).

The attempt to reform university administration should be seen in its historical context as one of many reforms of the Finnish system of education undertaken at the turn of the 1960s and 1970s. The comprehensive school reform had just been initiated and committees were also preparing a reform of upper secondary education (Kivinen, Rinne and Ketonen 1993). What was important about the reform of university administration was the fact that it prepared the political environment for the degrees reform even though it did not itself succeed as a reform.

4.1.2. The Process of the Degrees Reform: An Example of Central Steering
The degrees reform was launched according to normal procedure by appointing a committee in 1969 given the task of preparing a reform of university degrees in the field of the humanities and social sciences. The committee, which was known as FYTT (*Committee on Humanities and Social Science Degrees*), considered that its assignment went beyond the reform of a number of degrees. It set itself the goal of critically reflecting on the aims and purposes of higher education. The committee familiarised itself with foreign experiences (they visited the UK, Sweden, Germany and the Soviet Union) and used empirical studies as background material. The FYTT Committee published its report in 1972. It considered it important to support the values of the Humboldtian tradition and to promote cooperation between teachers and students. The FYTT Committee also saw it as important to increase goal-oriented studies and make learning objectives explicit at every phase of the curricula. It suggested the use of project-based studies because it saw combining theoretical knowledge and vocational skills with critical social attitudes and problem-solving skills as a key element of university education (Lahtinen 1988; Lampinen 2003). So far, so good?

The FYTT Committee also suggested that the previous degree structure of the BA, MA and licentiate degrees should be abolished and replaced with the MA as the basic academic degree. It should consist of one year of basic studies, two years of major subject studies and one year of more advanced studies. The FYTT Committee suggested that the unit of one study week should be used to measure the time used for teaching students.

After the publication of the FYTT Committee report, the Ministry of Education appointed its own *implementation committee* to analyse the feedback gathered from universities and various relevant actors and to plan the implementation of the reform. The general feeling of the feedback from the field of higher education was one of 'positive surprise', as Lahtinen (1988) has put it even though many commentators said that the report was too abstract and that its arguments were unclear. Universities representing mainly the opinions of the professors assumed a more critical attitude than the students and the trade union of junior academic staff (FUURT). Among the universities, traditional and well-resourced institutions (such as the University of Helsinki) were more critical of the suggested reform, whereas younger institutions adopted a more positive attitude towards it. Some critics even saw the report as an example of socialist values (Häikiö 1977 in Kivinen, Rinne and

Ketonen 1993). These right-wing critics said that the idea of the degrees reform originated in East Germany. The stage was set for the political play.

The implementation committee found it difficult to translate the abstract ideas presented in the FYTT Committee's report into practice. In the course of this translation, the original principles suggested by the FYTT Committee began to fade as they entered the political reality of higher education policy making. The implementation plan was approved by the Council of State and the implementation committee ordered that curricula should be planned as degree programmes. This replaced the traditional curriculum structure based on three levels of courses in each discipline. In fact, the new concept of degree programme (*koulutusohjelma* in Finnish) was translated from English, having not been used before in Finnish. The term discipline was replaced with that of study fields (Lampinen 2003; Kivinen, Rinne and Ketonen 1993).

According to the innovation strategy inspired by rational planning, national instructions for the reform were given by the Ministry of Education. They included general principles for every study field. The national planning and implementation of the reform were led by the Ministry of Education which issued detailed instructions covering each study programme. The students and university staff had their representatives on every national planning committee. The same procedure was repeated at the institutional level: each study field organised its local planning committee to look at each degree programme (Kivinen, Rinne and Ketonen 1993; Lampinen 2003).

The implementation committee also initiated an experiment in the Faculty of Social Sciences at the University of Jyväskylä in 1974. The objective was to gain experiences, analyse them and use the findings in the implementation of the reform. A follow-up research project was begun at the Institute for Educational Research in 1972 (see Välimaa 2000).[3] Both students and junior staff supported the experiment when it began. Quite soon, however, the supporters began to fade away and there was severe criticism of the overly rationalistic beliefs about planning underlying the reform, of the vocational orientation of the degree programmes and the mechanical standardisation of studies. This criticism did not, however, manage to postpone the reforms or to change the course of the planned actions (Lahtinen 1988; Lampinen 2003).

New national statutes were issued for the study fields of technology, medicine and law in 1974 and 1975. The implementation of the new degrees was, however, much more difficult in other study fields. In 1977, the Ministry of Education proposed a statute for the natural sciences, humanities and social sciences degrees. It was, however, fiercely opposed by the academics. As many as 120 university teachers demanded in public that the basic principles should be critically analysed. As a result of the protests, the Ministry of Education revised the statute and gave universities more power to decide on the contents of the degree programmes. The protests did not, however, lead to changes in the general aims of the reform. By 1979, all study fields had their statutes which stipulated that degrees consisted of basic studies, subject studies and advanced level studies.

4.1.3. The Outcomes of the Reform: Great Frustration With Mixed Performance
The degrees reform was opposed by Finnish academics throughout the 1970s. A professor of physics calculated that in one middle-sized university, some 1,000,000 working hours were wasted on sitting on degree reform committees (Konttinen and Välimaa 1990). This example illustrates the deep frustration felt by Finnish academics. Why were they frustrated?

The main reasons for their frustration were not only the process of the reform but also the strategy adopted to implement the reform. The reform was organised and led by the Ministry of Education. The implementation was left to the universities and academics with no opportunity to question the principles behind, or the applicability of, the reform. The course of the reform never changed even though most of the academic community resisted it. This was partly caused by the fact that to some politicians the reform had become a matter of honour (Lampinen 2003). The language of the reform was another source of frustration. The new, introduced concepts (degree programme, basic studies, subject studies and advanced level studies) challenged previous traditional academic terminology. As a consequence, the academics normally picked up the new concepts but left the curriculum structures intact (Lampinen 2003). This was, in turn, related to academic values. The reform was intended to replace disciplines – the heartland of academic identity as Henkel (2000) has shown – with degree programmes. In the context of academic identity it was very problematic that the focus of attention was shifted from research to teaching. The reformists also tried to start the pedagogical training of university teachers who found the idea particularly repugnant (Kivinen, Rinne and Ketonen 1993).

The reform was also seen as a threat to the main principles of the Humboldtian university ideal: institutional autonomy and academic freedom. During the reform, usefulness was defined by the Ministry of Education – the main criteria being the needs of society. These issues were soon translated into issues of power: who has the power to decide what is taught in the universities? It is not very surprising that this question led to bitter conflicts between the Ministry of Education and higher education institutions (Kivinen, Rinne and Ketonen 1993; Lampinen 2003; see also Cerych and Sabatier 1986).

However, the reform also had positive outcomes. It enabled new higher education institutions (established during the 1960s) to create their own curricula and free themselves from the traditional dominance of the University of Helsinki (Kivinen, Rinne and Ketonen 1993). One of the positive outcomes of the reform was also the introduction of the concept of a standardised study week (see earlier). This unit of measure made visible the simple fact that students have only a limited number of hours to use for their studies.

4.1.4. The Actors in the Degrees Reform
The analysis of the actors in the Finnish field of higher education reforms should begin with the analysis of the actors active during the degrees reform. The analysis must start with the *Ministry of Education,* which had just been reorganised in the 1960s. The Ministry of Education saw its role as that of the main promoter and

organiser of the reform. In this sense, the reform provides an example of a centrally planned and organised reform process.

There were, however, other players in this field of the degrees reform. Finnish *higher education institutions* were the second set of main actors in the field. They were responsible for the organisation of local planning committees which did the actual practical work. Finnish universities normally resisted the reform, which brought them into conflict with the Ministry of Education. The Ministry also recognised other players in the field. The most important of them were the *student organisations* and the *academic trade unions*. The Finnish Union of University Researchers and Teachers (FUURT) was established in 1967 and the Finnish Union of University Professors (FUUP) and the Finnish Union of University Lecturers (FUUL) in 1969. These groups were represented on both the national and institutional planning committees. At the beginning of the reform, students and junior staff took a positive attitude toward the reform, but it did not take long before they turned against it. FUUP resisted the reform for obvious reasons: the reform was seen as a threat to professors' traditional position of power. *Individual academics* also played a role in the resistance to the reforms. In addition to these academic groups, there were also other actors in the field interested in exerting influence on the reform process. One of the most prominent of them was KTTS, a research foundation established by *industry and right-wing political circles*. KTTS was a bitter critic of the reform and saw it as a threat to traditional universities and Finnish society (see Häikiö 1977). The *political parties* also showed an interest in the degrees reform.

According to Kivinen, Rinne and Ketonen (1993) the battle positions occupied during the fight against the reform of university administration were fully utilised during the degrees reform. This is evident especially as regards FUUP, which was established to resist the reform of university administration and to defend the status of professors. In fact, the academic trade unions arose as a response to the reforms of Finnish higher education. They became players in the field of higher education reform as soon as it emerged. Or, to put it in other words, the field of higher education reform emerged and developed when political and social needs arose to change the functioning of the Finnish higher education system. The social dynamics of the reforms required and generated the organisation of various interest groups to defend their stake in a situation where the traditional social order inside universities and the relationship between higher education institutions and society had changed. In this sense, the degree reform also offered a field to debate on and struggle for the ideals of the university.

The field of the degrees reform may be illustrated with the help of figure 1. The tensions in the field may be illustrated with the help of two main dimensions. The first tensions were created by the idea of the university. The modern idea of the university refers here to the need to reform universities in order to make them better respond to the needs of society, as they were understood at that time, whereas the traditional idea emphasises traditional Humboldtian values of universities, especially academic freedom. The second tensions were created by the differences in defining the social role of universities. Traditional academic relevance of universities refers to traditional academic production of knowledge in the spirit of Merton (1973), whereas the dimension of social relevance describes the need to produce a qualified labour force.

Figure 1. The field and actors in the degrees reform 1969–79

The idea of the university: Modern

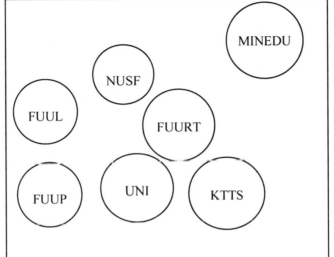

The role of
universities
in society:
Academic
relevance

Social
relevance

Actors: MINEDU (Ministry of Education), UNI (Universities), FUUP (Finnish Union of University Professors), FUUL (Finnish Union of University Lecturers), FUURT (Finnish Union of University Researchers and Teachers), KTTS (A foundation representing employers' perspectives), NUSF (National Union of Students in Finland)

4.2. Introducing the Self-regulative University: The Experiment With the Free Allocation of Teaching Resources

4.2.1. Background to the Reform: Difficulties in Planning and Allocating Resources

The 1980s saw a change in the system for steering Finnish higher education when the problems of central planning of the national higher education system became visible. There were two main sources of problems. First, it was realised that planning in a changing world should be based more on strategic thinking than on centrally steered measures (Kivinen, Rinne and Ketonen 1993). Secondly, there were the problems between the universities and the Ministry of Education stemming from rigid rules covering the use of money and inflexible regulations governing the academic work of university staff. The operations and activities of the universities were regulated chiefly through the structure of the state budget because the appropriations were bound to strict sub-items and could only be used for the purpose defined by each particular sub-item. The workload of university teachers was equally strictly regulated by and set down in statutes.[4] This practice both tied the hands of the Ministry of Education and made impossible any strategic planning of activities in universities. Therefore, there was a need to increase flexibility both in money allocations and in academic work. Towards the end of the 1980s, the Ministry of Education supported two separate experiments. The University of Joensuu was responsible for an experiment with lump sum budgeting and target negotiations (Joensuun yliopisto 1991), while two other higher education institutions experimented with flexible working conditions.

4.2.2. The Content and Implementation of the Experiment: More Responsibility and Flexibility

0In contrast to the degrees reform, launching the free allocation of teaching resources was not decided high up in the Ministry of Education or in the government but agreed to between the labour organisations and the Ministry during normal collective bargaining negotiations. The government and the three academic trade unions (FUUP, FUUL, FUURT) resolved that for a start the experiment would run for two years but later it would be extended to five years. A follow-up study of the experiment was launched at the same time. The aim of the follow-up study was to support national and local decision making by gathering and analysing data (Välimaa 1993).

The starting point of the free allocation of teaching resources experiment, initiated by the Helsinki School of Economics and Business Administration in 1988 and the University of Jyväskylä in 1989, was the basic concept that teachers' work would no longer be defined in terms of a given number of lecture hours but instead in terms of total annual working hours, set at approximately 1600 hours.[5] Further, the experiment would last five years, and include all university teachers: professors, lecturers, assistants and non-tenured part-time teachers. A safety clause was included in the collective bargaining agreement stating that if a teacher's teaching load was heavier than it was before, they would be paid a fee for the difference (Konttinen and Välimaa 1990).

Towards the end of 1991 the Ministry of Education wished to extend the experiment to other Finnish universities, mainly because 10 out of 20 institutions would have liked to join the experiment. However, the attempt did not succeed mainly because the trade unions of professors and lecturers opposed the suggestion, whereas FUURT supported it. Rhetorically, they argued that in the future someone would start to calculate the working hours, which would mean the end of academic freedom. They were also interested in having more detailed information on the results of the experiment (Välimaa 1993). In addition, the Ministry of Finance suspected that the experiment reduced the working hours of academics. Only the University of Joensuu was allowed to join the experiment to support it with lump sum budgeting which had started there earlier.

The resistance to the reform was rooted in fears of what would be the 'real future' of the experiment – both the academic trade unions and some university teachers were afraid of political confrontation and changes in the power structure within university departments. These suspicions were related to the earlier reforms, especially to the 1970s degrees reform (Välimaa 1993).

The experiment had no national level organising or planning committee. The practical organisation of the reform was left to the universities where the arrangements were never very rigid. The aim was rather to make the university community commit itself voluntarily to the experiment. The experiment's innovation strategy was based on the assumption that responsibility for the planning and implementation of innovations would be left to the faculties and the departments (Konttinen and Välimaa 1990).

4.2.3. The Outcomes of the Reform

During the experiment most teachers and departments were able to use the expanded autonomy to increase the time available for research and tutorial teaching. The teachers themselves considered this the most positive result of the experiment. Right from the start of the reform, the majority of the teachers were either very satisfied or satisfied (61%) with it; only 3.5 per cent were dissatisfied or very dissatisfied. In the same questionnaire, 83 per cent of the teachers said that they did not want to return to the previous practices. The academics were very satisfied with the increased scope for autonomy in the operations and activities of the basic units. However, the national trade unions opposed the experiment (Välimaa 1993). This proved a politically problematic situation for the trade unions, which were supposed to defend the interests of their members. Wishing to win more time, they made demands for information on the outcomes of the reform. As a consequence, in the collective bargaining negotiations it was decided to continue the experiment for another five years, until 1997. Finally it was agreed in 1998 that the experiment would be extended to all Finnish higher education institutions.[6] It was also agreed that the free allocation of teaching resources would be adopted in the polytechnics in 2004. In this sense, given its width, the reform for making academic work more flexible was quite successful.

The main reasons for these successes were not only the real need to make academic work more flexible but also the innovation strategy chosen. It was based on making academic communities commit themselves to the idea of reform and then supporting them when they carried it through. This was not a centrally steered reform but an experiment grounded on the ideas of departmental self-regulation. However, the reform did not reach all its goals. Finland was hit by one of the severest recessions, and higher education budgets were cut at the turn of the 1990s. These cuts significantly decreased the possibility to utilise increased flexibility in academic work.

4.2.4. The Actors in the Free Allocation of Teaching Resources Reform

The actors present during the processes of the free allocation of teaching resources reform were basically the same as in the degrees reform.

The *Ministry of Education* was one of the principal actors in favour of flexibility. It saw the experiment as one of the tools to enhance both institutional autonomy and the flexibility of academic work. The *Ministry of Finance* was also interested in the experiment. It was concerned about the potential reduction in academic working hours. As a consequence, Statistics Finland made a national survey of academic work (Statistics Finland 1993).

For obvious reasons, the *academic trade unions* were the second set of principal actors involved in the reform: the reform changed the nature of working conditions. The trade unions were very interested in seeing how changing the definition of work would affect the nature of the work. Finnish trade unions are not, however, a homogenous group. The Finnish Union of University Researchers and Teachers (FUURT) took the most positive attitude towards the reform because it saw that it could improve the working conditions of junior staff, whereas the Finnish Union of University Professors (FUUP) adopted a more critical attitude. The most conservative of all the trade unions was, however, the Union of Finnish University Lecturers (FUUL), which belongs to the Trade Union Education. This is the largest trade union in the field of education, most of its members being comprehensive school teachers. It was feared that once the system of total working hours was accepted in universities it would soon be extended to all schools.

Finnish universities saw the potential of this reform to make institutional and departmental planning more rational. After two years of implementation, in a questionnaire to the universities by the Ministry of Education, as many as half of them were interested in joining the reform. 'Finnish universities' refers here to those who represent the views of the universities in public. University staff in two higher education institutions taking part in the experiment also supported the reform.

Both local and national *student organisations* supported the experiment. The students were interested in the improvements in educational provision made during the experiment.

Follow-up research was also one of the actors during the reform through its provision of information on the various aspects of the reform.[7] The main message of the follow-up research was that university staff were very satisfied with the reform because it did not do any harm while offering an opportunity to make academic work more flexible (Konttinen and Välimaa 1990; Välimaa 1993).

The field of this reform may be illustrated with the help of figure 2 to describe the positions between the main actors. The field may be described with the help of two main conflicting dimensions. The idea of the university may be defined as the first dimension. Here the modern idea of the university describes the understanding of the university as a strategic actor which should have flexibility in the allocation of its resources, whereas the traditional view is rooted in the corporative ideas based on collective bargaining negotiations. The second main dimension may be found in the understandings on the nature of academic work. According to the promoters of the reform, academic work should be made more flexible to respond to the changing needs of society, whereas the resisters of the reform see no need for change. In this sense this dimension describes differences in defining the social role of universities.

Figure 2. The field and actors in the free allocation of teaching resources reform 1988–97

The idea of the university: Modern

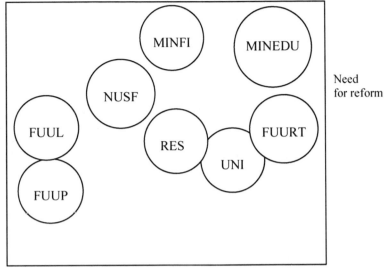

Actors: FUUP (Finnish Union of University Professors), FUUL (Finnish Union of University Lecturers), FUURT (Finnish Union of University Researchers and Teachers), MINEDU (Ministry of Education), MINFI (Ministry of Finances), NUSF (National Union of Students in Finland), RES (Researchers), UNI (Universities)

4.3. Globalising Finnish Higher Education: The Establishment of Polytechnics

4.3.1. Background to the Reform

The Finnish nation state was hit by a severe economic recession at the turn of the 1990s, the consequences of which were soon felt in higher education institutions as a part of budget cuts in the public sector. This context of a social crisis made new initiatives both politically and practically desirable. It was rather easy to reform doctoral training, which had been defined as problematic as early as the 1960s (Aittola and Määttä 1998; Määttä 2001; Lampinen 2003). In the context of crisis, however, the major reform introduced in the 1990s was the establishment of polytechnics in Finland.

4.3.2. The Reform Process

The Finnish government launched the polytechnics reform in 1992 by authorising 22 temporary vocational higher education institutions. In other words, the reform was initiated as an experiment because the decision makers were totally unprepared for such a grand move: "there was a lack of political maturity", as Lampinen (1998 in Nieminen and Ahola 2003) put it, to accept the rapid establishment of a new sector of higher education. The experimental institutions were located in all parts of the country and included practically all types of institution and study fields. Of the 22 vocational higher education institutions, 16 were organised as conglomerates of institutions representing different study fields while six offered only one study field (Ahola 1993).

From the perspective of governmental steering, the aims of the polytechnics reform were: to reconstruct the overall educational structure to meet the needs of society (students and the labour market); to expand and develop higher education to meet the needs of international economic competition and European integration; and to enhance educational provision and flexibility through more effective cooperation between institutions. A further aim was to increase the scope for individual choice. It was also assumed that a dual system would respond better to the needs of working life and society. According to the Ministry of Education, one of the main objectives of the reform was to "clarify and streamline the education system and to create a viable channel from secondary education to the university and non-university sectors" (Higher Education 1994: 13). Recent studies have revealed still further factors. According to Mäenpää (2000 in Nieminen and Ahola 2003), it is also possible to discern international pressures to reform Finnish higher education. The EU had issued a directive (89/48/ETY) stating that all three-year degrees should be recognised across the member states of the European Union. This boosted the development of vocational education in France, Belgium, Sweden and Finland (Teichler 1998). According to the then Minister of Education, Olli-Pekka Heinonen, the OECD country report on the polytechnics reform was used in these debates. This indicates a close relationship between Finnish higher education policy making and international models even though the outcome of the reform has been defined as a Finnish system more than a copy of international models (Liljander 2002).

According to the first plans, the polytechnics reform was meant to continue for at least five years before the first critical phase would have been reached. The plans were, however, rapidly revised. After a few years of experimenting, the government decided that the experimental polytechnics would be granted permanent licence to operate in the autumn of 1996. Originally, the idea was to give permanent licence only to those institutions which had started as temporary establishments. Instead, other institutions also received licences. However, after these first permanent licences were granted, an application system was developed. In accordance with official procedure, each temporary polytechnic applied for permanent status which was granted by the Council of State after an evaluation conducted by the Finnish Higher Education Evaluation Council (Välimaa in press).

The academics and the universities were initially critical of the establishment of a dual system, fearing that it would reduce the higher education budget. The resistance was not, however, systematic or sharply defined, possibly because of the obvious advantages that higher education institutions and individual academics foresaw with respect to the expansion of the educational market based on raising the qualification requirements of teachers in vocational higher education.

4.3.3. The Outcomes and Actors of the Reform

As a result of the reform there are 32 polytechnics located all over the country, most of which are multidisciplinary institutions. Since August 2000, all Finnish polytechnics operate on a permanent basis. Finnish polytechnics are normally local institutions run by an urban municipality, a federation of municipalities or a registered Finnish foundation or a limited company.[8]

Figure 3. The field and actors in the reform of polytechnics 1992–2000

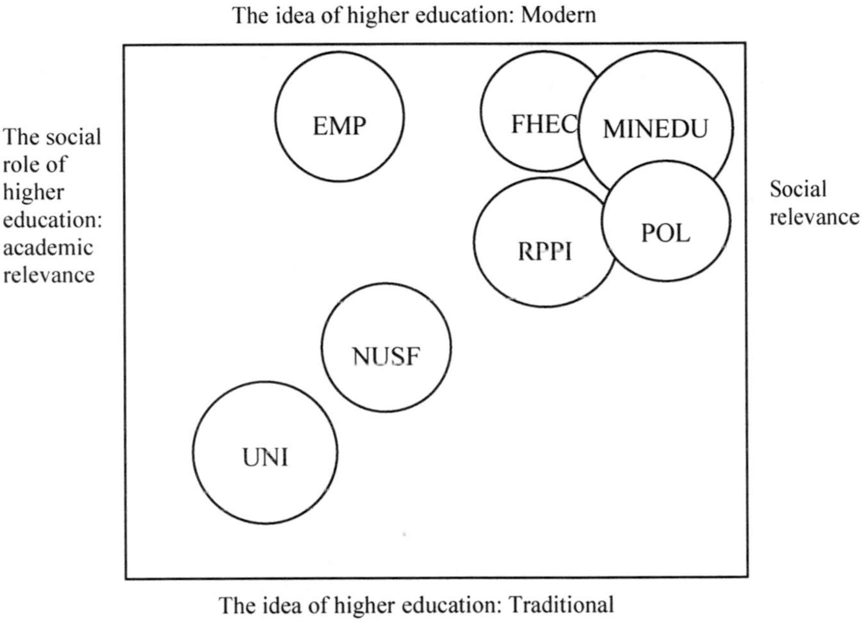

The idea of higher education: Modern

The social role of higher education: academic relevance

Social relevance

The idea of higher education: Traditional

Actors: FHEC (Finnish Higher Education Evaluation Council), EMP (Representatives of Employers), MINEDU (Ministry of Education), NUSF (National Union of Students in Finland), POL (New Polytechnics), RPPI (Representatives of Provinces and Provincial Institutions), UNI (Universities)

The main actors in the process of establishing the polytechnics were various. The context of recession made it necessary to take visible political action to address the economic problems. In this context, the government decided to establish a new sector of higher education. The ideas behind these institutions had been developed as early as the 1980s as a solution to problems besetting vocational upper secondary education. The *Ministry of Education* with its experienced civil servants was an important actor in the implementation of the reforms. The *Finnish Higher Education Evaluation Council* supported the Ministry of Education through evaluations of applications. No *political party* opposed the reform even though the establishment process was felt to be too rapid. The *representatives of provinces and provincial institutions* were in favour of raising the status of their upper secondary education institutions. They backed the new establishments. The *universities* normally resisted the establishment of polytechnics even though they actually had mixed feelings about the new sector of higher education, whereas the *vocational colleges* and the *emerging polytechnics* themselves supported the reform. Academic drift was thus one of the driving forces behind the reform. The *student organisations* were rather neutral on this topic, whereas the *representatives of employees* demanded that the polytechnics should have a practical and vocational orientation (Liljander 2002; Nieminen and Ahola 2003). The *researchers* conducting the follow-up study were not heard in the reform process.

The field of the polytechnics reform may be illustrated with the help of figure 3. The actors in the field may be illustrated with the help of two main conflicting dimensions. The first tensions were created by the idea of higher education. The 'modern idea' emphasises here the need to establish a dual system in Finland with polytechnics and universities. 'Traditional idea' refers here to universities as the main producers of new knowledge leaving no room for vocational educational establishments. The second tensions refer here to the social role of higher education institutions. 'Traditional academic' refers to universities as producers of high quality professionals and research, whereas the dimension of social relevance emphasises the need to produce a qualified labour force for the nation state.

5. DISCUSSION: THE FIELD OF FINNISH HIGHER EDUCATION POLICY MAKING

5.1. On the Nature of the Finnish Strategy of Gradual Reform

This study sought to demonstrate that the attempts to reform Finnish higher education have generated activities both for and against the reforms. These struggles can be described as constituting a field of social action, "where field is an institutionalised area of activity in which actors struggle about something that is of importance to them", as Kogan et al. (2000) defines the term. The field of higher education reforms emerged when there arose a social need to change the functioning of Finnish higher education. The social dynamics of the reforms generated various groups (universities, professors, lecturers, junior academic staff, students) who defended their interests in relation to the traditional social order inside universities as the relationship between higher education institutions and society were remodelled. This took place at the end of the 1960s.

There seems to be a causal regularity in the development of gradual reform strategy within higher education reforms. It first surfaced during the implementation of the degrees reform in the 1970s, when experiment as such was seen as a part of the reform even though the outcomes were mainly ignored by policy makers. The strategy was further developed during the free allocation of teaching resources reform when the experiment had an impact on the implementation of the reform process. Since then, the gradual reform strategy has been applied in all the reforms.

It is an essential aspect of this reform strategy that a reform is developed gradually on the basis of experiments in a few institutions after which it will be extended to the system of higher education as a whole. The main causal regularity behind the social dynamics of the field of Finnish higher education lies in the fact that there is no single centre of power capable of forcing the system to change. This state of affairs, in turn, creates a necessity to either negotiate or at least interact with many actors active in the field of Finnish higher education policy making. 'Negotiation' refers here to institutionalised forms of both asking statements from the actors and to collective bargaining negotiations, whereas 'interaction' refers to other forms of communication and debates over the objectives of reforms most often in the national media but also in various seminars and meetings. In this social context, on the one hand, all the actors can agree on an experiment because it is meant to be only an experiment, which can also fail. On the other hand, starting an experiment gives the different authors time to accumulate data and formulate an opinion about the experiment. These experiments are normally supported by follow-up studies which feed the actors with information. The critical moment in this strategy of gradual reform arrives when the promoter of the experiment wants to expand it into a system-wide practice. This is the point at which all the other actors must formulate their opinions. The polytechnics reform was, however, an exception to the rule because the decision to establish polytechnics on a permanent basis was made before any relevant empirical research findings were even published. The main factor prompting the decision was the political importance of this reform, which restructured the Finnish system of higher education. In this sense, it also reveals an essential feature of the Finnish strategy of gradual reform, that is, the experiments are not authentic trial runs because all the actors in the field know that sooner or later there will be an attempt to make the pilot reform a system-wide practice. For the same reason, the strategy of gradual reform has the advantage of making it possible to address obvious problems during the experimentation process. In the political reality of the field where higher education policy is formulated, this also makes any compromises easier to accept.

The study has also shown that it is an essential feature of this field of higher education policy making that all actors are not active in all reforms and that the importance of particular actors varies between reforms. This can be described in terms of social fields by saying that the distance between the actors varies in different reforms. However, the social dynamics of higher education reforms remain the same in all fields of reform.

On the basis of these case studies, the actors operating in the field of Finnish higher education policy are as follows (in the order of their general importance):

1. *The Ministry of Education.* The Ministry should not be understood as a monolithic entity, but, rather, as a collective actor representing various aims and goals and comprising persons who occupy different positions of power.
2. *Universities.* Finnish universities are neither homogenous interest groups representing monolithic policies nor do they have a strong buffer organisation to represent the perspectives of all universities. The conference of Finnish university rectors is more akin to a social club than a political actor. One contributing factor is the history of Finnish higher education: till the 1960s the University of Helsinki represented all Finnish

universities, and the Ministry of Education had close links with it. The second factor is a steering system called management by results which commenced in the 1990s. Each university 'negotiates' individually with the Ministry of Education, trying to advance its own aims.

3. *Trade unions.* Academic trade organisations are willing to be active actors in the Finnish field of higher education policy. They are active and also influential especially in those reforms which change the working conditions of academics defined in collective bargaining agreements.

4. *Student organisations.* The National Union of Students in Finland has traditionally been one of the most active and vocal actors in the making of higher education policy. Students are especially interested in all the reforms that influence their living conditions or studying in higher education institutions.

5. *Representatives of employers and private enterprise.* These two groups are united in this study because the perspectives of industrial enterprises and other private businesses are often articulated through their national organisations (KTTS in the 1970s after which they have been represented mainly by *TT teollisuus ja työnantajat* – Industry and Employers).

6. *The Ministry of Finance.* The Ministry has been the main initiator of the reform of Finnish public administration.

7. *Political parties.* The political parties are not very visible actors in the field of higher education policy. This is mainly because all political parties, whether right-wing or left-wing, share basically the same conviction that higher education benefits the development of the welfare state and the nation state. The differences lie, rather, in varying views on which steering mechanisms of the higher education system should be emphasised than different opinions on the aims of higher education. Right-wing parties are more in favour of market-like mechanisms than the other parties, even though no radical differences can be found (cf. Poropudas and Volanen 2003).

8. *Research and researchers.* In principle, the role of research is important during the experimentation processes. In practice, research findings are often used to promote each actor's own interests.

9. *Other more occasional actors.* This category includes all those other actors who are active either at the local level (such as private enterprises) or individuals who operate on their own without necessarily representing a united group.

The positions of actors in the illustrations have been shown in the initial phase of the reform (see figures 1–3), even though it should be remembered that the nature of the field is based on evolving processes. The illustrations, in turn, should be understood as heuristic devices in the analysis of reforms. The tensions in the reforms have been described with the help of two conflicting dimensions in order to describe the tensions of the field and to locate the actors in them. The first (vertical) dimension describes different ideas of the university because this topic normally lies at the heart of debates during the reforms. The continuum stretches from traditional to modern. 'Traditional' often takes support from the Humboldtian values, whereas 'modern' refers to attempts to make higher education as responsive to society as possible, no matter how 'modern' has been defined in each of the reforms. The second (horizontal) dimension refers to the role of higher education in society. Here emphases vary from being loyal to academic and epistemic traditions (academic relevance) to practical usefulness (social relevance) of higher education.

In this study, illustrations have been used to reveal the fact that actors influence each other in the field of higher education policy making. In fact, the illustrations should describe relationships in a three-dimensional field because there are many games going on in the same field. For example, during the free allocation of teaching resources reform, FUURT took a very positive attitude to the reform because they knew that FUUL would resist it together with FUUP. The trade union politics made it easier for them to play the role of reformer. However, these interactions and negotiations take place in a social context where all actors support the development of higher education and see it as important for the wellbeing and development of the Finnish nation state.

NOTES

[1] Cerych and Sabatier (1986) neither define a reform nor discuss its relationship with change. Instead, they combine reform and change by using 'scope of change' as an explanatory concept. Scope of change consists of three related elements: depth, breadth and level of change.

[2] The categories are as follows: 1) legislation for change; 2) management, finance and control; 3) access and wastage; 4) financial aid to students; 5) curriculum and teaching; 6) internationalisation

[3] A similar follow-up research strategy had been adopted earlier in the implementation of the comprehensive school reform in the 1960s.

[4] It was the duty of a professor to lecture 140 hours a year while associate professors had to teach 186 hours and lecturers 392 or 448 hours a year, depending on the title of their post.

[5] The figure of 1600 hours corresponds to the annual working time of a person who has served 10 years as a civil servant.

[6] *Yliopisto- ja tiedehallinnon tarkentava virkaehtosopimus* (agreement in bargaining negotiations) 3 June 1997.

[7] The researchers presented their findings in many national meetings and seminars arranged by student organisations, universities and academic trade unions (Välimaa 1993).

[8] The exceptions to the rule are two state-funded polytechnics (the Police College and National Defence College) and Ålands Yrkeshögskola, which is subordinate to the self-governing Åland Islands.

REFERENCES

Ahola, S. "Diversification and the Mass Higher Education System in Finland. Martin Trow Revisited." Paper presented at the 5th National Symposium on Higher Education Research, Jyväskylä, 19–20 August, 1993.

Aittola, H. and P. Määttä. *Tohtoriksi tutkijakoulusta. Tutkijakoulut tieteellisten jatko-opintojen uudistajina* (*Doctoral Education in Finnish Graduate Schools: Reforming Doctoral Studies in Finland*). Publication Series of the Institute for Educational Research, Research Report 3. Jyväskylä: University of Jyväskylä, 1998.

Becher, T. and M. Kogan. *Process and Structure in Higher Education*. 2nd edn. London and New York: Routledge, 1992.

Bourdieu, P. *Homo Academicus*. Trans. Peter Collier. Cambridge: Polity Press, 1984.

Cerych, L. and P. Sabatier. *Great Expectations and Mixed Performance: The Implementation of Higher Education Reforms in Europe.* Stoke-on-Trent: Trentham Books, 1986.

Clark, B.R. *The Higher Education System: Academic Organization in Cross-National Perspective.* Berkeley: University of California Press, 1983.

Eskola, S. "Tiedepolitiikka ja korkeakoulut." In Tommila, P. (ed.). *Suomen tieteen historia 4 (The History of Science in Finland, vol. 4).* Helsinki, 2000, 75–98.

Eurydice Studies. *Two Decades of Reform in Higher Education in Europe: 1980 Onwards.* Brussels: Eurydice European Unit, 2000.

Häikiö, M. "Tutkinnonuudistuksen taustaa: järjestelmäkeskustelua ja tutkintoasetuksia." In Häikiö, M., H. Rautkallio, P. Tuomikoski-Leskelä and J. Vuorinen (eds). *Korkeakoulut ja tutkinnonuudistus (Higher Education Institutions and Degree Reform).* KTTS:n julkaisuja 23. Helsinki: WSOY, 1977, 22–39.

Henkel, M. *Academic Identities and Policy Change in Higher Education.* London: Jessica Kingsley Publishers, 2000.

Higher Education. *Higher Education Policy in Finland.* Helsinki: Ministry of Education, 1994.

Hölttä, S. "Recent Changes in the Finnish Higher Education System." *European Journal of Education* 23 (1988): 91–105.

Honkimäki, S. (ed.). *Opetus, vuorovaikutus ja yliopisto (Teaching, Interaction and University).* Jyväskylä: Institute for Educational Research, University of Jyväskylä, 1999.

Joensuun yliopisto. *Yliopiston tuloksellisuus,* Näkökohtia, ehdotuksia *(The Accountability of Universities).* Hallintoviraston raportteja ja selvityksiä, no. 8. Joensuu, 1991.

Kivinen, O., R. Rinne and K. Ketonen. *Yliopiston huomen. Korkeakoulupolitiikan historiallinen suunta Suomessa (The Future of University. The Historical Direction of Higher Education Policymaking in Finland).* Helsinki: Hanki ja Jää, 1993.

Kogan, M., M. Bauer, I. Bleiklie and M. Henkel. *Transforming Higher Education. A Comparative Study.* London and Philadelphia: Jessica Kingsley Publishers, 2000.

Konttinen, R. and J. Välimaa (eds). *Pedagogiaa vai Byrokratiaa?* Työvelvollisuuskokeilun alku Jyväskylän yliopistossa *(Free Allocation of Teaching Resources as an Element of the Strategy of Self-regulation).* Publication Series B, Theory into Practice 49 (with English summary). Jyväskylä: Institute for Educational Research, University of Jyväskylä, 1990.

Lahtinen, I. *Tutkinnonuudistus – turvavaltion interventio yliopistoon.* Tutkimus tiedepolitiikasta ja Suomen yliopistojen 1970-luvun tutkinnonuudistuksesta *(The Degree Reform).* Jyväskylä: Jyväskylän yliopiston ylioppilaskunnan julkaisusarja 26, 1988.

Lampinen, O. *Suomen koulutusjärjestelmän kehitys (The Development of the Finnish System of Education).* Tampere: Gaudeamus, 1998.

Lampinen, O. *Suomalaisen korkeakoulutuksen uudistaminen.* Reformeja ja innovaatioita *(Reforming of Finnish Higher Education).* Helsinki: Opetusministeriön julkaisuja, 2003.

Liljander, J-P. (ed.). *Omalla tiellä.* Ammattikorkeakoulut 10 vuotta *(On Their Own Way. Ten Years of Polytechnics).* Helsinki: Arene and Edita, 2002.

Määttä, P. "Doctoral Studies in the 1990s: From Elite to Mass Training?" In Välimaa, J. (ed.). *Finnish Higher Education in Transition – Perspectives on Massification and Globalisation.* Jyväskylä: Institute for Educational Research, University of Jyväskylä, 2001, 139–155.

Mäenpää, H. Suomalaisen ammattikorkeakoulun synty, kasvu ja kehitys. *in Hämeen härkätieltä tiedon valtateille. Hämeen Ammattikorkeakoulun synty ja kasvu (The Establishment and Development of Häme Polytechnic).* Hämeenlinna, 2000.

Merton, R.K. *The Sociology of Science.* Chicago: University of Chicago Press, 1973.

Nieminen, M. and S. Ahola. *Ammattikorkeakoulun paikka.* Hakijanäkökulma suomalaiseen ammattikorkeakoulujärjestelmään *(The Position of Polytechnics).* Raportti 60. Turku: Research Unit for the Sociology of Education, 2003.

Poropudas, O. and M-V. Volanen. *Kohti Asiantuntijayhteiskunnan koulutuspolitiikka (Towards the Educational Policy of Expert Society).* Helsinki: Kirja kerrallaan, 2003.

Salminen, H. *Suomalainen ammattikorkeakoulu-uudistus opetushallinnon prosessina (The Reform of Finnish AMK-institutions).* Helsinki: Opetusministeriö, 2001.

Skocpol, T. "Emerging Agendas and Recurrent Strategies in Historical Sociology." In Skocpol, T. (ed.). *Vision and Method in Historical Sociology.* Cambridge: Cambridge University Press, 1984, 356–391.

Statistics Finland. *Statistics Finland: Science and Technology 2.* Helsinki, 1993.

Teichler, U. "The Changing Roles of the University and Non-university Sectors in Higher Education in Europe." *European Review, Interdisciplinary Journal of the Academia Europea* 6.4 (1998): 475–487.

Välimaa, J. (ed.). *Toimintaa vai terapiaa?* Työvelvollisuuskokeilu korkeakouluissa (*Action or Therapy? Free Allocation of Teaching Resources – Experimentation in Finnish Higher Education*). Publication Series B, Theory into Practice B 81. Jyväskylä: Institute for Educational Research, University of Jyväskylä, 1993.

Välimaa, J. "A Trying Game: Experiments and Reforms in Finnish Higher Education." *European Journal of Education* 29.2 (1994): 149–163.

Välimaa, J. "Higher Dead End?" In Schwarz, S. and U. Teichler (eds). *The Institutional Basis of Higher Education Research*. Dordrecht: Kluwer Academic Publishers, 2000, 247–258.

Välimaa, J. "A Historical Introduction to Finnish Higher Education." In Välimaa, J. (ed.). *Finnish Higher Education in Transition – Perspectives on Massification and Globalisation*. Jyväskylä: Institute for Educational Research, University of Jyväskylä, 2001.

Välimaa, J. "Three Rounds of Evaluation and the Idea of Accreditation in Finnish Higher Education." In Schwarz, S. and D.F. Westerheijden (eds). *Accreditation and Evaluation in the European Higher Education Area*. Higher Education Dynamics, vol. 5. Dordrecht: Kluwer Academic Publishers, ch. 5, 2004, 101–126.

Välimaa, J. and P. Vuorinen (eds). *Työvelvollisuuskokeilun rypäleitä ja kimaroita* (*Innovations in Teaching During the Experimentation of Free Allocation of Teaching Resources as an Element of Self-regulation Strategy*). Publication Series B, Theory into Practice 65. Jyväskylä: Institute for Educational Research, University of Jyväskylä, 1991.

Van Vught, F.A. "Creating Innovations in Higher Education." *European Journal of Education* 24.3 (1989): 249–270.

HANS PECHAR

BACKLASH OR MODERNISATION? TWO REFORM CYCLES IN AUSTRIAN HIGHER EDUCATION

1. INTRODUCTION

Over the last four decades Austria has experienced a series of higher education reforms. From an analytical point of view one can distinguish two reform cycles that strongly differed with respect to their underlying policy paradigms. During both periods a variety of measures was implemented according to a coherent background philosophy (see figure 1). In between the two reform cycles was about one decade of consolidation.

Figure 1. Major reform actions in Austrian higher education, 1960–2002

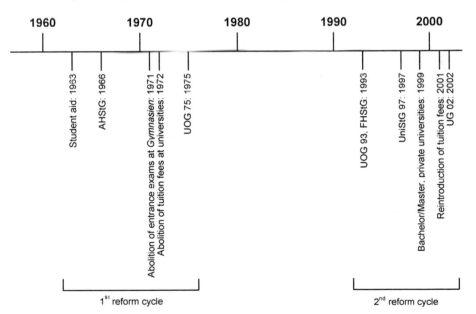

- The 1ˢᵗ reform cycle had its peak in the mid-1970s and can be characterised as an inclusion of higher education under the umbrella of welfare state policies. The policy catchwords were 'opening' and 'democratisation' of

Å. Gornitzka et al. (eds.), Reform and Change in Higher Education, 269-286.

higher education (emphasising student participation, integrating junior faculty into decision making, and broadening the fields of research).

- The 2nd cycle follows the international policy trends of the 1990s and has recently resulted (2002) in a reform that acknowledges the full legal entity status of universities (universities are no longer state agencies, but 'public enterprises'). The buzz words of this cycle are 'deregulation' and 'efficiency'.

Section 2 of this chapter characterises these two reform cycles in general terms. The third section highlights peculiar aspects, such as the student experience, structures of governance, and the working conditions of academics. The final remarks examine both the vast differences and the common aspects of the two reform cycles.

2. FROM STATE INTERVENTION TO DEREGULATION

Governments in the 1960s and 1970s had many good reasons to take action in higher education policy. In the mid 20th century, Austrian universities were in bad shape. They were elite institutions only in the sense of being very small and having student participation rates below 5%. However, one cannot apply the positive connotations of high quality which usually travel with the word elite. The glorious period of the late 19th and early 20th centuries, when some Austrian universities were eminent research institutions with worldwide reputations, was long gone. The political catastrophes of the 1930s and 1940s resulted in two waves of expulsion, for political and racial reasons, by which universities were deprived of many of their most able researchers (Stadler 1988). After the war, universities lacked the ability to renew themselves on their own. Only the most active Nazis were expelled, émigrés were rarely welcomed back. During the immediate post-war years, universities were more a place of intellectual narrowness than a source of innovation.

During the 1960s, new expectations of economic benefits which were roused by the promise of human capital theory moved education to the centre of policy making. Since it was now regarded as an important goal to raise the qualifications of the workforce, an outdated higher education system was no longer acceptable. The government set the course for educational expansion and modified the traditional chair system (*Ordinarienuniversität*). The overarching goal of the 1st reform cycle was to 'open up' the rigid structures of the elite system. Three dimensions to which this metaphor of 'opening' was applied (see Pechar 1996) can be distinguished:

- Most important was the goal to increase student participation. The (visible and hidden) gates which excluded large numbers of talented students should be opened. It was assumed that mainly financial barriers were responsible for the low participation rate.
- Another aspect was widening the spectrum of recognised disciplines and methodological approaches. For example, it was only in the late 1960s, that some social sciences such as sociology and political science were established at universities.

- Finally, the structures and procedures of self-governance at universities were made more democratic. Junior faculty and students were partially included in the procedures of academic self-governance.

Most key university actors did not welcome the new opportunities initiated by governments' reform policies. They felt that the prospect of growth would threaten the privileges of their sheltered institutions and responded negatively to the political request to open their gates. This situation differed from that in other countries, which in later years became a point of reference for Austrian higher education. North American universities had a long tradition of being responsive to external demands, simply because at no time did they have a benevolent patron who gave generous support to elite institutions – a commitment of the ruling elites *vis-à-vis* the cultural elites. Most American universities, particularly in the west, had to justify their existence and seek popular support. Hence they had little problem in accommodating the rising student demand when it eventually occurred. In contrast, Austrian universities were in the privileged position of having a benevolent state taking care of elite institutions. Hence they had little appetite for more students; instinctively they felt that expansion of student numbers would eventually abolish the privileges of elite institutions.

Unlike their counterparts in the UK they had no effective means to resist that demand. British universities were in a unique position. They could make autonomous decisions about student admission and yet they were not – until the 1980s – economically dependent on the number of students. Hence they could preserve their elite status for an unusually long period, until the government changed the architecture of the British system. Austrian academics were not in that position. Access was regulated by federal law; all graduates from the elite track of secondary education (*Gymnasium*) were entitled to enrol at any Austrian university. Reforms of secondary education which successfully widened access to the *Gymnasium* had inevitable consequences on first-year enrolments at universities. Austrian universities had no legal means to keep students out of the ivory tower. A totally different question was, of course: How would they welcome the undesirable students? How would academics treat students who increasingly came from family backgrounds without higher education? This became an issue in later decades when the controversy about mass higher education intensified.

Even stronger was the resistance of the academic oligarchy to all attempts aimed at introducing participatory decision-making structures within the university. The University Organisation Act 1975 (UOG 1975) which granted students and junior academics limited voting power in collegial bodies met stiff opposition from chairholders. When the law was passed a group of professors immediately – but without success – appealed against it in the high courts.

The 1980s can be characterised as an intermediate period without a strong distinctive profile in its own right. It was partly a time of consolidation after a period of severe change; but it was also a time of disappointment with respect to the high expectations triggered by the reforms. This reflected the mainstream development of most OECD countries. A naïve interpretation of human capital theory was suddenly confronted with the first signs of graduate unemployment. Higher education ceased to be a top priority of policy makers. As elsewhere, fiscal consolidation became the main concern of governments.

During the 1970s, the growth rate of expenditure for higher education matched that of student numbers. Higher education was then a high priority of the newly elected social democratic government which was strongly committed to the reform and expansion of universities. Starting in the late 1970s, the growth rate of higher education expenditure declined. The decline in per capita expenditure resulted in growing tension between the government and universities. In the second half of the 1980s, students and academics started a series of actions to direct public attention to the financial stringencies experienced by universities.

As a result of these policy shifts, the alliance between reform-oriented academics and policy makers gradually split. The change in the relations and interactions between government and universities during the 1st reform cycle became quite apparent. Much of what was formerly worked through in terms of implicit agreements was now based on formal rules and legal acts. Academics started to complain about excessive regulation and bureaucratic overload. The fact that universities were state agencies was now perceived as a burden. The key actors at universities drew a very dark picture. The dominant view was that universities were bound by a rigid state bureaucracy and hence could not develop their creativity. The academic mood at that time is portrayed in Rüegg (1987). A survey of expert opinion among 17 European states during the late 1980s came to the conclusion that Austrian experts in higher education had lost nearly all confidence in their system (see McDaniel 1992).The answer was for academics to liberate universities from state regulation. 'Autonomy' was the catchword in the policy debates at that time.

The 2nd reform cycle was triggered when some politicians and senior civil servants shared critical views concerning excessive state regulation of higher education. Policy makers increasingly felt overstretched by the complexity of a mass higher education system. It became obvious that they did not have the necessary means (sufficient information and influence to motivate actors at lower levels) to implement the 'best solutions'. Hence, the visions about the 'one best system' which requires central steering to be realised faded away. At the end of the 1980s, the government abandoned its former approach of stringent state regulation of all kinds of education institutions, universities included. The move towards deregulation was also facilitated by fiscal consolidation. Senior civil servants had no interest in being involved in the ugly details of executing cuts and became quite sympathetic to the arguments for increasing the autonomy of higher education institutions.

The change in the underlying paradigms of higher education policy gave rise to a new wave of reforms. Within only a few years the architecture of Austrian higher education was fundamentally changed. In the early 1990s, a non-university sector was established in order to provide a new educational profile (short-term studies, clear vocational orientation). With respect to management issues, *Fachhochschulen* were an unexpected break with the tradition of state agencies (see Pratt and Hackl 1999). In 1993, at the time of their establishment they were in many respects regarded as a model for universities.

Universities, however, offered stiff opposition. In 1991, the Ministry published a draft of an organisational reform which would liberate universities from most forms of governmental control and transform them into public enterprises (BMWF 1991). Policy makers claimed to be responding to the academic request for more autonomy by shifting decision-making power from the state to the universities (Pechar and Pellert 1998). However, the Ministry drew quite different conclusions from an assessment of the status quo which looked, at first glance, very similar to that of the academic critics.

Autonomy of universities can be interpreted in totally different ways by different actors. During the reform debate, three concepts of autonomy clashed:

- In the Humboldtian tradition, autonomy is mainly used as a synonym for academic freedom of the individual academic, that is to say, mainly the full professor. Many professors saw this kind of autonomy endangered, on the one hand, by state intervention and, on the other, by academic co-determination of students and *Mittelbau* (junior faculty). From their perspective, autonomy became a buzz word for a kind of restoration of the 'old regime' of academic oligarchy, of the *Ordinarienuniversität*.

- Junior faculty and students mainly favoured the concept of the autonomous collegial university. In their view, the focus of autonomy was not the individual academic but the collegial bodies in which they had some representation (after the democratic reforms of the 1970s). Those collegial bodies should govern the university without any interference from the state. Sufficient and unconditional funding by the government was simply taken for granted.

- Politicians and state bureaucrats advocated the concept of institutional autonomy; they wanted to turn universities into enterprises which were responsible not only for academic, but also for financial and administrative, affairs. This kind of autonomy had to go hand-in-hand with the development of professional management and a strengthening of external scrutiny by supervisory boards (Höllinger 1992).

It is easy to see that neither the concept of individual autonomy nor the concept of the autonomous collegial university is compatible with the ministerial reform approach. During the 1990s tension between governments and academics intensified. The areas of conflict were continual fiscal cuts combined with reinforced moves towards managerialism. There were misconception and paradoxical behaviour on both sides. Governments pushed universities to accept institutional autonomy but at the same time looked for loopholes to keep their old power. Academics fought against dull bureaucrats but at the same time desperately wanted to stick with the idea of the university as a state agency. In 2000, a new conservative government firmly changed the style of policy making. Former social democratic governments, even in the face of growing hostility, held on to the notion of consensus politics of the post-war years. The new government proudly announced a 'speed kills' approach. This enabled the government to enforce far-reaching changes in legislation within a few years. It remains to be seen to what extent this legislation will be successfully implemented.

3. FORTY YEARS OF REFORM: WHAT ARE THE RESULTS?

3.1. The Student Experience: Expansion, Diversification and Commodification

The 1st reform cycle was triggered by a remarkable policy shift: for the first time, education was not only regarded as a matter of culture but also as an economic benefit, as an important factor of economic growth and competitiveness. At that time, most political actors were convinced that the actual participation of students in the more advanced types of education did not keep pace with the demand from the labour market for graduates. For that reason, educational opportunities had to be expanded and access improved. In former times, policy makers took it for granted that the low participation rates in the elite tracks of secondary schools and in universities demonstrated lack of talent. In the 1960s these beliefs changed. It became obvious that the pool of talent by far exceeded the actual number of students who were enrolled in institutions of higher learning. It became a common phrase that a large 'potential of aptitudes' existed and the main policy goal of that time was to make use of that hidden resource.

During the 1960s, policy makers took two measures in order to raise student participation. On the one hand, they widened access to the *Gymnasium* and other types[1] of the elite track in secondary education, which were (and still are) the main route to higher education. Entrance exams to the *Gymnasium* – which were an effective gatekeeper for elite education enforced at the age of 10 – were relaxed during the 1960s and finally abolished in 1971. This was an important signal to those parents who previously would be deterred by selective procedures. Within only a few years, graduates from the secondary elite track (*Maturanten*) increased from 8% of the age cohort in 1960 to 17% in 1971; in 2000, 40% of the age group graduated from the secondary elite track.

The second policy to raise participation rates was to tackle potential financial barriers to the participation of low and middle income families.

- In the early 1960s, the system of student support was fundamentally changed. Formerly, grants for needy students were awarded at the discretion of university authorities. In 1963 a new Act was passed (*Studienförderungsgesetz 1963*) which for the first time gave a legal entitlement for grants to needy students who fulfilled certain minimal criteria of academic achievement. By establishing this new type of social grant (*Sozialstipendium*) policy makers did not aim to make students independent from their parents. Rather they instituted remedial measures for those low income families who could not afford to support the participation of their children in higher education.
- In 1972 tuition fees were abolished. In the 1950s, fees were indeed a significant financial barrier to low income families;[2] but by 1970 they were quite low since they were never adjusted for inflation. In any case, the abolition of fees was a signal that the government regarded higher education entirely as a public good.

During the 1970s, student numbers increased dramatically (see table 1). This extraordinary growth was caused by a combination of rising participation rates on the one hand, and the growing age cohorts of the baby boomers on the other. During the early 1970s, the growth was welcomed as the accomplishment of a successful policy. At the end of the 1st reform cycle, student expansion was looked at in a new perspective. Graduates were no longer considered to be in short supply; instead rumours about 'overeducation' were heard. This critical judgment about expansion was partly caused by the first indications of graduate unemployment and a re-assessment of the economic benefits of education. It also reflected a shift in policy orientation. The governmental commitment to expansion of higher education weakened.

Table 1. Total enrolments at Austrian universities, 1970–2002

Year	Women		Men		Total	
	No.	*% Increase*	*No.*	*% Increase*	*No.*	*% Increase*
1970	12.459		38.817		51.276	
1975	25.774	106.9	51.271	32.1	77.045	50.3
1980	43.586	69.1	66.930	30.5	110.516	43.4
1985	66.532	52.6	88.019	31.5	154.551	39.8
1990	81.999	23.2	104.608	18.8	186.607	20.7
1995	99.406	21.2	114.119	9.1	213.525	14.4
2000	113.224	13.9	108.281	-5.1	221.505	3.7
2002*	94.728	-16.3	85.238	-21.3	179.966	-18.8

*The decrease in student numbers in 2002 is due to the introduction of tuition fees in 2001–02 (see section 3.2)
Source: bm:bwk 2002: 163; author's calculations

Policy makers did not take hard measures against further expansion. Rather, they choose soft 'cooling out' strategies, mainly through increased 'counselling' activities, which emphasised the risks of graduate unemployment and pointed to the attractiveness of alternative vocational training opportunities. The retrenchment policy caused a serious deterioration of study conditions. Student aid, which was expanded during the 1970s, was now cut back. And yet, students and their families did not respond to such policy signals, they stubbornly continued to enrol in increasing numbers (even though the growth rate decreased from 50% during the early 1970s to 20% during the late 1980s) (see table 1).

One reason for the changing attitudes to expansion was the concern of policy makers for the high drop-out rates and the very long duration of studies.[3] Austrian universities were not sufficiently adapted to mass higher education. The increasing number of students did not fit into the traditional patterns of teaching and learning.

Many factors contribute to the weak educational outputs. Most important is that Austrian universities adhere to a laissez faire style of teaching and learning, which

was appropriate in a small elite system but caused chaos under the conditions of
mass participation:

- There is 'open access' in the sense that every citizen who has a final
  certificate of the elite track of upper secondary education is entitled to enrol
  at any Austrian university and in any field of study for an unlimited period.
  Universities are not allowed to reject students due to limited resources. The
  laissez faire conditions do not allow for resources to be made dependent on
  student numbers. This makes it easy for the government to adhere to an
  open access policy without feeling too much of an obligation to suffer the
  financial consequences. In particular, the teacher-student ratio has
  dramatically deteriorated over the last three decades. Involuntary waiting
  time of students due to lack of resources (e.g. waiting lines for laboratories,
  inadequate student-teacher ratios) contributes substantially to the long
  duration of studies.
- The liberal admission policy has its equivalent in the curriculum which is
  strongly shaped by the Humboldtian tradition. From the very first, semester
  students are treated like 'apprentice researchers' who are capable of
  conducting their studies in a completely independent manner. Students can
  either attend lectures and seminars or not. Equally relaxed are the
  obligations of academics *vis-à-vis* the students. A need for guidance and
  monitoring by the staff is not acknowledged. Students are not regarded as
  school children who need help; they are regarded as mature persons who
  are able to learn independently.
- A further aspect is the right to unrestricted length of study. It is up to
  students to take an exam at the end of the course or to delay this decision to
  a later semester – potentially an open-ended process. The high degree of
  liberty allows students to determine the pace of their studies and not all of
  them opt for vigorous learning. At first glance, this seems to be an
  incredible privilege for students, a dominant issue in the Austrian policy
  debate. However, this liberty is a double-edged sword. Since the university
  does not monitor the progress of students, it very easy for academics not to
  care about student needs. The laissez-faire conditions for students are
  matched by laissez-faire conditions for academics. Neither of the two sides
  has formal obligations *vis-à-vis* the other as occurs in some other higher
  education systems, mainly in the Anglo-Saxon world. In a sense, this is the
  core of the Humboldtian ideal of a university. The question of whether this
  remains a proper approach to mass higher education was never addressed in
  Austria.

While the 1980s were shaped by a rather sceptical, sometimes even disapproving
attitude towards expansion, the mood changed in the 1990s. Policy makers again
started to believe in the social and economic value of increased educational
aspirations and efforts of the population. Hence the subtle 'cooling out' strategies of
the former decade gave way to a more positive and optimistic assessment of student
expansion. During the 2nd reform cycle a variety of reforms was introduced which

aimed at making higher education more responsive to the needs of students and at enhancing 'throughput'. The policies regarding expansion differed compared to those of the 1st reform cycle – at the level of tacit assumptions as well as with respect to explicit organisational measures. Most important was the establishment of the *Fachhochschul* sector in 1993 and the re-introduction of tuition fees in 2001.

Austria was one of the few OECD countries which did not establish a non-university sector during the early stages of expansion. Attempts to create an alternative to universities in the early seventies failed (Lassnigg and Pechar 1988). Hence, expansion during the 1970s and 1980s took place almost completely within universities.[4] During the 2nd reform cycle, the homogeneous character of Austrian higher education was now seen as an obstacle for further expansion. The most important step to foster the diversification of the system was the establishment of a *Fachhochschul* sector in 1993. Its main mission was to provide vocationally oriented courses which could be effectively completed in three or four years (most *Fachhochschul* courses require a minimum length of study of four years). This called for a different culture of learning from that of universities. Students at *Fachhochschulen* are expected to take a normal workload. On the other hand, the institution must accept a high degree of responsibility for student needs. Experience suggests that few students drop out (10–20%) and most students complete their courses in 'standard time'. The new sector was not established by upgrading existing institutions but rather through the creation of completely new institutions. As a consequence, the *Fachhochschul* sector can only grow slowly and will be – in the short- and even mid-term perspective – much smaller than the university sector. For the academic year 2002–03, there were 125 *Fachhochschul* courses offered. The sector has about 17,000 students, and has produced 10,000 graduates. In only a few years the sector has built a high reputation amongst students, employers and the general public.

During the 1st reform cycle higher education was regarded as a pure public good. It was seen as the responsibility of the state to provide and fund all higher education. No tuition fees were charged. Commencing in the 1990s, the lack of public resources again stirred a debate on the need for possible additional revenue from private sources. In 2000, the newly elected conservative government decided to introduce tuition fees amounting to €363 per semester starting with the academic year 2001–02. The fee policy gave rise to criticism, some of it for good reasons:

- The fees were not additional income for the universities but collected by the treasury; it was a 'student tax' to facilitate fiscal consolidation, not to improve conditions at universities.[5]
- The 'flat fees' introduced by the government for all enrolled students do not differentiate between full-time and part-time students.[6] Students who combine study with work and hence need a longer duration of study pay more for their degree than full-time students.

The most important question is whether fees function as a social barrier for students from low income families. It is too early to answer this question based on empirical evidence. However, social selection due to fees is unlikely for the following reasons:

- The €363 fee per semester is relatively low. In addition, students who are eligible for student aid are exempt from fees.
- Evidence from the first three years suggests that fees did not result in a decline in the number of active students. At first glance, enrolment figures declined by more than 20% (see table 1). However, this decline can be explained in terms of the exit of non-active 'paper students' who under previous laissez-faire conditions stayed enrolled for various reasons. Estimates based on examination statistics concluded that the number of active students[7] remained stable (Pechar and Wroblewski 2002; bm:bwk 2002: 150). In 2001–02, when fees were charged for the first time, there was about an 8% decline in the number of first-year enrolments. However, this decline was compensated for in the following years with first-year enrolments higher than expected.

3.2. Governance: From State Agency to Public Enterprise

The traditional governance pattern of the elite system was characterised by a dualism between administrative and academic issues: the university was a state agency and subject to centralised decision making by legislation and state bureaucracy while all issues regarding teaching and research were in the hands of the academic oligarchy – each chairholder in charge of their own specialised field of research. The university as an organisation was weak. The most important issues were directly dealt with between the chairholding professors and the state bureaucracy. It was the self-image of the university to be a self-governing community of scholars held together by common values. The rector was regarded as *primus inter pares* to represent the university, not to govern, let alone manage it.

Academics usually did not strive for corporate autonomy of the university. The educated elite regarded it as a cultural obligation of the enlightened secular state (*Kulturstaat*) to provide beneficial circumstances for academic life. The state was seen mainly as a power to protect the integrity and autonomy of universities, not as a potential threat to their independence. Academics were civil servants with lifelong tenure. This status was supposed to secure academic freedom against outside pressure. The implicit precondition for this pattern of dual governance was mutual trust and respect between academics and policy makers. Of course, there were occasional conflicts between politicians and bureaucrats on the one hand, and academics on the other; but, for most of the time, the relationship was based on tacit understanding.

This period of implicit agreement between the state bureaucracy and senior academics was seriously disturbed during the 1st reform cycle. A majority of the academic oligarchy opposed the higher education reforms, in particular policies to increase student participation and to give junior faculty and students decision-making power in collegial bodies. The government had to enforce such policies by legislation and other means of regulation. During that period the mutual trust and respect between academics and policy makers started to erode. The tension was not immediately apparent due to the alliance between governments and reform-oriented academics. However, as soon as this alliance disintegrated (due to the retrenchment policy starting in the 1980s) it became obvious that the old pattern of smooth cooperation was gone. The fragile construction of an 'autonomous state agency' dissolved. The state was no longer regarded as a benevolent patron; academics no longer accepted and trusted decisions of policy makers.

The 2nd reform cycle can be interpreted as an attempt to split areas of administrative decision making at the system and institutional levels which formerly were intermingled (the 'autonomous state agency') but no longer fitted together. The government abandoned the *Kulturstaat* tradition and instead embraced the Anglo-Saxon policies of new public management (NPM). The first major step to apply NPM to higher education was the establishment of *Fachhochschulen* in 1993 (Pratt and Hackl 1999):

- For the *Fachhochschul* sector there were no legal ownership restrictions. All institutions were owned by 'quasi-private' associations or corporations and governed by professional management.
- The academic and non-academic staff of *Fachhochschulen* were employed and appointed by the institution.
- Students were admitted by the institution in accordance with available study places.
- Decisions on the curriculum were made by the responsible academics in cooperation with institutional management. The final responsibility for quality in the *Fachhochschul* sector was in the hands of an external professional body, the *Fachhochschulrat*. The *Fachhochschulrat* guaranteed minimal standards of quality. Furthermore, *Fachhochschulen* were expected to vary widely in terms of profile and quality of their education.
- From the federal government, *Fachhochschulen* received a lump sum based on student numbers. In addition, *Fachhochschulen* received funds from multiple public sources; not only the federal state, but also provinces and municipalities, and in some cases chambers, played a significant role.

It was much more difficult to apply the NPM approach to universities. In 1993, the Ministry drafted a reform Act which aimed to fundamentally restructure organisation and decision making at universities. The government wanted to strengthen the managerial elements at the top university level: the rector who represented the tradition of 'first among equals' should be replaced by a president who would not be dependent on collegial bodies; and governing bodies which represent relevant (and powerful) stakeholders should be established.

The majority of academics opposed the concept of institutional autonomy which was seen only as an excuse for the government to get rid of its financial responsibilities for higher education. As a response to this strong opposition the government softened its initial approach:

- The leadership positions at the top of the organisation were strengthened but their power was balanced by the significant influence of the collegial bodies.
- The influence of external stakeholders was reduced: no governing boards, but advisory bodies were introduced.

As a consequence, the Ministry refused to give a lump sum budget to universities; it assumed that universities did not have sufficient managerial structures to handle this kind of budget. The University Organisation Act of 1993 (UOG 1993) was a compromise between the proponents and the opponents of the reform and only a cautious step towards more institutional autonomy. It was easy to foresee that it was only an intermediary stage.

It was probably the most important consequence of the UOG 1993 that new types of actors emerged in higher education policy: the new rectors who – compared to the former type of rector – had significantly increased power; and the deans who became much more powerful than formerly. The emergence of this new group of academics, which was small but quite influential, significantly changed the power relations in the higher education policy networks. In many respects this group represented horizontal interests and positions in contrast to the usual vertical relationships between government and universities. It was important that the new senior academics became more sensitive to external needs and pressures; they could no longer be regarded as a group representing the internal interests of academe, but increasingly they were viewed as a mediating power block between internal and external pressures.

It was mainly this group that complained that the UOG 1993 was only a first step to efficient management structures. The new rectors wanted full legal entity for universities and a lump sum budget which would relieve universities of the state accountancy (*Kameralistik*). When the government took up this initiative and started to develop a new reform strategy it was not in the uncomfortable position of fighting alone against a united front of academic estates; rather, it had a powerful ally in the universities (who at least strove for the same goals). Some members of this group were actively involved in drafting the reform law (Titscher et al. 2000).

In 2002 the new Organisational Act (UG 2002) was passed by Parliament (see Sebök 2002). The implementation of the new Act started in 2004. The most important changes are:

- Universities cease to be state agencies and get full legal entity. However, universities will not be privatised; they remain in the domain of the public law, they are 'legal persons under public law' (*Körperschaften öffentlichen Rechts*).
- The federal government keeps the responsibility for basic funding, but universities are relieved from the fiscal regulations of the federal budget (*Kameralistik*) and instead receive a lump sum budget under their own discretion. Resources are allocated on the basis of performance contracts. Twenty per cent of the budget allocation will be based on indicators.

- The internal organisation of universities – other than the general regulations regarding the decision-making structure – is not prescribed by law. The organisational details should be determined by a statute (*Satzung*) decided by the academic senate.
- For each university a governing board (*Universitätsrat*) is established; the size of the board is to vary between five and nine members, according to the statute; half of the members should be elected by the academic senate, the other half appointed by the Minister.
- The position of the rector is strengthened against power struggles within the university; rectors are to be elected by the board and thus more independent of all collegial academic bodies than before. On the other hand they become more dependent on the board.
- The new university with full legal entity is the employer of all academic and non-academic staff. Academics are no longer civil servants but employed by private contracts.

The new organisational law is probably the most far-reaching reform since 1849, when Austria embraced the Humboldtian model. Austrian universities will cease to be state agencies and will acquire a kind of corporate autonomy unparalleled in the last 400 years. The new Act probably makes Austria a leader in the 'managerial revolution' on the European continent. Policy makers will regard this as a success. Most academics have mixed feelings.

3.3. Change in the Working Conditions and Career Patterns of Academics

During the past forty years working conditions of academics have changed dramatically. Most significant are changes for junior academics. In the elite system, their position was characterised by severe personal dependency on chairholders who were heads of academic units. All academic staff were subordinate to the chair. This dependency was increased by the fact that due to the lack of formalisation and legal regulation professors had a high degree of discretion. On the other hand, small elite systems were characterised by a low growth rate or almost stable conditions. In 1946, Austrian universities had 382 professors and 1060 assistants (BMfU 1969: 81ff). The ratio of professors to assistants was then 1 to 2.8. Under such circumstances, the majority of junior faculty had reasonable prospects to be promoted to full professorial status.

The expansion of student numbers since the 1960s led to an increase in work, tasks and complexity; new administrative functions arose. Universities could only cope with this burden by expanding the number of junior faculty. In the course of the expansion of higher education, non-professorial academic staff took on an increasing range of academic functions, many of them independently, without the guidance of a professor. The traditional assumption that the junior faculty may only engage in supportive services for the professoriate could no longer be maintained. As a consequence, junior faculty were partly included in self-governing bodies and collegial decision making.

Also with expansion, the notion of the 'chair' lost its original significance (although it never vanished completely). What remained was the steep hierarchy among professorial and non-professorial academics and the strict limitation of professorial posts. Professors belong to a fundamentally different group (*Kurie*) of academics than junior academics. Hence, regular promotion of junior faculty to professorship (as a result of individual academic success) is not possible.

Austria belongs to the group of countries that has an exceptionally long training period for academics. Belonging to the Humboldtian tradition, requirements for gaining full professional status included not only a doctoral degree, but in addition a *Habilitation*, a kind of second thesis. On average, junior academics finished their *Habilitation* at the age of about 40.[8] However, the completion of the *Habilitation* by no means guaranteed promotion to professorship. While within the group of non-professorial academics promotion depended on the individual academic success of each person, promotion to professorship is in principle of a different kind. Advancement to professorship requires an application for a new post; a precondition is that such a post is vacant. The collective chances of the junior faculty for promotion to full professorship mainly depend on the quantitative relation between the two groups. If the number of junior academics increases while the number of professors remains stable (or increases to a lesser degree), the (collective) chances for promotion decrease.

During the last decades the number of non-professorial academics increased faster than the number of professors, resulting in a growing mismatch of the two types of academic posts (see table 2). During the first years of expansion this was unavoidable, because there was an undersupply of experienced and trained academics who could serve the needs of an expanding institution. Hence, in the 1970s, the relation between professors and assistants (which was 1:2.8 during the late 1940s) changed to 1:4. To provide regular career options for these young academics it would have been necessary during the late 1970s and 1980s to expand the posts of professors accordingly. That never happened. In 2002, there were 4.2 assistants per professor.

Table 2. Academic and non-academic staff at research universities

Year	1970	1980	1990	1995	2000	2001	2002
Professors	906	1589	1732	1854	1854	1850	1850
Assistants	3653	4883	5434	6801	7335	7628	7696
Other non-professorial academic	317	690	727	746	763	748	746
Academic staff total	4876	7162	7893	9401	9952	10226	10292
Non-academic staff	3304	4316	5716	6743	8032	8073	8084
Total	8180	11478	13609	16144	17984	18299	18376

Source: bm:bwk 2002: 85

A necessary consequence of this development was that an increasing number of assistants with *Habilitation* could not be promoted due to a lack of professorial posts. Table 3 illustrates the quantitative dimension of that problem. One can assume that academics should have reached their full professional status at least by the age of 45. However, in 2001, there were 1672 assistants with *Habilitation* who were older than 45. They had the formal qualifications for promotion to professorship, but no such post was available in an academic system which has distinct *Kurien* instead of a continuous career scheme. This group of potential professors was almost as big as the group of 1850 full professors.

Commencing in 2004, the new university with full legal entity will be the employer of all academic and non-academic staff. Even in large and complex universities the institutional management will be much closer to the basic academic units and their work than the bureaucracy of the government; closer in terms of space, professional competence and shared academic values. This is a severe break with the Humboldtian legacy: the university as a whole used to be a fragile bundle of individuals and small units, striving in different, sometimes opposite directions, integrated by a common ethos and other rather symbolic mechanisms. In each specialised field, teaching and research were shaped by the ambitions and interests of single academics.

Table 3. Age distribution of assistants with habilitation in 2001

Age	Total	%
Younger	457	16
41–45	655	24
46–50	594	22
51–55	444	16
56–60	416	15
61–65	207	7
Older	11	0
Total	2784	100

Source: author's calculations

Now the 'principal' comes closer to the 'agent', possibly close enough to effectively influence their work. Not surprisingly, there is a lot of suspicion among academics of the organisational change and the corresponding decision-making structures. Rectors were regarded as *primus inter pares,* now they are 'bosses', 'superiors'; this is at odds with the traditional concept of academic autonomy which means: no subordination, no formal responsibilities *vis-à-vis* other academics, in particular for the members of the guild, the chairholders.

It is not yet possible to evaluate the consequences of the new law on academic working conditions. Many academics think that the new legislation has imposed the decision-making structures of the corporate world onto universities. They fear and expect a hierarchy which will not leave sufficient room for collegial decision making; an authoritarian mode of leadership which will not allow appropriate faculty influence. The mistrust mainly among junior faculty has been enhanced by repeated statements of representatives of the Ministry emphasising the importance of academic hierarchy and autocratic management. The new law has in any case lowered the status of non-professorial academics. They are now weakly represented in collegial bodies, and are no longer eligible for leading functions at all levels. It remains to be seen, to what extent the collective agreements between the universities and the union will revoke some of these developments.

4. FINAL REMARKS

It is commonplace among academics to emphasise the differences between the two reform cycles. Many regard the policies of the 2nd reform cycle as a backlash, as a destruction of all the advancements which were achieved during the previous reforms. Government representatives, on the other hand, claim that the 2nd reform cycle truly paved the way to the modernisation of Austrian higher education. Indeed, the underlying policy paradigms of the two phases differ in many respects. Yet, the two periods also have much in common. It could be that future historians of Austrian higher education emphasise the common characteristics of reform policies since the 1960s which stand in sharp contrast to the conditions of the former elite system.

The connecting common ground of the two reform cycles is the end of the government being a benevolent patron to universities. This pattern of cultural policy started in the second half of the 19th century, when Austria embraced the Humboldtian model. The precondition of this pattern was a small, homogeneous system of universities which was held together by the common values of the educated elite – including senior civil servants who provided beneficial circumstances in which elite institutions were supposed to prosper.

This pattern came to an end with the emergence of a knowledge-based economy which fundamentally and irrevocably changed the social foundations of universities. It tremendously increased the importance of research and teaching at universities, but at the same time abolished many privileges which were taken for granted during the elite period. Higher education ceased to be a 'luxury' and became a need, an absolute necessity in terms of social demand and economic competitiveness. During the 1960s and early 1970s it was easy to confuse the new economically driven reform policy with a continuation of former attitudes of the benevolent state (*Kulturstaat*); after all, governments increased funding and they awarded attention and importance to universities at a level unknown previously. However, the crucial difference, soon to become apparent, was that governments no longer gave unconditional support to elite institutions on mere cultural motivations (a kind of *noblesse oblige*), but that public funding from now on was based on the expectation of social and economic returns. Under this perspective the two reform cycles can be interpreted as two different policies with the common intention of making universities more responsive to social and economic demands.

NOTES

[1]   Such as BHS, the professional schools at the upper secondary level.
[2]   In the early 1950s, tuition fees amounted roughly to half an average monthly income.
[3]   Austria belongs to the countries with the highest drop-out rates (more than 50%) and the longest duration of studies (7.5 years for the first degree) within the OECD (see OECD 2003).

[4] There was always a tiny non-university sector (training for teachers at compulsory schools, social workers and para-medical professions) which was not regarded as part of higher education in Austria.
[5] This was changed in 2004; fees are now the income of universities.
[6] Austria has no formal part-time status for students. However, it is well known that at least half of the students are in fact part-time because they combine study with work.
[7] Active students' were defined as those who took at least one examination during a period of two years.
[8] There is some irony in the fact that Austrian higher education – embedded in the Humboldtian tradition – concedes the ability to independent learning at a very early stage to students, whereas independence of academics is significantly postponed. Students are considered as independent researchers from the very first semester, with the consequence that the university does not feel any responsibility to monitor their studies. Academics, on the other hand, acquire full professional status on average only in their 40s – with the side-effect that the university has an impressive number of helpful hands who may be called on to assist full professors.

REFERENCES

bm:bwk. *Hochschulbericht 2002*, vol. 2. Wien: bm:bwk, 2002.

BmfU. *Hochschulbericht 1969*. Wien: BmfU, 1969.

BMWF. "Die neue Universitätsstruktur. Reformkonzept" (Green Paper). Wien. BMWF, 1991.

Höllinger, Sigurd. *Universität ohne Heiligenschein. Aus dem 19. ins 21. Jahrhundert*. Wien: Passagen, 1992.

Lassnigg, Lorenz and Hans Pechar. "Alternatives to Universities in Higher Education." *Country Study: Austria*. Paris: OECD, 1988.

McDaniel, Olaf C. "The Direction of Higher Education." Short report of a DELPHI study, Zoetermeer, 1992.

OECD. *Education at a Glance*. Paris: OECD, 2003.

Pechar, Hans. "Die 'offene Gruppenuniversität' und ihre Grenzen." In Brandstaller, T. (Hrsg.). *Österreich 2 ½. Anstöße zur Strukturreform*. Wien: Deutike, 1996.

Pechar, Hans and Ada Pellert. "Managing Change: Organisational Reform in Austrian Universities." *Higher Education Policy* 11 (1998): 141–151.

Pechar, Hans and Angela Wroblewski. *Retrospektive Schätzung studienaktiver Studierender an Universitäten der Wissenschaften für den Zeitraum 1996/97–2000/01*. Wien: Gutachten im Auftrag des bm:bwk, 2002.

Pratt, John and Elsa Hackl. "Breaking the Mould in Austrian Higher Education." *Higher Education Review* 32.1 (1999): 34–54.

Rüegg, Walter. *Zementierung oder Innovation. Effizienz von Hochschulsystemen*. Wien: Österreichische Rektorenkonferenz, 1987.

Sebök, Martha. *Universitätsgesetz 2002. Gesetzestext und Kommentar*. Wien: WUV Universitätsverlag, 2002.

Stadler, Friedrich (Hrsg.). *Vertriebene Vernunft II. Emigration und Exil österreichischer Wissenschaft*. Wien: Jugend and Volk, 1988.

Titscher, S. et al. *Universitäten im Wettbewerb. Zur Neustrukturierung österreichischer Universitäten*. München/Mering: Rainer Hampp Verlag, 2000.

ELAINE EL-KHAWAS

THE PUSH FOR ACCOUNTABILITY: POLICY INFLUENCES AND ACTORS IN AMERICAN HIGHER EDUCATION

1. INTRODUCTION

Policy making for higher education in the United States poses a challenge for scholars seeking to develop coherent theories of the policy process. Under the federal system of American government, decisions over education matters are allocated to the individual states (Gladieux and Wolanin 1976; McGuinness 1981). Consequently, no single governmental body has jurisdiction over the 3000 universities and colleges located throughout the US. Historically, when the federal government exercised authority over higher education, it acted primarily on matters that have a clear interstate significance, for example, environmental and employment law, the nation-wide sponsorship of funding for scientific research, or the provision of student financial assistance that is 'portable' across the entire United States (Graham 1984; Wellman 2003).

Most universities and colleges in the US, therefore, are affected by multiple levels of policy governance. For public universities, state-level policy processes are of greatest importance. Traditionally, state legislatures and state agencies have primarily paid attention to financing and governance matters, while occasionally considering issues of institutional mission or the number and type of institutions that are needed. By and large, they did not extend their oversight into academic decisions on curriculum, academic hiring and graduation requirements (Hines 2000).

The last two decades have witnessed a trend toward a more active state role, with states pressing higher education institutions for greater accountability. These policy actions, which have dramatically altered the interaction between the state and higher education, are the basis for this analysis of policy implementation, US-style. This account, covering a twenty-year period and many different policy actions, is necessarily abbreviated. The objective has been to sketch the major outlines of the story of how accountability policies developed, recognising that many details cannot be covered.

From the perspective of policy theory, the analysis illustrates a pattern of policy development and subsequent modification, with evidence of significant impact. It describes a record of decades-long pressure by state policy makers, but also documents actions by several non-governmental policy actors. The analysis is thus

Å. Gornitzka et al. (eds.), Reform and Change in Higher Education, 287-304.
© 2007 Springer.

consistent with the recent interest in investigating policy making that involves multiple policy actors (Enders, Goedegebuure and Maassen 2003).

Section 2 offers a largely chronological description of policy formation and implementation related to higher education accountability during the last two decades. It specifically covers the trend toward using state-level performance indicators to monitor institutions of higher education, one of the major policy developments of the time in the US. Section 3 extends the narrative by assessing the contributions of each major policy actor. It also considers several contextual factors that influenced their actions. The analysis supports the recent arguments about policy theory that emphasise the importance of understanding advocacy networks and mutual influence patterns in implementation (Sabatier 1986; Sabatier and Jenkins-Smith 1999; Gornitzka, Kyvik and Stensaker 2002).

2. ORIGINS AND OBJECTIVES

In the early 1980s, a fundamental shift in the relationship between the state and higher education began to take form in the United States. State officials raised questions of institutional accountability by criticising low graduation rates for many collegiate programmes and by arguing that universities and colleges had inadequate concern for improving student achievement (Ewell 1985; Spangehl 1987). Several states initiated studies of higher education and many imposed new requirements on public institutions (Ewell 1993; Newman 1987; Gaither, Nedwek and Neal 1994).

Several governors took the lead in setting out new expectations. This shift can be seen in the speeches of a number of governors (Hines 1988; Krotseng 1990a) and in a 1986 report issued by the National Governors Association (NGA), titled *Time for Results*. This report, although mainly directed to NGA's campaign for reforms in elementary and secondary education, included a chapter on higher education that pointed to low performance and called for new standards of quality. Higher education was, for the first time, being scrutinised by public authorities for low performance. As Thomas Kean, then governor of New Jersey, stated:

> your critics ... say that higher education promises much and delivers too little ... They say your graduates can't write clearly or think straight. And they say you dare not assess your work, evaluate your product, or validate your claims (1987: 11).

As the report's title made clear, the governors expected results. NGA announced that it would issue yearly updates assessing progress with university efforts to improve performance. In 1989, governors joined with President George H.W. Bush in a highly publicised Education Summit that added further momentum toward education reform.

New initiatives were launched in a number of states (Newman 1987). Although varying in approach, they had a common goal: to raise student performance and achievement (Ewell and Boyer 1988). Implementing this new mandate often began with action by governors. In Missouri, for example, the governor took a personal approach. He invited university and college presidents to a meeting where he outlined improvement goals and told them to develop ways to meet these goals. During this period, many states followed this approach of not being specific but asking colleges and universities to develop new assessments (Hutchings and Marchese 1990).

Other states decided to develop achievement tests for college-level students (Banta and associates 1993; Gaither, Nedwek and Neal 1994). Georgia had already established its Regents Rising Junior Examination, focused on writing skills. In 1982, Florida introduced academic skills tests directed to 'rising juniors'. South Dakota developed its Higher Education Assessment Program, while Texas established an Assessment of Basic Skills (Ashworth 1994). New Jersey began developing an achievement test for students completing degree programmes (Jemmott and Morante 1993).

Tennessee took another approach, based on incentives. In 1982, it required that universities and colleges report their yearly performance on student completion and several other outcomes. Those with good results would receive additional funding (Bogue and Brown 1982; Banta and Fisher 1984; Bogue 2003). Other states also developed various incentive-based approaches during the early 1980s (Newman 1987).

By the early 1990s, a new phase in higher education accountability emerged (Ewell 1993; Gaither, Nedwek and Neal 1994). Most testing approaches were dropped, due both to funding difficulties and to controversies over test implementation. The emphasis on student assessment, and allowing universities to develop their own approaches, also lost favour. Instead, states began to adopt policies that required institutional reporting on student outcomes such as degree completion and graduate employment. Arkansas, Missouri and Ohio adopted information-reporting approaches during this time, after having examined Tennessee's experience (El-Khawas 1998). South Carolina and Virginia adopted 'report cards' on effectiveness during this period (Gaither, Nedwek and Neal 1994).

Compared to the earlier, generalised calls for attention to student assessment, this new generation of policies was targeted: definitions were spelled out for a common set of indicators, deadlines were established and state uses of the reports were formalised. Yearly progress was expected, and the use of multiple indicators put greater pressure on institutions to improve in several areas (Christal 1998; Ruppert 1994; Banta et al. 1996).

By 1992, two-thirds of the states required universities and colleges to report on their performance (Christal 1998; Burke and Serban 1998). In 1994, the Education Commission of the States issued a report with case studies of how ten states used performance indicators, with additional information on other states (Ruppert 1994).

Greater information disclosure occurred as a consequence of this move toward performance indicators. Traditionally, states had issued reports on higher education that only listed such information as enrolments, degrees awarded and the year an institution was established. Now, with information-reporting, many states began to issue detailed yearly reports on higher education. As a sign of how much state policy environments had changed, this detailed reporting was largely uncontested when introduced. A related factor, perhaps, had been the publication of annual college rankings by commercial news magazines, which began in 1983 and was widely debated in subsequent years (Rating the Colleges 1983; Bogue 2003).

Today, most states issue such reports. Directed to high schools, to the news media and to the general public, these reports typically include 'scores' on the performance of each public university and college (Bogue 2003; Schmidt 2002a). In December 2000, a policy centre extended this information-disclosure approach with what they called a report card for the states. Their report, called *Measuring Up*, assigned a letter grade (A to F) for each state's performance in five policy areas relevant to higher education: preparation for college study, participation rates, affordability, degree completion and benefits (National Center for Public Policy and Education 2000). An update was issued in 2002, part of the policy centre's strategy of keeping the policy debate focused on accountability in these five areas (National Center for Public Policy and Education 2002).

Another shift in the state approach to accountability became evident by the late 1990s. Many states moved toward a policy called performance funding (Burke and Serban 1998). Under these policies, states linked the yearly reports on performance to the state's process for allocating core funding. They also added financial sanctions: institutions could lose funds if they showed poor performance. This new approach was a logical progression from earlier state policies but it was influenced, too, by a trend toward performance-based financing for all public agencies (Osborne and Gaebler 1993).

Missouri was one of the first states to adopt this approach. Its performance-funding policy, begun in 1996, used several performance indicators (e.g. performance of graduates on national tests in their field; the number of degrees awarded in high-demand occupations; academic success of first-year students) and added about 2 per cent of state funding for institutions showing progress (Schmidt 2002b). South Carolina passed a similar policy in 1996, initially planning to base 100 per cent of an institution's funding on its performance on 37 different measures (Burke and associates 2002). Later, amidst problems with individual measures, this policy was scaled back so that 14 measures could affect 3 per cent of funds (South Carolina Commission on Higher Education 2001).

The trend toward performance funding spread quickly. In 1997, ten states had some form of performance funding (Burke and Serban 1998). By 2002, five years later, 36 states had performance-financing systems (Burke and associates 2002). Although approaches varied, most performance-funding policies linked performance data to funding on an agreed-upon formula. Other states, in an approach called performance budgeting, took performance measures into account during budget determinations, but not with a formula. Still other states set aside incentive funds tied to specific goals. In general, states used a small number of performance indicators to control about 3 per cent of state funding (Burke and associates 2002).

This chronology outlines the general story of policies to increase higher education accountability over the last two decades. Additional actions fill out this narrative, including actions of accrediting agencies, universities, independent policy groups and the federal government. The analysis turns to these developments.

Although most policy change centred in the states, the federal government was also active. Several new federal policies on accountability emerged. Some were tied to the use of federal funds for research, but others were linked to how universities and colleges administered US programmes of student financial aid. A federal advisory board sets criteria for and approves the accrediting agencies that can accredit institutions for federal purposes (Chambers 1983). In 1992, the US expanded this board's role (Gaither, Nedwek and Neal 1994; Wellman 2003) and assigned stricter requirements to accrediting agencies on institutional integrity and good performance. In 1998, they added further requirements on institutional monitoring of student progress and learning (Wellman 2003; Kezar and El-Khawas 2003).

The federal government also introduced an ambitious state-based policy for achieving accountability. In 1992 a new US law required each state to create State Postsecondary Review Entities (SPRE), a structure to monitor institutional operations on statistical indicators related to the proper management of student aid funds. If certain 'triggering' conditions were found, the state was required to conduct an in-depth visit and review of the institution (McGuinness 1999). By 1994, however, the US Congress had a change of heart and dropped all funding for the effort, effectively killing it (Wellman 2003).

Accrediting agencies are an important part of this accountability story. In the United States, a network of regional accreditation agencies, covering all US states, conducts evaluative reviews that provide quality assurance in higher education (Bemis 1983; Eaton 2003). More than 60 programme accrediting agencies review specific academic disciplines, especially programmes that prepare students for professions such as medicine, law, nursing and engineering (Glidden 1983).

During the 1980s and 1990s, as accountability policies were developing at the state level, accrediting agencies exerted independent pressure on institutions of higher education to improve performance and quality (Eaton 2001; Ewell 1993). Their objectives were similar, as they also focused on student progress and achievement.

The implementing mechanisms differed, however (Thrash 1988). Regional accrediting agencies required universities to conduct research and evaluation on 'student assessment' and 'student outcomes'. The primary purpose was for universities to use the research evidence in their own efforts to improve programmes (Ewell 1993; Thrash 1988).

This new emphasis on student 'outcomes' departed significantly from earlier accreditation procedures, which had been criticised for considering 'inputs' rather than outcomes (Dill, Massy, Williams and Cook 1996). Regional accreditation agencies introduced these requirements over several years, often revising them several times (Stanley and Patrick 1998; El-Khawas 2001).

The Southern Association of Colleges and Schools (SACS) was the first accrediting agency to act. In 1984, it adopted a new requirement on institutional effectiveness, requiring institutions to evaluate their success and use the results for planning and improvement (Bogue 2003). Other regional accrediting agencies followed with their own approaches. In 1990, the North Central Association (NCA) identified student achievement as a critical component in institutional effectiveness and, in 2000, it announced an Academic Quality Improvement Project (North Central Association 2000). At present, all of the regional accrediting agencies base their reviews on issues of student achievement and learning (Bogue 2003).

Programme-focused accrediting agencies also implemented accountability requirements. Several agencies – in business, engineering, nursing, physical therapy and architecture, for example – transformed their entire programme of study as well as accrediting requirements into a competency-based approach to student achievement (El-Khawas 1993). Under this approach, universities had to demonstrate that students completing their programmes met specific performance standards on the competencies deemed necessary for professional conduct.

Universities also were important policy actors on accountability. Separately and collectively, they actively worked to shape state policy and how state policies were implemented (Bogue 2003; Ewell 1993). In the early period, when governors and state agencies were introducing new calls for student achievement, universities often lauded the objectives but criticised details. They pointed to the difficulties of timely reporting and documenting student progress. Many complained that the states had unilaterally set new policies, disregarding the expertise of university officials (Hutchings and Marchese 1990). These arguments had some effect. Many states developed advisory mechanisms for accountability that included university representatives (Krotseng 1990b). These advisory groups helped shape the actual procedures that implemented performance indicator systems (Spangehl 1987; Banta et al. 1996).

Several policy-focused organisations were also active on accountability. Most had long histories of influencing policy developments affecting higher education. With respect to accountability, there were two subsets of active groups: those interested in improving state policy, and others primarily interested in improving practices within universities and colleges.

Several associations of universities and colleges were active, especially during the initial debates. The American Association of State Colleges and Universities (AASCU), for example, organised a special commission and issued a report with accountability recommendations (AASCU 1986). The Association of American Colleges issued a report (AAC 1985) emphasising the curricular issues in undertaking reform. The American Association for Higher Education (AAHE) was especially influential in helping to define the issues and the type of university responses that were appropriate. AAHE organised its first national conference on assessment in 1984 and has sponsored annual assessment conferences since then. AAHE also issued numerous reports and commentaries by respected experts on assessment. Its magazine, *Change,* became a must-read for those following accountability developments.

State-oriented policy organisations were also part of the accountability debate. Organisations pressing for vigorous state action during this period include inter state organisations such as the Education Commission of the States (ECS) and the State Higher Education Executive Officers (SHEEO). These groups issued reports, sponsored conferences and took other actions to spur accountability at the state level (Gaither, Nedwek and Neal 1994; ECS 1986).

By now, almost twenty years of US policy efforts have been directed toward the policy goal of making universities and colleges more accountable. What evidence is there on the impact of the varied efforts, by states and by other actors? Have these new policy initiatives brought lasting changes in state and university actions?

Answering such questions is difficult when many states and thousands of universities and colleges are involved, and when most state policies changed, sometimes dramatically, over this extended period. Realistically, too, any impact is likely to be indirect, especially when the policies allowed for local variation in how mandates are met (Ewell 1993).

Some perspective can be gained from reports on the extent of change that occurred:

- *State requirements for assessment.* By 1990, forty states had a policy that actively promoted assessment (Ewell, Finney and Lenth 1990). In 1992, more than 90 per cent of public universities reported that they faced requirements for state-mandated student assessment (El-Khawas 1992).
- *Accrediting requirements for assessment.* By the early 1990s, all six regional accrediting agencies had requirements that universities and colleges conduct assessment of student learning and outcomes, and use their assessment results to improve programmes (Ewell 1993).
- *Information reporting.* In 1992, thirty-nine states issued periodic reports to the public about the performance of the state's colleges and universities (Bogue 2003).
- *Performance financing.* In 2002, thirty-six states had performance-financing systems in which some portion of state funds was linked to statistical assessments of the performance of public colleges and universities. In 1997, only ten states had performance-financing systems (Burke and associates 2002).

This evidence documents major change in what states and accreditors require of universities and, in turn, a significant shift in how universities and colleges relate to such external bodies. All universities and colleges are now expected to offer explicit information about student assessment and learning to accreditors; most public universities and colleges must report such information to state agencies and, in most states, new fiscal consequences are attached to weak performance. This adds up to a substantial change in long-held 'rules of the game' with respect to higher education and the state. Back in 1980, none of these requirements was in place (Ewell 1993). Pertinent too is that compliance with (and acceptance of) the new rules is widespread. Most observers believe that public universities and colleges have become comfortable with these new policies (Bogue 2003; Gaither, Nedwek and Neal 1994).

However, there is little evidence of any systematic educational gains, and procedures for measuring performance remain contentious (Lingenfelter 2003; Schmidt 2002a). State agencies have achieved a system for pushing public universities and colleges to improve in specific areas, such as graduation and retention. These are useful, but they are less ambitious than original objectives. As the current head of SHEEO acknowledged: "... progress has been slow, both in developing satisfactory approaches and in improving performance" (Lingenfelter 2003: 20).

A broader perspective can also be taken. Aaron Wildavsky, in his classic book on *Speaking Truth to Power* (1979), offered a criterion for judging broad-scale policy initiatives. His question was whether different problems were being addressed after policies were in place, compared to before. On this criterion, it seems safe to say that the policy arena for higher education has been transformed over the last twenty years as a result of the push for accountability. New questions are raised about quality and accountability in higher education and sharper understandings of underlying problems have been achieved. Public universities and colleges face a different reality: they must comply with performance reporting on several indicators and, for most, state agencies link their performance to funding. Many state officials believe that, because of accountability policies, public universities and colleges today give more attention to state needs (Schmidt 2002a). This represents a significant change from the 1980s, when accusations abounded (Newman 1987) that public universities failed to take state needs seriously (Krotseng 1990b).

So too, the state role with respect to higher education has been transformed. Twenty years ago, states generally did not have the capacity to operate performance-based reporting systems, nor were such systems seen as appropriate for higher education; today, higher education agencies have talented staff, systems are in place, and their legitimacy is broadly accepted.

3. FACTORS AFFECTING IMPLEMENTATION

If state policies to increase higher education accountability have had some success, what accounts for this success? How can the shortcomings in implementation be understood? These questions are addressed by filling in key aspects of the policy context, including further analysis of the role of each major policy actor. Multiple policy actors – the states, the federal government, accrediting agencies, independent policy groups and universities and colleges themselves – influenced the implementation of higher education accountability measures during the last two decades (Ewell 1993; Marchese 1994).

The fact that policy implementation occurred primarily at the state level is advantageous for analysis of the policy process. It offers an appropriate setting, for example, for documenting the impact of contextual change, especially in economic conditions and in elected political leadership (Gaither, Nedwek and Neal 1994). Other contextual factors can also be identified, including shifts toward implementation modes that fit with state agency capabilities as well as shifts that responded to influence exerted by the state's universities and colleges (cf. Gornitzka, Kyvik and Stensaker 2002).

3.1. Factors Affecting State Actions

Accountability had an unusual origin compared to longstanding approaches to state policy making. Much of the impetus emerged from political agendas of several governors (Krotseng 1990a). During the early 1980s, these governors found that taking a special interest in education was politically popular. Although they had first sought to reform elementary and secondary education, higher education offered a natural extension of their push for reform (Ewell 1993). This link also affected the goals the governors selected, because student achievement and outcomes testing already were goals for elementary and secondary education (Kean 1987; Bogue 2003).

This active gubernatorial role was unusual for higher education policy, which usually worked through state-wide boards, agency heads and a few legislators on education committees. The unusual 'origin' of the accountability policy partly explains why its goals moved beyond the traditional policy areas – funding, facilities, capital improvements, mission differentiation, etc. – that were familiar to state-level policy officials.

The capabilities of state agencies also influenced policy implementation. Although their resources and the sophistication of their staff have increased, most state agencies in the early 1980s had limited resources and a small staff, and operated under informal norms that defined their roles as administrative – to allocate funds, gather information and prepare reports – not as advocates of change (Bender 1983).

Once the accountability process got underway, with required performance data, state agencies confronted a greatly increased technical workload. Limited agency capacity may have been a factor in the willingness of states to agree to university pressure to simplify requirements (Ewell 1993) and also in the failed federal attempt to establish state postsecondary review entities. For most states, the federal law would have required a substantial build-up in their administrative capacity (McGuinness 1999).

Significantly, state agencies had strong networks, both formal and informal. Heads of state agencies were members of the SHEEO, which sponsors annual conferences, information-sharing and other supportive services. Many heads of state agencies also were members of regional compacts that bring agency heads together. The Southern Regional Education Board (SREB) has actively promoted improvement in education at all levels. Other informal opportunities – conferences, meetings, special projects – also brought state agency officials into contact with counterparts in other states.

As a result, extensive 'policy borrowing' among the states, both on overall policy and on implementation details, played an important role in accountability reforms (Albright 1997). Tennessee's experience as a pioneer on performance indicators was watched closely by other states, even though few adopted the model in the early years. Other state actions were widely discussed. South Carolina contacted other states as it planned its performance indicators system in the late 1990s. As reflected in the phrase 'legislation by fax', it often seemed that accountability policies in one state were adopted with little independent analysis by other states (Gaither, Nedwek and Neal 1994).

State agencies are vulnerable to shifting priorities, however, and the accountability agenda was subject to considerable 'policy volatility' within the states during this period (Burke and associates 2002). Changes in the states' financial picture were a major source of volatility. Fiscal problems led to cutbacks in higher education funding in several states during the late 1980s and then again in the early 1990s (Hollander 1991; Gaither, Nedwek and Neal 1994). Some argue that these economic problems led to greater legislative interest in efficiency and productivity, which were added to the accountability agenda (Folger and Jones 1993).

For many states, legislatures often reversed gears or newly elected governors abandoned commitments made by previous governors. Arkansas initiated a policy on performance indicators in 1994, but dropped it in 1997. Kentucky started a performance funding policy in 1993, which was discontinued by the new governor in 1997. Similarly, the Minnesota legislature approved a performance funding policy in 1994 but suspended it in 1996. Missouri put its Funding for Results policy in place in 1994, but it was dismantled by a new governor facing budget problems in 2002 (Schmidt 2002c). Texas has discussed adopting several accountability policies but, each time, it has not moved forward (Ashworth 1994; Bogue 2003).

Central to the implementation process for accountability, consequently, was a substantial modification in procedures. State agencies had policy modifications imposed on them as economic or political circumstances changed. Also, they were open to change and regularly convened meetings to discuss procedures (Banta et al. 1996). Over the years, indicators, definitions and procedures changed, as did the funding consequences for good performance. This occurred even for states such as Tennessee, which kept a performance funding system in place continuously since 1982.

Universities and colleges actively pressed for changes, their approach varying by informal norms in each state (Hines 1988). Some states invited university representatives to discuss the new requirements and how to make them workable. Some states established advisory committees to air issues and work out implementation problems. In still other settings, issues were quietly discussed between individual presidents and state leaders.

3.2. Factors Affecting Federal Actions

The US government added its weight to the campaign to increase higher education accountability during the 1990s (Wellman 2003). This represented a departure from its earlier stance, in which the federal government limited its oversight, primarily focused on federal student aid programme (Graham 1984). This 'limited' scope became a substantial investment, however, as the aid programmes grew (Parsons 2000). Since the 1980s, about 40 per cent of all students each year receive federal student aid; the federal government spends close to $70 billion annually on its student grant and loan programmes. Aid recipients are dispersed throughout the US in 3000 colleges and universities but also in 14,000 other postsecondary institutions. The oversight task had become enormous.

The most visible federal action, legislation setting up State Postsecondary Review Entities, was a policy response to this genuine problem. Evidence had emerged of irregularities in how a small number of institutions managed student aid, and federal monitoring capabilities had been criticised for being slow to respond (McGuinness 1999). For beleaguered federal officials, new, state-level review agencies offered a logical mechanism to detect, and punish, bad practice. However, these new agencies were seen by higher education and by some states as a harsh policing device that would affect all institutions, not just those with flawed management. As already noted, the US Congress dropped its support for SPREs after hearing heated opposition (Wellman 2003).

In policy perspective, these new agencies would have imposed a major structural change and would have established a substantially new relationship between the states and the federal government on higher education matters. It required an uncomfortable 'policing' role to monitor administrative details, to inspect institutions and to penalise them where infractions were found. Most states at the time were already heavily invested in developing their performance indicator systems. For many, resources were stretched thin.

More broadly, the SPRE legislation challenged general norms about the respective roles of the federal government and the states. Longstanding agreements had been in place for the states, the federal government and accrediting agencies to take shared responsibility for oversight of American universities and colleges. Referred to as the 'program integrity triad' and described in Part H of the federal Higher Education Act, this agreement allocated responsibilities to each that fitted with their special role and capabilities (Gaither, Nedwek and Neal 1994). States had sole authority to authorise, or license, a new institution to begin operation (Bender 1983). Accrediting agencies were responsible for assessing quality once an institution was underway. The federal government monitored that universities and colleges followed all fiscal and regulatory requirements tied to the student aid programme (Chambers 1983). This agreement was subject to change, of course, but the SPRE approach had introduced an abrupt, one-sided change.

The federal government also placed additional responsibility on accrediting agencies. As a policy instrument, this was easy to implement. Accrediting agencies, already responsible for monitoring the quality of universities and colleges, accepted the new requirements, in part to uphold their commitment to the 'triad' concept and in part, too, as a preferred alternative to greater federal scrutiny of universities and colleges (Eaton 2001, 2003).

3.3. The Influence of Accrediting Agencies

US accrediting agencies actively promoted accountability during these decades. Their focus – on institutional effectiveness, student outcomes and processes of student assessment – differed from the state focus on performance, but accreditors put similar pressure on institutions to improve student progress and study completion (Ewell 1993). States and accreditors also relied on similar policy tools, primarily requirements with deadlines and institutional reporting.

In a contrast to state actions, accrediting agencies moved slowly to revise and strengthen their requirements. They followed longstanding procedures, allowed lengthy periods for comment and discussion, and introduced new rules over time (Eaton 2001; El-Khawas 2001). One factor may be that accrediting agencies have relatively small staff and a limited mandate, focused on cycles of institutional review. Another factor is their source of authority: while they serve a public purpose, they are voluntary organisations and depend on gaining acceptance for change. Unlike state agencies, accrediting agencies must build consensus, and obtain formal approval, before embarking on a reform (Thrash 1988; Stanley and Patrick 1998).

States and accreditors differed on approaches to accountability. States tended to rely on uniform criteria applied to all institutions and emphasised accountability over improvement. In contrast, accrediting agencies allowed performance to be defined according to institutional context, gave priority to self-review over uniform measures and, if pressed, emphasised improvement over accountability (Ewell 1993; Kezar and El-Khawas 2003).

The independent but complementary agendas of state agencies and accrediting agencies may have had a mutually reinforcing impact. For universities and colleges, the new accountability agenda was a strong departure from past practice, so institutions might have argued against it or adopted a wait-and-see approach, aware that many state policies do not last. Yet, the combined influence of both state and accrediting agency calls for accountability may have given a sense of inevitability to the push for change. Following initial questioning, most universities and colleges accepted the new calls for accountability from both states and accreditors (El-Khawas 1992).

3.4. Universities as Policy Actors

Universities have long been recognised as policy influentials at the state policy level (Hines 1988; Parsons 2000). In most states, a university president meets directly with state officials to discuss institutional needs. Many states have advisory committees of college presidents and most have boards (e.g. boards of trustees, boards of regents) that set policy and discuss institutional needs with state officials.

Although generalisation is difficult, university actions fell into several patterns as accountability policies developed. The initial response was largely rhetorical, expressing concern and pointing out shortcomings. A second phase was a pattern of university influence through consultation. State agencies, responding to criticism, opened their new procedures to discussion. Implementation difficulties were routinely aired and workable compromises identified, often resulting in weaker requirements (cf. Dill 1998). Tennessee, for example, made an early change from requiring a specific rate of degree completion each year to a new indicator calling for year-to-year progress on completion. Missouri's Funding for Results policy was designed with input from university and college leaders. As a result, it included a small number of indicators – more workable for institutions – and different indicators for two-year and four-year institutions. In another accommodation, state officials agreed that universities and colleges could receive additional money for good performance but would not face budget cuts for poor performance (Schmidt 2002b).

Few institutions openly 'resisted' accountability policies. Most took steps to comply with state requirements, expanding offices that gathered and reported information, and improving programmes to achieve gains on required indicators. However, as several studies have found, compliance was primarily at the administrative level. Little change occurred in academic programmes and among faculty (Bogue 2003; Banta et al. 1996; El-Khawas 1998). Also, university leaders continued to question the new policies. State officials have said that much policy 'volatility' and their retreats from stricter policies were largely due to the political influence of universities (Schmidt 2002b; Ewell 1993).

An interesting variation in university response occurred among those universities that embraced the accountability agenda. Truman State University and others recognised that this approach offered them a distinctive role, or 'niche', and could enhance their national reputation. Such responses, reflecting a resource dependency view (Gornitzka, Kyvik and Stensaker 2002), can be expected in a differentiated system of higher education. Universities will vary in their estimates of whether new ideas are profitable for them. They also vary in their response to different inducements. Reputational or prestige gains can be powerful inducements to action.

3.5. Independent Policy Organisations

Voluntary organisations were also prominent, most with nation-wide constituencies and reputations. These organisations took on policy roles (e.g. identifying problems and defining possible solutions) that a national government might otherwise exercise (El-Khawas 1997). Their combined actions lent legitimacy to the entire accountability agenda.

As already noted, two policy groups were influential in the accountability debate. In many respects they operated as two advocacy coalitions trying to shape policy response (cf. Sabatier and Jenkins-Smith 1999). The state-focused groups included the Education Commission of the States, SHEEO, NCHEMS, regional groups such as SREB and WICHE (the Western Interstate Consortium in Higher Education), and, recently, the National Center for Public Policy in Higher Education. Their assistance provided technical advice and moral support to state policy makers.

The institution-focused groups also promoted change through conferences and reports, but their attention was directed primarily to colleges and universities. Their messages differed from the state-oriented groups, with less emphasis on performance indicators and greater emphasis on issues of student learning and student outcomes. These associations did not argue against change, however. Indeed, AAHE adopted a strong reformist agenda, cooperating with state-focused groups on many occasions. It offered a reasoned voice for change, and a forum in which campus practitioners could exchange information and gain advice on implementing state mandates (cf. Hutchings and Marchese 1990).

Arguably, AAHE's continuing reformist role influenced the actions of many institutions across the US. AAHE argued for student assessment over a sustained period and provided both intellectual arguments and practical advice to shape its implementation. Its policy stance probably enhanced acceptance of both state and accrediting agency requirements for student assessment. Although it was critical of much statistical reporting, AAHE lent overall legitimacy to accountability policies, giving them an air of inevitability, and helped resolve operational issues that campuses faced in meeting state requirements.

4. CONCLUSION

US policy initiatives to promote higher education accountability have continued, albeit in differing forms, for two decades. They have had substantial impact. Today, state agencies, accrediting agencies and universities and colleges all operate with greater focus on accountability goals and have taken steps to enhance institutional quality and improve student learning.

One broad impact is that the external climate for higher education has changed. Following Wildavsky's questions, it is evident that different issues are on the table today, compared to two decades ago. Higher education pays greater attention to its external publics. Accountability issues are seen as legitimate objects of external attention. Considered in light of the longstanding tensions between academic and governmental values, this change in cultural assumptions is significant (cf. Gornitzka, Kyvik and Stensaker 2002).

Notably, it was the actions of multiple policy actors that created change. A 'cumulative effect' occurred, as individual groups and sectors collectively sustained the accountability effort (Ewell 1993). If states had taken the only policy action on accountability, the volatility and reversals that occur within state policy may have doomed the effort. The states gained support – and protection – from the parallel messages sent out by other states, by the federal government, by accreditors and by independent policy organisations.

This study offers several implications for further research on policy implementation. First, other studies are needed that look to multiple sources of policy influence in order to better discern the basis for survival of new policies. If this study had focused only on the state role, it would have missed the larger story of why the state policies were not opposed and, especially, why the university sector adapted to the new requirements. Similar studies are needed on different issues, in various settings.

Second, this study, by spanning two decades, helps demonstrate the important role of policy volatility. Further research should explore such volatility, perhaps documenting correlates of certain policy directions (e.g. more interventionist or more technical) with broader social and economic trends. The role of various actors in causing, or resisting, policy volatility also bears attention. Is there systematic support for the belief that newly elected or appointed officials typically introduce major policy shifts to put their own stamp on policy? How do the actions of long-term officials, elected or appointed, affect the continuity of policy initiatives?

Third, this study raises the question of how 'policy' should be defined. Is policy to be seen as a specific law or agency directive or, instead, as a sustained initiative? If the latter, how can a sustained effort be identified? If the focus is on governmental initiatives, should attention be limited to a single administrative term? Might it be tied to a particular issue, or location, or to the sustained efforts of a few actors? This study's focus on accountability at the state level was not limited to a specific state law or agency directive in order to show the effects of several, related initiatives on higher education institutions throughout the United States. Other policy research may also find it fruitful to examine a sustained, but decentralised, policy initiative. We need to understand better the ways in which such long-term policy initiatives are mounted, even as key actors change, venues shift and objectives change.

REFERENCES

Albright, B.N. "Of Carrots and Sticks and State Budgets." *Trusteeship: The Journal of the Association of Governing Boards of Colleges and Universities.* March/April (1997): 18–23.

American Association of State Colleges and Universities. *To Secure the Blessings of Liberty: Report of the National Commission on the Role and Future of State Colleges and Universities.* Washington, DC: AASCU, 1986.

Ashworth, K.H. "Performance-based Funding in Higher Education: The Texas Case Study." *Change* 26.6 (1994): 8–15.

Association of American Colleges. *Integrity in the College Curriculum.* Washington, DC: AAC, 1985.

Banta, T.W. and associates (eds). *Making a Difference: Outcomes of a Decade of Assessment in Higher Education.* San Francisco: Jossey-Bass, 1993.

Banta, T.W. and H.S. Fisher. "Performance Funding: Tennessee's Experiment." In Folger, J. (ed.). *Financial Incentives for Academic Quality.* New Directions for Higher Education. San Francisco: Jossey-Bass, 1984, 29–41.

Banta, T.W., L.B. Rudolph, J. van Dyke and H.S. Fisher. "Performance Funding Comes of Age in Tennessee." *Journal of Higher Education* 67.1 (1996): 23–45.

Bemis, J.F. "Regional Accreditation." In Young, K.E., C.M. Chambers, H.R. Kells and associates (eds). *Understanding Accreditation.* San Francisco: Jossey-Bass, 1983, 167–186.

Bender, L.W. "States and Accreditation." In Young, K.E., C.M. Chambers, H.R. Kells and associates (eds). *Understanding Accreditation.* San Francisco: Jossey-Bass, 1983, 270–288.

Bogue, E.G. *Quality and Accountability in Higher Education: Improving Policy, Enhancing Performance.* Westport, CT: Praeger, 2003.

Bogue, E.G. and W. Brown. "Performance Incentives for State Colleges." *Harvard Business Review* 60.6 (1982): 123–128.

Burke, J. and associates. *Funding Public Colleges and Universities for Performance.* Albany: The Rockefeller Institute Press, 2002.

Burke, J.C. and A.M. Serban. *Performance Funding for Public Higher Education: Fad or Trend?* New Directions for Institutional Research, No. 97. San Francisco: Jossey-Bass, 1998.

Chambers, C.M. "Federal Government and Accreditation." In Young, K.E., C.M. Chambers, H.R. Kells and associates (eds). *Understanding Accreditation.* San Francisco: Jossey-Bass, 1983, 233–269.

Christal, M.E. *1997 Survey on Performance Measures.* Denver: State Higher Education Executive Officers, 1998.

Dill, D.D. "Evaluating the Evaluative State: Implications for Research in Higher Education." *European Journal of Education* 33.3 (1998): 361–377.

Dill, D.D., W.F. Massy, P.R. Williams and C.M. Cook. "Accreditation and Academic Quality Assurance: Can We Get There From Here?" *Change* 28.5 (1996): 16–24.

Eaton, J. "Regional Accreditation Reform: Who is Served?" *Change* 33.2 (2001): 38–45.

Eaton, J. "The Value of Accreditation: Four Pivotal Roles." Washington, DC: Council for Higher Education Accreditation, 2003.

Education Commission of the States. *Transforming the State Role in Improving Undergraduate Education: Time for a Different View.* Denver, CO: ECS, 1986.

El-Khawas, E. *Campus Trends 1992.* Washington, DC: American Council on Education, 1992.

El-Khawas, E. "External Scrutiny, US Style: Multiple Actors, Overlapping Roles." In Becher, T. (ed.). *Governments and Professional Education.* London: SRHE/Open University Press, 1993, 107–122.

El-Khawas, E. "The Role of Intermediary Organizations." In Peterson, M.W., D.D. Dill and L.A. Mets (eds). *Planning and Management for a Changing Environment.* San Francisco: Jossey-Bass, 1997, 66–87.

El-Khawas, E. "Strong State Action But Limited Results: Perspectives on University Resistance." *European Journal of Education* 33.3 (1998): 317–330.

El-Khawas, E. *Accreditation in the United States: Origins, Development, and Future Prospects.* Paris: UNESCO/International Institute for Educational Planning, 2001.

Enders, J., L. Goedegebuure and P. Maassen. *Governance Shifts and Policy Implementation in Higher Education: A European Birds-Eye View.* Enschede, the Netherlands: Center for Higher Education Policy Studies, 2003.

Ewell, P.T. "Assessment: What's it all About?" *Change* 17.6 (1985): 32–36.

Ewell, P.T. "The Role of States and Accreditors in Shaping Assessment Practice." In Banta, T.W. and associates (eds). *Making a Difference: Outcomes of a Decade of Assessment in Higher Education.* San Francisco: Jossey-Bass, 1993, 339–356.

Ewell, P.T. and C.M. Boyer. "Acting Out State-Mandated Assessment: Evidence From Five States." *Change* 20.4 (1988): 40–47.

Ewell, P.T., J. Finney and C. Lenth. "Filling in the Mosaic: The Emerging Pattern of State-Based Assessment." *AAHE Bulletin* 42.8 (1990): 3–5.

Folger, J. and D. Jones. *Using Fiscal Policy to Achieve State Education Goals: State Policy and College Learning.* Denver: Education Commission of the States, 1993.

Gaither, G., B.P. Nedwek and J.E. Neal. *Measuring Up: The Promise of Performance Indicators in Higher Education.* ASHE/ERIC Research Report. Washington, DC: George Washington University, 1994.

Gladieux, L.E. and T.R. Wolanin. *Congress and the Colleges.* Lexington, MA: D.C. Heath, 1976.

Glidden, R. "Specialized Accreditation." In Young, K.E., C.M. Chambers, H.R. Kells and associates (eds). *Understanding Accreditation.* San Francisco: Jossey-Bass, 1983, 187–208.

Gornitzka, A., S. Kyvik and B. Stensaker. "Implementation Analysis in Higher Education." In Smart, J.C. (ed.). *Higher Education: Handbook of Theory and Research, vol. XVII.* Dordrecht: Kluwer Academic Publishers, 2002, 381–423.

Graham, H.D. *The Uncertain Triumph: Federal Education Policy in the Kennedy and Johnson Years.* Chapel Hill: University of North Carolina Press, 1984.

Hines, E.R. *Higher Education and State Governments: Renewed Partnership, Cooperation or Competition?* ASHE/ERIC Higher Education Report. Washington, DC: George Washington University, 1988.

Hines, E.R. "The Governance of Higher Education." In Smart, J.C. and W.G. Tierney (eds). *Higher Education: Handbook of Theory and Research, vol. XV.* New York: Agathon Press, 2000, 105–156.

Hollander, T.E. "States and College Reform: New Jersey's Experiment." *Planning in Higher Education* 19 (1991): 25–31.

Hutchings, P. and T. Marchese. "Watching Assessment: Questions, Stories, Prospects." *Change* 22.4 (1990): 12–38.

Jemmott, N.D. and E.A. Morante. "The College Outcomes Evaluation Program." In Banta, T.W. and associates (eds). *Making a Difference: Outcomes of a Decade of Assessment in Higher Education.* San Francisco: Jossey-Bass, 1993, 306–321.

Kean, T. "Time to Deliver: Before We Forget the Promises We Made." *Change* 19.5 (1987): 10–11.

Kezar, A. and E. El-Khawas. "Using the Performance Dimension: Converging Paths for External Accountability?" In Eggins, H. (ed.). *Globalization and Reform in Higher Education.* London: SRHE/Open University Press, 2003, 85–99.

Krotseng, M. "Of State Capitals and Catalysts: The Power of External Prodding." In Marcus, L.R. and B.D. Stickney (eds). *Politics and Policy in the Age of Education.* Springfield, IL: Charles C. Thomas, 1990a, 243–262.

Krotseng, M. "Profiles of Quality and Intrusion: The Complex Courtship of State Governments and Higher Education." *Review of Higher Education* 13.4 (1990b): 557–566.

Lingenfelter, P.E. "Educational Accountability: Setting Standards, Improving Performance." *Change* 35.2 (2003): 19–23.

Marchese, T. "Accountability." *Change* 26.6 (1994): 4.

McGuinness, A.C. "The Federal Government and Postsecondary Education." In Altbach, P.G. and R.O. Berdahl (eds). *Higher Education in American Society.* Buffalo: Prometheus Books, 1981, 157–179.

McGuinness, A.C. *Federal/State Partnerships in Postsecondary Education: SPRE as a Case Study.* Boulder, CO: NCHEMS, 1999.

National Center for Public Policy and Higher Education. *Measuring up 2000.* San Jose, CA: National Center for Public Policy and Higher Education, 2000.

National Center for Public Policy and Higher Education. *Measuring up 2002.* San Jose, CA: National Center for Public Policy and Higher Education, 2002.

National Governors Association. *Time for Results.* Washington, DC: National Governors Association, 1986.

Newman, F. *Choosing Quality: Reducing Conflict Between the State and the University.* Denver, CO: Education Commission of the States, 1987.

North Central Association. "Academic Quality Improvement Project." Revised. Chicago, IL: North Central Association, 2000.

Osborne, D. and T. Gaebler. *Reinventing Government: How the Entrepreneurial Spirit is Transforming the Public Sector.* New York: Penguin Books, 1993.

Parsons, M.D. "The Higher Education Policy Arena: The Rise and Fall of a Community." In Losco, J. and B.L. Fife (eds). *Higher Education in Transition: The Challenges of the New Millennium.* Westport, CT: Dergin and Garvey, 2000, 83–107.

Rating the Colleges. *US News and World Report,* 28 November, 1983, 41.

Ruppert, S.S. (ed.). *Charting Higher Education Accountability: A Sourcebook on State-Level Performance Indicators.* Denver, CO: Education Commission of the States, 1994.

Sabatier, P.A. "Top-down and Bottom-up Approaches to Implementation Research: A Critical Analysis and Suggested Synthesis." *Journal of Public Policy* 6 (1986): 21–48.

Sabatier, P.A. and H.C. Jenkins-Smith. "The Advocacy Coalition Framework: An Assessment." In Sabatier, P.A. (ed.). *Theories of the Policy Process.* Boulder, CO: Westview Press, 1999, 117–168.

Schmidt, P. "Most States Tie Aid to Performance Despite Little Proof That it Works." *Chronicle of Higher Education,* 22 February, 2002a, A20.

Schmidt, P. "Missouri's Financing System is Praised, But More for Longevity Than for Results." *Chronicle of Higher Education,* 22 February, 2002b, A21.

Schmidt, P. "Dashed Hopes in Missouri." *Chronicle of Higher Education,* 29 November, 2002c, A18.

South Carolina Commission on Higher Education. *Performance Funding at a Glance.* Columbia, SC: South Carolina Commission on Higher Education, 2001.

Spangehl, S.D. "The Push to Assess. Why it's Feared and How to Respond." *Change* 19.1 (1987): 35–39.

Stanley, E. and W. Patrick. *Quality Assurance in American and British Higher Education: A Comparison.* New Directions for Institutional Research, No. 99. San Francisco: Jossey-Bass, 1998.

Thrash, P.A. "Educational Outcomes in the Accrediting Process." *Academe* 74 (1988): 16–18.

Wellman, J. "Do Federal Spending and Regulation Produce Quality in Higher Education?" In Wolanin, T.R. (ed.). *Reauthorizing the Higher Education Act: Issues and Options.* Washington, DC: Institute for Higher Education Policy, 2003, 129–146.

Wildavsky, A. *Speaking Truth to Power: The Art and Craft of Policy Analysis.* Boston: Little, Brown, 1979.

RICHARD C. RICHARDSON JR AND ALICIA D. HURLEY

FROM LOW INCOME AND MINORITY ACCESS TO MIDDLE INCOME AFFORDABILITY: A CASE STUDY OF THE US FEDERAL ROLE IN PROVIDING ACCESS TO HIGHER EDUCATION

1. INTRODUCTION

In this chapter, we focus on a major turning point in US policy, the decision to shift most federal dollars for higher education from direct subsidies to institutions to need-based assistance to students. The shift was part of a strategy for transforming a meritocratic higher education system still trying to adjust to the imperatives of the civil rights era into one where the opportunity to attend higher education was the right of every individual without regard to race, gender or economic circumstances. Student decisions about where to attend college have subsequently come to determine in large measure the amount of federal aid to institutions and through this transition have helped to bring about the shift to quasi markets as a major influence on institutional decisions.

The story began with a near-national consensus (except among representatives of the higher education community) on the need to address past inequities in schooling opportunities and their impact on life chances by providing need-based financial assistance to students, remedial education in postsecondary institutions, and affirmative action to ensure faculty and student diversity. While this consensus gradually disintegrated over the ensuing years, the commitment to expanding educational opportunity through some form of individual need-based assistance has remained strong for more than two decades despite some twists and turns that surely were not anticipated by those who formulated the original policy reforms.

In this chapter, we draw on recent work by the Alliance for International Higher Education Policy Studies (AIHEPS) to describe the federal context for higher education in the US and to provide a brief overview of the foundations of the student funding reforms (Prisco, Hurley, Carton and Richardson 2002). We then provide a more detailed narrative of the development of the reform and the turns it has taken in the thirty years following the enabling legislation. We then show how federal policies interact with state policies to produce differential impacts on key outcomes in four US states. Finally, we report some of the changes in US higher education, both intended and unintended, that have accompanied the access reform.

305

Å. Gornitzka et al. (eds.), Reform and Change in Higher Education, 305-324.

2. THE FEDERAL CONTEXT

Because the Tenth Amendment to the US Constitution effectively delegates all authority for education to the 50 states, each defines and develops its own arrangements for higher education. With the exception of land grants and sporadic appropriations, a substantive federal role in higher education emerged only in the closing days of World War II with the passage of the Serviceman's Readjustment Act of 1944 (GI Bill). Along with the post-World War II baby boom, the GI Bill set in motion forces that culminated in a national transformation from elite to meritocratic, and then to mass or universal higher education. This transformation placed substantial pressure on states to create new and expand existing public institutions to absorb the enormous growth of new enrolments.

Until the mid-1960s, federal support for higher education consisted primarily of research, development and student or institutional subsidies in areas defined as national priorities. This changed with the Higher Education Act of 1965, an omnibus bill covering such items as community service and continuing education; library assistance, training and research; strengthening developing institutions; student assistance; teacher programmes; and facilities construction. To support these activities, Congress appropriated $804 million. Even with such unprecedented investment, the clear intent of federal policy makers was that higher education remain a federal concern but a state responsibility. To this end, the enabling legislation specifically stated that federal authority did not extend to the curriculum, administration, personnel or library resources of any institution.

While the most significant governance structures – for both public and private institutions – exist at the state and local levels, there are exceptions to the general rule of state dominance. Formal federal influence over institutions of higher education occurs in such areas as: (a) congressional legislative enforcement under the Fourteenth Amendment (equal protection); (b) research and development appropriations; and (c) matching funds generated by federal legislation in the area of loans for postsecondary students. Title VII of the Civil Rights Act of 1964, for example, makes no mention of higher education institutions, yet applies to all public institutions and private institutions receiving federal funds. Likewise, Title IX of the Education Amendments of 1972 (opportunities for women) and the Americans with Disabilities Act of 1991 further extend requirements for equal protection to groups of citizens for whom different treatment had been the norm.

The legacies of the GI Bill, the National Defense Education Act, and the Higher Education Act endure, serving as the foundation for current relationships between the federal government and higher education in the United States.

The federal government influences higher education behaviours and outcomes primarily through altering the terms under which financial resources are made available. To achieve national objectives, the federal government funds: (1) individual students directly via student financial aid; and (2) individual institutions (primarily for research) through incentive grants based upon a competitive proposal process. Attached to funding streams are regulatory requirements.

Both private (commonly referred to as 'independent') and public institutions receive federal funding and are therefore bound by the rules and regulations that accompany these funds. The federal government's policies are uniform for every state and for any institution that participates in the federal funding programmes. The states have general oversight over institutions within their borders, and exercise governing control over public colleges and universities. The degree to which private institutions follow state guidelines depends on state policies. Some states provide financial assistance to eligible residents regardless of whether they attend public or private institutions. A few provide direct subsidies to private institutions, either in the form of per capita grants based on the number of residents who attend or graduate, or through contracts for student spaces in such specialised programmes as engineering, medicine or dentistry. The more support a state provides to private institutions, the more likely it will exercise regulatory authority. Federal and state policies do not necessarily align and, in the words of a senior policy analyst interviewed for the AIHEPS study, "If they do, it is probably accidental".

US trends in funding for postsecondary education have shifted over the past 20 years. From 1975 to 1985, federal funding for higher education decreased by 27 per cent. From 1985 to 2000, it increased by 21 per cent (National Center for Education Statistics 2000). Both public and private institutions experienced a decrease in the percentage of their current fund revenues that came from government sources. The sources that have compensated for the shortfall are striking. The public sector has come to rely more on tuition revenue, while the private sector has become more reliant upon endowment income.

3. THE ACCESS REFORM IN CONTEXT

The National Defense Education Act of 1958 (NDEA) set in motion political forces that were to alter profoundly the relationship of the federal government to the nation's schools, colleges and universities (Brademas 1987: 8). Providing direct grants, loans and fellowships to college students for the first time, "the Act came closer to being an out-and-out education measure than any previous legislation" (Rivlin 1961: 119). The provisions for the student loan programme indicated congressional concurrence that helping undergraduates finance their education on a continuing basis was in the national interest. The NDEA also reinforced the federal government's use of higher education as a means to an end: national defence, while representing as well a quantum leap in the acceptable size and scope of the federal role in higher education (Gladieux and Wolanin 1976; Parsons 1997).

The following decade featured the Higher Education Act of 1965, which represented one facet of a much broader war on poverty and civil rights (McGuiness 1981). The package included a college grant programme, a subsidised loan programme, and a work-study programme. All were designed to extend educational opportunity more broadly to low and middle income families. "With the passage of the measure, Congress took on important new responsibilities in the sphere of higher education" (*Congressional Quarterly Almanac* 1965: 284). The rationale of equal educational opportunity proved to be a powerful vehicle for propelling increased federal activity, defining "a new and legitimate federal role in higher education, one which had attained widespread support in other functional areas at the time"

(Advisory Commission on Intergovernmental Relations 1981: 23). The late Senator Robert Taft expressed the consensus view: "Education is primarily a state function but in the field of education, as in the fields of health, relief and medical care, the federal government has a secondary obligation to see that there is a basic floor under those essential services for all adults and children in the US" (*Congressional Quarterly Almanac* 1965: 1374). Congress had in fact established a floor that would last for many years to come.

The Higher Education Act of 1965 was first amended in 1968, but the passage of the comprehensive Higher Education Amendments of 1972 broadened and elaborated the federal role in higher education to include new Basic Educational Opportunity Grants (BEOG) and direct institutional allowances to complement BEOG awards. In principle, every student who was financially needy would receive the federal grants due to the 'entitlement' nature of the new grant programme. The 1972 amendments were described as "truly a landmark in the history of higher education" and were particularly important to the US access agenda (*Congressional Quarterly Almanac* 1972: 198).

An important policy change to the need-based focus of the 1972 amendments came with the passage of the Middle Income Student Assistance Act (MISAA) in 1978 which changed the scope and direction of student aid programmes by opening up loan and grant programmes to middle income families. While education lobbyists criticised MISAA as "an undistinguished attempt to create loans of convenience for middle-class families" (Doyle and Hartle 1986), the then president, President Carter, called it "an historic expansion of federal assistance to education ... similar to the GI Bill as a landmark in the federal commitment" to aid college students (*Congressional Quarterly Almanac* 1978).

The 1980s brought a new administration determined to shrink domestic spending; not surprisingly, it was a period of increased scrutiny and accountability in federal spending for higher education and produced a shift in the primary source of federal support from grants to loans. Significantly, the policy focus moved from concerns about equity to such issues as academic performance and institutional improvement, a shift that public consensus seemed to support (Hansen and Stampen 1994).

At the beginning of the 1990s, 13.7 million students were seeking a postsecondary degree. By the end, that number had grown to 16 million (Gerald and Hussar 2000; US Census Bureau 2002). The American public also appeared more willing to take on debt for higher education. There was much concern about the imbalance between grant funding and loan funding and the amount of debt that students were accruing. In 1980, grants amounted to 55 per cent of the total federal student aid portfolio, while loans accounted for 42 per cent. By the end of the 1990s, this had shifted and grants accounted for 40 per cent, while loans had increased to 58 per cent (Ikenberry and Hartle 2000). But, with the perceived importance of higher education, Americans continued to borrow with the expectation that there would ultimately be a payoff.

Overtime, federal student assistance programmes have included federal Pell grants, Federal Family Education Loans (FFEL), the William D. Ford Federal Direct Loan Program, Income Contingent Loans (ICL), State Student Incentive Grants

(SSIG), Leveraging Educational Assistance Partnerships (LEAP),[1] Perkins Loans, Federal Work Study Grants and Federal Supplemental Educational Opportunity Grants (FSEOG). The last three programmes are distinguished as 'campus based'.

Now in existence for over three decades, the federal Pell grant programme serves as the foundation for need-based student aid. Pell grants are made directly to students based upon financial status as well as the cost of attendance. Increases in funding need-based aid suggest that the federal government has maintained its commitment to access and choice. However, funding levels have not kept up with increases in the costs of going to college. As a result, the buying power of the Pell grant has eroded both at public and private four-year institutions (see table 1). The Pell grant maximum would need to increase from $3750 to over $7000 to reach its 1975–76 buying power at a four-year public institution (Advisory Committee on Student Financial Assistance 2001). Although the Pell grant does not carry the purchasing power that it did upon its inception, it continues to serve as an important source of need-based assistance, and as a mechanism to correct the growing imbalance between grants and loans.

Table 1. Pell grant maximum award as a percentage of institutional cost of attendance

Year	Institution type	
	Public four-year %	Private four-year %
1975–76	84	38
1985–86	57	26
1995–96	34	13
1999–00	39	15

Source: College Board 2000a; National Center for Education Statistics 2001b quoted in Advisory Committee on Student Financial Assistance 2001

The Federal Family Education Loan (FFEL) programme subsidises and guarantees low-interest loans to students and parents. It remains the largest federal student assistance programme. The programme includes federal Stafford Loans (subsidised and unsubsidised), federal Parent Loans (PLUS) and federal Consolidation Loans. Private or commercial lending agencies make and manage the loans while the government backs or guarantees the loan. The only need-based element is the subsidised Stafford Loan, for which the student pays no interest while in school. The federal government pays interest subsidies to approximately 4100 lenders and guarantees loans against default through reinsurance programmes for 36 state and private, non-profit guarantee agencies that serve as intermediaries between the government and FFEL. Consolidation loans help student and parent borrowers consolidate several types of federal student loans with various repayment schedules into a single loan.

The State Student Incentive Grants (SSIG) programme, authorised in the 1972 Higher Education Amendments, provided federal grants to states to promote state-level, need-based grants and community service work-study assistance. Under the 1998 reauthorisation, SSIG became the Leveraging Educational Assistance

Partnership (LEAP) programme. Through the 1990s, federal funding for SSIG and LEAP consistently declined, although state governments continue to support the programme ardently. In 1997, states overmatched their federal SSIG (LEAP) funds by 20 to 1 (National Center for Education Statistics 2001a).

Three programmes, administered primarily by participating institutions, complete the picture of federal student assistance. The federal Perkins Loan is the largest and oldest. Enacted as National Direct/Defense Loans under the National Defense Education Act of 1958, the Perkins programme provides long-term, low-interest loans to graduate and undergraduate students. Undergraduate students are eligible to borrow up to $4000 and graduate students $6000 (National Center for Education Statistics 2001b).

Under the Work Study (College Work Study, Federal Work Study) Program, federal grants to institutions subsidise the salaries of on-campus student workers. Not all institutions participate in the programme. Eligible students begin the academic year with a specified work-study funding level. The funds are non-transferable and apply only to student salaries for part-time employment. Institutions provide matching funds equal to 25% of the total (prior to 1993 it was 30%) (National Center for Education Statistics 2001b). The Federal Supplemental Educational Opportunity Grant (FSEOG) programme is need based and provides assistance to both part- and full-time graduate and undergraduate students. Because the Student Loan Reform Act of 1993 stipulated that the federal portion of the grants could not exceed 75 per cent of the total, institutions must provide 25 per cent of the total amount awarded. Students receiving Pell grants are given FSEOG priority, although in contrast to Pell grants, not every eligible student receives the FSEOG. Those receiving an award are eligible for up to $4000 a year in funding.

Those responsible for providing need-based assistance in the form of grants and loans to low income students probably never envisioned rewarding families who could afford to pay for college with their own resources by providing deductions and credits on their annual income taxes. Even so, the rhetoric surrounding the passage of the Taxpayer Relief Act of 1997 emphasised the lack of direct funding to help needy families put their children through college. The legislation authorised HOPE Scholarships – $1500 tax credits for up to two years – to be offered to families with adjusted annual gross incomes no greater than $80,000 to $100,000. The Lifetime Learning proposal applied to families with the same income and allowed them to offset the cost of education by taking up to $10,000 a year in tax deductions. An IRA (Individual Retirement Account) provision eliminated penalties for account withdrawals if the money was used for postsecondary education. An extension of the legislation allowed workers to exclude from their income the cost of any graduate or undergraduate course work paid by their employer. Evidence available from a relatively brief experience with this act (figures 1 and 2) suggests that families in the income range of $60,000 to $79,999 reaped the largest benefits (US General Accounting Office 2002).[2] The focus on middle income families has been largely confirmed by subsequent data on use of the tax credits and deductions (US General Accounting Office 2002).

Many in the higher education community opposed these programmes, arguing that they were too expensive and will ultimately leave less funding available for need-based aid directed to low income students. In 1998, only about a third of the families who were estimated to be eligible actually claimed a federal education tax credit (including the HOPE Scholarship) and they claimed only $3.4 billion of an estimated $7 billion liability (Riley 2001).

Figure 1. HOPE credit and Title IV loans and/or grants for dependent students receiving both

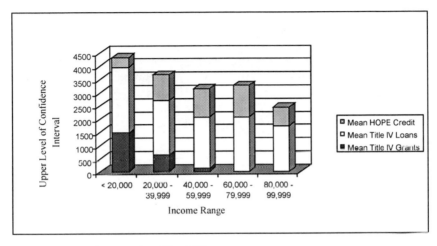

Source: US General Accounting Office 2002

Figure 2. Lifetime credit and Title IV loans and/or grants for dependent students receiving both

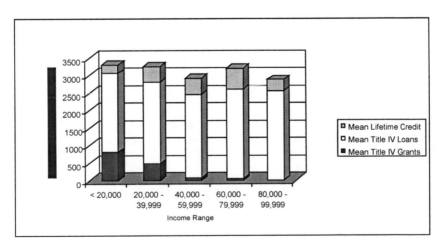

Source: US General Accounting Office 2002

4. RESULTS OF THE REFORM: THE NATIONAL PICTURE

In 1995–96, 50 per cent of all undergraduates received financial aid through programmes funded by the federal government, the states, the postsecondary institutions themselves, or other organisations. *Two-thirds* of all full-time students received financial aid (National Center for Education Statistics 1998). Federal student aid increased by 16 per cent during the 1990s (National Center for Education Statistics 2000). The $60 billion commitment during 2000–01 exceeds all other federal appropriations for higher education combined. During the 1990s, total aid nearly doubled (in constant dollars), while loan aid increased by 136 per cent (College Board 2000b).

Figure 3 summarises total Title IV federal student aid in current and constant dollars from before the inception of the policy reform to the current era with sufficient legislation noted.

Figure 3. Total Title IV federal student aid in current and constant dollars (1965–2000)

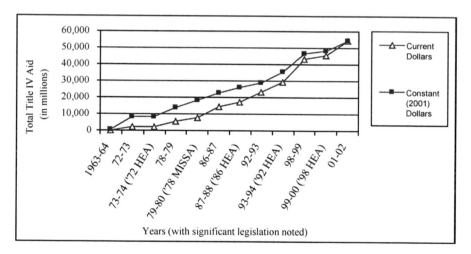

Source: College Board 2002

By 2001–02, the federal government was spending more than $60 billion on student aid. By any measure, this represented a considerable commitment (College Board 2002). Figure 4 summarises how the nature of federal aid has changed from 1965 to the present.

Clearly, grants have become less important as a strategy for achieving the access reform, while loans, which declined to almost parity with grants in 1978–79, have very nearly become as important in 2000–01 as they were prior to the 1972 amendments. Figure 4 significantly understates the role of tax credits because the data reflect the very early stages of this programme. Early projections suggest that tax credits may ultimately create a liability for the federal government equal to all other forms of aid combined.

Figure 4. Proportion of federal aid by type of aid (1965–2000)

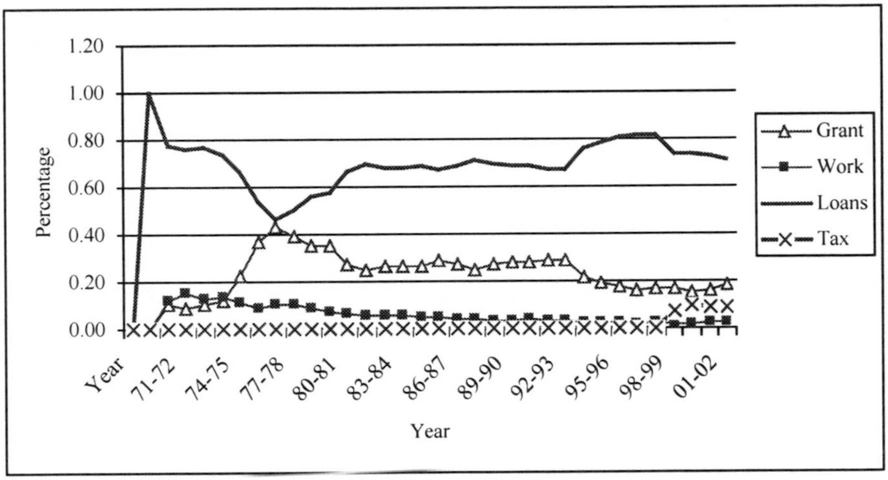

Source: College Board 2002

Table 2 illustrates changes (in millions of *current dollars*) in aid awarded to students during the past decade. Student loan volume soared following the 1992 amendments, which extended borrowing eligibility to middle and upper income groups. Federal student loans currently cover more than 68% of all student aid, compared to 40% in 1980, and 30% in 1970 (College Board 2000b). Since the inception of the federal education loan programme in the mid-1960s, students and their parents have borrowed more than $300 billion to finance the cost of college.

Table 3 summarises the substantial increases in average loan indebtedness occurring from 1992–93 to 1995–96.

Funding for merit-based programmes (grants and scholarships awarded based on academic criteria regardless of the student/family's ability to pay) also increased by 336% in real dollars from 1993 to 2000 (Advisory Committee on Student Financial Assistance 2001). By fall 1998, 13 states offered scholarships based on merit patterned after Georgia's HOPE Scholarship Program, which awards in-state students, who have at least a B average, their full tuition and fees at a public campus, or $3000 at a private campus in state regardless of family income. On average nationwide, 15 per cent of state aid awards currently are *not* based on need (National Center for Education Statistics 2001b). Such programmes are as much concerned with keeping higher performing students within their home state as with making higher education affordable (Schmidt 1999).

Concomitantly, the emphasis on merit-based aid also has increased at the institutional level, where the average grant for middle income students now exceeds that for low income students at private institutions (Advisory Committee on Student Financial Assistance 2001). The shift in federal student aid policy toward expanding eligibility to the middle class has been gradual but relentless over the last two decades (Spencer 1999). Nothing has exemplified that trend better than the federal HOPE Scholarship Program.

Table 2. Federal aid (in millions) used to finance postsecondary education expenses in current dollars 1992–93 to 2002–03

Programmes	1992/93	1993/94	1995/96	1997/98	1999/00	2000/01	2001/02	2002/03
Grants								
Pell Grants	6,176	5,654	5,472	6,331	7,208	7,956	9,975	11,716
SEOG	580	583	583	583	619	631	691	725
LEAP	71	72	64	50	25	37	46	66
Veterans	1,037	1,192	1,303	1,347	1,491	1,644	2,026	2,200
Military	393	405	438	463	534	559	638	811
Other Grants	162	167	230	233	248	279	290	309
Subtotal	8,419	8,074	8,089	9,006	10,125	11,106	13,665	15,826
Federal Work Study	780	771	764	906	917	939	1,032	1,218
Loans								
Perkins Loans	892	919	1,029	1,062	1,101	1,144	1,239	1,265
Subsidised Stafford	10,937	14,155	16,476	18,112	18,109	18,532	19,894	22,384
Unsubsidised Stafford	323	2,024	8,743	11,699	14,008	15,280	17,270	19,936
Plus	1,279	1,529	2,408	3,182	3,816	4,200	4,669	5,393
SLS	2,375	3,469						
Income Contingent Loans	5							
Other Loans	411	456	325	210	106	108	110	110
Subtotal	16,222	22,551	28,981	34,264	37,140	39,265	43,183	49,088
Education Tax Credits					4,772	4,851	5,205	5,437
Total Federal Aid	25,421	31,397	37,833	44,176	52,955	56,161	63,086	71,569

Source: College Board 2003

Table 3. Average loan indebtedness per student

Stafford Student Loans	1992–93	1995–96
Public 4-year Institutions	$7,400	$11,950
Private 4-year Institutions	$10,190	$14,290

Source: National Center for Education Statistics 1995, 1997

The purpose of the 1972 reform was to reduce the importance of family income as a determinant of who attended college and to increase the number of college-educated citizens. Figure 5 reports moderate success in attaining these objectives when looking at degree attainment.

Figure 5. Bachelors degree attainment by age 24 by family income quartiles (1970–2000)

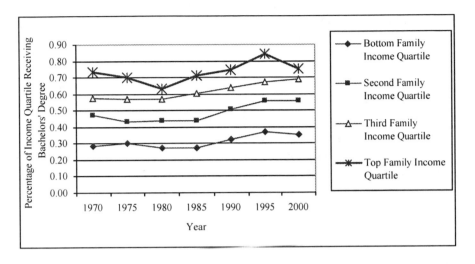

Source: Mortenson 2001

Again the evidence is mixed. The percentage of individuals from all family income levels receiving a bachelors degree increased, but the differences remained relatively constant. While the differences in proportions earning a degree had narrowed slightly by 2000, the results are less than those who sponsored the reform hoped. These results reflect in part the high numbers of poor and minority students who have chosen or been required to matriculate in community colleges. Transfer rates and degree achievement remain low for those starting in community colleges when compared to those who begin college in a baccalaureate degree-granting institution.

5. STATE VARIATIONS

We began this chapter by noting that higher education is a state responsibility in the US. While we report averages for the nation, these results conceal important variations produced by the unique circumstances of individual states. Delving very deeply into these differences is beyond the scope of this chapter, but selected examples help to underscore the complex environment within which judgments must be made about the answers to the three basic questions raised by Cerych and Sabatier (Cerych and Sabatier 1986).

State approaches in the US add to or subtract from the impact of federal higher education policy. Each state approach has weaknesses as well as strengths. The National Center for Public Policy in Higher Education developed a report card for comparing performance across state systems along five dimensions (National Center for Public Policy and Higher Education 2001). Three are arguably related to the access and opportunity reform:

1) • *Affordability* refers to the ability of families to pay for higher education (the family share, after financial aid, of higher education cost), state strategies to promote affordability, and the degree to which students rely on loans to finance their education.

2) • *Participation* is the extent to which young adults and working-age adults enrol in postsecondary programmes in their state.

3) • *Completion* involves the proportion of first-year college and university students who return for their second year and who complete their certificate or degree programme in a timely manner.

In the following discussion, we use the National Center's sub-categories for three of these report card measures to provide examples of how state policy interacts with federal policy to produce differing outcomes among these four states.

5.1. Affordability

Table 4 compares California, New Jersey, New Mexico and New York on the six variables used in awarding the affordability grade. Raw scores on each variable have been converted to a relative score that in theory can range from 0 to 100. Higher scores indicate better performance.

Table 4. Affordability

State	Family ability to pay costs of attending			Need-based financial aid	Low priced colleges	Low student debt
	Comm Coll	Public 4-Yr	Private 4-Yr			
California	66	62	42	35	215	71
New Jersey	75	67	54	100	50	86
New Mexico	91	72	46	26	100	91
New York	48	54	36	87	26	71

The impact of federal programmes shows most clearly in low student debt, the variable that is most influenced by need-based student assistance across all states. The state systems in California and New Mexico have historically followed a low-tuition access strategy. In contrast, New Jersey and New York have emphasised need-based student aid. New York alone awards nearly 1 billion dollars every year and guarantees that every low income student will receive an award equal to the tuition of the public university attended. These grants do not affect student eligibility for Pell grants, which are in addition to the state aid. New Mexico uses a combination of low tuition and scholarships (funded by lottery proceeds) available to every student who attends a public institution and achieves and maintains very modest academic performance to achieve the lowest level of student debt. New Jersey is close behind because of an extensive need-based student assistance programme.

5.2. Participation

Table 5 compares participation for the four states. Participation in some form of higher education does not vary that much across the states suggesting that the federal reform has had a significant levelling effect. At the same time, the impact of state policies can be seen as well. The three states that do best on the high school to college going rate all have strong programmes of need-based student assistance. By contrast, New Mexico relies on assistance awarded primarily on the basis of academic performance. In fairness, New Mexico is also a very large, sparsely populated state with the nation's highest concentration of American Indians living on reservations. Distances and demographics affect the enrolment of young adults in that state. Persistence as well as initial enrolments affect participation rates. New Jersey and New York, which rely heavily on need-based student aid, perform least well on the enrolment of working-age adults because tuitions in public institutions are higher than in California and New Mexico and because their need-based assistance programmes focus primarily on full-time students.

Table 5. Participation

State	HS graduates going directly to college (%)	HS freshmen enrolling in college within 4 years in any state (%): 1998	18–24 year olds enrolling in college (%): 1998–2000	25–49 year olds enrolled part-time in some type of post-secondary education (%): 1999–2000	Average of all scores
New Jersey	63.60	53.8	41.5	3.2	40.5
New York	63.90	43.5	37.4	3.4	37.0
New Mexico	58.90	37.3	29.8	6.0	33.0
California	47.70	34.5	35.9	4.9	30.7

5.3. Completion

Table 6 reports completion rates across the four states. New York outperforms the other states in the proportion of students earning bachelors degrees in 2002 as a proportion of the number of first-time freshman enrolled in four- and two-year degree granting higher education institutions in 1996. The lagged graduation rate measures system productivity in the award of bachelors degrees regardless of the type of institution where students begin. New Jersey also does well on this measure in part because of the emphasis placed by the two states on need-based aid for full-time students and to the high proportion of undergraduate students who attend independent institutions from which they are more likely to graduate. California forces nearly 67 per cent of its first-time college students to attend community colleges and as a result does not do nearly as well in the lagged degree completion category because of low graduation and transfer rates from community colleges. Lower performing New Mexico funds its institutions through a formula that encourages competition for enrolments, but does not address the issue of graduation.

The other three states have either divorced funding from enrolments entirely for baccalaureate institutions or administer state funding in a way that takes into account the readiness of students who are admitted to attempt college work as well as the number who complete. The California Master Plan for Higher Education requires students who are not initially eligible to attend a university to graduate from a community college to attain eligibility, an arrangement that helps bolster that state's associate degree graduation rate.

Table 6. Completion

State	Lagged grad rate %	Assoc 3yr grad rate %	Bach 6yr grad rate %	Average score %
California	47.3	44.00	59.20	0.502
New York	64.9	27.20	54.50	0.489
New Jersey	61.8	13.10	60.30	0.451
New Mexico	51.6	12.90	40.90	0.351

6. UNANTICIPATED DEVELOPMENTS

In the previous sections of this chapter we summarised evidence about the impact of policy reforms following passage of the Higher Education Amendments of 1972. In this section, we focus on some of the developments that have accompanied the implementation process that probably were not anticipated by those who supported the original legislation.

6.1. Financial Aid Abuses, Quality Concerns and Accountability Initiatives

The end of the 1980s and the early 1990s brought reports of scandals, fraud and abuse in student aid programmes. Thousands of proprietary (for profit) institutions, whose students had been eligible for federal student aid since 1972, emerged or expanded over the following years. Many of these institutions were criticised as being more interested in making money than in educating students, and many of the abuses to the aid programmes were attributed to this sector. High student loan default rates signalled that graduates were not getting jobs that provided sufficient compensation to repay their student loans, calling into question the quality of the education they had received. Institutions were also charged with illegally siphoning off dollars from the Pell grant programme, suggesting a weakness in the ability of the student aid systems to police against fraud.

The 1989 Budget Reconciliation Act set a 'default trigger' that restricted institutions with default rates over 30 per cent from participating in the federal student aid programmes. This meant that students who chose to attend those institutions would not be eligible for the federal student aid on which most proprietary institutions relied heavily (Harrison 1995). The 'Student Right to Know Act of 1990' set the government on a path to hold institutions accountable by means of information disclosure requirements. If federal lawmakers could not legislate the abuses out of existence, forcing disclosure of data to the public would at least in theory allow for informed decision making when prospective students were choosing which institutions to attend. Congress also placed the default issue on the agenda for the upcoming reauthorisation of the higher education bill so that the loan default discussion could take place within the broader context of all higher education funding programmes.

The Higher Education Amendments of 1992 included a series of modifications aimed at increasing oversight of the student aid programmes and higher education institutions. First, the legislation built on the idea behind the 'Student Right to Know Act of 1990' which had required institutions to disclose information to students in regard to both campus safety and the athletic programmes on campus. The 1992 legislation required institutions to report information such as college costs, additional campus safety information and student aid availability. The law also included provisions that set lower default rate triggers and called for more vigilant enforcement to rid the student aid system of schools that were not offering a quality education. Finally, the bill greatly enhanced the accrediting and auditing infrastructure in place to oversee higher education, and attempted to involve the states in the auditing process, an initiative that met with great resistance from the higher education community and was subsequently dropped when Republicans gained control of Congress (Congressional Record 1992a).

The federal changes had significant impact on accrediting agencies, which were required to devise outcome standards that would allow them to assess institutional quality and performance. Such standards, according to the law, should measure graduation and completion rates, performance on state licensure exams, job placement and other comparable indicators. Institutions underwent a 'programme review' to show they were in compliance in administering federal student aid programmes. Additionally, institutions were required to go through an annual (as opposed to biannual) audit that measured fiscal soundness.

The goals of the 1992 changes were realised at least in regard to ridding the higher education system of schools that had high numbers of student loan defaulters. By the end of the decade, there were 1500 fewer institutions in the higher education system. These 1500 institutions were primarily proprietary, for-profit institutions that provided training programmes that lasted one to two years. The default rate triggers rendered them and their students ineligible for federal aid, and they were forced to shut their doors.

In 1996, the Office of Inspector General testified before Congress that there were improvements in the areas in which Congress had legislated and that with the new standards of 1992, they were better able to measure success with respect to student achievement (US Department of Education Inspector General 1996). Also in 1996, the General Accounting Office (GAO) reported to Congress that abuses by proprietary schools had lessened; however, there were still ongoing concerns about the ability of proprietary school students to get jobs (US General Accounting Office 1996).

6.2. Cost Increases

From 1980 onward, college costs outpaced growth in median household income and increases in the cost of consumer goods. Even though studies were inconclusive, many policy makers came to believe that what they saw as disproportional increases in college costs were fuelled by increases in student financial assistance entitlements. The federal government with no constitutional control over postsecondary education has few viable options for controlling costs beyond the threat of shutting aid off for students at institutions where costs rise too precipitously. The government has yet to tie any sort of cost controls to an institution's eligibility to receive aid.

In 1992, Congress created a National Commission on the Cost of Higher Education that was responsible for conducting a two-year study and making recommendations for long-term restructuring of higher education (Congressional Record 1992b) an action that sent ripples through the higher education establishment. The National Commission's study would eventually reveal that attendance at the majority of colleges in the United States was in fact affordable (National Commission on the Cost of Higher Education 1998). In 1996, Congress authorised a Commission on College Costs to conduct a full analysis of college pricing structures, aid available and the notion of college costs (Congressional Record 1996).

The Commission's report was released in 1997, but the first version did not give the legislators (who were seeking ammunition to confront the higher education system) the data they sought. The legislators, in confidence, asked the Commission to do some rewriting and come up with different answers. The higher education community heard about this and the report's credibility suffered. The Commission's final report showed no dramatic crisis and noted that, except for certain institutions, the cost of college across the system was reasonable.

Members of Congress who called for the commission did not agree with recommendations that focused primarily on information disclosure and better understanding of what comprises the costs of a college education (National Commission on the Cost of Higher Education 1998). The final Higher Education Amendments of 1998 included legislation to hold colleges and universities accountable for tuition increases by requiring them to develop clear standards for reporting college costs and prices to students (Congressional Record 1998).

The 1998 amendments greatly expanded the data that institutions were required to report. Nevertheless, the higher education community saw the new requirements in a positive light, especially when contrasted with the alternative of price controls. Unfortunately, the amendments did little to contain costs, which continued to rise about five per cent annually (College Board 2000a). At the beginning of 2000, Congress held another series of hearings, but no new rules or legislation were forthcoming. The government continues to rely on access to information as a tool that students and families will hopefully use to make sound decisions about their investment in higher education. As this chapter is written, there is once again a movement in Congress to penalise institutions that raise tuition costs faster than increases in price indices. The discussion occurs in a context of draconian cuts to institutional budgets by beleaguered state legislatures and projected tuition increases of 30 per cent or higher.

6.3. Guaranteed Loans and National Service

Prior to 1992, federally guaranteed student loans were disbursed by private banks and guarantors, who relied on the government to 'back' the loans. A pilot programme was initiated in the 1992 Higher Education Amendments that put the government in the programme as a direct lender, thus eliminating the need for private lenders as well as the money the government paid to them. Bankers, understandably, mobilised to defeat or limit this option. The government programme also provided borrower repayment flexibility, a concept crucial to Clinton's national service plan.

Direct lending was designed to help moderate income families who had to rely extensively on loans by giving them borrower advantages. But, direct lending also required large system design changes – a new office, a new delivery system and a management structure. Direct lending also brought the Federal Department of Education into direct contact with student borrowers, not a typical relationship.

Political manoeuvring to win approval for Clinton's national service programme forced a direct lending programme still in its pilot stage with little chance of being fully implemented, into a full-fledged but inadequately conceived lending programme with significant implementation problems. Ironically, the unintended consequences of the direct lending programme were more significant than those intended. Loan repayment flexibility helped a number of students who would otherwise have defaulted on their loans. The new programme also provided a host of borrower benefits in terms of reduced interest rates due to competition between the federal government and traditional lenders who had to make their rates competitive to keep the business of the students. Of course, the government in turn had to offer the same benefits as private lenders.

7. CONCLUSION

We have traced the origins and evolution of the 1972 access and opportunity reform in the US outlining the official goals of the original legislation and providing data to show the outcomes of this reform over time. The intent of Congress in adopting the 1972 amendments was to guarantee low income, disadvantaged students the financial assistance they needed to attend any higher education institution that would admit them. This focus on promoting opportunity, achieving equity and providing affordable access through directing resources to low income families was evident in funding trends until the 1990s. During that decade, funding decisions significantly altered the balance toward affordability and choice for middle income students. As one example, both Republican and Democratic contenders in the presidential campaign of 2000 adopted a higher education agenda that focused on expanding tax benefits rather than need-based assistance. While programmes to help needy students also grew during the past decade, the expansion of eligibility parameters for

Pell grants and loan programmes, as well as a new tax package, signalled a clear shift of priorities toward helping middle income families.

At the turn of the century, there were a number of debates about the federal investment in higher education and whether it was enough to make a difference in the lives of low income families. As resources shifted away from the need-based programmes, the American higher education system showed signs of evolving into a two-tier system. Moderate income families were significantly more likely to attend elite institutions, while poorer students were increasingly concentrated in community colleges and public four-year institutions with low selectivity. Increasing college costs, declining state resources and enrolment management policies requiring most lower income and minority students to begin in community colleges all contributed to the trend. Low graduation and transfer rates from open-access or less selective institutions added to the degree of stratification.

The two-system phenomenon is also due to the lack of federal investment and intervention in K-12 education. Entire sectors – typically poor urban and rural areas – receive poor education and have few opportunities from the outset, and students from these areas stand little chance of being prepared financially or academically for postsecondary education. While families from the suburbs appear advantaged on both fronts, they are now the focus of much of the federal investment in resources. Given there are more people in the middle class in the US and, even more important, more who vote, it is not surprising that the 1972 access and opportunity reforms over time have been transformed into initiatives that offer more for the middle class than for the original targets.

It would, however, be misleading to conclude without noting that the US federal government, despite changes in party control of Congress and the White House, has for more than thirty years maintained a fundamental commitment to helping the most needy attend college. Clearly, there is within the US a widely shared consensus that the future of American society is inextricably linked to keeping the doors of higher education open to everyone who can benefit from the opportunity. Indeed, the argument is now shifting in the country as a whole and especially in California from a focus on access to a concern about access to the entire range of institutions that make up the US higher education scene (Gumport and Zemsky 2003).

NOTES

[1] LEAP was enacted in 1998 and replaced the SSIG programme.
[2] Figures are created based on GAO data taken from 1999–2000 NPSAS Data.

REFERENCES

Advisory Commission on Intergovernmental Relations. *The Federal Role in the Federal System: The Dynamics of Growth.* Washington, DC: Commission Report, 1981.

Advisory Committee on Student Financial Assistance. *Access Denied: Restoring the Nation's Commitment to Equal Education Opportunity.* A Report to the Congress of the United States. Washington, DC, 2001.

Brademas, J. and L.P. Brown. *The Politics of Education: Conflict and Consensus on Capitol Hill.* Norman, OK: University of Oklahoma Press, 1987.

Cerych, L. and P. Sabatier. *Great Expectations and Mixed Performance: The Implementation of Higher Education Reforms in Europe.* Stoke-on-Trent: Trentham Books, 1986.

College Board. *Trends in College Pricing.* New York: College Board, 2000a.

College Board. *Trends in Student Aid* (No. 989898). Washington, DC: College Board, 2000b.

College Board. *Trends in Student Aid.* Washington, DC: College Board, 2002.

College Board. *Trends in Student Aid.* New York: College Board, 2003, http://www.collegeboard.com.

Congressional Quarterly Almanac, vol. 21. Washington, DC: Congressional Quarterly, 1965.

Congressional Quarterly Almanac, vol. 28. Washington, DC: Congressional Quarterly, 1972.

Congressional Quarterly Almanac, vol. 34. Washington, DC: Congressional Quarterly, 1978.

Congressional Record. *Higher Education Amendments of 1992.* US House of Representatives Deliberations. Washington, DC: Cong. Rec, 1992a.

Congressional Record. *Higher Education Amendments of 1992: Conference Report.* US Senate Deliberations. Washington, DC: Cong. Rec, 1992b.

Congressional Record. *College Costs Skyrocket.* US House of Representatives, Hon. Joseph P. Kennedy II. Washington, DC: Cong. Rec, 1996.

Congressional Record. *Highlights of the Higher Education Amendments of 1998.* US House of Representatives Deliberations. Washington, DC: Cong. Rec, 1998.

Doyle, D.P. and T.W. Hartle. "Student-aid Muddle." *Atlantic* 17 (1986): 18–10, 54–56.

Gerald, D.E. and W.J. Hussar. *Projections of Education Statistics to 2010* (No. 065-000-01316-9). Washington, DC: National Center for Education Statistics, 2000.

Gladieux, L.E. and T.R. Wolanin. *Congress and the Colleges.* Lexington, MA: D.C. Heath, 1976.

Gumport, P.J. and R. Zemsky. "Drawing New Maps for a Changing Enterprise." *Change* 35.4 (2003): 32.

Hansen, L. and J.O. Stampen. "Economics and Financing of Higher Education: The Tension Between Quality and Equity." In Altbach, P.G., R.O. Berdahl and P.G. Gumport (eds). *Higher Education in American Society.* 3rd edn. Amherst, NY: Prometheus Books, 1994, 101–125.

Harrison, M. "Default in Guaranteed Student Loan Programs." *Journal of Student Financial Aid* 25.2 (1995): 25–41.

Ikenberry, S.O. and T.W. Hartle. *Where We Have Been and Where We Are Going: American Higher Education and Public Policy.* Washington, DC: American Council on Education, 2000.

McGuiness, A.C. "The Federal Government and Postsecondary Education." In Gumport, P.J. (ed.). *Higher Education in American Society.* Buffalo, NY: Prometheus Books 1981, 157–179.

Mortenson, T.G. *Bachelors Degree Attainment by Age 24 by Family Income Quartiles, 1970–2000.* Data from Census Bureau, 2001.

National Center for Education Statistics. *National Postsecondary Student Aid Study* (Report 95365). Washington, DC: US Department of Education, 1995.

National Center for Education Statistics. *National Postsecondary Student Aid Study* (Report 98073). Washington, DC: US Department of Education, 1997.

National Center for Education Statistics. *State Comparisons of Education Statistics: 1969–70 to 1996–97.* Washington, DC: US Department of Education, 1998.

National Center for Education Statistics. *Digest of Education Statistics 2000.* Washington, DC: US Department of Education, 2000.

National Center for Education Statistics. *The Condition of Education.* Washington, DC: US Department of Education, 2001a.

National Center for Education Statistics. *Federal Support for Education: Fiscal Years 1980 to 2001* (No. NCES 2002–129). Washington, DC: US Department of Education, Office of Educational Research and Improvement, 2001b.

National Center for Public Policy and Higher Education. *Measuring Up 2000: The State by State Report Card for Higher Education.* San Jose, California: National Center for Public Policy and Higher Education, 2001.

National Commission on the Cost of Higher Education. *Straight Talk About College Costs and Prices: Report of the National Commission on College Costs.* Washington, DC, 1998.

Parsons, M. *Power and Politics – Federal Higher Education Policy Making in the 1990s.* Albany: State University of New York Press, 1997.

Prisco, A., A.D. Hurley, T.C. Carton and R.C. Richardson. *Federal Policies and Higher Education in the United States.* New York: AIHEPS, 2002, http://www.nyu.edu/iesp/aiheps/research.html.

Riley, R. Remarks as Prepared for Delivery by US Secretary of Education Richard W. Riley. Washington, DC, 2001.

Rivlin, A.M. *The Role of the Federal Government in Financing Higher Education, vol. XII.* Washington, DC: Brookings Institution, 1961.

Schmidt, P. "A State Transforms Colleges with Performance Funding." *Chronicle of Higher Education* 45.43 (1999): 26–29.

Spencer, A.C. "The New Politics of Higher Education." In King, J.E. (ed.). *Financing a College Education: How It Works, How It's Changing.* Phoenix: The Oryx Press, 1999.

US Census Bureau. *Facts for Features: Back to School.* 2002, http://www.census.gov/Press-Release/www/2002/cb02ff12.html.

US Department of Education Inspector General. *Gatekeeping in the Student Financial Assistance Programs: Hearing Before the Subcommittee on Government Reform and Oversight.* Washington, DC, 1996.

US General Accounting Office. *Higher Education: Ensuring Quality Education From Proprietary Institutions* (No. GAO/T-HEHS-96-158). Washington, DC, 1996.

US General Accounting Office. *Student Aid and Tax Benefits* (No. GAO-02-751). Washington, DC, 2002.

SUSAN MARTON

IMPLEMENTING THE TRIPLE HELIX: THE ACADEMIC RESPONSE TO CHANGING UNIVERSITY–INDUSTRY–GOVERNMENT RELATIONS IN SWEDEN[1]

1. BACKGROUND

In the spring of 1993, the Swedish Parliament passed the Research for Knowledge and Progress bill. Using government funds amassed from the Wage Earners' Funds policy, approximately 15 billion SEK[2] were allocated as start-up capital to a number of newly created research foundations. The Swedish government outlined two major priorities for these research foundations: to concentrate research investments in 'strategic areas'; and to strengthen the cooperation between universities and business, and between universities and society in general. The government view at the time, as expressed in the bill to parliament, was that these funds would represent an extra injection into Swedish research funding in relation to direct state appropriations to university faculties (Marton 2000: 74).

The largest and most important foundations resulting from this decision include: 1) SSF, Foundation for Strategic Research (6 billion SEK start-up capital); 2) KK, Foundation for Knowledge and Competence Development (3.6 billion SEK); 3) MISTRA, Foundation for Strategic Environmental Research (2.5 billion SEK); 4) STINT, Foundation for International Cooperation in Research and Higher Education (1 billion SEK); and 5) Vårdal, Foundation for Health Care and Allergy Research (520 million SEK). In addition, the Bank of Sweden Tercentenary Foundation was awarded 1.5 billion SEK to start the 'Kulturvetenskapliga donationen' primarily for the benefit of the humanities.

Towards the end of the 1990s, the yearly support from these new foundations was reaching six to seven per cent of total research and research education income for Swedish universities. Support from older, private foundations (such as the Cancer Fund, Knut and Alice Wallenberg Foundation) reached ten per cent. Government agencies (such as Vinnova, FAS and Formas)[3] along with the new Swedish Research Council (Vetenskapsrådet) each contributed approximately ten per cent. Support from Swedish and foreign companies measured about four to five per cent (Sandström and Hällsten 2003: 1). Thus one can understand that by the start

Å. Gornitzka et al. (eds.), Reform and Change in Higher Education, 325-342.

of the new millennium, the government 'injection' of new foundation funds from 1993 was quite significant in the total financing package.

Such financing developments have contributed to the hotly debated topic of the autonomy of researchers in Sweden. Although an empirical investigation of this debate is beyond the task presented here, one should nevertheless be aware that such a debate exists (see e.g. Marton 2000; Benner 2001, 2002; Sandström 2002). Given the fact the funds available from the Swedish Research Council (Vetenskapsrådet) decreased (where funding decisions are made by a peer-review system) combined with the fact that direct allocations from the state to university faculties have also barely remained steady and at times decreased (while the number of doctoral students has increased by 18%),[4] the situation has worsened in recent years. Hällsten and Sandström (2002: 83) state that collegial, peer-reviewed research funds have decreased from 68% in 1993–94 to 55% in 2000 of the total income for research and research education. This leads them to conclude that no matter how one counts, "the results show a clear and precise downturn for 'researcher steered' [forskarstyrda in Swedish] funds. All indications show that the space for curiosity-driven research is shrinking" (Hällsten and Sandström 2002: 83).

2. THEORETICAL CONSIDERATIONS

2.1. The Triple Helix Connection

As noticed in the background section to this chapter, the Swedish government's priorities in the Research for Knowledge and Progress bill highlighted the three components captured by the 'Triple Helix' thesis: university–industry–government. As Etzkowitz and Leydesdorff (2000: 109) explain, "the Triple Helix thesis states that the university can play an enhanced role in innovation in increasingly knowledge-based societies". Instead of the firm having the central role in innovation, the focus instead is on "the network overlay of communications and expectations that reshape the institutional arrangements among universities, industries, and governmental agencies" (Etzkowitz and Leydesdorff 2000: 109). Thus, the thesis emphasises the role of the university in economic development and the institutional arrangements created between the three spheres of university, industry and government in order to generate economic growth and social transformation (Etzkowitz and Leydesdorff 2000: 118–119).

According to Etzkowitz and Leydesdorff (2000: 112), most countries are exhibiting characteristics of the Triple Helix, having a common objective of trying to realise an innovative environment "consisting of university spin-off firms, tri-lateral initiatives for knowledge-based economic development, and strategic alliances among firms (large and small, operating in different areas, and with different levels of technology), government labs, and academic research groups".

But how does the Triple Helix thesis relate to another well-known model for describing the recent changes taking place in research production and organisation, that of the shift from Mode 1 to Mode 2 knowledge production? Mode 1 emphasises the discipline as the centre of knowledge production whereas in Mode 2, there is a shift to a context of application and entrepreneurship (Gibbons et al. 1994). Etzkowitz and Leydesdorff (2000: 119) argue that, "When one opens the black-box [of the Triple Helix] one finds Mode 1 within Mode 2, and Mode 2 within Mode 1. The system is neither integrated nor completely differentiated, but it performs on the edges of fractional differentiations and local integrations".

Yet in order to evaluate this system, researchers have recently argued that a more intricate description of the Triple Helix system is warranted (Kaukonen and Nieminen 1999; Benner and Sandström 2000). A problem with the Triple Helix thesis, as explained by Benner and Sandström, is that it suggests "that the performance and regulation of university research is undergoing a change that will erode the organizational and normative boundaries of the university system". They question whether a new institutional order has developed by the integration of political, industrial and academic interests and whether all three spheres of the Triple Helix "have merged within the new organizational field ('knowledge-based economy') guided by a norm system stressing the importance of techno-economic renewal and market-determined success" (Benner and Sandström 2000: 292). The Triple Helix thesis would benefit from a "more specified model of the interplay between actors, organizations and institutions in this transition" (Benner and Sandström 2000: 292). Kaukonen and Nieminen (1999: 178) share this critique, stating that, "The development anticipated by the Triple Helix concept is not a simultaneous or even process in the whole disciplinary matrix". As they explain, by using funding statistics, the disciplines are able to be located in their macro-level network of actors, but not much can be said about the content of relationships between different actors.

This study will however attempt to do just that – to say something about the content of the relationships between the different actors by focusing primarily on two organisations under change: the university and its faculties.

2.2. Choice of Implementation Framework

In *Great Expectations and Mixed Performance*, Cerych and Sabatier focused their analysis on the original policy goals, how these compared with policy outcomes, and what factors contributed to or inhibited attainment of the goals along the way. With such an analytical framework, they attempted to evaluate whether there was a 'valid causal theory' which would provide officials responsible for programmes with "critical linkages to make possible the attainment of objectives" (Cerych and Sabatier 1986: 15). As Åse Gornitzka (in this volume) has pointed out, "The central characteristic for these kinds of studies was the belief that implementation processes could be centrally controlled and steered if just the number of relevant variables and their interconnectedness were disclosed".

Such a belief does not underline the research being presented in this chapter. Instead, the approach undertaken here relates more to a bottom-up approach where researchers ask questions about "how actors go about solving societal problems in different areas and see what role government measures play in that" (Gornitzka in this volume). There is no overarching aim in the study presented here to analyse policy success or failure according to a set of original policy or programme goals as in the Cerych and Sabatier study. Rather the theoretical framework adopted here finds its starting points in organisational theory literature with a new institutionalist base. Implementation in this case is viewed more as an organic and informal process, with actor constellations spontaneously arising from this process, and with the element of negotiation playing a strong role (Gornitzka in this volume).

Using DiMaggio and Powell's new institutional perspective on the Triple Helix processes, it can be argued that the three fields of the Triple Helix develop through a process of 'isomorphism' (Benner and Sandström 2000). As DiMaggio and Powell (1991: 66) explain, isomorphism occurs due to "forces pressing communities toward accommodation with the outside world". Under these pressures, the dissemination of routines, structures and norms of organisation results from coercive, normative and mimetic processes. Following Benner and Sandström's approach, the coercive forces in the university system are the criteria for resource allocation and the public regulation of the performance of research. The normative processes refer to the norms and values that regulate conduct within organisations – such as the collegial orientation of scientists and the procedures of peer review. The mimetic processes are expressed in the copying, by one organisation, of the daily routines of another, seen to be successful, organisation. This is exemplified by the way in which academics, research groups and universities deal with the pressure from outside sources (Benner and Sandström 2000: 292; see also Scott 1995).

The analysis in the case study presented below will pay particular attention to the three processes described above. First, how are universities and faculties responding to the coercive forces regarding resource allocation and public regulation? Second, are norms and values in conflict, and, if so, at what levels? To answer questions regarding the third process, that where universities and faculties attempt to copy successful organisations, a larger data set than that presented here would be necessary. However, within Göteborg University, the Faculty of Social Sciences is known for attracting high levels of external financing in comparison to the Faculty of Humanities. Thus a small investigation of mimetic processes is also possible.

3. RESEARCH ISSUE, RESEARCH DESIGN AND PURPOSE

This chapter will attempt to analyse in what way Swedish universities, and specifically university faculties, have responded to these changes in funding patterns described earlier in the background section. These changes are the underlying variable to this study. More specifically, the dependent variable can be defined as the university- and faculty-level response to the Triple Helix, which is operationalised by studying: a) views on and actions taken regarding changes in amounts and sources of funding; b) views on and steps taken towards multidisciplinarity; and c) views on and steps taken towards societal connections. The independent variables used to explain the responses of the university and the faculties are the new institutional processes outlined in the theoretical considerations (section 2.2). These processes are divided into coercive, normative and mimetic.

The goal of this chapter is to have an empirical base for comments regarding the relationships between the different actors in the process of implementing the Triple Helix. Furthermore, the chapter would like to contribute to the discussion of the Triple Helix thesis. Is there a new institutional arrangement between university–industry–government and, if so, is it based on a new norm system?

The research presented here is part of a larger, multidisciplinary team project established to investigate the role and influence of these new research foundations on Swedish research and on the Swedish higher education system in general. (The project's working name is 'Stiftelseprojektet 2004'.) Members of the team are currently working on separate knowledge areas (technology, natural sciences, medicine, social sciences and humanities) at seven institutions. Research results are to be published in the fall, 2004. In the case study presented here, the Faculty of Social Sciences and the Faculty of Humanities at Göteborg University will be studied between the years 1997 and 2002.

4. EMPIRICAL CASE

The empirical evidence for this chapter relies on data collected through the annual reports of Göteborg University, as well as the annual reports, activity reports, external evaluations and strategic plans of the boards for the Faculty of Social Sciences and the Faculty of Humanities. In the text below, the usage of the term *'faculty' should be read as a reference to the decision-making faculty 'board'*. (All documents have been translated from Swedish by the author.)

4.1. Göteborg University

Göteborg University dates back to 1891 when the university first operated as a private college. In 1954, with the combination of Göteborg College and Göteborg Medical College, university status was granted. The university expanded in 1967 with the opening of the School of Odontology and again in 1971, with the incorporation of the School of Economics and Commercial Law. Today Göteborg University has more than 40,000 students of which 2580 are PhD candidates. Göteborg University has approximately 5100 employees, consisting of 2400 academic staff (410 of these are professors) and 1700 technical/administrative staff.

4.1.1. The Funding Situation
In 1997, the university's view towards external funding was positive and it is clearly expressed that increasing the level of externally financed activities has been a goal of the university in recent years. It is recognised that funds from the research councils have decreased, but the effect is compensated for by the increase in other types of external funds. In particular, the annual report highlights funds from the Foundation for Strategic Research (SSF) and from the Foundation for Health Care and Allergy Research. At the faculty level, notice is given to the Faculty of Social Sciences and to the Humanities Faculty for having increased their external financing

approximately 30%, although from significantly different starting points (*Göteborgs universitet årsredovisning* 1997).

By 1998, Göteborg University recognised that the recent increases in external financing were not without problems. For the entire university, external financing represented 47% of total funds available for research and research education, but the variation between faculties was quite large. At faculties where external funds dominated, discussions were underway regarding the proper balance between internally and externally initiated research. Furthermore, it was recognised that the demands from external financers for their funding to be matched with university funds were causing further restrictions in the use of state-appropriated funds to the faculties (*Göteborgs universitet årsredovisning* 1998). These changing funding patterns were contributing to difficulties in university-wide planning and budgeting work and, by 2000, Göteborg University recognised that the internal follow-up of economic developments must be improved. New requirements for quarterly economic reports were enacted (*Göteborgs universitet årsredovisning* 2000).

The problems relating to these changing funding patterns appear to have peaked in 2002. In the annual report, it was clearly stated that "An increase in state appropriations to research is necessary to prevent the impoverishing of the research connection to undergraduate education" (*Göteborgs universitet årsredovisning* 2002: 25). Furthermore, the effects of the changing funding patterns on academics was described in detail, such as:

> In order to maintain competence within their scientific area, teachers are having to take responsibility themselves for financing their research and development ... Projects with external financing set demands on the purpose of the research and the time conditions. To combine project research with teaching places high demands on teachers (*Göteborgs universitet årsredovisning* 2002: 25).

The data below illustrate the problem. In table 1, it can be seen that external financing is playing a larger role in the total picture of funds available for research and research education. The fact that increases in state appropriations to the faculties have been marginal (given an increasing cost structure at the universities and increases in student numbers) does not improve the situation.

Table 1. Göteborg University, external funds to state appropriations for research and research education, 1997–2002 (SEK thousands, current prices)

	1997	1998	1999	2000	2001	2002
External funds	696	695	738	753	849	892
State appropriations	724	786	798	799	827	875
Total	1420	1481	1536	1552	1676	1767
% Relation	49%	47%	48%	48%	51%	51%

Note: % Relation is percentage of external funds to total
Source: *Göteborgs universitet årsredovisning* 2001: 42, 45

4.1.2. The Emphasis on Multidisciplinary Research
By 2000, it was clear that multidisciplinary programmes were receiving increasing interest, evidenced by a university-sponsored investigation of the situation. The annual report highlighted the importance of the Göteborg Environmental Sciences Center (GMV). The centre was organised to incorporate all environmentally related teaching and research under one structure and represents a cooperation between Göteborg University and Chalmers University of Technology. Further intensification of the university's role in multidisciplinary research occurred in 2001 with the founding of a university 'scientific council' which would establish guidelines for 'matrix research'. In addition, a special unit for short-term research projects was established. One can read in the annual report that:

> With this [initiative] the university takes a thorough approach to the issue of multidisciplinary research, from both the researcher's perspective and from a more comprehensive perspective. The new organization challenges all faculties to increase cooperation between scientific boundaries (*Göteborgs universitet årsredovisning* 2001: 4).

In 2001, the Swedish government established 16 national 'research schools' with the task of increasing cooperation between different universities and colleges on basic research, and in a cross-department environment. Göteborg University agreed to be the host university for two such research schools, one in genomics and bioinformatics and the other in language technology.

Furthermore, with financial support and guidance from the Vårdal Foundation, Göteborg University (together with Lund University) was named host for the Vårdal Institute. Additional financing was provided by the regional government organisations 'Västra Götaland' and 'Skåne'. The Institute is to provide a national environment for research and development in the field of health care, with close collaboration with the local county and municipal authorities.

Although continuing to be emphasised, the Göteborg University policy toward the development of multidisciplinary programmes and centres appears to have taken a twist in 2002. To begin with, it is interesting to note that the terms used to describe these programmes are now a combination of both interdisciplinary ('tvärvetenskaplig') and multidisciplinary ('mångvetenskaplig') research (instead of just one of these terms as in the past), but no elaboration of what this means for the research programmes is evident. Second, the annual report states that the university board has decided that efforts to enhance these programmes, previously conducted at the university level, would now be primarily transferred to the faculties (*Göteborgs universitet årsredovisning* 2002: 27). There is no elaboration of why this is so.

4.1.3. The Societal Network Relations
In discussing cooperation with the surrounding society, the 1997 annual report referred to the university 'vision' document that explains that the university shall be 'an open university' – spreading knowledge and insights. In this regard, the university concentrated efforts on providing research information and research databases to the public. Communicating with local and regional businesses was made a priority and the university established a business advisory board. The university also took an active role in the commercialisation of research results by

establishing Göteborg University Holding Company. Not only were connections with business in focus, but also the municipalities around Göteborg and the local trade unions worked together to form a 'Regional Center for School Development' (financing for this initiative was provided by the National Agency for Education) (*Göteborgs universitet årsredovisning* 1997).

Throughout the late 1990s, new forms of cooperation with society were evident. Specifically, in the area of local museums, the university had been engaged in two large projects. For example, in 1998, an interdisciplinary project for education and research called 'Museion' began in cooperation with the new World Cultures Museum in Göteborg. In 2000, the National Science Center, 'Universeum' opened in Göteborg with much expert advice provided by members of the Faculty of Natural Science. In line with the university's goal to contribute to economic development, the Business School intensified its relationship with West-coast companies by starting a 'Partnership Program' for education and research. In addition, to assist in the start-up of companies and the commercialisation of research ideas, a unit was established (with primarily external funds) to provide researchers and students with advice on patent law, business development and business law.

4.2. The Faculty of Social Sciences

In 2002, approximately 4300 full-time undergraduate students and 263 PhD candidates studied at the Faculty of Social Sciences. On staff were 307 teachers and researchers, 99 faculty-financed doctoral students and 113 technical and administrative personnel. In 1999, the School of Economics and Commercial Law and the School of Education separated from the Social Sciences Faculty and established their own faculties. Currently, the faculty is comprised of nine departments, three research centres and one institute of public opinion.

4.2.1. The Funding Situation at the Social Sciences Faculty

As early as 1997, the faculty reports described the external funding situation as one of a 'balance problem'. The levels of external financing as a percentage of all funding for graduate education and research was approximately 54% in 1997. Basic research was seen as falling behind for more applied research activities such as investigations and evaluation studies. The hollowing of state appropriations to the faculty during the recent years had also contributed to the fact that vacant post-doc research positions were not filled (*Samhällsvetenkapliga fakultetsnämndens verksamhetsberättelse* 1997: 8). By 1999, the amount of post-doc positions had fallen 50% compared to the levels in 1995 (*Samhällsvetenkapliga fakultetsnämndens verksamhetsberättelse* 1999: 5). Every activity report between 1998 and 2000 continued to refer to this problem. The faculty clearly stated that the simplest solution to this problem was to "restore state appropriations to a level where every subject area involved in doctoral education has the possibility to hire at least one post-doc researcher" (*Samhällsvetenkapliga fakultetsnämndens verksamhetsberättelse* 1998: 4–5). In relating this problem to external funds, the report pointed out that:

Even if the proportions of external funding has increased and therewith the possibilities for the continuation of research financing, this can not completely replace the position of post-doc researcher [paid for by the faculty]. With a continuation of such developments, the system of recruiting positions financed through state appropriations is in threat of total collapse (*Samhällsvetenkapliga fakultetsnämndens verksamhetsberättelse* 1998: 8–9).

At the same time, it can be seen that these reports did not contain any comments for a strategy on how the faculty should handle these problems in the future. The strategic investments made by the faculty during the years 1997–99 were primarily in the areas of internationalisation and gender equality programmes. Yet during 1999, a Strategic Plan for the faculty was finalised.

The 1999 Strategic Plan began by recognising that the high level of external funds was an indication of confidence in the research carried out in the faculty from both the research world as well as other areas of society. Due to the increases in external financing, the number of PhD degrees could be increased. Yet the plan highlighted the seriousness of the financial situation, describing "a situation that is therefore completely unsustainable in the long-run" (*Strategisk plan för samhällsvetenskapliga fakultetsnämnden åren 2000–2002* 1999: 1). The Plan highlighted that the departments responded by not hiring post-doc researchers, and instead, post-docs worked on external projects with short-term contracts (*Strategisk plan för samhällsvetenskapliga fakultetsnämnden åren 2000–2002* 1999: 4).

At this point, the strategy was to "actively work for compensation against the hollowing of state appropriations" and to "effectively use resources in general, and to co-ordinate across department borders" (*Strategisk plan för samhällsvetenskapliga fakultetsnämnden åren 2000–2002* 1999: 4). This was seen as necessary in order to conduct basic research. But at the same time, the document stated that contacts with society must be furthered in order to discover new fields of research and to find cooperative partners and financers, and that, at a minimum, the level of external financing must be maintained. In addition, discussions must commence regarding eventual research profile areas. The Strategic Plan identified two measures for the faculty to accomplish: 1) research strategies up to the present time should be mapped and evaluated; and 2) the visibility of research should be improved through contacts and improved information (*Strategisk plan för samhällsvetenskapliga fakultetsnämnden åren 2000–2002* 1999: 12–13).

In this regard, the Strategic Plan highlighted the point that cooperation with surrounding society was a natural occurrence for a Social Sciences Faculty, and that "cooperation in a direct or an indirect form is an integrated part, not in the least [when considering] the stage of problem formulation" (*Strategisk plan för samhällsvetenskapliga fakultetsnämnden åren 2000–2002* 1999: 6). This was further developed with the following reflection, "Maybe the difference between 'steered' research and 'contract' research should be underlined in this context. The faculty takes the position naturally that researchers can answer the questions generated directly by the financer; however, the freedom in providing the answer, along with space for the free formulation of questions, must be protected" (*Strategisk plan för samhällsvetenskapliga fakultetsnämnden åren 2000–2002* 1999: 6). Yet the

Strategic Plan presented quite a confusing picture of what the real problem was. Later in the document, one could read:

> The all the more diffuse situation in regards to research financing – many sources with different principles for the awarding of resources – presents a threat against the collegial, critically reviewing, academic judgment system. It is of utmost importance to counteract this (*Strategisk plan för samhällsvetenskapliga fakultetsnämnden åren 2000–2002* 1999: 10).

The measure adopted in the Strategic Plan was that an external evaluation would be conducted.

The external evaluation was delivered in August 2000. The reviewers completely agreed with the faculty that the largest problem was that of decreased state appropriations and the growing dependence on external funding. Yet according to the reviewers, the faculty had not presented a strategy to meet these problems and the faculty's steering of research and research education had been relatively weak (Kristensen, Niemi and Åberg 2000: 19). Recognising that it was at the department level that initiatives for new projects were taken, the evaluators realised that the faculty played little role in the department's research and research education (especially when, for some departments, external funding provided more than 60% of the total available resources for research). The capacity of the faculty leadership to prioritise and re-direct resources was very limited, given that the state appropriations were directed towards paying primarily professors' salaries. The reviewers also pointed to the shrinking roll for discipline-oriented research, and agreed with the faculty that researchers were seeking money wherever it was to be found, thus contributing to the fragmentation of research environments with negative implications for the department's intellectual environment (Kristensen, Niemi and Åberg 2000: 25).

Furthermore, the reviewers addressed the issue of faculty leadership and its relation to Göteborg University. Although recognising that Göteborg University had a very decentralised management tradition, the reviewers suggested that the faculty should work on its image and roll in relation to the entire university. Accordingly, a more thorough and well-articulated argumentation for the usefulness and strengths of the faculty was needed. Given the political situation in Sweden, with a Minister of Education who believed that "Free research in competition is better than increased state appropriations", the reviewers questioned whether the faculty was prepared to handle the competition. The fact that almost all initiatives were at the department level was worrying to the investigators. It was suggested however that the departments consider more carefully what type of external funding was most beneficial for them. Support for research programmes and research schools, which increased the departments' ability to consolidate research in its priority areas, was seen as most advantageous.

The external reviewers recommended various measures, among them the following proposals for improvement: a) create a faculty research education board; b) strengthen connections and cooperation with other departments; c) strive to acquire external funding which supports disciplinary-based research and set aside faculty-level funds to support the writing of grant applications; d) create an incentive system to encourage researchers to apply for external funds; e) evaluate the strategic investments which have already taken place; and f) clarify the faculty's role in a strategic plan given that the existing management style is based on bottom-up principles (Kristensen, Niemi and Åberg 2000: 26, 30).

How did the faculty respond to the external evaluation? The main problem (i.e. that the Swedish government did not intend to increase the state's appropriations to the faculty) continued to be interpreted in the same way. Yet steps for better use of resources were taken, such as the appointment of a coordinating advisor for graduate education. Furthermore, the 2001 activity report mentioned that the faculty would carry out a thorough analysis of the model for the distribution of state appropriations from the faculty level to the departments. This is seen as especially important in light of the fact that some departments would not survive without constant reliance on external funds.

By 2002, very little progress had taken place on the measures outlined by the reviewers in the evaluation report. Under discussion were ways in which the faculty could support a further development of research and identify profile areas, but no concrete plan had been written. Neither had any steps been taken to provide incentives for writing grant applications, but the report did state that external funding "creates an undesired dependence, not in the least in the demands for the continuous search for research money to finance the activities" of the departments (*Samhällsvetenskapliga fakultetsnämdens verksamhetsberättelse* 2002: 17). By the end of 2002, external funds as a percentage of the total faculty funds available for research and research education was 56% (up 2% since 1997) and there was still no new model for the distribution of faculty funds to the departments.

4.2.2. The Emphasis on Multidisciplinarity at the Social Sciences Faculty

The activity reports describe a long tradition of multidisciplinary research through, for example, the Institute for Society, Opinion and Mass Media and through the research centres, such as the Center for European Research, Center for Research on the Public Sector and the Nordic Center for Media and Communication Research. During the time-frame of this study, a growing emphasis on multidisciplinary research was evidenced and the reporting of these activities covered more pages in the activity reports over time. In particular, the launching of the Vårdal Institute (for multidisciplinary health care research) and the Center for Handicap Research was cited, as well as the start in 2002 of the Institute for World Studies of Human Conditions.

4.2.3. The Societal Network Relations at the Social Sciences Faculty

There are many illustrations of connections with societal interests described in the activity reports. For example, the Göteborg-Region Municipal Association had a contract with the School of Public Administration with the purpose of strengthening research on the public sector as well as improving undergraduate education. In 1998, municipalities in the region financed two professorships in the School of Public Administration. Furthermore, the family which publishes the largest daily newspaper in the area, Göteborgs Posten, funded a professorship in journalism. In the 2002 report, two events were highlighted: a) the founding of the Vårdal Institute (see description above in section 4.1.2); and b) a new cooperation with the municipality of Göteborg for a 'Forum for Research on a Safe and Secure City', jointly conducted with Chalmers University of Technology (*Samhällsvetenskapliga fakultetsnämdens verksamhetsberättelse* 2001: 14–23).

4.3. The Faculty of Humanities

The Faculty of Humanities listed 4700 full-time undergraduate students and approximately 200 PhD candidates as enrolled during 2002. On staff were 243 teachers and researchers, 106 faculty-financed doctoral students and 93 technical and administrative personnel. At the time of writing, the faculty is comprised of 18 departments, three research centres[5] and one national research school (Graduate School of Language Technology).

4.3.1. The Funding Situation at the Humanities Faculty

In reviewing the funding situation at the Humanities Faculty, the starting point in 1997 was a very difficult period, with the faculty trying to recover from large budget deficits from previous years. Such a situation made the availability of funds for new strategic investments impossible, and the faculty focused instead on providing funds for its previous strategic commitments (*Humanistiska fakultetsnämnden årsredovisning* 1998: 12–14). A positive exception however was a large investment from Göteborg University's central administration in order to start an Institute for Swedish as a Second Language (under the Swedish Language Department). The task of the institute was to conduct development and research work regarding the Swedish language and teaching for immigrants. Within the budget of the institute, six peer-reviewed, interdisciplinary projects were selected for research financing. In addition, the National Agency for Schools financed three development projects (*Humanistiska fakultetsnämnden årsredovisning* 1998: 7).

The annual report was clear in stating the difficulties for conducting research. All research beyond that automatically included in professors' and doctoral students' positions was conducted almost entirely with external funds. The report pointed out that this type of research was not planned by the faculty, but was based on other factors such as the individual researcher's own special competencies and ability to write applications for grants. Even as early as 1998, the faculty report stated that "national competition for external funds will increase as a result of an increase in grant applications and that the amount of money available for distribution from the research councils has decreased" (*Humanistiska fakultetsnämnden årsredovisning* 1998: 15). The faculty actively tried to increase funds from external sources and began, in the budget year 1995–96, to implement a faculty model for the distribution of state appropriations, which included a plus factor for departments which attracted external funds. The result was positive, with external funds doubling between 1994–95 and 1997. For 1997, external funds as a percentage of total funds for research and doctoral education was 35% (*Humanistiska fakultetsnämnden årsredovisning* 1998: 15).

In 1999, the faculty published 'Research Strategies and Strategies for Knowledge Development at the Humanities Faculty 2001–2004'. The major problem outlined was the lack of financial resources for prioritised research areas. In addition, it was no longer possible to ensure that every subject area with graduate education would also have a post-doc research position financed by the faculty (*Forskningsstrategier och Strategier för Kunskapsutveckling vid Humanistiska Fakulteten 2001–2004* 1999: 1–4).

Thus the faculty identified six research profiles for the future and emphasised that the traditional division between the language sciences and the historical-philosophical sciences would not be maintained. Instead a broader perspective was necessary in order to create faculty-wide research environments and common graduate education courses (*Forskningsstrategier och Strategier för Kunskapsutveckling vid Humanistiska Fakulteten 2001–2004* 1999: 5).[6] Yet, the faculty recognised that it would need more state appropriations in order to plan for its own investments, stating that, "otherwise the situation can be one where one more or less must accept that the research profiles are steered by external funds. We are already now in a situation where some of our 'profiles' are involuntary" (*Forskningsstrategier och Strategier för Kunskapsutveckling vid Humanistiska Fakulteten 2001–2004* 1999: 6).

One year after this internal document was put in place, the external reviewers presented their evaluation report. An overview of the problems identified included: a) the lack of multidisciplinary initiatives; b) the lack of clear incentives for cooperation across departments; c) an unclear task for the faculty; and d) lack of clear policies in key areas such as staff recruitment. In addition, the reviewers concluded that there still remained much work to be done in formulating the faculty's research tasks and that the leadership for research and graduate education remained unclear, even if steps in the right direction had begun.

The evaluation report advised the faculty to aggressively seek other sources of funding than just that from the Swedish Research Council and the Bank of Sweden Tercentenary Foundation. It was suggested that a strategy based on receiving financing from the new research foundations and from other external financers, such as the Swedish Federation of Municipalities and the Swedish Federation of County Councils be adopted. The evaluators explained that, "It is clear that the process can not solely be expected to occur through self-organizing at the bottom by the researchers, which is however also a necessary condition" (Sörlin et al. 2000: 31). The report emphasised that the faculty leadership would need to use careful judgment in combining the priorities of the faculty and university, as well as in listening to and supporting the curiosity and activities of the researchers (Sörlin et al. 2000: 31–34).

The reviewers advised the faculty to form a strategy for external funding in cooperation with central university administration. Such a strategy could ensure that the university leadership was fully supporting the research being conducted. Other important suggestions included establishing: a) a reward system for departments, and even researchers, who take the responsibility to develop and lead research programmes; b) a plan for staff recruitment; c) a review of faculty organisational forms/structures; d) a more complete plan for differentiating the tasks for the various subject areas under the faculty's responsibility; and e) an investment in outward communication and contacts (improved information, web pages, media contact, etc.) (Sörlin et al. 2000: 130–131).

In May 2001, the faculty wrote a new research strategy 'programme' and argued strongly for the internal integration of research in order to attract more external financing. The faculty outlined a plan to provide financing for three to five research programmes, spanning a five-year period. Two to three of these would be multidisciplinary. In principle, every multidisciplinary programme would be required to attract external financing to match the investment by the faculty. In addition to these research programmes, the faculty suggested a concentration on profile areas, with financing spanning a ten-year period. These programmes would be required to play a central role in the development of the faculty's contacts with other universities in Sweden and internationally. An investigation into the ability of the faculty to start more national graduate schools was also presented (*Humanistiska Fakultetsnämndens Forskningsstrategiska Program 2002–2005* 2001: 2).

The faculty Strategic Plan included two more measures, one relating to recruitment and the other dealing with the budget system. As for recruitment, the situation had improved recently with the establishment of ten post-doc positions. For the long-term, the faculty worked out a three-year plan for recruiting younger academics to the faculty. Finally, in regard to the division of resources, the faculty adopted a more performance-oriented system to allocate funds to the departments. This new system would include not only the number of PhDs awarded and the amount of external research funding, but also the levels of published research works and the level of accomplishment of PhD students (*Humanistiska Fakultetsnämndens Forskningsstrategiska Program 2002–2005* 2001: 4).

The annual reports for 2001 and 2002 provided evidence of a strengthening of state appropriations to the faculty as well as increases in external funds. The faculty interpreted positively the increased appropriations from the state as a sign that the state was preparing for the future generational shifts in higher education staffing. However, there appeared to be uneasiness with the rise in external funds (up 2% since 1997 to 37% of total funds available for research and research education). The annual report stated, "Economically it is of course positive, but at the same time, the organization is more vulnerable to external market conditions and more steering from outside" (*Humanistiska fakultetens årsredovisning* 2002: 17).

4.3.2. The Emphasis on Multidisciplinary Research at the Humanities Faculty
Between 1997 and 2000, the faculty strategy was to try to maintain the existence of previous multidisciplinary investments (under conditions of limited resources). However, relatively little attention was paid to this topic in the annual reports. Only in conjunction with the Iberian-American Institute (founded in 1939) can a reference be found to an extensive 'interdisciplinary' research environment.

After the external reviewers' critique from 2000, the most recent strategy 'programme' from 2001 clearly advocated a multidisciplinary perspective: "We have a responsibility as much within our own disciplinary area as with other disciplinary areas to conduct research which contributes to a humanistic perspective" (*Humanistiska Fakultetsnämndens Forskningsstrategiska Program 2002–2005* 2001: 2). In addition, the 2002 annual report recorded the progress of the six multidisciplinary research programmes started by the faculty as a result of the strategy programme. Cooperation began also with Oslo University and with the Faculty of Social Sciences at Göteborg University on research projects involving mass communications, as well as area studies for Africa and Asia in cooperation with relevant language departments.

4.3.3. The Societal Network Relations at the Humanities Faculty

Scanning the annual reports from the faculty, it appears that between 1997 and 2001 almost no attention was paid to recording cooperation and connections with the surrounding society. The 1999 annual report only mentions that a policy document is on the way. It arrived in 2000.

The policy document opened with a background discussion of what cooperation with society would mean, and warned against "the typical understanding that it means cooperation with business/societal interests which will have deciding influence over the university's activities in a type of one-way communication with the university from outside" (*Humanistiska fakultetens strategi och handlingsprogram för samverkan med det omgivande samhället* 2000: 1). Instead, the faculty outlined the following objectives: a) to establish new channels for outward communication (such as better web pages, press releases, public events); b) to make humanities education more available to a wider audience through different types of study forms (i.e. distance, part-time); and c) to increase consideration of the knowledge needs of the surrounding society (more external education courses, better marketing to businesses) (*Humanistiska fakultetens strategi och handlingsprogram för samverkan med det omgivande samhället* 2000: 1).

In the 2001 annual report, some evidence of external education for government authorities is provided. By 2002, the annual report for the first time devoted a special section to this topic. One can read of activities such as public seminars, open houses and radio programmes, along with information on the faculty's work with the local schools and with a project from the municipality on 'Attractive Schools'.

5. CONCLUSIONS

Earlier in this chapter, it was argued that the developments anticipated by the Triple Helix may not be simultaneous or linear across the whole range of disciplines. With the incorporation of a new institutional perspective, three processes were identified for further study – coercive, normative and mimetic.

In the empirical case presented here, the strongest 'coercive force' has been the restructuring of research finance in Sweden. The changes in the amount of state appropriations to universities and faculties are viewed by all actors as the primary problem. This has led to what is interpreted at times as a further 'coercive force' – the need to acquire funds from external financers. Connected to this are demands for advanced economic accounting systems and follow-up reports, as well as the need for promises from the university and faculties to provide matching funds in order to receive external grants. In addition, the government's policy to establish national research schools is a coercive force on the universities. At the faculty level, university policies to establish 'scientific councils' provide another example of a coercive force.

At the normative level, the norms and values that regulate conduct within the organisations (both university and faculty levels) appear to be in tremendous flux. During the six years under study here, it was impossible to identify a common position among the actors on how to deal with these coercive forces. Annual reports and policy papers fluctuated between viewing external funds as a type of recognition for the high status of research (and thus it is a benefit to get more) versus a concerned view over the proper balance of internal and external funds, the role of a research connection to higher education, and the long-term sustainability of departments' research profiles. However, there does seem to be agreement among the actors that the researchers seek money wherever it may be found. Occasionally, there is evidence of an awareness that different types of external financers provide funds under different sets of norms (peer-review and collegial versus applied), but strategies on how to address this issue seem to be lacking.[7]

The limited case data presented here do not allow for an extended analysis of the mimetic processes between organisations, but it does seem clear that the Faculty of Social Sciences and the Humanities Faculty at Göteborg University have responded in quite varying ways to the coercive forces described above. Three prominent differences are: 1) the Humanities Faculty's strong efforts to form a faculty-wide research strategy and their willingness to invest faculty funds in identified research profiles versus the Social Sciences Faculty's continuous discussions of the matter without a resulting policy; 2) the Humanities Faculty's policy on performance-based distribution of funds to the departments versus the Social Sciences Faculty's discussion of the matter; 3) the strong emphasis on both multidisciplinary research and connections with society from the Social Sciences Faculty versus the very little attention given to these topics by the Humanities Faculty.

Thus, given this theoretical framework, it can be concluded that the coercive forces in the university system in Sweden seem to be the strongest element of change in a process of 'isomorphism' of the Triple Helix. Certainly, there is no support for the idea that a new institutional order has developed to integrate the political, industrial and academic interests into the spheres of the Triple Helix so that a new organisational field ('the knowledge economy') can develop. The normative boundaries of the university are in flux, but there is no evidence that a system of norms based on market-determined success has taken over. The case study presented here shows that there is quite a distance to go before a new institutional order is reached.

NOTES

[1]   The author would like to acknowledge financial support for this research from the consortium of financers supporting the 'Stiftelseprojektet 2004' based at SISTER (Swedish Institute for Studies in

2   Education and Research). In addition, many thanks are extended to CEFOS (Center for Public Sector Research at Göteborg University) for office space and a rewarding intellectual environment.

2   At the time of writing, one Euro equals approximately nine Swedish crowns.

3   English names in order of appearance: Swedish Agency for Innovation Systems; Swedish Council for Working Life and Social Research; and the Swedish Research Council for Environment, Agriculture Sciences and Spatial Planning.

4   Nationellt Uppföljningssystem, Swedish National Agency for Higher Education, category 'active researcher students', 1994 to 2002.

5   SKI (Center for Interdisciplinary Research, Center for Cultural Studies, and Institute for Studies of Knowledge Production).

6   The six areas identified were: 1) The Swedish Word Bank; 2) gender research; 3) regions; 4) middle ages; 5) modern culture; and 6) schools and learning.

7   Henkel (2000: 264) suggests that accommodating new modes of management in higher education may not be so much a question of a final solution, but rather that of a provisional strategy, with the implications slow to emerge. This observation seems to hold in the case study presented here.

REFERENCES

Benner, M. *Kontrovers och consensus: Vetenskap och politik i svensk 1990-tal.* Stockholm: Nya Doxa SISTER Rapport 1, 2001.

Benner, M. "Ställningskrig: Reflektioner kring debatten." In Sandström, U. (ed.). *Det nya forskningslandskapet. Perspektiv på vetenskap och politik.* Stockholm: Nya Doxa SISTER Skrifter 5, 2002, 67–75.

Benner, M. and U. Sandström. "Institutionalizing the Triple Helix: Research Funding and Norms in the Academic System." *Research Policy* 29 (2000): 291–301.

Cerych, L. and P. Sabatier. *Great Expectations and Mixed Performance: The Implementation of Higher Education Reforms in Europe.* Stoke-on-Trent: Trentham Books, 1986.

DiMaggio, P. and W. Powell. "The Iron Cage Revisited. Institutional Isomorphism and Collective Rationality in Organization Fields." In Powell, W. and P. DiMaggio (eds). *The New Institutionalism in Organizational Analysis.* Chicago: University of Chicago Press, 1991, 63–83.

Etzkowitz, H. and L. Leydesdorff. "The Dynamics of Innovation: From National Systems and 'Mode 2' to a Triple Helix of University–Industry–Government Relations." *Research Policy* 29 (2000): 109–123.

Forskningsstrategier och Strategier för Kunskapsutveckling vid Humanistiska Fakulteten 2001–2004, 1999.

Gibbons, M., C. Limoges, H. Nowotny, S. Schwartzman, P. Scott and M. Trow. *The New Production of Knowledge: The Dynamics of Science and Research in Contemporary Societies.* Thousand Oaks: Sage, 1994.

Göteborgs universitet årsredovisning, 1997, 1998, 2000, 2001, 2002.

Hällsten, M. and U. Sandström. "Högskoleforskningens nya miljarder." In Sandström, U. (ed.). *Det nya forskningslandskapet. Perspektiv på vetenskap och politik.* Stockholm: Nya Doxa SISTER Skrifter 5, 2002, 79–97.

Henkel, M. *Academic Identities and Policy Change in Higher Education.* London: Jessica Kingsley Publishers, 2000.

Humanistiska fakultetens strategi och handlingsprogram för samverkan med det omgivande samhället, 2000.

Humanistiska fakultetsnämnden årsredovisning, 1998, 2002.

Humanistiska Fakultetsnämndens Forskningsstrategiska Program 2002–2005, 2001.

Kaukonen, E. and M. Nieminen. "Modeling the Triple Helix from a Small Country Perspective: The Case of Finland." *Journal of Technology Transfer* 24 (1999): 173–183.

Kristensen, B., P. Niemi and R. Åberg. *Samhällsvetenskapliga fakulteten i Göteborg: En utvärdering.* Göteborg: Samhällsvetenskapliga fakulteten, 2000.

Marton, S. *The Mind of the State: The Politics of University Autonomy in Sweden, 1968–1998.* Göteborg: BAS Publishers, 2000.

Samhällsvetenkapliga fakultetsnämndens verksamhetsberättelse, 1997, 1998, 1999, 2001, 2002.

Sandström, U. "Forskningsdebattens långa vågor." In Sandström, U. (ed.). *Det nya forskningslandskapet. Perspektiv på vetenskap och politik.* Stockholm: Nya Doxa SISTER Skrifter 5, 2002, 49–66.
Sandström, U. and M. Hällsten. "Företagens finansiering av universitetsforskning." SISTER Working Paper 25, 2003.
Scott, W.R. *Institutions and Organizations.* Thousand Oaks: Sage, 1995.
Sörlin, S., S. Johansson, F. Karlsson, H. Montgomery, T. Nordenstam and M.S. Jensen. *Den humanistiska cirkelns kvadratur: om humanioras möjligheter och framtid: rapport från Humanistiska fakultetens nordiska bedömargrupp.* Göteborg: Humanistiska fakulteten, 2000.
Strategisk plan för samhällsvetenskapliga fakultetsnämnden åren 2000–2002, 1999.

INGVILD MARHEIM LARSEN AND LIV LANGFELDT

PROFILING COMPREHENSIVENESS?
STRATEGY FORMULATION AND EFFECTS OF
STRATEGIC PROGRAMMES AT TRADITIONAL
UNIVERSITIES

1. INTRODUCTION

During the last decades, strategic planning and profiling have been regarded as a necessity for higher education institutions to meet a situation characterised by changing environments and increased competition (Dill 1996; Neave 1995; Schmidtlein and Milton 1990). Since the beginning of the 1980s, it has been claimed that the period of incremental planning has passed, and that the universities have to implement strategic decision making (Keller 1983). This chapter presents a study of strategic work and strategic programmes at Norwegian universities. The research questions of the project include:

- How should we understand the concept of 'strategy' in a university setting?
- Why do the institutions formulate strategic plans and strategic programmes, and what is the content of such strategies?
- What are the criteria for selecting 'strategic programme areas' and how are strategic programmes organised?
- How are strategic plans implemented and what effects may they have on practice?
- Do strategic plans and strategic programmes reflect institutional ambitions for increased steering capacity or are they a mere 'window-dressing' response to national authorities' demands for reforms at the institutions?

In presenting the study, we first briefly discuss the concept of strategy in a university setting and give a short introduction to the literature on strategic planning in higher education. We then give an overview of our case studies in a short presentation of the Norwegian higher education system and the national policy that relates to the strategy formulation of the universities. The overview also incorporates the results of a survey that include academic staff opinion about strategic planning. Thereafter, we present empirical findings on strategic plans and strategic programmes. In the final section of the chapter, possible explanations of the findings are discussed.

Å. Gornitzka et al. (eds.), Reform and Change in Higher Education, 343-362.

2. WHAT IS STRATEGY AT A UNIVERSITY?

The concept of strategy is ambiguous. What is meant by strategy formulation and strategic programmes at universities? According to Mintzberg (1983) we may set up 5 Ps for strategy each defining a different meaning of the concept (he also gives examples where the concept is used in each of these five ways):

Plan	intended course of action made in advance of actions, often stated in formal documents
Ploy	a manoeuvre intended to outwit an opponent or competitor
Position	a viable position, that is, occupying a niche in the environment or the market
Pattern	consistency in behaviour, whether intended or not
Perspective	an integrated way of perceiving the world; like culture, ideology or a paradigm.

All these concepts may relate to university governance. Here we shall link the concept of strategy to the first three Ps: plan, ploy and position. We think a combination of strategy as plan, ploy and position is what explicit strategy formulation at today's universities is about: it deals with the formulation of plans for securing the future position of the university in its environment. How to deal with opposing forces and competing institutions (ploy) are natural parts of such plans – though how to outwit 'enemies' is of course not stated in official documents.

Patterns of behaviour and the *perspectives* behind the behaviour are central elements of theories concerning higher education and the sociology of science, but have, as we see it, less to do with the concept of strategy underlying today's 'strategic work' at academic institutions. We therefore do not include here patterns and perspectives in the *concept* of strategy, though the patterns and perspectives at academic institutions may be elements of the analysis, trying to explain the universities' accomplishments related to strategy formulation.

3. THE USE AND USEFULNESS OF STRATEGIC PLANNING IN HIGHER EDUCATION

The use of strategic planning in higher education institutions started in the US and goes back to the 1960s, and represents a practice borrowed from the private business sector (Maassen and Van Vught 1992). As in the US, both authorities and higher education institutions in many European countries see strategic planning as a useful tool to handle shifts in the environment and increased competition. Also, when the need to reform higher education institutions is on the agenda, strategic planning has been regarded as a useful tool (Powers 2000). Furthermore, strategic planning can be a response to fiscal crises and decreases in the number of students as well as an instrument to assess the weaknesses and strengths of institutions.

Even though strategic planning is a widely accepted tool, the history of strategic planning in higher education institutions is a mixed experience and there are a number of criticisms as to its usefulness for universities. Since the end of the 1990s, there has been an increasing scepticism towards strategic planning in the higher education sector in the US, both because of the premises of strategic planning as well as observed experiences. Despite the enthusiasm in the 1980s, there has been a lot of frustration in institutions because many feel strategic planning is both time-consuming and not very useful (Presley and Leslie 1999).

It has been argued that characteristics of higher education institutions are incompatible with strategic planning objectives. Universities as 'professional bureaucracies' (Mintzberg 1983) and 'organised anarchies' (March and Olsen 1976) are well-known labels for describing universities. According to Mintzberg (1983), strategy more or less looses its importance in professional bureaucracy since it is hard to agree upon any common goal in this kind of organisation as goal ambiguity is one of the chief characteristics of academic organisations. Not only are goals unclear in organised anarchies, they are also highly contested when they are specified (Baldridge 1971). As a consequence of these characteristics, it could be questioned whether a university's research strategy can possibly be something more than the sum of the strategies of all the professors who carry out research. To understand the failure of strategic planning we also have to understand the decision-making processes in academia. Since scholarly authority is located at the lower levels in professional bureaucracies and decision making in higher education institutions favours broad participation, it is difficult for leaders at the central level to steer the organisation.

Strategic planning is often regarded as a tool for handling the surroundings. On the other hand, it has been argued that the level of environmental control is rather limited (Maassen and Van Vught 1992). Consequently, strategic planning fits best when there is some predictability in the environment, while change is an obvious tendency in today's society. Furthermore, studies have also demonstrated mixed experiences with strategic planning for universities with economic problems (Presley and Leslie 1999: 209). As well, Schuster et al. (1994) emphasised that institutions meet problems regarding strategic planning in periods of economic recession. On the other hand, such planning processes were more or less unproblematic as long as the system was growing and had broad support in the environment. It is also emphasised that the surroundings often changed in directions that strategic planners could not foresee.

According to Schmidtlein and Milton (1990) many institutions have implemented planning procedures recommended by external consultants. The result is often frustration and disappointment since it is difficult to agree upon common goals, sub-units refuse to discuss the important questions and the expectations go beyond available resources.

As a consequence of characteristics of higher education institutions, plans are often general and vague, and consequently they do not function as a guide to future decisions. This leads us to the implementation of strategic plans as another critical point. First, directions or procedures for implementation are often absent in the plans. And second, fragmentation and diffusion of power in higher education make it difficult to effect change. The individual professor's autonomy over research and teaching makes it difficult to formulate plans and even more difficult to implement them.

In a study of strategic planning in French higher education institutions, Musselin and Mignot-Gérard (2002) emphasise three main reasons for the discrepancy between higher education institutions' ability to make and implement decisions. First, absence of implementation may be explained by individual resistance and individual autonomy. Second, the leadership does not pay enough attention to the implementation process. And thirdly, insufficient communication of the strategy within the university community seems to be a common phenomenon.

In addition to ambiguous goals, March and Olsen (1976) have pointed to the fact that universities have an unclear technology, in the sense that there is not a very sophisticated understanding of the relationship between means and ends. Consequently, if the organisation is able to agree upon a common goal, nobody knows how to achieve it. Hardy et al. (1984) have claimed that as a result of lack of implementation, much of central university planning has been decorative.

According to Dill (1996) planning processes are often superficial exercises which attempt to avoid difficult decisions, and plans for implementation and reallocation of resources are often neglected or underestimated. On the other hand, some of the leading American universities have implemented strategic plans which promoted internal and permanent change. These universities' relative success in strategic planning is explained by planning processes that harmonise with and support the organisations in which they are embedded. Dill emphasises that it is necessary to design a process that integrates the organisation and encourages cooperation. If the planners succeed in incorporating these elements, strategic planning could be an important tool in integrating highly fragmented organisations such as universities (Dill 1996: 51).

4. OVERVIEW OF THE EMPIRICAL STUDY

In 2003, Norway has four universities, six specialised university colleges, as well as two art schools with the same status as a specialised university college. In addition, there are 26 university colleges in different regions of Norway. They are all public institutions, mainly funded by the Ministry of Education and Research. The private higher education sector in Norway is rather limited in size.

During 2003, the so-called Quality Reform of Higher Education will be implemented in the higher education system in Norway (St.meld.nr 27 2000–2001). This is a comprehensive reform affecting most parts of the university system. A new degree structure, a new funding model, heavy emphasis on internationalisation, changes in the governance structure and new systems for evaluating the students as well as the institutions, are all elements of the reform. According to this reform, the six specialised university colleges will be allowed to call themselves universities, and those state colleges that have the right to offer at least five master programmes and four doctorate programmes will be able to apply for designation as universities. While the Norwegian universities today offer a full range of subjects, the future universities are meant to be more specialised institutions.

This study concentrates on today's four Norwegian universities. In 2001, the four universities had 75,000 students, the six specialised university colleges 7000 students, the 26 state colleges 75,000 students, and the 26 private colleges 20,000. The four universities differ in size, history and to some extent scholarly profile, but they are all research-based comprehensive universities (see table 1 for an overview of their main characteristics).

Table 1. Main characteristics of the four Norwegian universities

	UiOslo	UiBergen	NTNU	UiTromsø
Year founded	1811	1946	1996*	1968
Number of academic positions 2001	3816	1798	2169	979
Number of students, Autumn 2002	32 617	17 921	20 669	6496
Doctoral degrees 2002	231	158	203	55
R&D expenditure 2001, million kr	1.904.8	1.118.1	1.211.9	623.8
Organisation	8 faculties	7 faculties	7 faculties	6 faculties

*NTNU (Norwegian University of Science and Technology) is an amalgamation of two higher education institutions located in Trondheim

The Norwegian university system is part of a state hierarchical structure, but norms of self-governance run deep in the institutions. With the exception of some private university colleges, all are state-run, but have considerable academic and administrative autonomy. However, there is an ongoing debate in Norway whether higher education institutions should be organised according to enterprise principles or persist as state agencies.

The University and College Act places the board at the top of the institutional pyramid (Larsen 2002). The board at the institutional level has the overall responsibility for academic as well as administrative affairs. The Act identifies five areas where the board has particular responsibility. One of these tasks is highly relevant for this study, namely, that the board shall 'draw up a strategy for the institution's educational programme, research and other academic activities'. The university board also exercises authority over allocation of financial resources.

According to the Act, all decision-making authority at the faculty and department level is a consequence of delegation from the university board. From 2003 on, the board determines the institution's internal governance structure at each level; the only precondition is that the students and employees have a say in decisions.

4.1. Increased Demands for Strategy Formulation

During the past years there have been many calls for universities to institute strategic planning. Since the beginning of the 1990s, white papers on research and higher education from the Ministry of Education and Research state that the universities should focus on strategic planning and increased steering and profiling of their scholarly activity (Larsen 2000). The emphasis on strategy in higher education is not a distinctly Norwegian matter, but in line with international trends in higher education.

In Norwegian higher education the concept of strategy was first introduced in the context of planning and priorities for research activities, and is now also applied in the context of education activities. Through the past years the explicitness of the demands has increased. The reports from the early 1990s contained general demands and signals about strategy formulation, whereas in the latest reports, demands for strategy formulation are linked to explicit demands for increased capacity for reforms. Furthermore, the government is changing organisational and financial structures to increase the universities' steering capacity (with a new funding model and increased authority to the university board, as stated above). The rationale for demanding increased steering capacity seems to be to ensure the institutions' ability to reallocate resources and to respond to the changing environment, and more generally to promote scholarly progress.

4.2. Academic Staff Opinion About Strategic Planning

A recent survey at all four Norwegian universities investigated staff opinion on strategic planning at the university. Table 2 shows that more than half of the academic staff fully or partly agreed that there was a need for more long-term planning of research activities at the university, while scarcely 20 per cent fully or partly disagreed. The comparisons between different fields of learning show that staff in the medical sciences are more positive to the planning of research activities than staff in other fields.

Whether the departmental leadership should influence the scholarly profile of the department or not, is another question in the survey. While 42 per cent fully or partly disagreed that the head of department should have strong influence on the scholarly profile of the department, 37 per cent fully or partly agreed (table 3). Due to the traditional freedom of individual staff members to choose the subject of their research activities, it could be argued that it is somewhat surprising that almost 40 per cent supported the view that the head should have strong influence on the department's profile (Larsen 2003). It is less surprising that faculty members in the humanities and social sciences are more sceptical about a situation in which the head influences the department's academic profile, as responsibility for research and teaching is traditionally a more individual activity in these fields of learning. Research cooperation is more widespread in experimental subjects, and staff in the medical sciences are also the most positive in this respect.

What do these data tell us about the conditions for implementing strategic plans at Norwegian universities? The academic staff do not seem entirely opposed to more scholarly leadership at the departmental level and a majority see the need for long-term planning of research. This indicates conditions in favour of implementing departmental research plans. On the other hand, there is no question in the survey dealing explicitly with strategic plans for the scholarly activity of the entire university. Our guess is that the attitudes towards such plans might be rather negative – unless of course these plans are built strictly on plans originating in the departments, thus giving them legitimacy.

Table 2. Statement: 'There is a need for more long-term planning of research activities at the university'. The opinion of academic staff in Norway 2001, by field of learning (%)

	Humanities	Social sci.	Natural sci.	Medical sci.	Engineering	Total
Fully agree	18	21	24	29	19	22
Partly agree	38	36	31	41	35	36
Neither agree nor disagree	23	24	23	19	25	23
Partly disagree	13	12	13	8	16	12
Fully disagree	8	7	8	4	6	7
Sum	100	100	99	101	101	100
(N)	(401)	(432)	(560)	(381)	(146)	(1920)

Source: NIFU (Norwegian Institute for Studies in Research and Higher Education) University Staff Survey

Table 3. Statement: 'The head of department should have strong influence on the scholarly profile of the department'. The opinion of academic staff in Norway 2001, by field of learning (%)

	Humanities	Social sci.	Natural sci.	Medical sci.	Engineering	Total
Fully agree	8	8	13	13	10	11
Partly agree	24	19	28	32	28	26
Neither agree nor disagree	19	22	19	21	30	21
Partly disagree	26	31	24	21	22	25
Fully disagree	24	20	16	12	11	17
Sum	101	100	100	99	101	100
(N)	(409)	(435)	(557)	(381)	(147)	(1929)

Source: NIFU University Staff Survey

5. EMPIRICAL FINDINGS

5.1. The Strategic Plans of Norwegian Universities

The first strategic plans at Norwegian universities appeared around 1990 – except for the NTNU (Norwegian University of Science and Technology), a university that was not established until 1996. The strategic plans are quite comprehensive. They cover a broad set of topics and contain strategies for the research activity, the research profile of the university, the education activity, the surroundings and the internal infrastructure (see table 4). However, the strategic plans are general rather than specific. They deal with challenges and express 'wishes' and vary regarding the focus on what to do and how to obtain the goals. And, as discussed below, it is not easy to say whether they have had any effect.

For all four Norwegian universities the stated purpose of formulating their strategic plans is some variant of the argument that they need strategies to meet the challenges from their surroundings. More specifically, they intend to formulate a strategy to help retain the ideals of the university in a time of increased competition and increased internationalisation. In interviews, strategic plans are described partly as a response to challenges from public authorities and comparative advantages and partly as a result of scholarly choice. The leadership also describes the plan as a tool to help the organisation achieve its goals and objectives. Informants also refer to the new funding model, which intends research to be strategically justified. Despite the fact that strategic plans often are externally motivated, the processes generate internal reflections over questions like 'What kind of university do we want to be?' and 'How may traditions and norms be best defended?'

Table 4. Topics covered by strategy documents of Norwegian universities (first year topic covered)

Topic	UiB	UiO	UiTø	NTNU*
Scholarly activity				
Research	1988	1990	1992	1998
Education	1988	1990	1992	1998
Supplementary education	1988	1990	1992	1998
Research profile, strategic programmes	1988	1990	1992	1998
Vision/values		2000		1998
Surroundings				
Relation to surrounding/popularisation	1988	1990	1992	1998
Internationalisation/international strategy	1988	1990	1992	2001
Internal infrastructure/administration	1988	1990	1992	1997

*Established in 1996 as an amalgamation of two higher education institutions located in Trondheim

Vision, values and 'communication platform' are among the newer topics of the strategic plans. Provided that these terms are more than an adaptation to a trendy vocabulary and have some bearing on the substance of the universities' strategies, the emphasis on values and communication underlines that sustaining values and handling the surroundings are important aspects of the strategy formulation.

5.2. Strategic Programmes at Norwegian Universities

The strategic plans contained strategies for the research profile and strategic areas of the universities. The implementation of the plans included university research programmes – programmes that allocated grants for selected research areas.

The *University of Oslo* was the first Norwegian university with strategic research programmes that distributed internal grants to research projects. These strategic programmes lasted from 1995 to 1999. NOK 23 million from the university budget was spent on four research programmes that comprised: ethics, clinical communication, communication, technology and culture, and environmental research.[1]

Next was the *NTNU*, which in total granted NOK 24 million to projects of an internal interdisciplinary research programme in the period 1998 to 2001. From 2000 on, the NTNU has four strategic programmes relating to their science and technology profile in addition to this interdisciplinary programme.

The *University of Bergen* has no specifically defined internal 'programme', but marine research and development research are defined as their long-term strategic areas. For the period 1999 to 2003, the University of Bergen has earmarked NOK 102 million for strategic research areas.

Norway's smallest university, the *University of Tromsø*, has pointed out several 'strategic research areas' originating in their geographical position in Northern Norway. Figures from this university show internal allocations to two of these areas in the period 1999–2003 totalled NOK 5.6 mill.

To measure the relative importance of the strategic programmes, the grants for these programmes can be looked at in relation to the universities' total R&D expenditures. In total, we have identified NOK 21 million as internal university allocation to strategic programmes in 1999, whereas the universities' total R&D expenditures in 2003 was NOK 4.6 billion. This means that internal strategic programmes cover only about half a per cent of the research at the universities.[2] External funds, on the other hand, finance about a third of all university R&D in Norway.

5.3. Close-up of a Strategic Programme

In this section, we outline the details of one particular strategic programme: the Programme for Interdisciplinary Research at the NTNU. The first programme period was from 1998 to 2002, and the second from 2003 to 2006.

Why does the NTNU have a strategic programme devoted to interdisciplinary research? The history of this programme started as the NTNU was established in 1996. The white paper that reported on the foundation of the NTNU demanded that the new university actively promote cooperation across disciplines and across department borders. As the NTNU was not a new institution but a reorganisation of the former University of Trondheim (which consisted of two separate units with different origins – the Norwegian Institute of Technology and the College of Arts and Science), this requirement for interdisciplinarity was a challenging demand. The programme for interdisciplinary research was a direct response to this external demand (Langfeldt 2002).

The processes defining the content of the programme started in 1996, when the university board decided to prioritise areas for interdisciplinary research. Four broad thematic areas were defined through a process including various seminars and workshops at the ground level of the institution:

- Sustainable development and consumption
- Infrastructure and quality of life
- Technology, art and cultural change
- Information, communication and competence.

Directors for each thematic area were appointed from senior faculty at the NTNU. These directors prepared programme descriptions, and the board of the NTNU allocated a sum from the university budget to the programme. The programme got its own board constituting the four directors of the thematic areas and chaired by the pro-rector (vice president) of the NTNU.

The first call for applications in 1997 resulted in 128 responses for the interdisciplinary programme. The success rate was not high, nor were the grants for each project large. Twenty-four per cent of the applications received grants from the programme, in total NOK 23 million (€2.8 million) for the first four years. This means on average NOK 192,000 (€23,000) per project a year – which is not really much for an interdisciplinary project, as far as it was supposed to include participation from both sides of the divide, that is, between the humanities and the social sciences on the one hand and technology and the natural sciences on the other, and produce results from such interdisciplinary research.[3]

Regarding the question of implementation, the NTNU case tells us that when there is some external pressure and the ground level is involved in the formulation of the programme, a university may succeed in implementing a broad interdisciplinary research programme that includes a number of research projects across the organisational divisions – though in size the effort might seem small compared to the 'normal' research of the university.

6. DISCUSSION

6.1. The Processes Formulating the Content and the Organisation of the Strategic Programmes

How are strategic programmes selected? In most cases, the selection processes seem to involve the basic scholarly units at the university (departments), whose suggestions are coordinated at the intermediate level (faculty/school), while the whole process is initiated, controlled and finalised at the central level (rector, the university board and the university research board).

The degree of 'top-down' or 'bottom-up' in the processes varies, interestingly, for each university. It seems common that the ongoing process for formulating strategic plans is to some degree a reaction to experiences in the former process. This implies that a top-down process is followed by a process more open to suggestions from the sub-units; thus it is organised more as a bottom-up process. And vice versa – a bottom-up process for one strategic plan leads to the next process, which is organised more from the top-down. During the planning process, a new rector also seems to be of significance in the sense that new leaders want to influence the direction of the university; they do this by introducing additional elements to the plan.

In a more overall analysis of the stated criteria and the outcome of the processes we ask: What are a university's criteria for selecting 'strategic programme areas'? And: How do these criteria relate to the outcome of the programme selection? We find that the expressed criteria encompass comparative advantages, possibilities for external funding, nationally defined strategic areas, European priorities, nationally defined specific tasks/'duties' of the university, interdisciplinarity, scientifically interesting areas and societal needs. These are much the same priority criteria as those behind Norway's *national* strategic research areas. The resulting programmes are also close to these nationally defined strategic areas: marine research, information and communication technology, medicine and health, and environment and energy. In conclusion, we can say that in a national context the strategic programmes of the universities are marginal – the small amount of internal funds that the universities are able to allocate to their own strategic programmes are, by and large, allocated to research areas that already are national priorities. There are still substantial differences in the profiles of the universities. The NTNU has a distinctive scholarly profile as Norway's technological university, the University of Tromsø as the polar university, the University of Bergen as the west-coast university and the University of Oslo as the largest and most comprehensive university. These profiles are historically and geographically given and the small internal sums allocated to strategic programmes do not add enough research activity to affect these profiles.

6.2. Implementation of Strategic Plans

To produce specific effects, strategic plans require implementation. Two questions arise from this statement. First: What actions do the Norwegian universities take to implement their strategic plans? And second: Are strategic plans at Norwegian universities actually implemented?

Our data indicate that many elements in the Norwegian universities' strategies are implemented, not as a consequence of direct implementation of the strategic plan, but as a result of the ongoing quality reform of higher education in Norway. As one of the informants stated: "There has been a lucky concurrence between the strategic plan and the quality reform". This point is true for teaching and learning, but not to the same extent when it comes to strategic areas in research since the reform is more focused on teaching and learning than on research.

Norwegian universities have also taken other moves to put the plans into effect. While some of the strategic plans include direction on who is responsible for following up the various objectives, others work out a separate plan for action and a schedule for implementation. The administration must regularly report to the university board about the status quo of the implementation process. Strategic plans are also meant to be an important rationale for the budget process, since resources often are a precondition for putting the plans into effect. On the other hand, the informants from the universities emphasised that the connection between plan and budget was not fully developed. Furthermore, seminars are arranged to communicate the university plan to leaders at different levels and in different units. The aim is for leaders at all levels to feel committed to the plan and function as agents for its implementation. Informants admit that while most leaders at different levels are familiar with the strategic plan, academic staff in general will have little knowledge of the content of the plan. In addition to making the plan known internally, implementation of strategic plans includes external marketing. The departments of information at the different universities play a central role in 'selling' the plans to different stakeholders.

The universities' strategies for research are often expressed in the establishment of strategic programmes. We may identify some kind of activity within all these programmes. Allocation and reallocation of recruitment positions are often used as an instrument to implement strategic programmes. In fact, such allocation may constitute the core factor in the implementation of a programme.

The question is whether this is sufficient to say a strategy has been implemented. As we have seen, resources channelled from the institution to the strategic programme are often limited. It is therefore relevant to ask how significant a strategic programme needs to be before it can be rated as part of the implementation of a strategy. This leads to another question of vital importance: How to decide when a plan is implemented and when it is not?

6.3. The Effects of the Strategic Programmes

The size of the grants from the Programme for Interdisciplinary Research at the NTNU illustrates a central point in our data. The universities are seldom able to allocate substantial internal funds to their strategic programmes. They are very aware of this, and an explicit objective of the strategic programmes is to attract external funds. (About half of the projects funded by the Programme for Interdisciplinary Research at the NTNU succeeded in attracting external funds.) University priorities are in this way 'strategic moves' to attract external funds, and priorities set by the surroundings are important for the strategic priorities of the university. In the case of the interdisciplinary programme at the NTNU, the strategic programme was also a response to the external demands on the scholarly profile of the new university.

The small strategic programmes at Norwegian universities can be seen as a simple solution to the task of being both profiled and comprehensive. The programmes *make visible the stated research profile of the university*, but do not endanger the comprehensiveness of the university – as such small programmes have little bearing on the overall activities of the institution. As stated above, each university has a particular scholarly profile which is historically and geographically given. Strategic programmes may draw attention to this profile, but hardly change it.

The programmes may still have other kinds of effects. One special challenge regarding the implementation of strategic programmes is that they are often interdisciplinary and as such involve more faculties and departments. This may consequently imply cooperation between units that traditionally have little contact. The NTNU programme, presented above, had such cooperation as a main objective, while other programmes are more directed towards research achievements within a defined thematic field and such cooperation is more a precondition and effect than a central aim of the programme. These kinds of impacts of strategic programmes should be further investigated.

6.4. The Effects of National Demands for Institutional Policy Formulation and Firmer Steering of the Universities

Do strategic plans and strategic programmes reflect institutional ambitions for increased steering capacity or are they mere 'window-dressing' responses to national authorities' demands for institutional reform and international trends in higher education? Cohen and March (1974), for instance, point to the symbolic role of strategy – strategy as a way of impressing external interests – whereas universities themselves may state ambitions for increased steering capacity (as their strategy formulation otherwise would seem somewhat meaningless).

Different decision-making models give different answers to questions about the central decision-making capacity of an institution. In a 'collegial model' the strategic plan of an institution is the sum of the plans of its various basic units. In a 'political model' the strategic plan of an institution is the result of bargaining and reflects the views of the most powerful coalition. In a 'hierarchical model' the strategic plan of an institution is the outcome of top-down decision making at the university. In a 'garbage can model' the strategic plan of an institution is the outcome of more or less randomly connected problems, solutions and actors. Below we discuss strategy formulation at universities in relation to these models.

Decision making in higher education institutions is traditionally characterised by consultation and shared leadership. In his study of entrepreneurial universities, Clark (1998) emphasises that there is a need for a strong element of collegial participation in the governance of universities; on the other hand, it must be organised in a way that does not slow down decision making. Clark argued that there has to be a balance between participation of academic staff and decision-making capacity. The first three models presented here provide different answers to this demand. The collegial model and the hierarchical model represent the extreme points, while the political model may be more of a mix between participation and central decision making.

6.4.1. The Collegial Model

How are different levels in the organisation involved in formulation and implementation of the university strategy? Are the studied processes in line with a 'collegial model' in which the strategic plan of an institution is the sum of individual plans? The question is whether a complex organisation, such as a university where staff traditionally have individual freedom in scholarly activities, can formulate a shared strategy that is more than just a collection of the plans of the different departments and units. Furthermore, is there any conflict between the planning processes at the central level and the planning processes in the sub-units? A study from the US has demonstrated that the university plan suppressed the plans of the single unit, and that the processes at different levels were not coordinated in time, focus or content (Presley and Leslie 1999). Furthermore, broad participation and decision-making processes are vital for the legitimacy of the process and the plan. Consequently, according to this model, comprehensive planning processes that profile all the characteristics of comprehensive universities are necessary. The collegial model is an internal bottom-up model. The model means governance according to the norms of the scientific community, implying academic freedom and a 'hands off' approach to academic affairs. Consequently, there are no norms capable of guiding strategy formulation. According to the model there is not much room for institutional ambitions for increased steering capacity at a university.

Bottom-up decisions in heterogeneous institutions are unlikely to call for increased steering capacity – because increased steering capacity would imply more top-down decisions, which normally is perceived to be contrary to the interests of the decision makers (i.e. the basic units). This implies that so long as collegial decision making results in strategic plans for institutions, these plans are more likely to express a 'window-dressing' response to external demands than internal ambitions for increased steering capacity.

As for the studied Norwegian universities, most basic units at the universities have their separate strategic plans, and involvement/consultation of the basic units seems to be a fundamental principle of the processes in which the overall strategic plans of the institution are formulated. The basic units are involved in the formulation of both strategic plans and strategic programmes. Looking at the contents and stated rationales of the strategic plans of the studied universities, we find that these are built on historical and geographical bases and the traditional values of the institutions. This makes the collegial model relevant for understanding the strategy formulation at these universities.

Dill (1996) emphasises that the planning processes at successful universities in the US such as Michigan, Minnesota, Princeton and Stanford all take place in accordance with academic tradition and values. He stresses that all these universities have implemented strategies that have resulted in substantial changes.

6.4.2. The Political Model

Are the studied processes in line with a 'political model' in which the strategic plan of an institution is the result of bargaining and reflects the views of the most powerful coalition? The political model also includes external interests, as some of the coalitions may have allies outside the university with the power to affect the outcome of the process. In many countries universities are under increased pressure to cooperate with different actors in their surroundings. Such cooperation is supposed to bring new and more resources to the university.

In the political model, the strategic plans and strategic programmes do not reflect institutional ambitions for increased steering capacity, nor are they 'window-dressing' responses to national authorities' demands for institutional reform. They are better described as a response to, and compromise between, different internal and external interests.

Central characteristics of the studied strategic programmes identify the political model as relevant for understanding the strategic work of the studied Norwegian universities. The programmes are broad and seem designed to encompass divergent scholarly interest – their contents appear to be a compromise between different scholarly interests of selected basic units and external interests. As external interests are included and all internal interests are not, the political model rather than the collegial model appears to have more sway.

Studies of strategic planning in higher education institutions in the US have demonstrated that since the end of the 1970s the processes increasingly include the institutions' relationship to the environment. This new orientation in strategic planning has resulted in separate assessments of the universities' environment as an obligatory part of the planning process (Presley and Leslie 1999: 204). Consequently, strategic planning can be seen as an antenna tuned to pick up changes in the environment. In their classical study from 1974, Cohen and March demonstrated that strategic plans are more symbolic than instrumental and are regarded as a tool to impress external stakeholders.

6.4.3. The Hierarchical Model

Are the studied processes in line with a 'hierarchical model' in which the strategic plan of an institution is the outcome of top-down decision making at the university? Seen as part of the state hierarchical system, an *external* top-down model is relevant for understanding strategy formulation at universities. Seen as autonomous institutions, an *internal* top-down model is relevant, provided that the universities have substantial steering capacity at the institutional level.

According to an external top-down model, the strategic plans and strategic programmes of an institution are supposed to reflect external authorities' demands. According to an internal top-down model, the strategic plans and strategic programmes of an institution may reflect institutional ambitions for increased steering capacity or be mere 'window-dressing' responses to demands from external authorities. Strategic planning and strategic leadership are often emphasised when change and reform are on the agenda, more specifically, the need for strategic change. Accordingly, we can ask whether such a development means concentration of power and authority at the institutional level – a strengthening of the hierarchical structure – and as such could this be regarded as a sign of stronger coordination of the institution's scholarly activities.

Elements of both an external and an internal top-down model may prove relevant for understanding the strategy formulation at Norwegian universities. The initiation of the strategy formulation agrees with the *external* top-down model, as national authorities demanded the universities formulate a strategy for their scholarly activities. The completion of the strategic plans, on the other hand, indicates some *internal* top-down decision-making capacity. Without a minimum of decision-making capacity at the institutional level, it is hard to see how the processes involving the various basic units could have decided on a common strategy for the academic activity. But, of course, the level of decision-making capacity needed depends on whether the strategy is seen to have substantial effects or not. To decide upon a strategy that is expected to be implemented and to cause some changes in the activities of the university definitely demands more decision-making capacity than to decide upon a strategy that is perceived to be mere window-dressing towards the surroundings and not bring about substantial change.

According to a neo-institutional perspective, mimicking is a basic mechanism that couples environmental demands and pressure for organisational change (DiMaggio and Powell 1991). Since organisations attempt to align their structure with their institutional environment, the result is conformity or apparent conformity between organisations (Meyer and Rowan 1977). An analysis of the content of the strategy in higher education institutions in the US showed that they were remarkably similar. A mission statement is also required of the British universities. However, these seem to have little effect as tools to profile the institutions since more than 100 institutions produced almost similar documents (Gornitzka, Maassen and Nordgård 2001: 51).

Decoupling between formal structure and actual behaviour is another element in neo-institutional theory. Thys-Clement and Wilkin (1998) demonstrated how strategic planning could function as window-dressing. While all the studied institutions (18 universities in 10 European countries) had formulated strategic plans, less than half had implemented the plans one year later. Also, Dill (1996) came to the conclusion that at many universities in the US strategic plans were more symbolic than real; planning processes were often superficial exercises, and discussion of the more difficult topics was avoided.

In Clark's study (1998) of European entrepreneurial universities, a strengthening steering core is one of the common characteristics of the universities labelled as entrepreneurial. Inter alia, this means that leadership has played a central role in the process. This study partly demonstrates the relevance of the hierarchical model, both in the sense that the universities included in the study were all under pressure from government to reform themselves and that institutional leadership played a central role in the transformation process.

6.4.4. The Garbage Can Model

Are the studied processes in line with a 'garbage can model' in which the strategic plan of an institution is the outcome of more or less randomly connected problems, solutions and actors? In a garbage can model timing is important to understand the official strategy; problems, solutions and actors will be coupled in a decision-making process more or less accidentally. A common institutional goal is often regarded as a precondition in strategic processes. To promote a common vision and mission is not an easy task in an academic setting where the organisation is complex, fragmented and loosely coupled (Cohen and March 1974). According to the 'garbage can model' the strategic plans and strategic programmes of an institution are not likely to reflect institutional ambitions for increased steering capacity, nor are they likely to be 'window-dressing' responses to national authorities' demands for reforms at the institutions – such outcomes would reflect a kind of intentionality for which there is not much room in the garbage can model.

Leslie (1996) asks whether a system like higher education can make strategic decisions. He emphasises that the characteristics of universities contradict the basic precondition of strategic planning. While strategic planning is a rational governing system, decision making in higher education is not particularly rational. Consequently, it is questionable whether a loosely coupled organisation such as a university could use strategic planning in a sensible way. Furthermore, comprehensive universities do not have sufficient information at the institutional level to formulate a unified strategy for the whole institution (Presley and Leslie 1999). In other words, there can be a substantial element of arbitrariness in the outcome. For instance, what other issues happen to be on the agenda, and which persons happen to be present, may affect what information attracts attention and what information does not.

As indicated above, while the plans may not reflect institutional ambitions for increased steering, they may be regarded as 'window-dressing' responses to national authorities' demands for universities to formulate such plans. The traditions of Norwegian universities support academic autonomy and not increased steering. The referred survey certainly showed that more than half of the academic staff fully or partly agreed that there was a need for more long-term planning of research activities, but, as noted earlier, it is likely the result would be more disagreement if the question were about increased *central* planning of research activities.

It should be added that, in another perspective, the contents of the plans may be interpreted as integrating the overall interests of the institution and searching for a way to preserve the ideals of the institution in a time of changing environments. And external demands for strategic plans may be important only for initiating the process, not for the result.

In any case, the garbage can model does not seem the most relevant model for understanding strategic plans.

7. IN CONCLUSION

- The strategic *plans* are not very specific and it is therefore not easy to measure what impact on institutional activity they may have produced.
- The processes that formulate the strategies indicate the relevance of the collegial model.
- The content of the strategic *programmes* indicates the relevance of the political model.
- The correspondence between national priorities and the strategic programmes at the universities highlights the relevance of the hierarchical model.
- The study demonstrates that there is a mixture of collegial, political as well as hierarchical elements working in decision making in higher education institutions.
- Measured in project grants, the strategic programmes are too small to have actual effects on the scholarly profile of the universities, that is, the strategic programmes may highlight the research profiles of the universities in terms of visibility, but, most likely, they have no substantial impact on the profile or comprehensiveness of the university.

7.1. Reflections on Future Change – Towards a More Hierarchical Model in More Competitive Environments?

The Norwegian universities are now in a process of reform that was initiated by an external top-down model (*the quality reform of higher education*, described above). The reforms are perceived to produce substantial effects in many respects, inter alia, they aim to strengthen the academic leadership functions at different levels. Furthermore, the system with shared leadership between academic leaders and administrative leaders will be replaced by a unified leadership system where the administrative leaders are subordinate to the academic leaders. Such strengthening of the academic leadership may imply the strengthening of the institution's steering capacity. However, academics (also as leaders) are often defenders of democracy and broad participation in decision making – values and norms that often are seen as obstacles to a strengthened steering core.

As mentioned, the ongoing reform allows for more universities in Norway. As a consequence of more universities, the coming years will probably include more competition for both students and research grants. Even though the future universities are not meant to be comprehensive, they will be more equal competitors as universities than as state colleges. Higher education institutions on the international scene may also be more real competitors for the Norwegian universities in the future. Consequently, there are reasons to believe that increased competition will be the situation for the four universities in Norway. This implies that it may be of vital importance that the single university has the ability to profile their education and research in a way that is attractive to different stakeholders. Since the Norwegian universities vary in size (see table 1) it is reasonable to believe that profiling will be more challenging for an institution the size of the University of Oslo with more than 30,000 students than for the University of Tromsø with about 6000 students.

NOTES

[1]   These programmes were terminated in 1999 and new programmes commenced in 2001.
[2]   These figures are tentative as there are no set rules for the registration of these kinds of internal allocations. At any rate, the total amount seems marginal compared to other resources.
[3]   The total project funds for the first four years of the programme amount to NOK 23.8 million (€2.9 million). Dividing this amount among 46 projects gives an even lower average amount per project a year: NOK 129,000 or €15,700.

REFERENCES

Baldridge, J.V. *Power and Conflict in the University*. New York: Wiley, 1971.
Clark, Burton R. *Creating Entrepreneurial Universities. Organizational Pathways of Transformation*. Paris: IAU Press, 1998.
Cohen, Michael D. and James G. March. *Leadership and Ambiguity. The American College President*. New York: McGraw Hill, 1974.
Dill, David. "Academic Planning and Organizational Design: Lessons From Leading American Universities." *Higher Education Quarterly* 50 (1996): 35–53.
DiMaggio, P.G. and W.W. Powell (eds). *The New Institutionalism in Organizational Analysis*. Chicago: University of Chicago Press, 1991.
Gornitzka, Åse, Peter Maassen and Jorunn Dahl Nordgård. "Nasjonal prioritering og arbeidsdeliing i høyere utdanning – internasjonale erfaringer." Oslo: NIFU skriftserie 9/2001, 2001.
Hardy, Cynthia, Ann Langley, Henry Mintzberg and Janet Rose. "Strategy Formation in the University Setting." In Bess, James L. (ed.). *College and University Organization: Insights from the Behavioral Sciences*. New York/London: New York University Press, 1984, 169–210.

Keller, George. *Academic Strategy. The Management Revolution in American Higher Education.* Baltimore: The Johns Hopkins University Press, 1983.

Langfeldt, Liv. "Evaluering av NTNUs program for tverrfaglig forskning." Oslo: NIFU skriftserie 21/2002, 2002.

Larsen, Ingvild Marheim. "Research Policy at Norwegian Universities – Walking the Tightrope Between Internal and External Interests." *European Journal of Education* 35.4 (2000): 385–402.

Larsen, Ingvild Marheim. "Between Control, Rituals and Politics: The Governing Board in Higher Education Institutions in Norway." In Amaral, A., G. Jones and B. Karseth (eds). *Governing Higher Education: National Perspectives on Institutional Governance.* Dordrecht: Kluwer Academic Publishers, 2002, 99–119.

Larsen, Ingvild Marheim. "Departmental Leadership in Norwegian Universities – In Between Two Models of Governance?" In Amaral, A., V.L. Meek and I.M. Larsen (eds). *The Higher Education Managerial Revolution?* Dordrecht: Kluwer Academic Publishers, 2003, 71–88.

Leslie, David W. "Strategic Governance: The Wrong Questions?" *Review of Higher Education* 1 (1996): 101–112.

Maassen, P.A.M. and F. van Vught. "Strategic Planning." In Clark, Burton and Guy Neave (eds). *The Encyclopedia of Higher Education, vol. 2, Analytical Perspectives.* Oxford: Pergamon Press, 1992, 1483–1494.

March, James G. and Johan P. Olsen. *Ambiguity and Choice in Organizations.* Bergen: Universitetsforlaget, 1976.

Meyer, J.W. and B. Rowan. "Institutionalized Organizations: Formal Structure as Myth and Ceremony." *American Journal of Sociology* 83 (1977): 340–363.

Mintzberg, Henry. *Power In and Around Organizations.* Englewood Cliffs: Prentice-Hall, 1983.

Musselin, Christine and Stéphanie Mignot-Gérard. "The Recent Evolution of French Universities." In Amaral, A., G. Jones and B. Karseth (eds). *Governing Higher Education: National Perspectives on Institutional Governance.* Dordrecht: Kluwer Academic Publishers, 2002, 63–85.

Neave, Guy. "The Stirring of the Prince and the Silence of the Lambs: The Changing Assumptions Beneath Higher Education Policy, Reform, and Society." In Dill, D. and B. Sporn (eds). *Emerging Patterns of Social Demand and University Reform: Through a Glass Darkly.* Oxford: Pergamon Press, 1995, 54–71.

Powers, Joshua B. "The Use of Institutional Incentive Grants for Strategic Change in Higher Education." *Review of Higher Education* 23.3 (2000): 281–298.

Presley, Jennifer B. and David W. Leslie. "Understanding Strategy: An Assessment of Theory and Practice." In Smart, John C. (ed.). *Higher Education: Handbook of Theory and Research, vol. XIV.* New York: Agathon Press, 1999, 201–239.

Schmidtlein, Frank A. and Toby H. Milton. *Adapting Strategic Planning to Campus Realities.* San Francisco: Jossey-Bass, 1990.

Schuster, J.H., D.G. Smith, K.A. Corak and M.M. Yamada. *Strategic Governance: How to Make Big Decisions Better.* Phoenix: Oryx Press, 1994.

St.meld.nr 27. "Gjør din plikt – Krev din rett. Kvalitetsreformen i høyere utdanning." *Kirke-, utdannings- og forskningsdepartementet.* 2000–2001.

Thys-Clement, Francoise and Luc Wilkin. "Strategic Management and Universities: Outcomes of a European Survey." *Higher Education Management* 10.1 (1998): 13–28.

Higher Education Dynamics

Printed in the United States
72653LV00002BA/34-54